MATHEMATICS

People · Problems · Results

Edited by Douglas M. Campbell
and John C. Higgins

Brigham Young University

Wadsworth International
Belmont, California
A Division of Wadsworth, Inc.

Acquisitions Editor: John Kimmel
Production Editor: Andrea Cava
Copy Editor: Ann Draus
Cover Designer: Catherine Flanders
Interior Designer: Leigh McLellan

Printed in the United States of America

1 2 3 4 5 6 7 8 9 10—88 87 86 85 84

ISBN 0-534-03200-1 (hardback)

ISBN 0-534-03203-6 (paperback)

Library of Congress Cataloging in Publication Data
(Revised for vol. 2)
Main entry under title:

Mathematics : people, problems, results.

1. Mathematics—Addresses, essays, lectures.
I. Campbell, Douglas M. II. Higgins, John C., 1935–
QA7.M34466 1984   510   83-17039
ISBN 0-534-03200-1
ISBN 0-534-03203-6 (pbk.)

Contents

part one   The Nature of Mathematics

3   Mathematics and Creativity   *Alfred Adler*

11   The Meaning of Mathematics   *Morris Kline*

19   Mathematics as a Creative Art   *P. R. Halmos*

30   Definitions in Mathematics   *Émile Borel*

37   The Role of Intuition   *R. L. Wilder*

46   Mathematics—Our Invisible Culture   *Allen L. Hammond*

61   On the Present Incompleteness of Mathematical Ecology   *L. B. Slobodkin*

68   Preface to *The Common Sense of the Exact Sciences*   *Bertrand Russell*

part two   Real Mathematics

74   The Early History of Fermat's Last Theorem   *Paulo Ribenboim*

83   π and e *E. C. Titchmarsh*

89   Geometrical Constructions. The Algebra of Number Fields   *Richard Courant and Herbert Robbins*

101   Bicycle Tubes Inside Out   *Herbert Taylor*

104   The Calculus According to Newton and Leibniz   *C. H. Edwards, Jr.*

112   Non-Euclidean Geometry   *Stephen F. Barker*

128   The Idea of Chance   *Jacob Bronowski*

136   Hilbert's 10th Problem   *Martin Davis and Reuben Hersh*

149   The Riemann Hypothesis   *Philip J. Davis and Reuben Hersh*

154   The Four-Color Problem   *Kenneth Appel and Wolfgang Haken*

174   Group Theory and the Postulational Method   *Carl H. Denbow and Victor Goedicke*

part three   Foundations and Philosophy

183   The Three Crises in Mathematics: Logicism, Intuitionism, and Formalism   *Ernst Snapper*

194   Proofs and Refutations   *Imre Lakatos*

209   Mathematics and Computer Science: Coping with Finiteness   *Donald E. Knuth*

223   Are Logic and Mathematics Identical?   *Leon Henkin*

233   C. S. Peirce's Philosophy of Infinite Sets   *Joseph W. Dauben*

248   Proof   *Philip J. Davis and Reuben Hersh*

251   Impossibility   *Ian Richards*

262   Analogies and Metaphors to Explain Gödel's Theorem   *Douglas R. Hofstadter*

part one

The Nature of Mathematics

SUPPOSE THAT BY the rarest of happenstance the body of a senior, most learned priest of the Egyptian empire were discovered in a sealed and airless tomb and that by some miracle of medical science, this person were awakened after 4,000 years of hibernation with all of his faculties in perfect order. Now further suppose that after some period of initiation into the learning and language of our society we were to ask him to explain to us the nature of mathematics as it was understood in his long-departed world. Since this priest would be a man of great personal intelligence and urbanity, he would most likely begin by observing that Egyptian society then had no term equivalent to our word mathematics. And that fact would itself speak volumes about the nature of mathematics.

To the best of our ability to determine matters of this sort, mathematics as it is understood today began with the Greeks in their golden age. While many earlier cultures had a substantial trove of mathematical truths, they generally seemed to view these ideas as inextricably linked with the real world situations that inspired them. Such is the viewpoint of the school child who can count, add, and subtract apples or oranges but not abstract numbers. This is not to say that the ancient Egyptians or Chinese did not possess the abstract ideas of number; they most emphatically did. What those cultures seemed to lack is the notion that such arithmetic ideas have a life of their own—that irrespective of any applicability or potential cosmic significance, they may be created, examined, compared, expounded, and generalized in an amazing number of ways, and that this process generates an intellectual discipline worthy of the most careful and serious investigations.

Such a difference in viewpoint suggests that the nature of mathematics has changed over time as profoundly as has the subject itself. To the extent that pre-Greek cultures had any opinion on the nature of mathematics it would be that mathematics is a part of nature. Mathematics was viewed as an empirical science that one simply observes as one examines the surrounding world. This viewpoint is very plausible; the vast majority of the current population of the world, if forced to ponder the matter, would arrive at the same conclusion.

The ancient Greek viewpoint, in contrast, was at once more sophisticated and more radical than this rather pragmatic approach. Briefly—and in brevity there is some inaccuracy—the Greeks held that mathematics is reality. They felt that to know mathematics is to comprehend the immediate world of sense experience and much more besides. To the Greeks, mathematics is not something that evolves from one's observations of the world, but rather one's observations of the world evolve from mathematics. The Greeks felt that the world of observation and experience is formed from the interaction of more fundamental ideas, which are intrinsically mathematical. At the very least the Greek view suggests that mathematical ideas are not *like language, a transitory convenience, created to aid our understanding of a permanent physical reality, but are intrinsically embedded in any permanent reality, physical or mental.*

It is not surprising that the Greek view dominated Western thinking on the nature of mathematics until the nineteenth century. While it is true that various Christian theologians at one time or another did express different opinions on the nature of mathematics, these seem to have had relatively little impact for at least two reasons. First, the theologians did not care very much about mathematics. Second, the Greek achievements so dominated the subject of mathematics that the Greek views on its nature seemed the most plausible. The theme of mathematical ideas as essential truth was accepted and developed by Western philosophers up to the end of the nineteenth century. However, as with so many of the fixed notions of other earlier traditions, the last half of the nineteenth century produced a variety of mathematical results that made the Greek position untenable.

Among the most surprising and disturbing of the findings of the "new" mathematics was the proof that the geometric axioms of Euclid are not essential. Specifically, mathematicians were able to show that if one replaces the parallel axiom with a different postulate the resulting system is as "true" mathematically as the old Euclidean geometry had been. By "true" they meant that this new non-Euclidean geometry is not inconsistent and that there exists a model or example of a system that obeys these new rules. But clearly there cannot be two different and mutually contradictory geometric descriptions of ultimate reality. Since the new system is as valid as the old, it is evident that there is no necessary geometry embedded in our collective experience but instead a variety of creatable geometries that may or may not have any meaning in terms of physical reality. The impact of this discovery both inside and outside of mathematics was quite profound and continues to this day.

Thus the view that mathematics is necessary truth was dealt a disabling if not fatal blow by the development of non-Euclidean geometry. The void that this created in the philosophy of mathematics has been filled by a variety of plausible descriptions of the nature of mathematics and its relationship to human experience. Some of these views are presented in the essays that comprise this part. To date there is no universal consensus as to what is the real nature of mathematics in the modern age. Indeed, the upsets that attended the dismantling of the old ideas at the turn of the century so influenced succeeding generations of mathematicians that they prefer not to think about such matters. The complexity, beauty, and power of mathematics are so profound that most active mathematicians are content to leave discussions of ultimate meaning to the theologians. If ultimately they are drawn to discuss the philosophy of mathematics it is only after they are no longer able to create it.

Mathematics and Creativity

Alfred Adler

Alfred Adler was born in Germany in 1930. He received his Ph.D. in mathematics from U.C.L.A. in 1956. He has held positions at M.I.T., Rutgers, University of Bonn, and Purdue and has been professor of mathematics at S.U.N.Y., Stonybrook, since 1967.

Why are almost all famous mathematicians eldest sons? This intriguing question is posed by Alfred Adler in this essay on mathematics and creativity. In fact, the author does not give an answer to that question nor to a number of other more profound and penetrating questions relevant to the nature of mathematics. While this may be frustrating to those who like things all neatly tied up, it is a very honest approach. And the questions themselves may tell us more about Adler's view of mathematics than answers ever could.

There are a number of assertions in this essay that would surely be the subject of heated debate if raised in a company of mathematicians. For example, "There is little haste to be credited with results before someone else is . . ." is a statement to which we as the editors of this volume feel we can find exceptions in every decade of the past 300 years. Yet Adler's observations are very much worthy of consideration despite the personal hurt that is caused by such statements as "Each generation has its few great mathematicians, and mathematics would not even notice the absence of the others. They are useful as teachers, and their research harms no one, but it is of no importance at all."

MATHEMATICS, LIKE CHESS, requires too direct and personal a confrontation to allow graceful defeat. There is no element of luck; there are no partners to share the blame for mistakes; the nature of the discipline places it precisely at the center of the intellectual being, where true cerebral power waits to be tested. A loser must admit that in some very important way he is the intellectual inferior of a winner. Both mathematics and chess spread before the participant a vast domain of confrontation of intellect with strong opposition, together with extreme purity, elegance of form, and an infinitude of possibilites. Mathematics is pure language—the language of science. It is unique among languages in its ability to provide precise expression for every thought or concept that can be formulated in its terms. (In a spoken language, there exist words, like "happiness," that defy definition.) It is also an art—the most intellectual and classical of the arts. And almost no one is capable of doing significant mathematics. There are no acceptably good mathematicians. Each generation has its few great mathematicians, and mathematics would not even notice the absence of the others. They are useful as teachers, and their research harms no one, but it is of no importance at all. A mathematician is great or he is nothing. Perhaps that is where the purity of the discipline begins. In mathematics, no one can be fooled; there is never the remotest chance of great work's suddenly being done by a previously uninspired man; everyone recognizes mathematical genius immediately, and without bitterness or reservation. So it is tempting to ap-

Source: Alfred Adler, "Mathematics and Creativity." © 1972, The New Yorker Magazine, Inc. Reprinted by permission.

proach the nature of mathematical creativity by describing the nature of creative mathematicians. But that is the wrong way to go about it. For example, the approach cannot explain the fact, amusing at first and then puzzling, that nearly all mathematicians are eldest sons. The few exceptions tend to be mathematicians whose older brothers are mathematicians, too. Mathematical gifts cannot be unique to oldest sons. It must be that the discipline itself is crucial—that it provides a domain in which mental power and creativity can be wielded in a manner congenial to the special qualities of men who for a time, at least, were the only sons in their families.

The logical way to begin is to describe what mathematics is and what mathematicians do. But this is probably impossible. Almost certainly, any two mathematicians would disagree in significant ways if they were asked to give such a description, and a day later each would disagree with what he had said the day before. It can be said that mathematics is whatever mathematicians are doing. This sounds circular, and in some respects it is. But there is never any doubt about who is and who is not a creative mathematician, so all that is required is to keep track of the activities of these few men. A stronger case can be made for the assertion that mathematics is in large part the discovery and study of analogies. Mathematicians will consider two mathematical objects and ask whether they are similar in some significant way, and whether there are other objects that are like those two in the same significant way, and then, perhaps, whether there are among these objects further similiarities, which have not yet been discovered. It is almost impossible to give examples of this. Mathematics is at a stage where the apparently simple and easily posed problems are too difficult to approach, so it is necessary to construct elaborate mathematical objects with a great variety of special properties before there is any possibility of discovering fundamental relationships between the objects. Then, there are the branches of mathematics concerned with foundations. At one level, they deal with the nature of logic itself. At another level, they deal with numbers—the basic units of mathematics, and perhaps of all human thought. Often, the problems can be simply stated and yet are profoundly dif-

ficult—in fact, usually impossible even to begin to solve. Here is an example of the kind of question that is asked. A number is called a prime if it is divisible only by the number itself and the number one. So the numbers two, three, five, seven, eleven are primes, and the number six is not a prime. It seems apparent that all composite numbers are products of primes, as twelve is the product of two and two and three. It is another matter, but not a difficult one, to prove that this is so. Primes, then, are the building blocks of the whole number system, and mathematicians pursue their special properties. How many primes are there? Are they finite in number, or can primes of arbitrarily large size be found? A shrewd guess will not do. What is required is an assertion, together with its proof. Perhaps the reader can supply it. If so, he will have proved a theorem of Euclid, and will have discovered a fundamental property of the number system.

There are two simple and ruthless ethical standards by which the purity of any discipline can be determined. Mathematics has at times seemed almost alone in the attainment of these standards. What is required is, first, an institutionalized indifference to men whose work has been completed—a disregard or contempt for those who have accomplished much but who have lost the will to create and whose major accomplishments are of the past. This applies perfectly to mathematics. There is in mathematics no repressive establishment of older men, no traditional way to do mathematics and so to become an important member of the mathematical community, no shortage of room for the rapid progress of gifted men, none of the slavish behavior toward academic superiors which is common in many other disciplines. What is also required is the institutionalized conviction that accomplishment is important only if it advances the discipline in some significant way. Competition must exist for creative achievement only—with and for the discipline itself, rather than with competitors. This, too, applies perfectly. Plagiarism among mathematicians is essentially nonexistent. There is little haste to be credited with results before someone else is, because it simply does not matter who achieves results as long as someone does achieve them. This is not at all in the spirit of "The Double Helix," a book that, perhaps unfairly, indicts biochemistry as a field in which a major concomitant of success is a cynical attempt to keep others unaware of what is being done, and, when this attempt fails, to mislead and misdirect them. Science simply cannot function in this manner, and mathematics is a science.

The mathematical life of a mathematician is short. Work rarely improves after the age of twenty-five or thirty. If little has been accomplished by then, little will ever be accomplished.If greatness has been attained, good work may continue to appear, but the level of accomplishment will fall with each decade. Perhaps this is due to an early failure of the nerve for excellence. It is easy to believe that life is long and one's gifts are vast—easy at the beginning, that is. But the limits of life grow more evident; it becomes clear that great work can be done rarely, if at all. Moreover, there are family responsibilities and there are professional sinecures. Hard work can certainly continue. But creativity requires more than steady, hard, regular, capable work. It requires total commitment over years, with the likelihood of failure at the end, and so the likelihood of a total waste of those years. It requires work of truly immense concentration. Such consuming commitment can rarely be continued into middle and old age, and mathematicians after a time do minor work. In addition, mathematics is continually generating new concepts, which seem profound to the older men and must be painstakingly studied and learned. The young mathematicians absorb these concepts in their university studies and find them simple. What is agonizingly difficult for their teachers appears only natural to them. The students begin where the teachers have stopped; the teachers become scholarly observers.

One quality, that of absolute skepticism, is organically a part of mathematics more than of most other disciplines. Not that the world is deficient in this quality; every thinking person possesses it. But where most of life's encounters invite skepticism, mathematics, by its nature, forces skepticism on its students as a first requirement. This can be put more strongly: Mathematics is a field in which much that appears obviously true is in fact false. (A natural corollary would be that mathematics is a field in which very little is known, and this is indeed so, but the statement is equally true of every other domain of human thought.) The ambient uncertainty is apparent even at an elementary level. For example, nothing could seem more reasonable than the assertion that every surface—every page of a book, say—has two sides. It is reasonable, but it is false. The Möbius band, a figure produced by twisting a strip of paper and then gluing the ends together, has only one side. This is no trick, no joke, no semantic sport. It is an aspect of reality that cannot be dismissed, and therefore no proof of anything can ever make use of the falsehood that all surfaces have two sides. Another example: It is easy to sketch a curve with an angle in it (for instance, the letter v). It is just as easy, if more time-consuming, to sketch one with three angles (the letter w), or twenty, or ten million. The process becomes absurd, however, when one is asked to construct a curve consisting entirely of angles, or corners. Absurd, and yet it can be done. About a century ago, the mathematician Weierstrass gave an example of a curve consisting of angles, or corners, and nothing else. It cannot be sketched, but its equation can be written down, and can be comprehended by most college juniors and seniors. The examples proliferate. They cannot be avoided, for they lurk in every branch of mathematics, and the mathematician learns early to accept no fact, to believe no statement, however apparently reasonable or obvious or trivial, until it has been proved, rigorously and totally, by a series of steps proceeding from universally accepted first principles.

And even the first principles have been exposed as uncertain. Again, it is not a matter of semantics. Nor is it a matter of the pronouncement that it is fallible human beings who are doing the thinking and hence the product of their thought is fallible. This is true, but too obvious to be very fruitful—not a statement likely to force us to take a large piece of our picture of ourselves and of our world and alter it radically. Goedel's Theorem does precisely that. It proves that there exist meaningful mathematical statements that are neither provable nor disprovable, now or ever—neither provable nor disprovable, that is, not simply because human thought or knowledge is insufficiently advanced but because the very nature of logic renders them incapable of resolution, no matter how long the human race survives or how wise it becomes. There is no way to escape this conundrum. It is not a question of sophistry of any kind. The theorem itself was proved some decades ago, and recently the first example of an undecidable mathematical statement was found. Called the Continuum Hypothesis, it is the assertion that in a set-theoretic sense there exist no sets with more elements than the integers but fewer than the set of all real numbers. So there it stands—an assertion that to the end of time cannot be proved and yet cannot be disproved. The philosophical implications are devastating.

The mathematician's disciplined skepticism and creative imagination might seem enough to guarantee success in the non-mathematical world. Mathematicians are often expected to manage brilliantly in the fields of business and finance. Of course, they do nothing of the kind. Their non-mathematical efforts are, on the whole, pitifully inept. The qualities embedded in the mind of the mathematician by the discipline of mathematics fail to extend beyond the boundaries of mathematics. It appears to be mathematics itself, rather than any inner constraint, that anchors the mathematician to caution and rational thought in his professional work—a measure of the astonishing power of the discipline. For example, departmental and mathematics-society meetings are occupied mainly with talk—aimless and pedantic talk, billowing with Latinisms. Little of substance is ever accomplished, or even intended. The financial adventures of mathematicians consist of wildly speculative stock-market excursions—always exciting but usually unsuccessful—rationalized by elaborate but irrelevant formulas and systems. Almost no mathematicians are to be found in banking or finance, the two fields to which one might suppose them to be ideally suited. Nor do mathematicians distinguish themselves by their political activities, at any level. They have been known for their radical positions, usually on the left but sometimes on the right—positions defended emotionally and often irrationally. There is no reason to expect mathematicians to do well in politics, true. However, their aversion to any but extreme and speculative positions has caused

them to forfeit even the modest power and influence due them in bureaucratic affairs, where, consequently, mathematics at all levels is much less influential than any of the other sciences and much less influential than its scientific importance and its procedural virtues warrant. All this contrasts vividly with the achievements of mathematicians when they do mathematics: meaningful results of brevity and simplicity, accomplished by an insistence on total rationality both in hypotheses and in proofs. The professional restraints are so severe that the reaction is too powerful. As soon as the bonds are loosened, mathematicians adopt careless procedures that, together with a vast self-esteem and a conviction of intellectual superiority, cause them to overlook crucial aspects of whatever they are doing—to lose the mental self-control essential to almost every successful human effort.

Why do otherwise rational men fail to see what is happening to them? It may be because the non-academic world makes it easy for them to succeed in very minor ways—to fulfill small ambitions and a greed for acclaim. Perhaps mathematicians, lacking the imagination to appreciate the scope and sophistication of the outside world, confuse minor success with real achievement and are satisfied with it. Then, too, they seldom recognize failure when they are confronted by it; rather, they tend to think of it as simply one more betrayal by a society that usually patronizes them while elevating armies of patently inferior claimants. In the academic world, on the other hand, mathematicians often enjoy rewards that they do not merit. They are engulfed by admirers from the departments of philosophy and the social sciences, disciplines that suffer from a dangerous confusion of thought; namely, that the presence and the casual contributions of scientists certify them as sciences. Mathematicians are too vain to assess such admiration at its true worth.

Mathematicians as teachers are another matter entirely. There is no reason to expect good mathematicians to be good teachers, any more than to expect them to be good financiers, or even good philosophers. These subjects all rely to a large extent on mathematical reasoning and techniques but involve other talents as well. Nevertheless, almost every good mathematician is also a good teacher, while almost no mediocre mathematician can teach the subject adequately even at an elementary level. This phenomenon is easier to recognize than to explain. Students, even though in most cases they do not know what constitutes good mathematics or which are the best mathematicians they have encountered, will unfailingly pick out the best mathematicians when asked to identify their best mathematics teachers. Love of mathematics and active involvement in its development forge ties between the teacher and his students; the latter are rarely fooled by style or dramatic effect. The usual confusions are absent: confusions between content and presentation, between the subject and the man, between profound inspiration and trivial manipulation—in short, those confusions common in the classrooms of so many other subjects, and common, in fact, in so great a part of life. There is no such thing as a man who does not create mathematics and yet is a fine mathematics teacher. Textbooks, course material—these do not approach in importance the communication of what mathematics is really about, of where it is going, and of where it currently stands with respect to the specific branch of it being taught. What really matters is the communication of the spirit of mathematics. It is a spirit that is active rather than contemplative—a spirit of disciplined search for adventures of the intellect. Only an adventurer can really tell of adventures.

There is no Nobel Prize in mathematics. In view of the record of the Nobel committee, this doesn't matter very much. But it is an indication of what all mathematicians eventually learn to expect, and even take for granted—that successful research and teaching are the only rewards they will ever receive. Money? Salaries are adequate but never have been and never will be generous enough to permit more than a modest middle-class way of life. Power? It is almost ridiculous to speak of any relationship between mathematics and secular power. Of course, money and power are only superficial rewards, and it is possible to live without them; less tangible rewards, those of recognition and understanding, are what make effort and accomplishment rich and fulfilling when things are going well, and effort and failure bear-

able when things are going badly. But mathematicians cannot expect these, either. For example, it would be astonishing if the reader could identify more than two of the following names: Gauss, Cauchy, Euler, Hilbert, Riemann. It would be equally astonishing if he should be unfamiliar with the names of Mann, Stravinsky, de Kooning, Pasteur, John Dewey. The point is not that the first five are the mathematical equivalents of the second five. They are not. They are the mathematical equivalents of Tolstoy, Beethoven, Rembrandt, Darwin, Freud. The geometry of relativity—the work of Riemann—has had consequences as profound as psychoanalysis. The mathematical equivalents of Mann, Stravinsky, and the others would be Bochner, Thom, Serre, Cartan, and Weil, and it is all but certain that the reader is unfamiliar with every one of these names. There is really no reason he should be. But that is precisely the cruelty of the situation. All professions reward accomplishment in part with admiration by peers, but mathematics can reward it with admiration of no other kind. It is, in fact, impossible for a mathematician even to talk intelligently to non-mathematicians about his mathematical work. In the company of friends, writers can discuss their books, economists the state of the economy, lawyers their latest cases, and businessmen their recent acquisitions, but mathematicians cannot discuss their mathematics at all. And the more profound their work, the less understandable it is; a spirited high-school teacher can regale his audience with puzzles and magic squares, but there is no way for the serious mathematician to talk to the non-mathematician about his latest results on the homotopy groups of spheres. Few laymen are really interested enough to distinguish between real mathematicians and fools who can multiply six-digit numbers in their heads. Even a well-educated layman is generally willing to grant, at most, an hour's time to the consideration of the implications of the last half century of mathematical discovery, and then only if he is in a benign humor and the explicant is eloquent and talks philosophy rather than mathematics. The listener will then almost certainly leave without any understanding of what is going on in mathematics, because he has not cared to expend any effort on understanding mathematics by first learning a bit about it; that is, by learning it as a language. The most rudimentary requirement for comprehending a language is a knowledge of its vocabulary, and acquiring a vocabulary demands some hard work. The mathematician can take it for granted that acquiring the vocabulary of mathematics is simply out of the question for his friends, acquaintances—nearly anyone.

And yet the language of mathematics is so natural and so simple in comparison to the spoken languages that the resistance it encounters is difficult to understand. All children learn to count, and most seem to enjoy it. Perhaps incompetent teaching spoils mathematics for them early. Elementary-school teachers know all about arithmetical and algebraic techniques, but not many are able to alert their students to the power and beauty of mathematics, at which these techniques can only hint. Algebra, geometry, calculus— some of the most profound residues of human thought—are taught simply as trades. The operational methods of mathematics become a calculating aid. Yet it is operational methods that distinguish one language from another, that give each language its particular "feel" and, in many ways, endow nationalities with their divergent patterns of thought. The operational methods of mathematics are designed to refine and simplify the search for analogies. Their purposes are to abstract, to generalize, to compress, to isolate, and to expose.

The first abstraction, that of number, is perhaps the most profound. There exist cultures that have not discovered numbers—cultures that can speak of "one" and "many" but of nothing between. Most attempts at a definition of the concept of number seem reasonable at first but prove unsatisfactory on close inspection. Not until this century, in fact, was the first logically acceptable definition found. A further abstraction is that of algebra. This requires speaking of numbers as a whole, rather than of specific numbers, so letters—called variables—are introduced to take the place of particular numbers. The letter t might represent time—not one second or thirty hours but any amount of time whatever. The letter h might represent height—any height—and the letter w any weight. In this way, the concept of

numbers is abstracted to that of variables. And it is possible to go much further. A first generalization is accomplished by the recognition that the variables t, h, and w are simply special cases of a more general phenomenon, that of mathematical functions. A second generalization occurs with the observation that functions need not be restricted to real values, such as lengths or widths, but can be given meaning for other mathematical objects as well. One can consider collections of functions, and then speak of functions of functions, and so on. In short, by abstracting and generalizing first the concept of number, then the concept of the variable, and then the concept of function, it is possible to arrive at an extremely abstract and general level of thought, and so to isolate the kernel of subtlety and difficulty that the less abstract levels obscure.

Then, there is the method of accommodation. The mathematical language is continually being altered to fit new results, to simplify new techniques. In this respect, it differs from the spoken languages, which usually resist accommodation. It is a commonplace that human thought is often bent by the accumulated meanings of words, instead of bending the words to denote refinements of their old meanings. Mathematics does not suffer from this weakness. In the calculus, for instance, the derivative was at one time denoted by a Newtonian symbol—adequate but uninspired. Another notation, introduced by Leibnitz, denoted the derivative by the symbol dy/dx, which looks like a fraction but is nothing of the kind. It is only a symbol, and the two ds cannot be cancelled, as they could if the dy/dx were a fraction. The Leibnitz notation nevertheless suggests that in some sense derivatives can be expected to behave like fractions, even though they are not fractions. But can they really? Do they satisfy some of the usual rules for fractions? It became the task of mathematicians to find out. They can and do. The appropriate notation thus led directly to a collection of results that had been hidden by inappropriate notation. One good definition is worth three theorems.

Finally, there are the methods of compression and referral, typified by the evolution of the theory of tensors. The original theory, still in use among some scientists, emphasizes the manipulation of tensors, which are enormously complicated variables, involving elaborate arrays of subscripts and superscripts. The modern theory derives from the observation that these complications are not essential—that the theory would remain intact, and, in fact, would be greatly advanced, if the complicated objects (tensors) representing something simple (numbers) were replaced by simple objects (called forms) representing something complicated (called matrices). It does not really matter whether the reader is familiar with the technical concepts; the significant thing is the method. What has been accomplished is a compression of the notation into one that is easy to manipulate mathematically, together with a referral of the difficulties to the one place where they really belong (the theory of multilinear algebra) and away from the subscripts and superscripts, which serve only to obscure the basic problems.

It is all very simple: Each of these methods results in the isolation and, finally, the exposure of some essential—which is to say difficult—mathematical problem. It is axiomatic among mathematicians that only difficult tasks are worth doing. A difficult problem will lead to important results; a truly intractable problem is one that is worth any amount of time and effort. The most exasperating questions promise the most significant mathematical answers. For example, one of the first results of the theory of integrals is a formula for powers of x. The formula, which is simple, is valid for all powers except the power -1. Therefore, precisely this power must be the important one. Why does the formula break down? Where is one to look for a resolution of the special case? Is there some mathematical object whose importance has never been fully appreciated and which is suddenly signalling its hidden meanings? The answer is known: the formula for the case -1 requires the introduction of the logarithm—the logarithm of high-school algebra, which in high school is usually relegated to a computational role. Why should it appear among the formulas of the theory of integrals, when it really belongs to algebra? What in the world is the logarithm doing in so diverse a pair of domains? These are among the next questions that must be asked about this most important mathematical object. It is difficult to believe that anyone would not wish to know the answers.

Nothing ventured, nothing gained. It is time now to propose the existence of a pattern in all that has been said: The essential feature of mathematical creativity is the exploration, under the pressure of powerful implosive forces, of difficult problems for whose validity and importance the explorer is eventually held accountable by reality. The reality is the physical world. Mathematics allows great speculative freedom, but in the end each mathematical theory must be relevant to physical reality, either directly or by relevance to the main body of mathematics, which, in turn, has direct physical origins. There is perhaps no other way to force the distinction between style and substance, and so to purify a discipline periodically of stylistic eccentricities and of trivial but fashionable diversions. The forces that exert the pressure have been described. There is the constant awareness of time, of the certainty that mathematical creativity ends early in life, so that important work must begin early and proceed quickly if it is to be completed. There is the focus on problems of great difficulty, because the discipline is unforgiving in its contempt for the solution of easy problems and in its indifference to the solution of almost any problems but the most profound and difficult ones. There is the pressure of the nature of mathematics itself—of the elusiveness of truth, of the ever-present necessity for skepticism. And, finally, there is the non-mathematical world, in which the mathematician appears unable to find success, and which at almost all points accords the mathematician a monolithic indifference. So there is no way out for mathematicians; there is no place for them to turn but to other mathematicians and inward on themselves. The insanity and suicide levels among mathematicians are probably the highest in any of the professions. But the rewards are proportionately great. A new mathematical result, entirely new, never before conjectured or understood by anyone, nursed from the first tentative hypothesis through labyrinths of false attempted proofs, wrong approaches, unpromising directions, and months or years of difficult and delicate work—there is nothing, or almost nothing, in the world that can bring a joy and a sense of power and tranquility to equal those of its creator. And a great new mathematical edifice is a triumph that whispers of immortality. What is more, mathematics generates a momentum, so that any significant result points automatically to another new result, or perhaps to two or three other new results. And so it goes—goes, until the momentum all at once dissipates. Then the mathematical career is, essentially, over; the frustrations remain, but the satisfactions have vanished. It has been said that no man should become a philosopher before the age of forty. Perhaps no man should remain a mathematician after the age of forty. The world is, after all, full of worlds to conquer.

The Meaning of Mathematics

Morris Kline

Morris Kline was born in New York City and did his undergraduate and graduate work in New York City at N.Y.U. He has been associated with N.Y.U. almost continuously from 1930 and was appointed emeritus professor in 1976. He has been a Fulbright and a Guggenheim fellow.

Morris Kline is an American commentator on the nature and history of mathematics. His books, which include Mathematics in Western Culture *and* Mathematics and the Physical World, *have been widely accepted both as popular exposition and as college texts in mathematics history. He is well qualified to present a historically comparative discussion of the nature of mathematics.*

Kline has firmly held the view that mathematics can successfully develop only if there is constant and vigorous interaction between the worlds of mathematics and the physical sciences. In his opinion whenever mathematics has been isolated from physical reality and developed purely as formal abstraction it has quickly become sterile. In short order, Kline feels, this sterility is followed by the decline of mathematics and the threat of its extinction. Mathematics, at these times, has been saved from extinction only by heroic effort engendered by the vital insights obtained from fresh physical problems. This view is by no means universal, but it has been persuasively argued by Kline in a number of public lectures.

MATHEMATICS IS UNDOUBTEDLY one of man's greatest intellectual achievements. In addition to the knowledge which the subject itself offers, its language, processes and theories give science its organization and power. Mathematical calculations dictate engineering design. The method of mathematics has inspired social and economic thought, while mathematical thinking has fashioned styles in painting, architecture and music. Even national survival depends today upon progress in mathematics. Finally, mathematics has been a major force in molding our views of the universe and of man's place and purpose in it.

The paradox of how such an abstract body of thought can give man an ever-widening and deepening grip on the physical world and work its influences on almost all phases of our culture tantalizes the nonmathematician. We propose therefore to examine the nature of mathematics and to see why the subject possesses such astonishing effectiveness.

The distinguishing feature of mathematics is its method of reasoning. By measuring the angles of a dozen or so triangles of various shapes and sizes a person would find that the sum in any one triangle is 180 degrees. He could then conclude by inductive reasoning that the sum of the angles in every triangle is 180 degrees. One can also reason by analogy. The circle plays about the same role among curves that the sphere does among surfaces. Since the circle bounds more area than any other curve with the same perimeter, a person might conclude that the sphere bounds more volume than any other surface with the same area.

Reasoning by induction and by analogy calls for

Source: Morris Kline, "The Meaning of Mathematics." Reprinted from *The Saturday Evening Post* © 1960, The Curtis Publishing Company.

recourse to observation and even experiment to obtain the facts on which to base each argument. But the senses are limited and inaccurate. Moreover, even if the facts gathered for the purposes of induction and analogy are sound, these methods do not yield unquestionable conclusions. For example, though cows eat grass and pigs are similar to cows, it does not follow that pigs eat grass.

To avoid these sources of error, the mathematician utilizes another method of reasoning. He may have the fact that $x - 3 = 7$ and wish to find the value of x. He notes that if he adds 3 to both sides of this equation he will obtain $x = 10$. May he perform this step? He knows that equals added to equals give equals. He knows also that by adding 3 to both sides of the original equation he is adding equals to equals. Hence he concludes that the step is justified. The reasoning here is deductive. As in the present case, so in all deductive reasoning the conclusion is a logically inescapable consequence of the known facts. Hence it is as indubitable as these facts.

Since deduction yields conclusions as certain as the initial facts, the application of this process to known truths produces new ones. The latter may then be used as the premises of new deductive arguments. Every conclusion so obtained may not be significant, but the end result of ten or twenty such arguments could be. If so, it is labeled a theorem. The series of deductive arguments which lead to the theorem is the proof.

Though mathematical proof is necessarily deductive, the creative process practically never is. To foresee what to prove or what chain of deductive arguments will establish a possible result, the mathematician uses observation, measurement, intuition, imagination, induction, or even sheer trial and error. The process of discovery in mathematics is not confined to one pattern or method. Indeed, it is in part as inexplicable as the creative act in any art or science.

The requirement that mathematical reasoning be deductive was laid down by the Greeks. The Greek mathematicians were also philosophers and as such were concerned with truths. They saw clearly that only deductive reasoning could supply certainties. By recommending mental exploration of the riches contained in some available truths, a most reasonable people carved out a new intellec-

tual world and made reason a vital factor in western culture.

The plan to obtain truths by deduction presupposes some initial truths. These the Greeks found in the domains of number and geometrical figures. It seemed axiomatic that equals added to equals should yield equals, that the whole is greater than its parts and that two points determine a straight line. Hence mathematics was built on the axioms of number and geometry. Mathematicians as mathematicians do not reason about forces, weights, sound, light, chemical mixtures or the goal of life.

There were other reasons for the decision to concentrate on number and geometrical figures. The triangle formed by a piece of land and the triangle formed by the earth, sun and moon at any instant are both subsumed under the abstract geometrical concept of triangle. Study of the properties of this concept would yield knowledge about these two physical triangles and about hundreds of others in one swoop. What the Greeks saw, in other words, was that number, size and shape are fundamental properties. In fact, the Greeks believed that the universe was mathematically designed, and so the phenomena of nature could be understood only in terms of number and geometry.

The third feature of mathematics is its highly symbolic language. There is, however, nothing deep or complicated about this language, for it is only a shorthand and, in fact, an easier one to learn than that employed by stenographers. Such symbols as $+$ for addition, x for an unknown quantity, and x^2 for x times x, are, of course, well known. Letters are used for several purposes, and the context usually tells us what is intended. Suppose, for example, we take a famous mathematical statement which describes the result of some experiments made by Galileo about 350 years ago: The number of feet which an object falls in any given number of seconds is 16 times the square of the number of seconds it has been falling. Symbolically this statement is written as $d = 16t^2$ wherein t stands for any number of seconds and d the corresponding distance fallen in these t seconds. Thus, if an object falls for 5 seconds, simple arithmetic shows that it has fallen 400 feet.

Why is symbolism used so extensively? Brevity,

precision and comprehensibility are the three major reasons. The brevity is apparent. Precision is aided because many important words of ordinary discourse are ambiguous. The word "equal," for example, can refer to equality in size, shape, political rights, intellectual abilities, or other qualities. Hence the assertion that all men are born equal is vague. As used in an expression such as $d = 16t^2$, the equals sign stands for numerical equality. The comprehensibility gained through symbolism derives largely from the fact that the mind easily carries and works with symbolic expressions, but has considerable difficulty even in carrying the equivalent verbal statement.

Our discussion of the method of proof, subject matter and language of mathematics gives some indication of its nature. It is but a step from this point to see some of the sources of the power of mathematics. Number and geometrical figures, and the relationships built on these abstractions, such as formulas, embody the essence of hundreds of physical situations. Any knowledge acquired about these abstractions is many times more potent than that acquired about any particular situation, just as any fact applicable to all men is more powerful than a fact about John Jones. A second source of strength derives from the reliability of deductive proof. Hence the conclusions derived by the Greeks are still acceptable as logical consequences of the axioms and will be a thousand years from now.

But the power of mathematics rests on still another ground. The mathematician is the professional reasoner who devotes his life to learning what has been accomplished in his subject and to extending the results by new reasoning. Moreover, all of the results obtained by one generation are passed on to the next, and this one carries on from where the preceding generation left off. Each generation adds a story to the structure.

To appreciate the full power of mathematics we must examine its role in science. In the seventeenth century, when modern science was founded and received its first great impetus, several major physical laws were obtained by induction and experimentation. Of these we shall be concerned with the second of Newton's three laws of motion and with Newton's law of gravitation. These laws involve a few, by now, common concepts—force, mass and acceleration. Newton's second law of motion states that any force applied to a mass gives it an acceleration, and the quantitative relation among the amount of force F, the amount of mass m, and the amount of acceleration a is

$$F = ma. \tag{1}$$

The Newtonian law of gravitation states that any two pieces of matter in the universe exert a force of attraction or gravitational force on each other and that the quantitative expression for this force is given by the formula

$$F = \frac{G\,mM}{r^2} \tag{2}$$

In this equation F is the amount of force exerted; m is the amount of mass in one body; M is the amount of mass in the second body; r is the distance between these bodies; and G is a constant, that is, the same quantity no matter which masses are involved and whatever the distance between them.

These laws concern force, mass and acceleration, which are physical concepts, and the obtainment of relationships among such quantities is the task of the scientist. However, formulas (1) and (2), regarded in and for themselves, are merely algebraic equations relating variables, and it is legitimate to ask the mathematician whether he can draw upon his stock of theorems and processes to deduce new significant equations from (1) and (2). He can. He observes first of all that it is mathematically correct to write formula (2) in the form

$$F = m\left(\frac{G\,M}{r^2}\right). \tag{3}$$

He then compares (1) and (3) and observes that the two formulas have the same algebraic form. Moreover, formula (1) applies to any force and so, in particular, applies to the force of gravitation. Since the quantity which multiplies m in (1) is acceleration, the quantity which multiplies m in (3) must also be acceleration. That is, the acceleration which the gravitational force F between M and m imparts to m is

$$a = \frac{G\,M}{r^2}. \tag{4}$$

Next let us apply this formula to a particular situation. Let M denote the mass of the earth. Equation (4) now gives the acceleration which the gravitational force of the earth imparts to any other mass, the acceleration which causes the mass to fall if released from a point above the surface of the earth. It is a fact that the earth acts as if all its mass were concentrated at the center. Then for objects near the surface of the earth the quantity r in (4) is the radius of the earth. The quantity G, as noted above, is a constant under all conditions. Hence, all quantities on the right side of (4) are constant no matter which mass m near the surface of the earth is involved. We may conclude that all bodies fall to earth with the same constant acceleration, a famous result which Galileo discovered experimentally, but which we have deduced from the second law of motion and the law of gravitation.

Now, says the mathematician, we can go a step further. If the quantities a, G and r in (4) are known, then (4) may be regarded as a simple first-degree equation in the unknown M, and M can readily be calculated. For, correct algebraic steps yield that the mass M of the earth is

$$M = \frac{ar^2}{G}. \tag{5}$$

Let us see if we do know the several quantities which appear on the right side of (5). Since the acceleration of all bodies falling to earth is the same, one could take any falling body and measure its acceleration. This quantity had been measured by Galileo and is 32 feet per second each second. The quantity G is a constant under all conditions. It can be and has been measured many times in a laboratory where the conditions are at the experimenter's convenience. Its value is 1.07 divided by 1,000,000,000. The value of the earth's radius r can be determined by a simple application of geometry and was first obtained by the Greek Eratosthenes about 250 B.C. This radius is 4000 miles or 4000×5280 feet. After the known numerical values are substituted for a, G, and r in (5) one finds that

$$M = 131 \times 10^{23} \text{ pounds.} \tag{6}$$

(The symbol 10^{23} stands for the product $10 \times 10 \times 10$ . . . containing 23 factors.) The mass of the earth is a staggering number, but what is more staggering is how easily one finds it.

With essentially such simple tools, Isaac Newton, his contemporaries and his immediate successors calculated the masses of the sun and the several planets, the paths of comets, the motion of the moon and the rise and fall of the tides. In particular, Newton showed that the Keplerian laws of planetary motion, which Kepler had obtained merely by induction from data, were logical consequences of the laws of motion and the law of gravitation. Thus the key laws of the heliocentric theory of planetary motion, which up to that time were unrelated to any basic physical principles, received indisputable support.

The work we have just described belongs to celestial mechanics, a field which has come to the fore again to treat the motion of satellites. It was followed by the construction of equally majestic theories for light, sound, electricity and magnetism, electromagnetic waves (which comprise the radio waves, the very existence of which was predicted mathematically); the flow of fluids and gases as applied to the design of ships and airplanes; relativity, atomic structure, molecular structure (now basic in modern chemistry); the biological science of mathematical genetics and the statistical treatment of social and medical problems. In all these domains the union of mathematics and science has been most fertile.

The contributions of a special, functional language and the deductive processes are a small part of the mathematical largess. Science seeks to obtain knowledge of the physical world, but that knowledge would be useless if unorganized. A mass of disconnected results is no more science than a collection of bricks is a house. The major results of scientific work are theories. In each of these, hundreds of results are organized in a deductive structure very much like Euclidean geometry. At the head of the structure are basic physical principles which play the role of axioms. From these axioms the various laws of any one theory are deduced. The large and overriding fact is that the entire structure of a scientific theory is held together by a series of mathematical deductions. The mortar which binds the bricks, or individual laws, one to another is mathematical deducibility. A scientific theory is, so to speak, a branch of mathematics whose axioms state quantitative relationships among physical concepts, whose structure is a series of mathematical deductions and whose theorems are mathematical affirmations about these concepts.

Mathematics plays still another role in science. The central concept in the most impressive and most successful body of science, mechanics, is the force of gravitation. This force, when exerted by the earth, pulls objects to the earth and, when exerted by the sun, keeps the planets in their paths. What is the mechanism by which the earth and the sun exert their respective attractive forces? Newton had considered this very question and, having failed to answer it, uttered his famous "I frame no hypotheses." The history of this subject is extensive, but the upshot of it is that no explanation of the action of the force of gravitation has ever been given.

What then do we know about the force of gravitation? The answer is formula (2) above. We have a quantitative law which tells us how to calculate this force and from which we can deduce how bodies will move, what paths they will take, and where they will be at particular instants of time. We have not a shred of insight into the physical nature of the force itself; it can with full justification be regarded as sheer fiction.

In the Newtonian age mathematics mounted the steed of science and took the reins in its own hands. Since the seventeenth century the physical behavior of nature has become less and less clear despite the vast expansion of the sciences, and mathematical laws have become the essence and goal of science. The mathematical conquest of science has by now proceeded so far that in our own century the late Sir James Jeans, the noted astronomer and physicist, claimed that the mathematical description of the universe *is* the ultimate reality. The pictures and models we use to assist our understanding are a step away. We go beyond the mathematical formula at our own risk.

While mathematical physics was growing to manhood, mathematics began to exert a formative influence on numerous other branches of our culture. Revival of interest in the physical world caused the Renaissance painters to abandon the unrealistic, highly symbolic style of medieval painting and to seek a veridical depiction of nature. To solve the problem of presenting on a flat surface scenes which would create the same visual impression as the three-dimensional world itself, the painters created a mathematical system of perspective painting. This introduction of depth, solidity, mass and consequent realism is the key contribution to Renaissance painting.

The mathematical treatment of matter in motion engendered the now famous philosophical doctrines that every phenomenon in the universe can be reduced to matter and motion, that all matter, including man's body, follows invariable and immutable mathematical laws, that man's will is bound fast, and that thought is but a mechanical reaction to material sensations impressed on the brain through the sense organs. Inspired by the success of the mathematical method in the physical sciences and enthusiastic about the power of reason exercised through mathematics, leading eighteenth-century thinkers undertook a rational approach to social problems and launched the sciences of government and economics. The spread of this same rational spirit freed man from superstitions and groundless fears and permitted him to breathe in a more tolerant atmosphere.

The proliferating demands of science, which first became urgent during the seventeenth century, stimulated an enormous expansion in mathematics proper. To obtain a deeper appreciation of the nature of modern mathematics we must look into these more recent developments. The mathematics which the Europeans possessed by 1600 consisted of algebra, Euclidean geometry and the beginnings of trigonometry. In the seventeenth century the need to study curves—whether the paths of light through lenses, the paths of cannonballs, the paths of ships at sea, or the paths of the planets—prompted René Descartes and Pierre de Fermat to create an algebraic method of representing curves so that algebra could be used to deduce the properties of curves. This creation is known as co-ordinate or analytic geometry.

The need to calculate varying velocity, force, pressure, and other physical quantities in problems of celestial mechanics as well as in navigation and gunfire was met by the creation of a new concept, the concept of a limit, and a new method called differentiation. This is the substance of the differential calculus. To obtain the sum of an infinite number of small quantities, for example, the sum of the gravitational forces which each bit of earth exerts on some external mass, the integral calculus was created.

The calculus was the beginning of a series of new branches commonly grouped under the name of analysis. Differential equations, infinite series, differential geometry, the calculus of variations, functions of a complex variable and vector and tensor analysis are but a few of the subdivisions of analysis. The domain of algebra was likewise extended to include such abstractions as complex numbers, vectors, hypernumbers, matrices, abstract sets and the theory of structures of algebra known as abstract algebra. Projective geometry, non-Euclidean geometry, algebraic geometry and topology joined Euclidean geometry.

The major motivation for all these creations was to further the leading physical studies of the eighteenth and nineteenth centuries—the strength of beams in structures, the motion of ships, the flow of the tides, the development of steam as a source of power, the generation and utilization of electrical power, the improvement of optical instruments, ballistics, and dozens of other new or growing scientific interests. But we should not overlook the fact that mathematicians enjoy the creative mathematical activity itself, the intellectual challenge, the satisfaction of accomplishment and the beauty of proofs and results. Given the themes suggested by physical problems, mathematicians develop these far beyond the needs of science, often to find that they have anticipated other needs or have unintentionally supplied the concepts and frameworks for new physical theories.

While the proliferation of mathematics is a phenomenon of our modern culture, an even more startling development has been the realization that mathematics is not an absolute, all-embracing truth, or description of reality, in the sense that man had until recently thought it was. For 2000 years the axioms of number and geometry were accepted as self-evident truths. Since the theorems are logically necessary consequences of the axioms, the theorems, too, were believed to be incontrovertible truths.

The creation of non-Euclidean geometry had the unintended effect of thrusting mathematics off this pedestal. Historically, non-Euclidean geometry was the result of attempts to find a simpler version of the Euclidean parallel-line axiom which postulates, in effect, that through any point in a given plane there is one, and only one, line parallel to a given line. In the course of this research, mathematicians deliberately adopted an axiom on parallel lines which contradicted Euclid's axiom. From this new axiom and the remainder of Euclid's axioms they proceeded to deduce theorems. They expected to arrive at inconsistencies within the new geometry; that is, they expected to find some theorems contradicting others because they had started with an axiom, which, so they thought, denied the truth. But these contradictions failed to appear!

The supreme mathematician of the nineteenth century, Karl Friedrich Gauss, was the first to see the handwriting on the wall. He realized that Euclidean geometry could no longer be regarded as the only geometry of physical space and that a non-Euclidean geometry might do as well. Further, his efforts to test experimentally which of the geometries, Euclidean or non-Euclidean, fits the physical world better, ended in failure. The situation became even more unsettled when Bernhard Riemann created additional non-Euclidean geometries. The potential applicability of all the non-Euclidean geometries was increased when mathematicians recognized that the physical "straight" lines used in the most weighty scientific work are not stretched strings or rulers' edges but paths of light rays. Since these paths are generally not straight, the geometry whose axioms fitted their behavior and the behavior of figures formed by such "lines" could very well be one of the non-Euclidean varieties. The mathematicians were ultimately forced to admit that there was no reason to believe in the exclusive truth of any one of these geometries. When the theory of relativity made use of a non-Euclidean geometry, the point was driven home.

Some mathematicians sought refuge in those portions of mathematics which rest on the number system and maintained that these at least offer truths. However, this thesis is also indefensible, for we now see more clearly that while the arithmetic we ordinarily use fits the common situations involving quantity, there are other arithmetics and their algebras which fit other situations. To mention a trivial example, an alternative arithmetic fitting a real situation is used when we state that four hours after nine o'clock the hour will be one o'clock rather than thirteen o'clock.

A word of comfort here to the nonmathematician who fears that he may have learned the rudiments of arithmetic and geometry in vain—or suspect that my earlier statements concerning the validity of mathematical processes are now contradicted. "Two plus two equals four" is still a valid deduction from the axioms of arithmetic just as the theorems of Euclidean geometry are still valid deductions from Euclid's axioms. However, the arithmetic and geometric conclusions can be applied only where experience tells us that the axioms are applicable. Thus we shall still use the fact that 2 dollars plus 2 dollars are 4 dollars, but not that 2 raindrops added to 2 raindrops are 4 raindrops. Two raindrops plus 2 raindrops make a puddle. Again, if we mix 2 cubic inches of hydrogen and 1 of oxygen, we obtain not 3 but 2 cubic inches of water. Philosophically this suggests that "truth" in mathematics, as in all human processes, is a many-faceted thing.

Recognition of the shattering fact that mathematics, which had always been regarded as the anchor of truth and as conclusive evidence that man can attain truths, rests on pragmatic grounds was a direct result of the nineteenth-century questioning of man's assumptions concerning the physical world. Mathematicians had believed that the assumptions or axioms—and therefore the logical consequences—were truths. It was now realized that such axioms are man-made inferences based on limited sense data and are only approximations of what happens in the physical world. In fact, the word "axiom" should now be taken to mean assumption, rather than self-evident truth. We continue to use the axioms and conclusions, even though they are not truths, because they do offer some highly useful knowledge about the physical world—the best knowledge, in fact, that man possesses.

Oddly, though truth, the most prized possession of mathematics, was taken from it, the subject emerged richer for the loss. Axioms palpably untrue had led to geometries which proved use-

ful. This experience justified the exploration of any system of axioms, however unpromising for application it might seem at the outset. Mathematics, which had been fettered to the physical world, passed from serfdom to freedom.

There is no doubt of the positive value of the new freedom. From the unrestricted play of mathematical imagination have come and will continue to come systems of thought which may prove to be far more valuable in representing and mastering the physical world than could have come from concentration on the two original systems of number and Euclidean geometry. So it was, when Einstein needed to know the structure of a particular four-dimensional, non-Euclidean geometry, that he found the information at hand.

Examination of the newer mathematics reveals another gradual change in its nature. The early concepts of mathematics, the whole number, the fractions and the several geometrical figures, were clearly suggested by immediate experiences. Mathematicians later found themselves developing and applying such abstract extensions of the idea of number as irrational, negative and complex numbers. Because they did not at first understand these new types of numbers or recognize their usefulness, even the greatest ones resisted their introduction. Having worked for centuries with numbers and geometrical figures which were suggested directly by physical objects, mathematicians had implicitly and unconsciously concluded that their concepts must be "real." What was involved in the acceptance of new types of numbers was a sharp break from concepts grounded directly in experience. Mathematicians have since learned the deeper meaning of the statement that mathematics is an activity of the human mind and now grant that any concept which is clear and fertile should be explored whether or not it has an apparent physical basis.

Paradoxically, to obtain insights into the physical world, we must plunge deeper into human minds, consider abstractions that are remote from reality, and explore the implications of axioms that not only transcend but even appear to deny our sense impressions. Though recourse to higher and higher abstractions seems regrettable, the case for it was superbly stated by the distinguished philosopher, Alfred North Whitehead:

"Nothing is more impressive than the fact that as mathematics withdrew increasingly into the upper regions of ever greater extremes of abstract thought, it returned to earth with a corresponding growth of importance for the analysis of concrete fact. . . . The paradox is now fully established that the utmost abstractions are the true weapons with which to control our thought of concrete fact."

The pleasures and pains of mathematical activity have been recommended largely on the ground that they help us to achieve knowledge of the physical world. Why do we seek this knowledge? The ultimate goal of scientific activity is man himself. He wants to know the meaning of his own life and seeks the answer by attempting to understand the world in which he finds himself.

Mathematics mediates between man and nature, between man's inner and outer worlds. What mathematical concepts and methods have achieved in rationalizing nature have yielded our clearest and most weighty scientific doctrines. When solely for mathematical reasons Copernicus and Kepler adopted a new mathematical scheme by which to organize the observations of the heavens and placed the sun rather than the earth in the center, they caused man to recognize that he was an insignificant creature whirling through vast spaces rather than the central figure in the drama of nature. When Newtonian mechanics revealed a universe firmly controlled by definite mathematical laws and functioning both in the past and in the future to no end other than the fulfillment of mathematical laws, man had to cope with the implication that he was without will or purpose. If more recent creations such as quantum theory have cast in doubt the bleak, mechanical, deterministic implications of earlier theories and have given man some hope of reinstatement in an important role, it is still true that his outlook is confined and directed by mathematical chains of thought.

Science provides the understanding of the universe in which we live. Mathematics provides the dies by which science is molded. Our world is to a large extent what mathematics says it is. This body of man-made abstractions, wherein as Bertrand Russell put it, we never know what we are talking about nor whether what we are saying is true, this practical tool, model of all intellectual enterprises, and essence of our knowledge of nature leads through science to man himself.

Mathematics as a Creative Art

P. R. Halmos

Paul R. Halmos was born in Budapest, Hungary, and received his Ph.D. in mathematics from the University of Illinois. He has held professorial positions at the University of Chicago, University of Michigan, and University of Hawaii. He is currently professor of mathematics at the University of Indiana. He is the author of numerous books and research articles in pure mathematics.

Suppose that while you are walking down a street, a man steps out from the shadows and thrusts a microphone at your face. He demands your answer to the following question: "Is mathematics more like poetry or plumbing?" Relieved that you are not being mugged, you respond, "More like plumbing." "Just what I supposed, not a mathematician," he sniffs and retreats into the shadows.

A little annoyed at being startled and dealt with so abruptly, you shout at the retreating figure, "What do you know about it, jerk? Plumbers use numbers and make angles. What do poets do? Count how many words per line?" While continuing to walk away, the retreating figure throws a glance over his shoulder and condescendingly replies, "With the thought process that you exhibit, I can see I would waste my time by trying to explain my answer."

P. R. Halmos, whom we met in Volume I, now tries to convince us that the man with the microphone is not, after all, such a jerk. Mathematics is indeed more like poetry than plumbing, more creative art than applied science. Halmos is perfectly capable of speaking for himself so this introduction will present no synopsis of his arguments. It is interesting, however, to contrast his attitude with that of Kline in the previous article. The approach that each takes to the subject is surely, in some sense, colored by his own interests and indeed by his own successes and failures in creating and applying mathematics.

DO YOU KNOW any mathematicians—and, if you do, do you know anything about what they do with their time? Most people don't. When I get into conversation with the man next to me in a plane, and he tells me that he is something respectable like a doctor, lawyer, merchant, or dean, I am tempted to say that I am in roofing and siding. If I tell him that I am a mathematician, his most likely reply will be that he himself could never balance his checkbook, and it must be fun to be a whiz at math. If my neighbor is an astronomer, a biologist, a chemist, or any other kind of natural or social scientist, I am, if any-

thing, worse off—this man *thinks* he knows what a mathematician is, and he is probably wrong. He thinks that I spend my time (or should) converting different orders of magnitude, comparing binomial coefficients and powers of 2, or solving equations involving rates of reactions.

C. P. Snow points to and deplores the existence of two cultures; he worries about the physicist whose idea of modern literature is Dickens, and he chides the poet who cannot state the second law of thermodynamics. Mathematicians, in converse with well-meaning, intelligent, and educated laymen (do you mind if I refer to all non-

Source: P. R. Halmos, "Mathematics as a Creative Art," *American Scientist* 56 (1968): 375–389.

mathematicians as laymen?) are much worse off than physicists in converse with poets. It saddens me that educated people don't even know that my subject exists. There is something that they call mathematics, but they neither know how the professionals use that word, nor can they conceive why anybody should do it. It is, to be sure, possible that an intelligent and otherwise educated person doesn't know that Egyptology exists, or haematology, but all you have to tell him is that it does, and he will immediately understand in a rough general way why it should and he will have some empathy with the scholar of the subject who finds it interesting.

Usually when a mathematician lectures, he is a missionary. Whether he is talking over a cup of coffee with a collaborator, lecturing to a graduate class of specialists, teaching a reluctant group of freshman engineers, or addressing a general audience of laymen—he is still preaching and seeking to make converts. He will state theorems and he will discuss proofs and he will hope that when he is done his audience will know more mathematics than they did before. My aim today is different—I am not here to proselyte but to enlighten—I seek not converts but friends. I do not want to teach you what mathematics is, but only *that* it is.

I call my subject mathematics—that's what all my colleagues call it, all over the world—and there, quite possibly, is the beginning of confusion. The word covers two disciplines—many more, in reality, but two, at least two, in the same sense in which Snow speaks of two cultures. In order to have some words with which to refer to the ideas I want to discuss, I offer two temporary and ad hoc neologisms. Mathematics, as the word is customarily used, consists of at least two distinct subjects, and I propose to call them *mathology* and *mathophysics*. Roughly speaking, mathology is what is usually called pure mathematics, and mathophysics is called applied mathematics, but the qualifiers are not emotionally strong enough to disguise that they qualify the same noun. If the concatenation of syllables I chose here reminds you of other words, no great harm will be done; the rhymes alluded to are not completely accidental. I originally planned to entitle this lecture something like "Mathematics is an art," or "Mathematics is not a science," or "Mathematics is useless," but the more I thought about it the more I realized that I mean that "Mathology is an art," "Mathology is not a science," and "Mathology is useless." When I am through, I hope you will recognize that most of you have known about mathophysics before, only you were probably calling it mathematics; I hope that all of you will recognize the distinction between mathology and mathophysics; and I hope that some of you will be ready to embrace, or at least applaud, or at the very least, recognize mathology as a respectable human endeavor.

In the course of the lecture I'll have to use many analogies (literature, chess, painting), each imperfect by itself, but I hope that in their totality they will serve to delineate what I want delineated. Sometimes in the interest of economy of time, and sometimes doubtless unintentionally, I'll exaggerate; when I'm done, I'll be glad to rescind anything that was inaccurate or that gave offense in any other way.

What Mathematicians Do

As a first step toward telling you what mathematicians do, let me tell you some of the things they do not do. To begin with, mathematicians have very little to do with numbers. You can no more expect a mathematician to be able to add a column of figures rapidly and correctly than you can expect a painter to draw a straight line or a surgeon to carve a turkey—popular legend attributes such skills to these professions, but popular legend is wrong. There is, to be sure, a part of mathematics called number theory, but even that doesn't deal with numbers in the legendary sense—a number theorist and an adding machine would find very little to talk about. A machine might enjoy proving that $1^3 + 5^3 + 3^3 = 153$, and it might even go on to discover that there are only five positive integers with the property that the equation indicates (1, 370, 371, 407), but most mathematicians couldn't care less; many mathematicians enjoy and respect the theorem that every positive integer is the sum of not more than four squares, whereas the infinity involved in the word "every" would frighten and paralyze any ordinary office machine, and, in any case, that's probably not the sort of thing that the person who relegates mathematicians to numbers had in mind.

Not even those romantic objects of latter day science fiction, the giant brains, the computing machines that run our lives these days—not even they are of interest to the mathematician as such. Some mathematicians are interested in the logical problems involved in the reduction of difficult questions to the sort of moronic baby talk that machines understand: the logical design of computing machines is definitely mathematics. Their construction is not, that's engineering, and their product, be it a payroll, a batch of sorted mail, or a supersonic plane, is of no mathematical interest or value.

Mathematics is not numbers or machines; it is also not the determination of the heights of mountains by trigonometry, or compound interest by algebra, or moments of inertia by calculus. Not today it isn't. At one point in history each of those things, and others like them, might have been an important and non-trivial research problem, but once the problem is solved, its repetitive application has as much to do with mathematics as the work of a Western Union messenger boy has to do with Marconi's genius.

There are at least two other things that mathematics isn't; one of them is something it never was, and the other is something it once included and by now has sloughed off. The first is physics. Some laymen confuse mathematics and theoretical physics and speak, for instance, of Einstein as a great mathematician. There is no doubt that Einstein was a great man, but he was no more a great mathematician than he was a great violinist. He used mathematics to find out facts about the universe, and that he successfully used certain parts of differential geometry for that purpose adds a certain piquancy to the appeal of differential geometry. Withal, relativity theory and differential geometry are not the same thing. Einstein, Schrödinger, Heisenberg, Fermi, Wigner, Feynman—great men all, but not mathematicians; some of them, in fact, strongly antimathematical, preach against mathematics, and would regard it as an insult to be called a mathematician.

What once was mathematics remains mathematics always, but it can become so thoroughly worked out, so completely understood, and, in the light of millenia of contributions, with hindsight, so trivial, that mathematicians never again need to or want to spend time on it. The celebrated Greek problems (trisect the angle, square the circle, duplicate the cube) are of this kind, and the irrepressible mathematical amateur to the contrary notwithstanding, mathematicians are no longer trying to solve them. Please understand, it isn't that they have given up. Perhaps you have heard that, according to mathematicians, it is impossible to square a circle, or trisect an angle, and perhaps you have heard or read that, therefore, mathematicians are a pusillanimous chicken-hearted lot, who give up easily, and use their ex-cathedra pronouncements to justify their ignorance. The conclusion may be true, and you may believe it if you like, but the proof is inadequate. The point is a small one but a famous one and one of historical interest: let me digress to discuss it for a moment.

A Short Digression

The problem of trisecting the angle is this: given an angle, construct another one that is just one third as large. The problem is perfectly easy, and several methods for solving it are known. The catch is that the original Greek formulation of the problem is more stringent: it requires a construction that uses ruler and compasses only. Even that can be done, and I could show you a perfectly simple method in one minute and convince you that it works in two more minutes. The real difficulty is that the precise formulation of the problem is more stringent still. The precise formulation demands a construction that uses a ruler and compasses only and, moreover, severely restricts how they are to be used; it prohibits, for instance, marking two points on the ruler and using the marked points in further constructions. It takes some careful legalism (or some moderately pedantic mathematics) to formulate really precisely just what was and what wasn't allowed by the Greek rules. The modern angle trisector either doesn't know those rules, or he knows them but thinks that the idea is to get a close approximation, or he knows the rules and knows that an exact solution is required but lets wish be father to the deed and simply makes a mistake. Frequently his attitude is that of the visitor from outer space to golf. (If all you want is to get that little white ball in that little green hole, why don't you just go and put it there?)

Allow me to add a short digression to the digression. I'd like to remind you that when a mathematician says that something is impossible, he doesn't mean that it is very very difficult, beyond his powers, and probably beyond the powers of all humanity for the foreseeable future. That's what is often meant when some one says it's impossible to travel at the speed of sound five miles above the surface of the earth, or instantaneously to communicate with someone a thousand miles away, or to tamper with the genetic code so as to produce a race of citizens who are simultaneously intelligent and peace-loving. That's what is belittled by the classic business braggadocio (the impossible takes a little longer). The mathematical impossible is different: it is more modest and more secure. The mathematical impossible is the logical impossible. When the mathematician says that it is impossible to find a positive number whose sum with 10 is less than 10, he merely reminds us that that's what the words mean (positive, sum, 10, less); when he says that it is impossible to trisect every angle by ruler and compasses, he means exactly the same sort of thing, only the number of technical words involved is large enough and the argument that strings them together is long enough that they fill a book, not just a line.

The Start of Mathematics

No one knows when and where mathematics got started, or how, but it seems reasonable to guess that it emerged from the same primitive physical observations (counting, measuring) with which we all begin our own mathematical insight (ontogeny recapitulates phylogeny). It was probably so in the beginning, and it is true still, that many mathematical ideas originate not from pure thought but from material necessity; many, but probably not all. Almost as soon as a human

being finds it necessary to count his sheep (or sooner?) he begins to wonder about numbers and shapes and motions and arrangements—curiosity about such things seems to be as necessary to the human spirit as curiosity about earth, water, fire, and air, and curiosity—sheer pure intellectual curiosity—about stars and about life. Numbers and shapes and motions and arrangements, and also thoughts and their order, and concepts such as "property" and "relation"—all such things are the raw material of mathematics. The technical but basic mathematical concept of "group" is the best humanity can do to understand the intuitive concept of "symmetry" and the people who study topological spaces, and ergodic paths, and oriented graphs are making precise our crude and vague feelings about shapes, and motions, and arrangements.

Why do mathematicians study such things, and why should they? What, in other words, motivates the individual mathematician, and why does society encourage his efforts, at least to the extent of providing him with the training and subsequently the livelihood that, in turn, give him the time he needs to think? There are two answers to each of the two questions: because mathematics is practical and because mathematics is an art. The already existing mathematics has more and more new applications each day, and rapid growth of desired applications suggests more and more new practical mathematics. At the same time, as the quantity of mathematics grows and the number of people who think about it keeps doubling over and over again, more new concepts need explication, more new logical interrelations cry out for study, and understanding, and simplification, and more and more the tree of mathematics bears elaborate and gaudy flowers that are, to many beholders, worth more than the roots from which it all comes and the causes that brought it all into existence.

Mathematics Today

Mathematics is very much alive today. There are more than a thousand journals that publish mathematical articles; about 15,000 to 20,000 mathematical articles are printed every year. The mathematical achievements of the last 100 years are greater in quantity and in quality than those of all previous history. Difficult mathematical problems, which stumped Hilbert, Cantor, or Poincaré, are being solved, explained, and generalized by beardless (and bearded) youths in Berkeley and in Odessa.

Mathematicians sometimes classify themselves and each other as either problem-solvers or theory-creators. The problem-solvers answer yes-or-no questions and discuss the vital special cases and concrete examples that are the flesh and blood of mathematics; the theory creators fit the results into a framework, illuminate it all, and point it in a definite direction—they provide the skeleton and the soul of mathematics. One and the same human being can be both a problem-solver and a theory-creator, but, usually, he is mainly one or the other. The problem-solvers make geometric constructions, the theory-creators discuss the foundations of Euclidean geometry; the problem-solvers find out what makes switching diagrams tick, the theory-creators prove representation theorems for Boolean algebras. In both kinds of mathematics and in all fields of mathematics the progress in one generation is breath-taking. No one can call himself a mathematician nowadays who doesn't have at least a vague idea of homological algebra, differential topology, and functional analysis, and every mathematician is probably somewhat of an expert on at least one of these subjects—and yet when I studied mathematics in the 1930's none of those phrases had been invented, and the subjects they describe existed in seminal forms only

Mathematics is abstract thought, mathematics is pure logic, mathematics is creative art. All these statements are wrong, but they are all a little right, and they are all nearer the mark than "mathematics is numbers" or "mathematics is geometric shapes." For the professional pure mathematician, mathematics is the logical dovetailing of a carefully selected sparse set of assumptions with their surprising conclusions via a conceptually elegant proof. Simplicity, intricacy, and above all, logical analysis are the hallmark of mathematics.

The mathematician is interested in extreme cases—in this respect he is like the industrial experimenter who breaks lightbulbs, tears shirts, and bounces cars on ruts. How widely does a reasoning apply, he wants to know, and what happens when it doesn't? What happens when you weaken one of the assumptions, or under what conditions can you strengthen one of the conclusions? It is the perpetual asking of such questions that makes for broader understanding, better technique, and greater elasticity for future problems.

Mathematics—this may surprise you or shock you some—is never deductive in its creation. The mathematician at work makes vague guesses, visualizes broad generalizations, and jumps to unwarranted conclusions. He arranges and rearranges his ideas, and he becomes convinced of their truth long before he can write down a logical proof. The conviction is not likely to come early—it usually comes after many attempts, many failures, many discouragements, many false starts. It often happens that months of work result in the proof that the method of attack they were based on cannot possibly work, and the process of guessing, visualizing, and conclusion-jumping begins again. A reformulation is needed—and—and this too may surprise you—more experimental work is needed. To be sure, by "experimental work" I do not mean test tubes and cyclotrons. I mean thought-experiments. When a mathematician wants to prove a theorem about an infinite-dimensional Hilbert space, he examines its finite-dimensional analogue, he looks in detail at the 2- and 3-dimensional cases, he often tries out a particular numerical case, and he hopes that he will gain thereby an insight that pure definition-juggling has not yielded. The deductive stage, writing the result down, and writing down its rigorous proof are relatively trivial once the real insight arrives; it is more like the draftsman's work, not the architect's.

The Mathematical Fraternity

The mathematical fraternity is a little like a self-perpetuating priesthood. The mathematicians of today train the mathematicians of tomorrow and, in effect, decide whom to admit to the priesthood. Most people do not find it easy to join—mathematical talent and genius are apparently exactly as rare as talent and genius in painting and music—but anyone can join, everyone is welcome. The rules are nowhere explicitly formulated, but they are intuitively felt by everyone in the profession. Mistakes are forgiven and so is obscure exposition—the indispensable requisite is mathematical insight. Sloppy thinking, verbosity without content, and polemic have no role, and—this to me is one of the most wonderful aspects of mathematics—they are much easier to spot than in the non-mathematical fields of human endeavor (much easier than, for instance, in literature among the arts, in art criticism among the humanities, and in your favorite abomination among the social sciences).

Although most of mathematical creation is done by one man at a desk, at a blackboard, or taking a walk, or, sometimes, by two men in conversation, mathematics is nevertheless a sociable science. The creator needs stimulation while he is creating and he needs an audience after he has created. Mathematics is a sociable science in the sense that I don't think it can be done by one man on a desert island (except for a very short time), but it is not a mob science, it is not a team science. A theorem is not a pyramid; inspiration has never been known to descend on a committee. A great theorem can no more be obtained by a "project" approach than a great painting; I don't think a team of little Gausses could have obtained the theorem about regular polygons under the leadership of a rear admiral anymore than a team of little Shakespeares could have written *Hamlet* under such conditions.

A Tiny and Trivial Mathematical Problem

I have been trying to give you a description of what mathematics is and how mathematicians do it, in broad general terms, and I wouldn't blame you if you had been finding it thoroughly unsatisfactory. I feel a little as if I had been describing snow to a Fiji Islander. If I told him snow was white like an egg, wet like mud, and cold like a mountain water fall, would he then understand

what it's like to ski in the Alps? To show him a spoonful of scrapings from the just defrosted refrigerator of His Excellency the Governor is not much more satisfactory—but it is a little. Let me, therefore, conclude this particular tack by mentioning a tiny and trivial mathematical problem and describing its solution—possibly you'll then get (if you don't already have) a little feeling for what attracts and amuses mathematicians and what is the nature of the inspiration I have been talking about.

Imagine a society of 1025 tennis players. The mathematically minded ones among you, if you haven't already heard about this famous problem, have immediately been alerted by the number. It is known to anyone who ever kept on doubling something, anything, that 1024 is 2^{10}. All cognoscenti know, therefore, that the presence in the statement of a problem of a number like $1 + 2^{10}$ is bound to be a strong hint to its solution; the chances are, and this can be guessed even before the statement of the problem is complete, that the solution will depend on doubling—or halving—something ten times. The more knowledgeable cognoscenti will also admit the possibility that the number is not a hint but a trap. Imagine then that the tennis players are about to conduct a gigantic tournament, in the following manner. They draw lots to pair off as far as they can, the odd man sits out the first round, and the paired players play their matches. In the second round only the winners of the first round participate, and the former odd man. The procedure is the same for the second round as for the first—pair off and play at random, with the new odd man (if any) waiting it out. The rules demand that this procedure be continued, over and over again, until the champion of the society is selected. The champion, in this sense, didn't exactly beat everyone else, but he can say, of each of his fellow players, that he beat some one, who beat some one, . . ., who beat some one, who beat that player. The question is: how many matches were played altogether, in all the rounds of the whole tournament?

There are several ways of attacking the problem, and even the most naive one works. According to it, the first round has 512 matches (since 1025 is odd and 512 is a half of 1024), the second round has 256 (since the 512 winners in the first round, together with the odd man of that round, make 513, which is odd again, and 256 is a half of 512), etc. The "etcetera" yields, after 512 and 256, the numbers 128, 64, 32, 16, 8, 4, 2, 1, and 1 (the very last round, consisting of only one match, is the only one where there is no odd man), and all that is necessary is to add them up. That's a simple job that pencil and paper can accomplish in a few seconds; the answer (and hence the solution of the problem) is 1024.

The mathematical wiseacre would proceed a little differently. He would quickly recognize, as advertised, that the problem has to do with repeated halvings, so that the numbers to be added up are the successive powers of 2, from the ninth down to the first,—no, from ninth down to the zeroth!—together with the last 1 caused by the obviously malicious attempt of the problem-setter to confuse the problem-solver by using 1025 instead of 1024. The wiseacre would then proudly exhibit his knowledge of the formula for the sum of a geometric progression, he would therefore know (without addition) that the sum of 512, 256, . . . , 8, 4, 2, and 1 is 1023, and he would then add the odd 1 to get the same total of 1024.

The trouble with the wiseacre's solution is that it's much too special. If the number of tennis players had been 1000 instead of 1025, the wiseacre would be no better off than the naive layman. The wiseacre's solution works, but it is as free of inspiration as the layman's. It is shorter but it is still, in the mathematician's contemptuous word, computational.

The problem has also an inspired solution, that requires no computation, no formulas, no numbers—just pure thought. Reason like this: each match has a winner and a loser. A loser cannot participate in any later rounds; every one in the society, except only the champion, loses exactly one match. There are, therefore, exactly as many matches as there are losers, and, consequently, the number of matches is exactly one less than the membership of society. If the number of members is 1025, the answer is 1024. If the number had been 1000, the answer would be 999, and, obviously, the present pure thought method gives the answer, with no computation, for every possible number of players.

That's it: that's what I offer as a microcosmic example of a pretty piece of mathematics. The example is bad because, after all my warning that mathematicians are interested in other things than counting, it deals with counting; it's bad because it does not, cannot, exhibit any of the conceptual power and intellectual technique of non-trivial mathematics; and it's bad because it illustrates applied mathematics (that is, mathematics as applied to a "real life" problem) more than it illustrates pure mathematics (that is, the distilled form of a question about the logical interrelations of concepts—concepts, not tennis players, and tournaments, and matches). For an example, for a parable, it does pretty well nevertheless; if your imagination is good enough mentally to reconstruct the ocean from a drop of water, then you can reconstruct mathematics from the problem of the tennis players.

Mathology vs. Mathophysics

I've been describing mathematics but, the truth to tell, I've had mathology (pure) in mind, more than mathophysics (applied). For some reason the practitioners of mathophysics tend to minimize the differences between the two subjects and the others, the mathologists, tend to emphasize them. You've long ago found me out, I am sure. Every mathematician is in one camp or the other (well, almost every—a few are in both camps), and I am a mathologist by birth and training. But in a report such as this one, I must try not to exaggerate my prejudices, so I'll begin by saying that the similarities between mathology and mathophysics are great indeed. It is a historical fact that ultimately all mathematics comes to us, is suggested to us, by the physical universe: in that sense all mathematics is applied. It is, I believe, a psychological fact that even the purest of the pure among us is just a wee bit thrilled when his thoughts make a new and unexpected contact with the non-mathematical universe. The kind of talent required to be good in mathology is intimately related to the kind that mathophysics demands. The articles that mathophysicists write are frequently indistinguishable from those of their mathological colleagues.

As I see it, the main difference between mathophysics and mathology is the *purpose* of the intellectual curiosity that motivated the work—or, perhaps, it would be more accurate to say that it is the *kind* of intellectual curiosity that is relevant. Let me ask you a peculiar but definitely mathematical question. Can you load a pair of dice so that all possible rolls—better: all possible sums that can show on one roll, all the numbers between 2 and 12 inclusive—are equally likely? The question is a legitimate piece of mathematics; the answer to it is known, and it is not trivial. I mention it here so that you may perform a quick-do-it-yourself psychoanalysis on yourself. When I asked the question, did you think of homogeneous and non-homogeneous distributions of mass spread around in curious ways through two cubes, or did you think of sums of products of twelve numbers (the twice six probabilities associated with the twice six faces of the two dice)? If the former, you are a crypto-mathophysicist, if the latter you are a potential mathologist.

How do you choose your research problem, and what about it attracts you? Do you want to know about nature or about logic? Do you prefer concrete facts to abstract relations? If it's nature you want to study, if the concrete has the greater appeal, then you are a mathophysicist. In mathophysics the question always comes from outside, from the "real world," and the satisfaction the scientist gets from the solution comes, to a large extent, from the light it throws on *facts*.

Surely no one can object to mathophysics or think less of it for that; and yet many do. I did not mean to identify "concrete" with "practical" and thereby belittle it, and equally I did not mean to identify "abstract" with "useless." (That $2^{11213} - 1$ is a prime is a concrete fact, but surely a useless one; that $E = mc^2$ is an abstract relation but unfortunately a practical one.) Nevertheless, such identifications—applied-concrete-practical-crude and pure-abstract-pedantic-useless—are quite common in both camps. To the applied mathematician the antonym of "applied" is "worthless," and to the pure mathematician the antonym of "pure" is "dirty."

History doesn't help the confusion. Historically, pure and applied mathematics (mathology and mathophysics) have been much closer to-

gether than they are today. By now the very terminology (pure mathematics versus applied mathematics) makes for semantic confusion: it implies identity with small differences, instead of diversity with important connections.

From the difference in purposes follows a difference in tastes and hence of value judgments. The mathophysicist wants to know the facts, and he has, sometimes at any rate, no patience for the hair-splitting pedantry of the mathologist's rigor (which he derides as *rigor mortis*). The mathologist wants to understand the ideas, and he places great value on the aesthetic aspects of the understanding and the way that understanding is arrived at; he uses words such as "elegant" to describe a proof. In motivation, in purpose, frequently in method, and almost always in taste, the mathophysicist and the mathologist differ.

When I tell you that I am a mathologist, I am not trying to defend useless knowledge, or convert you to the view that it's the best kind. I would, however, be less than honest with you if I didn't tell you that I believe that. I like the idea of things being done for their own sake. I like it in music, I like it in the crafts, and I like it even in medicine. I never quite trust a doctor who says that he chose his profession out of a desire to benefit humanity; I am uncomfortable and skeptical when I hear such things. I much prefer the doctor to say that he became one because he liked the idea, because he thought he would be good at it, or even because he got good grades in high school zoology. I like the subject for its own sake, in medicine as much as in music; and I like it in mathematics.

Let me digress for a moment to a brief and perhaps apocryphal story about David Hilbert, probably the greatest mathematician of both the nineteenth and the twentieth centuries. When he was preparing a public address, Hilbert was asked to include a reference to the conflict (even then!) between pure and applied mathematics, in the hope that if anyone could take a step toward resolving it, he could. Obediently, he is said to have begun his address by saying "I was asked to speak about the conflict between pure and applied mathematics. I am glad to do so, because it is, indeed, a lot of nonsense—there should be no conflict, there can be no conflict—there is no conflict—in fact the two have nothing whatsoever to do with one another!"

It is, I think, undeniable that a great part of mathematics was born, and lives in respect and admiration, for no other reason than that it is interesting—it is interesting in itself. The angle trisection of the Greeks, the celebrated four-color map problem, and Gödel's spectacular contribution to mathematical logic are good because they are beautiful, because they are surprising, because we want to know. Don't all of us feel the irresistible pull of the puzzle? Is there really something wrong with saying that mathematics is a glorious creation of the human spirit and deserves to live even in the absence of any practical application?

Mathematics Is a Language

Why does mathematics occupy such an isolated position in the intellectual firmament? Why is it good form, for intellectuals, to shudder and announce that they can't bear it, or, at the very least, to giggle and announce that they never could understand it? One reason, perhaps, is that mathematics is a language. Mathematics is a precise and subtle language designed to express certain kinds of ideas more briefly, more accurately, and more usefully than ordinary language. I do not mean here that mathematicians, like members of all other professional cliques, use jargon. They do, at times, and they don't most often, but that's a personal phenomenon, not the professional one I am describing. What I do mean by saying that mathematics is a language is sketchily and inadequately illustrated by the difference between the following two sentences. (1) If each of two numbers is multiplied by itself, the difference of the two results is the same as the product of the sum of the two given numbers by their difference. (2) $x^2 - y^2 = (x + y)(x - y)$. (Note: the longer formulation is not only awkward, it is also incomplete.)

One thing that sometimes upsets and repels the layman is the terminology that mathematicians employ. Mathematical words are intended merely as labels, sometimes suggestive, possibly facetious, but always precisely defined; their everyday connotations must be steadfastly ignored. Just as

nobody nowadays infers from the name Fitzgerald that its bearer is the illegitimate son of Gerald, a number that is called irrational must not be thought unreasonable; just as a dramatic poem called *The Divine Comedy* is not necessarily funny, a number called imaginary has the same kind of mathematical existence as any other. (Rational, for numbers, refers not to the Latin *ratio,* in the sense of reason, but to the English "ratio," in the sense of quotient.)

Mathematics is a language. None of us feels insulted when a sinologist uses Chinese phrases, and we are resigned to living without Chinese, or else spending years learning it. Our attitude to mathematics should be the same. It's a language, and it takes years to learn to speak it well. We all speak it a little, just because some of it is in the air all the time, but we speak it with an accent and frequently inaccurately; most of us speak it, say, about as well as one who can only say "*Oui, monsieur*" and "*S'il vous plaît*" speaks French. The mathematician sees nothing wrong with this as long as he's not upbraided by the rest of the intellectual community for keeping secrets. It took him a long time to learn his language, and he doesn't look down on the friend who, never having studied it, doesn't speak it. It is however sometimes difficult to keep one's temper with the cocktail party acquaintance who demands that he be taught the language between drinks and who regards failure or refusal to do so as sure signs of stupidity or snobbishness.

Some Analogies

A little feeling for the nature of mathematics and mathematical thinking can be got by the comparison with chess. The analogy, like all analogies, is imperfect, but it is illuminating just the same. The rules for chess are as arbitrary as the axioms of mathematics sometimes seem to be. The game of chess is as abstract as mathematics. (That chess is played with solid pieces, made of wood, or plastic, or glass, is not an intrinsic feature of the game. It can just as well be played with pencil and paper, as mathematics is, or blindfold, as mathematics can.) Chess also has its elaborate technical language, and chess is completely deterministic.

There is also some analogy between mathematics and music. The mathologist feels the need to justify pure mathematics exactly as little as the musician feels the need to justify music. Do practical men, the men who meet payrolls, demand only practical music—soothing jazz to make an assembly line worker turn nuts quicker, or stirring marches to make a soldier kill with more enthusiasm? No, surely none of us believes in that kind of justification; music, and mathematics, are of human value because human beings feel they are.

The analogy with music can be stretched a little further. Before a performer's artistic contribution is judged, it is taken for granted that he hits the right notes, but merely hitting the right notes doesn't make him a musician. We don't get the point of painting if we compliment the nude Maya on being a good likeness, and we don't get the point of a historian's work if all we can say is that he didn't tell lies. Mere accuracy in performance, resemblance in appearance, and truth in storytelling doesn't make good music, painting, history: in the same way, mere logical correctness doesn't make good mathematics.

Goodness, high quality, are judged on grounds more important than validity, but less describable. A good piece of mathematics is connected with much other mathematics, it is new without being silly (think of a "new" western movie in which the names and the costumes are changed, but the plot isn't), and it is deep in an ineffable but inescapable sense—the sense in which Johann Sebastian is deep and Carl Philip Emmanuel is not. The criterion for quality is beauty, intricacy, neatness, elegance, satisfaction, appropriateness—all subjective, but all somehow mysteriously shared by all.

Mathematics resembles literature also, differently from the way it resembles music. The writing and reading of literature are related to the writing and reading of newspapers, advertisements, and road signs the way mathematics is related to practical arithmetic. We all need to read and write and figure for daily life: but literature is more than reading and writing, and mathematics is more than figuring. The literature analogy

can be used to help understand the role of teachers and the role of the pure-applied dualism.

Many whose interests are in language, in the structure, in the history, and in the aesthetics of it, earn their bread and butter by teaching the rudiments of language to its future practical users. Similarly many, perhaps most, whose interests are in the mathematics of today, earn their bread and butter by teaching arithmetic, trigonometry, or calculus. This is sound economics: society abstractly and impersonally is willing to subsidize pure language and pure mathematics, but not very far. Let the would-be purist pull his weight by teaching the next generation the applied aspects of his craft; then he is permitted to spend a fraction of his time doing what he prefers. From the point of view of what a good teacher must be, this is good. A teacher must know more than the bare minimum he must teach; he must know more in order to avoid more and more mistakes, to avoid the perpetuation of misunderstanding, to avoid catastrophic educational inefficiency. To keep him alive, to keep him from drying up, his interest in syntax, his burrowing in etymology, or his dabbling in poetry play a necessary role.

The pure-applied dualism exists in literature too. The source of literature is human life, but literature is not the life it comes from, and writing with a grim purpose is not literature. Sure there are borderline cases: is Upton Sinclair's "Jungle" literature or propaganda? (For that matter, is Chiquita Banana an advertising jingle or charming light opera?) But the fuzzy boundary doesn't alter the fact that in literature (as in mathematics) the pure and the applied are different in intent, in method, and in criterion of success.

Perhaps the closest analogy is between mathematics and painting. The origin of painting is physical reality, and so is the origin of mathematics—but the painter is not a camera and the mathematician is not an engineer. The painter of "Uncle Sam Wants You" got his reward from patriotism, from increased enlistments, from winning the war—which is probably different from the reward Rembrandt got from a finished work. How close to reality painting (and mathematics) should be is a delicate matter of judgment. Asking a painter to "tell a concrete story" is like asking a mathematician to "solve a real problem."

Modern painting and modern mathematics are far out—too far in the judgment of some. Perhaps the ideal is to have a spice of reality always present, but not to crowd it the way descriptive geometry, say, does in mathematics, and medical illustration, say, does in painting.

Talk to a painter (I did) and talk to a mathematician, and you'll be amazed at how similarly they react. Almost every aspect of the life and of the art of a mathematician has its counterpart in painting, and vice versa. Every time a mathematician hears "I could never make my checkbook balance" a painter hears "I could never draw a straight line"—and the comments are equally relevant and equally interesting. The invention of perspective gave the painter a useful technique, as did the invention of 0 to the mathematician. Old art is as good as new; old mathematics is as good as new. Tastes change, to be sure, in both subjects, but a twentieth century painter has sympathy for cave paintings and a twentieth century mathematician for the fraction juggling of the Babylonians. A painting must be painted and then looked at; a theorem must be printed and then read. The painter who thinks good pictures, and the mathematician who dreams beautiful theorems are dilettantes; an unseen work of art is incomplete. In painting and in mathematics there are some objective standards of good—the painter speaks of structure, line, shape, and texture, where the mathematician speaks of truth, validity, novelty, generality—but they are relatively the easiest to satisfy. Both painters and mathematicians debate among themselves whether these objective standards should even be told to the young—the beginner may misunderstand and overemphasize them and at the same time lose sight of the more important subjective standards of goodness. Painting and mathematics have a history, a tradition, a growth. Students, in both subjects, tend to flock to the newest but, except the very best, miss the point; they lack the vitality of what they imitate, because, among other reasons, they lack the experience based on the traditions of the subject.

I've been talking *about* mathematics, but not *in* it, and, consequently, what I've been saying is not capable of proof in the mathematical sense of the word. I hope just the same, that I've shown you that there is a subject called mathematics (mathology?), and that that subject is a creative art. It is a creative art because mathematicians create beautiful new concepts; it is a creative art because mathematicians live, act, and think like artists; and it is a creative art because mathematicians regard it so. I feel strongly about that, and I am grateful for this opportunity to tell you about it. Thank you for listening.

Definitions in Mathematics

Émile Borel

Émile Borel lived from 1871 to 1956. His name is one that forever belongs to the settled vocabulary of mathematics. He did his graduate work at the École Normale in Paris and from that time until his death he was connected with the École Normale in some official capacity. Borel's accomplishments in integration theory and functions of a complex variable are mathematical achievements of enduring stature. During World War I he served as Secretary General in the cabinet under Prime Minister Painleve (who was also a mathematician). Disillusioned by the decimation of a generation of his students, Borel switched after World War I from analysis to the theory of probability.

Among the most fundamental processes in mathematics is the creation of definitions. Mathematics begins with primitive, or undefined, terms and properties of those terms (axioms). For example, in the usual set-theory approach to mathematics the terms set, element, *and* inclusion *are undefined. To the nonmathematician the use of undefined terms may seem absurd at first, but a brief analysis shows that they are essential. For example, to define* democracy *what words do we use? Now how do we define those words? And the words used to define those? The problem is obvious. Dictionary definitions are either circular (a set is a collection; a collection is a set) or involve an infinite regression. Since infinite dictionaries don't exist and circular definitions are meaningless, we are compelled to recognize the fact that some terms must remain undefined. Clearly the number of such terms should be as few as possible. Virtually all of modern mathematics can be developed using only* set, element, *and* inclusion *as primitive terms.*

With the primitive words we may define other terms and ideas using logic and the axioms that describe the fundamental properties of set, element, *and* inclusion. *And now a problem arises. Having defined something, say the counting numbers 1, 2, 3, . . . , do we really understand our definition? This essay, by one of the great mathematicians of modern time, suggests that such understanding does not always follow.*

I

"MATHEMATICS IS THE science in which one never knows what one is talking about, nor whether what one is saying is true."

This sally of Bertrand Russell tends to emphasize the fundamental role that arbitrary definitions play in mathematics. But one could just as well say: "Mathematics is the only science in which one always knows exactly what one is talking about and in which one is certain that what one says is true." Of course, if we are discussing the properties of a line, the expression *straight line* does not have the same meaning in the geometries of Euclid, Riemann, or Lobachevsky; however, if a line is defined in conformity with the postulates of this or that geometry, then we will know exactly what we are talking about and we will be

Source: Émile Borel, "Definitions in Mathematics," in F. Le Lionnais, ed., *Great Currents of Mathematical Thought* (New York: Dover Publications, 1971). (References omitted.)

assured of the truth of this or that theorem: for example, the sum of the angles in a triangle is always equal to two right angles, or it is always greater than two right angles, or it is always less than two right angles. Although these theorems appear contradictory, each of them is true in one of the geometries, i.e., the one with the appropriate definition of a line.

Mathematics is coming to appear more and more as the science which studies the relations between certain abstract entities defined in an arbitrary manner, restricted only in that these definitions must not lead to a contradiction. However, to avoid the risk of confusing mathematics either with logic or with games such as chess, we must add that these definitions were suggested first of all by analogies to real objects; such is the case for the straight line, for the circle, for the rigid body of dynamics, etc. On the other hand, complex numbers, transfinite numbers and many other mathematical entities are pure creations of the human mind. They are justified by the fact that they permitted an easier solution of problems posed by mathematicians or physicists and clarified difficulties which they faced.

In addition, a distinction must be made between those definitions which can be called general, such as those of a function of a real or complex variable, and the particular definitions which allow one to single out classes of functions having a special interest, such as continuous functions of a real variable, discontinuous functions of the first Baire class, etc., and, among the functions of a complex variable, entire functions, meromorphic functions, Abelian functions, Fuchsian functions, etc. Finally, one can specialize still further and define individual functions, such as the exponential function, trigonometric functions, etc. The situation is similar in geometry and in all the other branches of mathematics. Of course, there is a certain degree of arbitrariness in the choice of the definitions considered to be interesting, but we cannot discuss this question here since it would entail a critical study of the entire field of mathematics, a task requiring numerous volumes, even supposing that an author could be found with sufficient competence to write it.

Therefore, we shall limit ourselves to these general statements on axiomatic definitions and go on to study in more detail some problems concerning those definitions which can be called individual and which define a specific mathematical entity rather than a class of such entities.

II

Let us start out with the simplest definitions of arithmetic, those of the integers, the rational numbers and the irrational numbers. Each of these defines a *set* of numbers and permits a precise, unambiguous definition of certain elements of these sets. For example, 3, 17, 10^{100}, $2^{10,000}$ are specific integers; their precise definition is obtained from the conventions relating to decimal representation and integral exponents. Similarly, 3/4, 5/7 or 0.3427 are well-defined rational numbers. We also know that $\sqrt{2}$, $\sqrt[3]{7}$, e and π are irrational numbers. The principal question which first arises is the following: which numbers can be *well defined* in this way? It is clear that a solution of this question would lead to a solution of the analogous questions that could be posed for all mathematical entities. For example, a circle is defined if its center and radius are given; moreover, two circles of the same radius are equal and are regarded as identical in Euclidean geometry; but to give the radius, a number must be given and we are back to the problem of the definition of number.

Let us first consider the integers.

By means of mathematical symbols it is easy to define arbitrarily large integers; if, for example, $\phi_1(n)$ denotes the number 10^n; $\phi_2(n)$ the number $\phi_1[\phi_1(n)]$; $\phi_k(n)$ the number $\phi_1[\phi_{k-1}(n)]$; etc.; the number $\phi_k(n)$ will be a very large number, if k and n are themselves very large. Then we could take $\psi_1(n) = \phi_n(n)$ as our point of departure and obtain still larger numbers, and so on. However, it seems that those numbers having an incalculable number of digits are exceptional among the numbers having a very large number of digits. It would be completely impossible for a man to write a number with several billion digits, if he were actually required to write down all these digits. But it is nevertheless conceivable, if the number n were defined as the billionth prime number, that the number n is well defined, for all mathematicians would be sure that they were talking of the same number when they talked of n. However, it is beyond the present capacity of the science to actually write down the number n, although it is known to have only 10 digits; the computation would take too long. This reasoning applies a fortiori to the 10^nth prime number N. But it is not absurd to think it will be possible someday to demonstrate certain specific properties of the numbers n and N.

If we limit ourselves to integers with a relatively small number of digits—for instance, not exceeding 50 or 60—then it would appear simple at first glance to define any one of them, since we could write down a sequence of 50 or 60 digits chosen arbitrarily. However, it could just as well be said that it is easy to write down a sequence of 40 or 50 letters of the French alphabet in such a way as to obtain an Alexandrine verse. And yet it is certain that the French language will have ceased to exist, at least in its present form, before all the French verses of twelve syllables have been written. It is as inconceivable that we could know all the numbers of 60 digits as it is to suppose that we know all the French verses of twelve syllables. For the man who knows all the properties of numbers, two integers of 60 digits would be as distinct from one another as a beautiful line by Victor Hugo and a random collection of 46 letters would be. However long mankind endures, men will not be able to define more than a very few of the 60-digit numbers, and will choose among them those which have special or interesting properties, just as they will not write more than a very tiny part of the prose and poetical works which possibly could be imagined.

Let us say a few words about artificial and meaningless combinations. If we apply a coding procedure to a French text, we will obtain an incomprehensible grouping of letters of no interest to anyone who does not have the key to the code. For example, two given texts could be summed letter by letter; that is, on encountering the third and fourth letters of the alphabet one above the other, the seventh letter would be written; if the total exceeded 26, then 26 would be subtracted, i.e., the 15th plus the 17th would give the 6th. One could proceed in the same way with num-

bers: after defining a number with a very large number of digits by a simple arithmetic formula, say 2^{100} or 3^{117}, another number could be obtained from one of these by replacing the figure 5 everywhere by the figure 7 and conversely, or an *artificial sum* of two numbers could be formed by agreeing that if the two digits 2 and 7 occur one below the other, then the sum would be written down as the digit 4, the last digit of 14. Artificially defined numbers really seem to have as little interest for mathematicians as cryptograms have for readers of literature. However, for the sake of completeness it was necessary to mention artificial numbers, since they incontestably satisfy the first condition that we have required of a correct definition: the number that they define is certainly *the same* for all mathematicians; they can be discussed without the risk of any ambiguity. The trouble is that there is nothing to say about them.

It is interesting to try to classify the integers which can be defined in terms of the time required to define them, assuming that a word can be spoken or a digit written each second. If the decimal system is used, then about the same number of seconds as digits would be needed, if it is agreed purely and simply to say these digits one after the other. Of course, certain numbers with a very large number of digits can be defined more simply by arithmetic formulas, such as 2^{100} or 257! (which denotes the product of the first 257 natural numbers). One can also speak of the prime number of rank equal to one of the numbers previously defined. We shall call the minimum time necessary to define an integer its *height* (expressed in seconds in accordance with the preceding conventions).

Let us try to give an idea of the actual extent of the set of integers which have been studied by mathematicians, i.e., for which they know some property. The construction of tables of prime numbers, more than anything else, has yielded knowledge of the arithmetic properties of a very large number of integers. Tables of primes have been calculated up to 10 million and these also give the divisors of numbers which are not prime. These tables would permit by means of laborious but not completely unmanageable calculations the decomposition into prime factors of a number having not more than 14 digits. But if a number is written with 30 digits chosen at random, then it would be impossible to decompose it into prime factors or to know if it were prime.* The same is true for integers defined by arithmetical procedures as soon as the height reaches 20 or 30. Thus, the problem (interesting from many points of view) of finding the divisors of numbers of the form $2^n + 1$, where n is a power of 2, has been solved only for relatively small values of n. The height of these numbers, however, exceeds that of n only by four; i.e., it is 7 if n has 3 digits. For instance, we would say: 2 to the exponent 512 plus 1.

To sum up, the number of integers that could be defined is unlimited in the sense that, having defined a certain number, we could always define one more, but in practice it is limited to a relatively small number because of the short duration of human life and the fact that the great majority of men have other things to do than to define integers other than the ones needed in their daily life. In fact, most of the integers which have been defined by mathematicians appear in the various numerical tables which have been published, notably in the tables of primes. To these can be added the ones which appear in the numerous statistical and financial publications, although the latter do not appear to have been studied for their arithmetical properties and, therefore, are not of interest to mathematicians. On the whole, although certain of these numbers exceed a billion and although mathematicians have frequently considered much larger numbers, defined by means of the exponential or other notations, the total number of integers actually defined is certainly much less than a billion. The creative imagination of man has been much more prolific in the domain of language, since the number of lines of all the volumes that have been printed is of the order of magnitude of a thousand billions and, as

we have already observed, each line is as complex as a number of several tens of digits.

III

The detail with which we discussed the integers will permit us to be much more brief in regard to the other numbers, rational or irrational, since it is only by taking the integers as the point of departure that one can precisely define these other numbers.

This is evident for the rational numbers, which are the quotients of two integers; this is also the case for the algebraic numbers, which are the roots of algebraic equations with integral coefficients. Such numbers are well defined when the integers on which they depend are themselves well defined.

Let us now move on to the irrational numbers. The simplest and most important of these are defined by series or by differential equations. Such is the case for the number e and the number π; such is also the case for the trigonometric ratios, sine or cosine. It must be noted, however, that for $\sin x$ and $\cos x$ to be well defined, it is necessary that the argument x be itself a well-defined number. The same is true for the values of the elliptic functions (provided the value of the modulus is itself well defined) and of other functions conceived by mathematicians.

More generally, if we consider an algebraic differential equation with coefficients which are well-defined numbers, and if equally well-defined initial conditions are given, then the value of the integral will be itself well defined for a well-defined value of the variable.

The idea of height established for the integers can be readily extended to all the numbers defined in terms of integers; their height will be the sum of the heights of the integers which are involved in their definition. In the case of numbers defined by a series it suffices, of course, to give the law for the series.

Finally, if it is considered worthwhile, artificial definitions analogous to those of cryptograms can be added to these natural definitions; for example, from a number such as $\sqrt{2}$ or π written approximately in the form of a finite decimal, another

---

*If we consider a number N chosen at random, it is very likely that it will have a certain number of prime factors that are smaller than 1000 or 10,000. It is not very difficult to find these prime factors, and by dividing N by these prime factors, a considerably smaller number will be obtained. However, if N is prime, or has several sufficiently large prime factors, the calculations cannot be carried out in practice.

number can be derived by replacing everywhere the digit 3 by the digit 8, and conversely. However, such artificial numbers do not have any other known properties than the one expressed in their definition, and so they are without interest for mathematicians. It is thus hardly likely that they will ever cease to be anything but mere curiosities.

Is it now possible to go further and to *define* other irrational numbers? Naturally, one can imagine many artificial arithmetic definitions; for example, a decimal whose digits are the sequence of natural numbers:

$$x = 0 \; 1 \; 2 \; 3 \; 4 \; 5 \; 6 \; 7 \; 8 \; 9 \; 10 \; 11 \; 12 \; 13 \; 14 \; 15 \; 16 \; 17 \; 18 \; 19, \text{ etc.}$$

The definition of a number such as x can be varied in many ways, but it is scarcely likely that such a number would ever play a role in mathematics, since for that the discovery of a special property beyond that of its definition would be required.

It is equally easy to *define* certain sets of numbers and to demonstrate properties which belong to all the numbers of one of these sets. An example is the set of all real numbers between 0 and 1; such is also the case for many sets that can be obtained by means of a finite or infinite number of operations. For instance, such an operation might consist in removing from a given set the points included in a given interval whose end points are well-defined numbers. The set is then well defined and can be the object of further study which might make possible statements of certain properties common to all of its points. However, if one desires to speak of a particular point of this set, is it sufficient to designate it by the letter x in order to consider it well defined? This is what certain mathematicians appear to believe; for my part, I cannot consider x as well defined if, when I discuss x with another person, I cannot be certain that we understand one another, i.e., that we are speaking of the same number.

Of course, just as in certain cases one can demonstrate properties common to all the points x of a set E, it would be possible to demonstrate properties common to all pairs of points x and y with the sole condition that x is different from y. However, this last condition does not at all entail the conclusion that x and y are well defined; neither of them has any real individuality if all that is known about them is that they belong to the same set and that they are distinct.

When the notion of a well-defined number is made precise, as we have done, we arrive at the somewhat paradoxical conclusion that the well-defined irrational numbers actually considered by mathematicians are, in fact, far fewer in number than the well-defined integers. For, if we take the example of the algebraic numbers, only a minute number of the innumerable equations of degree less than one thousand and with coefficients less than one million have been actually studied or even written down. As for the transcendental numbers, only a very small number have been considered or studied apart from the values of certain functions for which tables have been calculated.

I shall not insist upon an answer to the following question: What is the order of infinity of the transcendental numbers which could be well defined, if human life were of unlimited duration and, hence, arbitrarily large integers could be used? Actually, this question would be connected with the subject of trans-finite numbers and would require a lengthy development.

IV

Before concluding, let us say a word about a difficult question. We have made clear what is to be understood by a well-defined number and we have required that when two mathematicians discuss such a number a, they be sure that they are discussing the *same* number. Should it not be added that when two numbers a and b are well defined, it should be known with certainty whether the two numbers are equal or unequal? This problem can be posed in the following way. Let us consider the integer $N = 145! + 1$, that is, the product of the first 145 natural numbers, increased by one. We do not know whether this is prime, but there is no information to the contrary. If N is prime, then well-known formulas of analysis allow the approximate calculation of its rank in the sequence of primes; this rank is certainly between $a - b$ and $a + b$, if b is sufficiently small with respect to a. Now, if we define N' as the prime number of rank a, then it is possible that N' equals N, but it is also possible that they are not equal; in the present state of the science the calculations necessary for this decision cannot be carried out practically. Ought one then to regard N and N' as well defined?

The same question can be posed in a different form for the irrational numbers, even in the case in which their height is relatively small. If two such numbers a and b are defined in a simple manner permitting their methodical calculation, as is the case for e, π, π^2, . . . , for example, it will be possible, if they are unequal, to determine this after a finite number of operations; but if they are equal, this can never be certainly known unless it can be demonstrated by an analytic method. Actually, agreement for any number of digits whatsoever would not suffice to demonstrate it.

For example:

$$\pi = 3.1415926 \ldots$$
$$\frac{355}{113} = 3.1415929 \ldots$$

If only six decimal places had been calculated, it might have been believed that these two numbers were equal. Similarly, certain people seeking to square the circle observed that

$$\pi = 3.14 \ldots$$
$$\sqrt{2} + \sqrt{3} = 3.14 \ldots$$

and concluded that these two numbers are equal.

In the two preceding cases anyone knowing that it is impossible to square the circle (since π cannot be the root of any algebraic equation with integral coefficients) could have asserted without any calculation that the two numbers whose first few decimal places were the same were certainly not equal. However, it is very rare that a demonstration of this type is available.

There are many ways to define the number π by means of a series or a definite integral. If we set

$$s = 1 - \frac{1}{3} + \frac{1}{5} - \frac{1}{7} + \frac{1}{9} - \frac{1}{11} + \ldots,$$
$$t = \int_0^1 \frac{dx}{\sqrt{1 - x^2}},$$

then we know that

$$s = \frac{\pi}{4}; \qquad t = \frac{\pi}{2}.$$

Let us suppose that some mathematicians, not aware of the preceding results, had sufficient curiosity to compute the values of $2s$ and t to a large number of decimal places. They would observe, for instance, that the first twenty decimal places of these values are the same. Could they then conclude without further calculation that $2s$ is exactly equal to t? In the present state of the science the answer to such a question must be in the negative. However, one cannot doubt that the mathematician who had obtained such a result would eagerly seek a rigorous demonstration of the equality $2s = t$, and, if he was not able to obtain it immediately, would have posed this problem to other mathematicians until such a demonstration was found. For, even lacking such a rigorous demonstration, he would nevertheless have been convinced that the agreement of the initial decimal places was not fortuitous and that the following decimal places would also coincide.

However, it would be absurd to claim that two irrational numbers with a large number of decimal places in common must necessarily be equal; in fact, nothing prevents us from defining an irrational number x as being obtained by increasing or decreasing by one the thousandth decimal place of π; the numbers x and π would thus have 999 decimal places in common but would still not be equal.

The great difference that exists between the comparison of $2s$ and t and that of x and π is that, in the first case, we are dealing with numbers defined in a simple manner by means of formulas which can be stated in a few words, whereas the number x is obtained from π in an artificial manner and its very definition implies that x is not equal to π.

It would, therefore, be very interesting to be able to demonstrate a general proposition which would permit us to state in interesting cases analogous to that of $2s$ and t that what everyone feels is true is actually true. For this it would be necessary to start from the following observations. After defining precisely the height of an irrational number, it would be observed that the number of numbers of height less than *h* is certainly finite. As a consequence, the minimum difference between two of these numbers is a quantity $\phi(h)$ which may be very small, but is not zero. It would now be a question of determining the function $\phi(h)$ or at least a function $f(h)$ such that $f(h)$ is definitely less than $\phi(h)$. Then, if two numbers of height less then *h*, which were defined by different methods had a difference less than $f(h)$, one could be sure that they were exactly equal.

Liouville's theorems on algebraic numbers and more recent work on the number *e* are a first step toward the determination of the function $f(h)$. This determination would constitute great progress in our knowledge of the arithmetic properties of numbers.

V

I would like, in conclusion, to say a few words about those "definitions" that could be called enigmatic, i.e., those which suppose an enigma has been solved to which we do not have the key. Certain of these definitions have a mathematical appearance; for some of them there is hope that the progress of the science will allow the resolution of the enigma, although that appears quite unlikely.

For example, let us define the number *x* in the following manner: in the decimal expansion of π we replace the billionth digit by a zero. Thus, if this digit is a zero, *x* will equal π; if not *x* is different from π. Those adept in the logic of Brouwer would say that we have here a case in which the law of the excluded middle does not apply and that neither of the propositions "*x* equals π" and "*x* differs from π" is either true or false.

The case in which the enigma posed is unrelated to mathematics is still less interesting; it is not defining a number to say that it is equal to 0 or 1 according to whether the number of Frenchmen killed at the battle of Waterloo was even or odd, or according to whether Bacon was or was not the collaborator of Shakespeare.

One could even "define" a number by defining its successive digits, the value of each depending on the solution of a scientific or historical enigma. Knowledge of this number would thus give the solution of the entire denumerable infinity of enigmas that could be posed in the domains of science, history, metaphysics or popular imagination. All this is pure fantasy. The interesting domain of research which remains open to mathematicians in regard to the definition of numbers and other mathematical entities is sufficiently vast so that one may easily forego an artificial extension of it.

The Role of Intuition

R. L. Wilder

Raymond Louis Wilder was born in 1896 in Massachusetts. He received his doctorate in 1923 from the University of Texas. He was a member of the National Academy of Sciences and also president of the American Mathematical Society from 1955 to 1956 and president of the Mathematical Association of America from 1965 to 1966. He received the Lester R. Ford Award from the Mathematical Association of America in 1973.

Popularly, mathematics is viewed as the ultimate rational activity, so analytical as to be nearly inhuman. Nonmathematicians are often proving things "mathematically" or decrying the "callous mathematical attitudes" of the latest bureaucratic regime. However, previous essays have already developed a fair case for mathematics as a most human activity. Whether it is viewed as creative art or the ultimate expression of self-awareness, mathematics is a uniquely human creation. Far from being the mechanically derived deductions of a programmed automaton, the ideas of mathematics flow in fits and starts from virtually inexpressable feelings about how the world is and what may help to order it. It should come as no surprise then that an important ingredient for the successful creation of mathematics is a talent for the correct guess. Wilder in this essay calls this talent "mathematical intuition" and introduces us to its nature and development.

I CAN RECALL that when I was a doctoral student, I was admonished again and again by my advisers, "Don't let your intuition fool you." I cannot, however, remember just what I took this to mean; I probably thought it meant, "Don't let your imagination lead you astray; what you think is true may very possibly turn out to be false."

One of my favorite articles in this connection is a transcription of a lecture by Hans Hahn, entitled "The Crisis in Intuition," in the anthology edited by J. R. Newman entitled *The World of Mathematics*. This article echoes the warnings of my early teachers, and especially the admonition that "what you think is true may very possibly turn out to be false." In fact, one can easily get the impression from Hahn's article that "intuition" is a thoroughly unreliable guide and that one should regard it with suspicion even when its every suggestion has been rigorously checked.

Now insofar as checking carefully the suggestions of one's intuition is concerned, no one would quarrel with this, I believe. But as for intuition being thoroughly unreliable, I am of the opinion that this mental quality, whatever it is, has been too much maligned. Indeed, I would go so far as to say that without it, mathematical creation would well-nigh cease, and modern methods of teaching would be difficult to justify.

Nature of Mathematical Intuition

In order to support these contentions, it must be made clear just what is meant, in mathematics, by "intuition."

Not so long ago, those who were trying to test intelligence got into a predicament because they ignored the problem of defining exactly what they

Source: R. L. Wilder, "The Role of Intuition," *Science* 156 (5 May 1967): 605–610. Copyright 1967 by the American Association for the Advancement of Science. (Some references omitted.)

meant by "intelligence." Subsequently, these testers came up with a number, the "intelligence quotient" or I.Q., and it was demonstrated that the student with the higher I.Q. would, generally speaking, do better in his studies than the one with lower I.Q. But the concept of the I.Q. as a measure of something called "native intelligence," that is, the intelligence bequeathed to the individual by his heredity, had to be abandoned. After numerous experiments, especially with inductees during World War I, it became clear that the cultural environment so modifies this native intelligence as to render the I.Q., at most, a measure of the combined effect of heredity and environment on the individual's capacity for learning, his perception, and his degree of conformity to cultural directives. And an I.Q. could, over a period of time, be lowered or raised by the environmental factors active during the period.

Coming back to mathematical intuition, we might expect to find an analogous situation. I believe that the intuition about which some philosophers speak is—if not wholly, at least partially—a "native intuition." Thus Descartes stated:[1] "By *intuition* I understand, not the fluctuating testimony of the senses, nor the misleading judgment that proceeds from the blundering constructions of imagination, but the conception which an unclouded and attentive mind gives us so readily and distinctly that we are wholly freed from doubt about that which we understand." And Kant, as I interpret him, conceived of the concepts of both time and space as deriving from an a priori intuition which is independent of experience. Among the more modern philosophers, especially those of a mystical bent, knowledge imparted by this native intuition may be considered more valid than that gained from observation and experience. The "intuitionism" of Brouwer and Poincaré, insofar as it conceived of the natural numbers as "intuitively given," seems to proceed from this native intuition.

I do not believe that my teachers had in mind anything like this native intuition. Moreover, I have always doubted whether they ever tried to analyze just exactly what they meant by "intuition." But I believe that they associated it, in some way, with experience—mathematical experience, to be more precise—and that the more experienced the mathematician became, the more reliable did his "intuition" become. That is, mathematical intuition, like intelligence, is a psychological quality which stems possibly from a hereditarily derived faculty, but which is, at any given time, principally an accumulation of attitudes derived from one's mathematical experience. This should not be taken to mean that mathematical intuition is something which already contains one's attitude toward a mathematical situation which one has never faced before. Indeed, in this day of widely diversified branches of mathematics, a mathematician may be expected to have little or no intuition regarding a branch of mathematics in which he has never worked; his intuition is of use chiefly in those areas with which he has had some experience. There is some agreement between this assertion, I think, and the one with which Hahn concluded his article, namely, that intuition "is force of habit rooted in psychological inertia."[2] Like intelligence, and I refer here to the kind that I.Q. testers have in mind, intuition is greatly influenced, possibly wholly formed, by the cultural environment— probably even more so than is intelligence. For I believe, in particular, that the average nonmathematician has no mathematical intuition at all, except that nebulous quality of the mind which, if nourished by experience with mathematics, would develop into what we call mathematical intuition.

Individual Versus Collective Intuition

I have used the word "psychological" with reference to intuition (from here on, "intuition" will mean "mathematical intuition"). I wish to emphasize that my ultimate concern is with the intuition of the individual mathematician. I am not unaware of the fact that concerning certain questions there is essentially what might be called a collective or cultural intuition. For instance, before Weierstrass gave his example of a real continuous function having no derivative at any point of its interval of definition, probably almost every mathematician felt intuitively that such a function could not exist; this intuition had become a cultural attitude, a common belief. But consider the four-color map problem: I doubt if the average mathematician today has any intuitive feeling regarding whether there exists or does not exist a map that cannot be colored with at most four colors—simply because he has never worked on the problem. And an analogous statement can be made about the so-called "last theorem of Fermat," as well as a host of other problems. Before one can have a really intuitive feeling about such problems, one must have worked on them. But everyone who has gone very far in mathematics will have worked with functions of a real variable and can be expected to have developed an intuition for them. A similar remark holds for the structure of the real-number continuum. So far as those mathematical concepts that form part of the equipment of every mathematician are concerned, there can be expected to exist a kind of intuition that is common to most members of the mathematical community. But as soon as one goes beyond these concepts to mathematical specialties—particularly to their frontiers—then the intuition becomes a quite individual affair; and it is this intuition that is of immediate importance in creative work.

But this is entirely in accord with the concept of mathematical intuition as an accumulation of attitudes derived from one's experience. Regarding matters of common knowledge, such as function theory, the attitudes we acquire are determined by our teachers, and the relation to the general mathematical culture of the time is apparent. But when one cultivates a special area of interest, and especially as he becomes involved in research on its frontiers, then one develops his own attitudes in the light of his own personal experiences. Only he can make the educated guess, since he has developed his own intuition. And although the connection with the current cultural atmosphere is still traceable, it is much less direct.

Coming to my main topic—the role of intuition—it is advisable, I believe, to look at some specific examples first. And since the manner in which intuition exerts its influence varies according to whether it is collective (cultural) or individual, and whether it is true or false, I shall separate my examples along those lines.

Examples

Let us first consider the intuition apparently possessed by the Greeks, and certainly by their medieval successors, that the parallel axiom was true. I use the word "true" in the absolute sense in which *they* seem to have used it. This was an intuitive belief possessed by all mathematicians, since during the period involved everyone who professed to be expert in mathematics was expected to be familiar with Euclid's *Elements*. It was an instance in which the collective intuition was a false guide—a case typical of those which Hahn cited in his article. It is interesting, however, to try to assess the overall influence which this intuition had on mathematics. That an intuition was false is not sufficient reason to conclude that it was bad. And in this case, I believe that the influence was highly beneficial. For if it had not been for the conviction that the parallel axiom could be proved from the other axioms of Euclid—and this conviction was a direct result of the common intuition concerning its truth—then possibly the appearance of the non-Euclidean geometries together with their effect on all mathematics and philosophy might have been delayed. Of course the non-Euclidean geometry would most certainly have been discovered sooner or later, if for no other reason than that the axiomatic method, as Hilbert, for example, conceived it in his *Foundations of Geometry*, was already beginning to emerge in the work of such mathematicians as Boole, Hamilton, and others. And someone would no doubt ultimately have experimented with alternatives for the parallel axiom, just as Hamilton and Grassmann experimented with denials of the commutative laws of algebra. But because of the special position held by Euclidean geometry, not only in philosophy, but as part of the general mathematical curriculum, the impact of the eventual realization of the independence of the parallel axiom on the mathematical and philosophical community started a chain of research, the effects of which caused a virtual revolution in philosophical and mathematical thought.

I have already mentioned the intuition, also false, which underlay the conviction that every continuous function must have a derivative at some point of its interval of definition. I am confident that, if a study were made of the historical background preceding publication of Weierstrass's example, it would be found that the influence of this false intuition had had its beneficial aspects. I can immediately recall Lagrange's proposed method for calculating derivatives by expanding functions in Taylor's series; thereby making a start on the theory of analytic functions. If he had known, as we now know, that most continuous function ("most" in the sense of the Baire category) have no derivatives anywhere in the interval of definition, might he not have been deterred from proposing a method which he considered applicable to all continuous functions?

To take a more recent case, consider the general "closed curve"; more specifically, a curve which is a common boundary of two domains in the plane. There was more general interest in this topological configuration 65 years ago than now, since both the Jordan curve theorem and Peano's space-filling curve had stimulated interest in plane curves. Although we now know quite simple examples of closed curves which have complementary domains other than the two of which they are the common boundary, apparently around the turn of the century the common intuition was that there could be only two such domains, an "inside" and an "outside." Just how much influence the proving of the Jordan curve theorem had on this intuition we can only surmise. At any rate, Schoenflies, who had recently given such a proof and who could be considered an expert on the topology of the plane, as well as one of the principal founders of the topology of Euclidean spaces, published a number of results in which he took it for granted, as intuitively clear, that a closed curve could have only two complementary domains. Now this was bad, of course; but was its influence on the development of mathematics bad? I think not. For example, it evidently came to the attention of L. E. J. Brouwer, the "father" of modern Intuitionism, and inspired him to look into the validity of the assumption. I surmise that this helped arouse Brouwer's interest in topology (although that interest possibly had other stimuli too), and that his classical work in this regard (giving counterexamples which included closed curves which are the common boundaries of an

arbitrary countable number of domains) influenced his continuing interest in topology. In particular, it led to his interest in the topological invariance of closed curves. In the proof of this, which he was the first to give, he started a chain of ideas which led to the extension of homology theory to general spaces. For several years thereafter he was quite active in this branch of mathematics, finding a number of results which have become classical (such as his fixed point theorems and work on mappings of locally Euclidean manifolds), and which were not fully appreciated in the mainstream of topology until over a decade later.

Common Features of the Examples

All three of the examples of collective intuition that I have mentioned were false, yet it is difficult to believe that their influence was entirely bad. It is curious how much good mathematics can be done even when the collective intuition concerning basic matters is false. This is most striking during the period preceding Weierstrass's example. For during that period the collective intuition concerning continuity, existence of derivatives, infinite series, the real-number system, and a host of other fundamental concepts was at best faulty and usually full of error. Yet on such a basis much of classical analysis was built up. It would be quite as apt to speak of the "modern miracle" as we do of the "Greek miracle."

Speaking of the "Greek miracle" recalls the classical crisis regarding commensurability. Here again, the collective intuition regarding number and magnitude, according to which all magnitudes were commensurable, though false, was able to support the creation of much good mathematics. Moreover, the ultimate discovery of their true character led, in all these cases, to very fruitful periods of mathematical activity. It is my individual opinion that they all represent natural phenomena in the evolution of mathematics. In each case, the evidence is strong that the discovery of the error in the basic intuition was about to burst forth through the medium of several mathematical leaders, all working independently.

In the case of the discovery of incommensurability, some have attributed it to Pythagoras himself, others to Hippasus (a student of Pythagoras); but the truth is that nobody really knows. However, since the Pythagorean theorem had become known quite generally at that time, the incommensurability between the diagonal and side of a square could not have been long concealed, no matter who first detected it. In the case of the parallel axiom, Gauss, Bolyai, and Lobachewski all discovered the facts at about the same time. We now know that Bolzano had an example similar to Weierstrass's. And about the same time that Brouwer found his example of a "pathological" closed curve, a Japanese mathematician, Wada, also apparently produced one. And no one knows how many other individual mathematicians were either working on, or had produced examples, proving the faulty character of each of these collective intuitions. The discovery of the space-filling curve, which I mentioned above only incidentally, was evidently another typical case. Parametric representation of plane curves had proved extremely useful, although evidently its introduction (possibly by Cauchy) was made under the influence of the intuitive belief that such curves would always be curves of the intuitively accepted kind—that is, having no "breadth" or "thickness." The usual pattern of events followed. After much good research based on the concept, almost simultaneously Peano, E. H. Moore, and Hilbert came up with examples showing that the intuition underlying the concept of parametric representation was false. There followed a period of 40 years or so of research in plane topology and problems related to it. The pattern is quite typical.

Role of Intuition in Evolution of Concepts

What do these case histories indicate concerning the manner in which mathematical concepts evolve on the cultural level? I am asking this question with a twofold purpose in mind. Thus far I have recounted only cases in which the collective intuition was false—I have not given any cases where it was true—and mathematical intuition is not always wrong, fortunately. Consequently I would like to cite some cases where the intuition was correct; but at the same time I would like to consider how these cases dovetail, so to speak, with the former cases in forcing the formulation of new concepts.

Let me begin with the most basic concept of all, namely number; more specifically, the "counting" or "natural" numbers, 1, 2, 3, ... The Intuitionist philosophy regards the origin of these to be in man's intuition of "fundamental series" of mental acts, consisting of a first act, a second act, a third act, and so on. I presume this must have been an intuition which was derived from the physical and cultural environment. More specifically—and this can be inferred from a study of the forms of primitive number-words, as well as of the practice of tallying—the use of one-to-one correspondence to compare collections of physical objects, along with the repetitive character of the actual determination of such correspondences, built up a set of attitudes which formed, ultimately, the intuition of fundamental series. And I presume this was an intuition on the cultural level, shared by virtually all who found it necessary to engage in the primitive forms of counting. Probably an analogous kind of intuition was involved in the genesis of geometry, where it became necessary to compare lengths and areas. All of this is very conjectural, of course, but it seems fairly representative of what occurred prior to those periods for which the historical records are more complete. And it is our earliest example of how correct intuition on the collective level serves to build the mathematical edifice.

However, it was an intuition which finally led to concepts that produced the "Greek crisis"; and it was necessary for Eudoxus and his contemporaries to create a new conceptual framework which, while containing the major part of the old, rejected the parts that had been found false. There followed that flowering of activity that we call the "Greek miracle," based on a new intuition of the number concept—the so-called geometric "magnitudes"—which permitted a further construction of mathematical theory atop the old of the Pythagoreans. Although couched in the language of geometry, this intuition comprised virtually a complete theory of the real-number system. Unfortunately, the course taken by Western culture precluded further development of the Greek intuition. And it was not until early times that activity in mathematical analysis, based on the foundation laid by the Greeks and their successors (who added new symbolic representations for number), brought to light the inadequacy of the intuition created by the work of Eudoxus. By the latter half of the 19th century, real analysis had reached a more precise formulation of the real-number continuum with the notion of set. The so-called "arithmetization of analysis" by Weierstrass and others provided a new conception of the real continuum and made possible the theory of measure and the brilliant researches of the first half of the present century in both analysis and topology.

But this new conception of the real continuum gave birth to a new intuition—that of the theory of sets. The work of Cantor was the classical formulation of this new intuition. Some of its faults were discovered early, in the guise of the set-theoretic contradictions. By now, the mathematical world had developed new standards of rigor, and it was realized that the remedy must be sought in a more precise formulation of the theory of sets. The axiomatic method, used by the Greeks to avoid the Zeno paradoxes and the commensurability assumption, was approaching a new maturity and again offered a method for attaining the desired precision. For most ordinary purposes, axiomatic systems for set theory provided quite a satisfactory basis. But so far as a unique formulation of general set theory is concerned, we are today in little better position than were the Pythagoreans with respect to geometry, or the early analysts with respect to the real continuum. Our knowledge of the axiom of choice, for instance, is purely intuitive. We have an accumulation of good mathematics based upon its use, but we feel uneasy about its paradoxical consequences, such as the Banach-Tarski theorem. The same holds for the continuum hypothesis, although this is perhaps not so serious for most of us. It does serve as a reminder, however, that our intuition of the real continuum was not thoroughly clarified by the work of Weierstrass and his contemporaries. They, of necessity, brought into being a new intuition—the theory of sets—and so long as this

theory has only an intuitive base, so must all the mathematics dependent upon it.

I think that there is only one conclusion that we can draw from all this, namely, that so far as mathematics being ultimately based on intuition is concerned, the Intuitionists are correct. But the mathematical intuition, as I have used the notion, is not precisely that of Intuitionism; and, moreover, the methods which the majority of mathematicians use are not those of the Intuitionistic doctrine.

But to summarize the role of the mathematical intuition in the evolution of mathematical concepts—our collective intuition of basic concepts has grown by a series of discoveries of faulty features in the current concepts, with ultimate replacement by new concepts which not only clear up the faults, but lead to feverish activity on the new foundation with consequent creation of much good mathematics. Ultimately, the new concepts begin to reveal faults; in particular, we discover that they have brought in with them new intuitions which have to be made more conceptually precise. And the cycle goes on.

Role of Intuition in Research

I come now to the role of intuition in research. The biographical comments in Poincaré's writings, and the more complete work of Hadamard, embody a good account of how intuition works on the individual level in creative work. As I remarked before, this is intuition which is of a highly specialized nature. It relates to the particular problem on which only the individual, or a few individuals, are working. It is true, of course, that in their background is collective intuition, and they are certainly influenced by it. In particular, their choice of the problems on which they work is guided by what the collective intuition deems the most fruitful direction for research. But once having selected the particular problem, the individual begins to build new concepts and their resultant intuitions. In a way, he repeats the experience of the general mathematical culture, but on a different level and at greater rates of change. His false intuitions are usually recognized to be such in a relatively short time ("relatively short" can be as much as several years, of course), and they are patched up by correct conceptual material.

These remarks apply, too, in the case of problems that remain unsolved for many years and become "classical." The experienced individuals may have stopped working on them, having found their efforts at solution frustrated, and therefore have gone on to problems promising quicker results. I believe that what happens here is that the collective intuition in the field of a particular problem continues to grow, being passed on by the older workers to the younger. Ultimately, due to a combination of a more mature collective intuition (which has been growing unnoticed), new methods, and individual genius, someone (usually a younger mathematician, relatively new in the field, and possessing a fresh individual intuition) is able to solve the problem. That feeling of awe, which I am sure many older creative mathematicians must get regarding the powers of the younger generation of creative workers, has a firm basis. The younger man has not only come into the particular field without having to clutter up his brain with concepts and methods which served their purpose and are now discarded, but using new concepts and methods he has built up an individual intuition which forms a platform from which he can regard his field of research with an eye undimmed by the recollection of earlier and faulty intuitions. The director of his first research has no stronger responsibility than that of guiding and steering this young intuition into the most up-to-date conceptual channels. It is almost a truism that without intuition, there is no creativity in mathematics.

Role of Intuition in Teaching

Like collective intuition, individual mathematical intuition is not a static but a growing thing. It starts developing when we are children, during the time when we learn to distinguish shapes and sizes (geometric intuition) and to count (arithmetic intuition). We are not born with it, for without a cultural basis for its development, there can apparently be no mathematical intuition. By the time the child starts school in our culture, however, he usually has some basis to build on—his parents have probably taught him to count, for example—and the continuing development of this basis undoubtedly forms one of the central responsibilities of primary teachers.

By the time the student reaches high school he should have a fairly substantial intuitive base from which to work. Presumably his teachers have used his arithmetic intuition to develop both higher arithmetic and algebra, and—at least under new curricular ideas—his geometric intuition, not only to develop elementary geometric facts but to aid in solving arithmetic and algebraic problems. And in this process, the teacher should have added to the intuitive base. In short, as the student comes to the high school teachers, his mathematical equipment should have two main components—the intuitive component and the knowledge component. These are difficult to separate, particularly since the intuitive component is dependent for its growth on the knowledge component.

Perhaps I can make this clearer by stating my conception of what the new curricula being developed today should accomplish in contrast to the old, standard, mathematical curriculum. The old curriculum was designed chiefly for the knowledge component; the student was taught how to perform arithmetic and algebraic operations and how to prove theorems. But little conscious development of mathematical intuition took place; what there was of this seemed to find expression chiefly in the problems that were given to be solved. But insofar as these were mechanical repetition of the operations or modes of proof that had been taught, they added little or nothing to the intuitive component. In contrast to this, the new curricula should try to turn teaching of the knowledge component into a process whereby the student's intuition is actually used and developed further in acquiring the new knowledge.

For example, while under the old system the student was *told* the formula for carrying out a process, under the new he should be invited to do a little guessing as to what form the process should take. This guessing and the accompanying experimentation, resulting in a decision as to the final result, develops and strengthens his mathematical intuition. In an embryonic way, the procedure is precisely the same as that pursued by the research mathematician, and in my opinion the teacher who cultivates it is doing creative teaching. And I believe that all concepts should be introduced in this way. To explain a concept to a student adds to his knowledge component, perhaps, but does not strengthen his intuition. Probably the worst example of this kind of thing is the writing of a definition on the board, then explaining what it means and how it is used.

For example, consider the mathematical induction principle. One can proceed by first writing it on the blackboard in the form in which it is usually stated, as an axiom; secondly, by explaining what it means; and thirdly, by showing how to use it in proof of simple arithmetic formulas. This is followed by homework in which the student applies the process much as a proof algorithm, imitating what the teacher has done. The brighter students will not have any trouble with this, perhaps, but the average ones will be beset by minor questions such as: "How do I find the $(n + 1)$st term?"—questions which are largely due to the algorithmic character of what they have been taught.

Now this kind of teaching is certainly not going to help the student recognize, when he later comes to a problem in which mathematical induction is a natural mode of proof or definition, that the mathematical induction principle may be called upon. For while he may "know" mathematical induction he has not acquired any intuitive feeling for it. If, on the other hand, his teacher had given him credit for knowing how to count and having an intuition of "fundamental series," and if the teacher had proceeded from there to guide him to the *discovery* of the mathematical induction principle, then the student would have acquired not only a knowledge of the principle, but also an intuitive base for later recognizing instances when the principle could be applied. In this way, the intuition would be permitted to play its proper role in creative teaching.

Perhaps most experienced teachers already use such creative teaching methods, and they would not think of presenting a definition without first calling upon the student's intuitive powers to help

formulate the definition. However, two matters worry me: First, that they may find, under the pressure of crowding a certain amount of material into a given amount of time, that it is necessary to resort to the old mode of teaching which consists of (i) statement of the definition, (ii) explanation of it, and (iii) application of the concept to a particular problem. In discussing the so-called "Moore method" of teaching—which exemplifies much of what I have been saying—Moise commented that "sheer knowledge does not play the crucial role in mathematical development that most people suppose."[3] And a propos of the time lost in using the Moore method, he stated: "The resulting ignorance ought to be a hopeless handicap, but in fact it isn't; and the only way that I can see to resolve this paradox is to conclude that mathematics is capable of being learned as an *activity*, and that knowledge which is acquired in this way has a power which is out of all proportion to its quantity." And in the second volume of Polya's recent book *Mathematical Discovery*, there is the quotation from the 18th-century German physicist Lichtenberg: "What you have been obliged to discover by yourself leaves a path in your mind which you can use again when the need arises."[4] This is an expressive way of saying that you have added to the accumulation of your mathematical intuition.

The second matter that worries me is related to the use of the axiomatic method in secondary school teaching, particularly where the function is that of definition. What I said before regarding mathematical induction applies here. The student should not be introduced to a theory by means of axioms. Consider the arithmetic of integers. Here is a theory with which the student is already familiar, a circumstance which makes it an excellent subject for a proper introduction to axiomatics. But before stating a single axiom, the teacher ought to respect the student's imagination enough to tell him something about the purpose of axiomatics. In particular, he should be told that one wishes to seek out certain specific aspects of the arithmetic of integers from which the other aspects can be derived; for having done so, then not only can one test the accuracy of an operation against the axiomatic base, but one can also try out one's imagination by finding models for all or some of the axioms other than that of the arithmetic of integers—as, for example, the arithmetic of rationals, elementary algebra, and the like.

After having decided to try to list axioms, the student should be encouraged to discover suitable axioms himself—under the guiding hand of the teacher, of course. It should go without saying, however, that if these matters are too advanced to be comprehended by the student, then the axiomatic method should not be introduced at all. Nor should axioms be sneaked in under the guise of so-called "laws" presumably handed down by some obscure mathematical Moses.

Most of this applies, I believe, to college teaching—certainly up to the end of the first two years of college. As the student goes on to more advanced work, the intuitive component of his training begins to assume more importance. At this stage of his career it may be assumed that he is possibly going on to do some kind of creative work, if not in mathematics, then in some other science. And it is desirable that his teachers have had some experience with creative work. This does not mean that the teacher must have a Ph.D. degree; this is a fetish I wish we could get rid of. I would much prefer a teacher without a Ph.D. who is excited about mathematics and can teach creatively, than a teacher with a Ph.D. who is neither enthusiastic about mathematics nor capable of inspiring his students. Naturally, as the student progresses into graduate work, most of his teachers will, as a matter of course, have Ph.D.'s, since they should themselves either be doing creative work, or at least have done sufficient work to realize the role of intuition in such work and the importance of using methods that will develop it. The student in the graduate stage should be capable of adding to his knowledge component on his own; his mentor's responsibility is chiefly to nourish his mathematical intuition, for it is this that is going to be of greater importance in his career as a mathematician.

Summary

"Intuition," as used by the modern mathematician, means an accumulation of attitudes (including beliefs and opinions) derived from experience, both individual and cultural. It is closely associated with mathematical knowledge, which forms the basis of intuition. This knowledge contributes to the growth of intuition and is in turn increased by new conceptual materials suggested by intuition.

The major role of intuition is to provide a conceptual foundation that suggests the directions which new research should take. The opinion of the individual mathematician regarding existence of mathematical concepts (number, geometric notions, and the like) are provided by this intuition; these opinions are frequently so firmly held as to merit the appellation "Platonic." The role of intuition in research is to provide the "educated guess," which may prove to be true or false; but in either case, progress cannot be made without it and even a false guess may lead to progress. Thus intuition also plays a major role in the evolution of mathematical concepts. The advance of mathematical knowledge periodically reveals flaws in cultural intuition; these result in "crises," the solution of which result in a more mature intuition.

The ultimate basis of modern mathematics is thus mathematical intuition, and it is in this sense that the Intuitionistic doctrine of Brouwer and his followers is correct. Modern instructional methods recognize this role of intuition by replacing the "do this, do that" mode of teaching by a "what should be done next?" attitude which appeals to the intuitive background already developed. It is in this way that understanding and appreciation of new mathematical knowledge may be properly instilled in the student.

Notes

1. R. Descartes, in *The Philosophical Works of Descartes*, E. S. Haldane and G. R. T. Ross, Trans. (Cambridge Univ. Press, Cambridge, 1911).
2. J. R. Newman, *The World of Mathematics* (Simon and Schuster, New York, 1956), pp. 1956–1976.
3. E. E. Moise, *Amer. Math. Mon.* 72, 4 (1965).
4. G. Polya, *Mathematical Discovery* (Wiley, New York, 1965), vol. 2, p. 103.

Mathematics—Our Invisible Culture

Allen L. Hammond

Allen L. Hammond was born in 1943 and received his Ph.D. in applied mathematics in 1970 from Harvard. He has served as Research News Editor for the American Association for the Advancement of Science since 1970. He has been a consultant for the Rand Corporation.

This essay treads on what by now ought to be rather familiar ground. Hammond speaks of the vigor of modern mathematics and the virtually exploding universe of its creations. But a dark shadow hangs over the essay: the concern for the lack of general interest in or even knowledge of this priceless cultural treasure. However, these now familiar themes are only the backdrop for a most insightful discussion of the problems and triumphs of modern mathematics from three genuinely distinct perspectives. The essay revolves around a nearly verbatim account of a discussion involving a widely respected older member of the international mathematical establishment, a most promising young member of the American mathematical community, and a high school student of demonstrated mathematical ability but little formal training. The interaction among these three points of view is most enlightening and provides an entertaining introduction to "our invisible culture."

AN INQUIRY INTO mathematics and mathematicians might begin with certain curious facts. One is that mathematics is no longer an especially uncommon pursuit. Never mind that a multitude of mathematicians seems a contradiction in terms. The universities are simply teeming with them. The latest figures compiled by the National Science Foundation show that there are as many mathematicians in the United States as there are physicists or economists. Mathematicians are not a rare breed, simply an invisible one. It is a multitude singularly accomplished at keeping out of the public eye. Who has ever seen a mathematician on television, or read of their exploits in the newspapers?

A second fact about this reticent profession is even more startling. All those people are busy doing something, including some very remarkable somethings. In all its long history extending back 25 centuries, mathematics has never been more vigorous, more active than now. Within this century mathematicians have experienced philosophical upheavals and intellectual advances as profound as those that have catapulted physicists into fame or transformed economists into the indispensable advisors of governments. The foundations of mathematics itself have been challenged and rewritten, whole new branches have budded and flourished, seemingly arcane bits of theory have become the dicta for giant industries. Yet this drama has been played out in near obscurity. The physical concepts of relativity and subatomic particles have entered the language, the gross national product is reported to millions of living rooms, but it is as if the very texture of mathematics is antithetical to broad exposure. What is it in the nature of this unique field of knowledge, this unique human activity that renders it so re-

Source: Allen L. Hammond, "Mathematics—Our Invisible Culture," in *Mathematics Today— Twelve Informal Essays* (Springer-Verlag, 1978), pp. 15–34. Copyright by CBMS. (Some references omitted.)

mote and its practitioners so isolated from popular culture?

In searching for a foothold to grapple with this elusive subject, an Inquirer is struck by the contradictions that abound. For example, mathematics is nearly always described as a branch of science, the essence of pure reason. Beyond doubt mathematics has proved to be profoundly useful, perhaps even essential, to the modern edifice of science and its technological harvest. But mathematicians persist in talking about their field in terms of an art—beauty, elegance, simplicity—and draw analogies to painting, music. And many mathematicians would heatedly deny that their work is intended to be useful, that it is in any sense motivated by the prospect of practical application. A curious usefulness, an aesthetic principle of action; it is a dichotomy that will bear no little scrutiny in what is to come.

A further contradiction arises from the stuff of mathematics itself. It is in principle not foreign to our experience, since the root concepts are those of number and of space, intuitively familiar even to the child who asks "how many" or "how large." But the axiomatization and elaboration of these concepts has gone quite far from these simple origins. The abstraction of number to quantitative relationships of all kinds, the generalization of distance and area first to idealized geometrical figures and then to pure spatial forms of diverse types are large steps. Somewhere along the lengthy chains of logic that link modern mathematics to more primitive notions, a transmutation has occurred—or so it often seems to outsiders—and we can no longer recognize the newest branches on the tree of mathematics as genetically related to the roots. The connection is obscured, the terminology baffling. Is any of it for real? Do these abstractions and elaborations genuinely expand our understanding of number and of space, or do they amount to an empty house of theorems?

Mathematicians bristle at such questions. But it is not surprising that there is a popular tendency to dismiss much of this unfamiliar stuff as the subtle inventions of clever minds and having no important relationship to reality. What is surprising is that mathematicians do not agree among themselves whether mathematics is invented or discovered, whether such a thing as mathematical reality exists or is illusory. Is the tree of mathematics unique? Would any intelligence (even a nonhuman one) build similar structures of logic? How arbitrary is the whole of mathematical knowledge? These too are points worth additional inquiry.

We might also learn something of the end result, however incomprehensible, if we could see the process by which it is made and know more of the makers. Should we pity the poor mathematicians, condemned to serve his or her days bound to a heavy chain of cold logic? How does that image jibe with the white-hot flashes of insight, the creative "highs," so often reported, or the intensely human character of mathematicians in the flesh? Clearly, a suitable subject for this inquiry is the nature of mathematicians themselves, their motivations, their trials, their rewards, and how they spend their days.

A final question might be directed toward the place of mathematics in our culture. There are those, including Plato, who have identified mathematics with the highest ideal of civilization—a lofty claim indeed. A claim more often made and subscribed to by mathematicians is that mathematics is one of the finest flowerings of the human spirit, a cathedral of enduring knowledge built piece by piece over the ages. But if so it is a cathedral with few worshipers, unknown to most of humankind. Mathematics plays no role in mass culture, it cannot claim to evoke the sensibilities and inspire the awe that music and sculpture do, it is not a significant companion in the lives of more than a very few. And yet it is worth asking whether mathematics is essentially remote, or merely poorly communicated. Perhaps it is a remediable ignorance, not an inability, that now limits appreciation and enjoyment of mathematical intuitions by a wider audience; perhaps our culture is only reaching the stage at which mathematics can begin to penetrate a larger consciousness.

Three Mathematicians

This Inquirer was himself originally trained in a mathematical subject. But he does not—as mathematicians say—*do* mathematics and he approaches this inquiry from the great camp of outsiders. The principal sources of information that he consulted and here reports on are of two kinds: what mathematicians of note have written about themselves and their craft, unfortunately a sparse literature; and three live data points, talking mathematicians, captured in a joint conversation before an inquiring microphone. Let us introduce them. In order of descending age, we have: Lipman Bers, a professor of mathematics at Columbia University; Dennis Sullivan, a professor of mathematics at the Institute des Hautes Etudes Scientifiques in Bures-sur-Yvette, France; and Miller Puckette, a mathematics special student at the Massachusetts Institute of Technology.

"Papa" Bers, as he is known to his students, was born in Latvia. He evokes the filmmaker's European emigree with his accent and continental manners, an image that is enhanced by his small mustache, greying hair, and glasses. He is a kindly man, active in the cause of scientists imprisoned abroad, and enthusiastic when he speaks of mathematics. His research is in analysis, a branch of mathematics that began in Newton's time with the calculus but now spans a range extending from numerical and algebraic subjects at one extreme to geometric and spatial subjects at the other.

Sullivan is one of the world's experts on things spatial; he is a topologist, a field sometimes described as an essay on the word "continuous" because it deals with the properties of objects undergoing transformations in their shape that do not involve cutting or tearing. Sullivan is a vigorous man who gestures and moves his body when he speaks. He fairly radiates intensity; with his long untamed locks, full beard, and glasses, he is a fierce, almost primal figure on first meeting. His laughter, however, turns out to be rich and infectious and frequently punctuates the discussion.

Puckette is trim and clean-shaven, bright-eyed in his youth. He is intent on the discussion but not seemingly fazed by his elders. Puckette is not yet a practicing mathematician but is well launched in that direction; in high school he was twice a member of the U.S. team entered in the International Mathematics Olympiad. He is

studying combinatorics—one of the newer branches of mathematics on the numerical side of the family which deals with how objects are distributed into classes. For the sake of the completeness that mathematicians hold dear, he is to represent the class of things numerical.

The diversity of backgrounds and personal styles, deliberately contrived for this inquiry, emphasize what is all too easily forgotten. Mathematics is universal and unified, but those who do it are varied indeed. For all its abstractness, it is a very human endeavor. As the four of us sit down in Bers' office at Columbia to begin our discussion,* trucks whine by on the highway below the window and the heating system hisses continually. The high-ceilinged old room is a bit bleak, but the atmosphere is warm, almost jovial.

"I sometimes work like I used to do when I was young, in long stretches, thinking only about the same problem. Sometimes I have to force myself to sit down to write down something or to read something. In general, one waits—I don't know how long for other people—one waits for the few pleasant moments when suddenly something that was obscure and mysterious becomes clear."

Bers is talking about how he spends his time, what he actually does when he does mathematical research. His description hints at the mental self-discipline and intensity of thought required. Listen to Sullivan:

"In one period I would work like this. I would wake up in the morning thinking about something, and think about it until I ran into some other talking mathematician, then I would start talking about it. I would talk about it all day long, go through all kinds of deformations and interactions about what I was doing. I would go home in the evening to my family, have supper, do what I had to do to lead a normal life, then sit on the couch and start thinking about it again. I would think about it until I fell asleep, then start over again the next day. It's this very funny process, slowly the topic is revolving and changing, but there is never any rhyme or reason about it. You must follow different trains of thought; they

---

*In what follows, individual comments have been lightly edited and sometimes excerpted to focus the discussion.

don't always lead to something. It's sort of a recycling process. I keep thinking things over and over again for years, maybe not always the same things, but mixed in with other things."

It is a picture of single-minded pursuit. The question arises as to whether the thinking process is consciously organized, directed by some plan of attack.

"You have to have an overall prejudice or goal," Sullivan says. "But I see the process as sort of eating [mathematics], seeing new examples; I sort of like the examples, the phenomena of mathematics, like different types of entertainment."

BERS (interjecting):   Do you invent or do you discover? What is your gut feeling? [See p. 50.]

SULLIVAN: Sometimes you come upon something sort of natural, it's like you're discovering it. But sometimes you just make something up out of thin air, so to speak; maybe force it a little bit.

BERS: What gives you more pleasure, inventing or discovering?

SULLIVAN: I haven't invented very often, so that was very, very pleasurable. I would say that inventing and discovering give different kinds of pleasure. Most mathematicians are basically driven in their desire to simplify, to understand. You need a balance. The ideal situation is where you have a rich set of phenomena and you vaguely feel that you are about to understand it, but if you understand it too well, then it gets a little low on entropy. This sort of paradoxical situation is the best. By the way, would you prefer to find an example or prove a theorem?

BERS: I want to know the truth.

SULLIVAN: But suppose I gave you a choice, to find an example or to prove that there is no such example, which would you prefer?

BERS: I cannot imagine myself having this power. Only one thing is true.

INQUIRER: Does the understanding that results from a new mathematical example or theorem reflect an aspect of reality, an innate truth about the universe, or is it an aspect of an arbitrary, invented system?

BERS: I'm not sure we can answer this question. I was educated in a philosophical tradition, logical positivism, that leads me to believe that evolution developed the human mind to understand nature, and that nature is written in the language of mathematics, as Galileo said. But when I actually do mathematics, I have the subjective feeling that there is a real world to discover, the world of mathematics, which is much more eternal, unchangeable, and real than are the accidents of physical reality. This is the feeling that I have. I actually feel a little embarrassed: here I am, a grown up man, worrying about whether the limit set of a Kleinian group has positive measure and willing to invest a great deal of effort to find the answer.

SULLIVAN: I prefer to talk from the point of view that there are two kinds of textures in mathematics. One is the context of structure of mathematics: if you see the structure unfolding, you feel, "that's something that is there." Then the idea of examples, of phenomena—that's like something you invented. I mean you just write it down; it's pretty inventive.

BERS: The human mind is made so that when we do mathematics, we have the feeling that we are dealing with some reality. There are some parts of mathematics that are more real than others. To me the value of a mathematical theory depends on how much it deals with things made, in some sense, by God and not by man.

SULLIVAN: I have a more down-to-earth feeling. First of all, the whole of mathematics is built up from essentially two concepts. One is number, and one is space. Both of these things are part of reality. I think that mathematics is very much tied to physical reality by these two concepts. In fact, mathematics always had these two sides. The more sophisticated side is often attached to number, the more intuitive side is often attached to

Discovery or Invention?

The argument among mathematicians over whether mathematical truths are invented or discovered has been going on a long time. It is not an argument that is easily resolved but it is revealing of how mathematicians think about their work.

The two points of view are at first glance quite distinct. One holds that mathematicians discover a piece of reality no less firm than physical reality, a truth not of their own making but rather an inherent part of the universe. "God made the integers," as one nineteenth century mathematician put it—they did not arise out of some Greek geometers' fertile imagination but rather from human experience. Hence the properties of the integers encompassed in simple arithmetic and in the more sophisticated theorems of number theory are viewed by most mathematicians in much the same way as astronomers think of the planets—discovered elements of the heavens. This absolutist or Platonist viewpoint—mathematics as reality revealed—extends to other areas of mathematics as well and is in fact the dominant dogma in the mathematical community. But even among the integers there lurk some telltale signs of human inventiveness. The Arabic number system we use today, including the concept of the number zero, was invented by mid-eastern mathematicians during the Middle Ages and has had a substantial impact on mathematics ever since, making possible such things as the binary arithmetic of computers.

The second point of view emphasizes the role of human creativity in inventing mathematical structures. Clearly there is an element of human creativity involved, but how much, where to draw the line? Any system of mathematics rests ultimately on a series of axioms, for example, and there is in many instances an element of choice as to which axioms to use. Euclidean geometry was based on five supposedly basic and self-evident axioms about the nature of space, but just how arbitrary such choices can be was shown by the discovery (in physics, not in mathematics) that space is not Euclidean after all but rather Riemannian—that an alternate set of axioms due to Riemann provided a geometry that corresponds more to physical reality than that of Euclid's. Other mathematicians have since invented and explored the properties of still other geometries, all good mathematics, but with an element of choice. Nor is this element of human inventiveness confined to geometry; there exist alternate, "nonstandard" models of the real number system too. Even the laws of logic on which all of mathematical reasoning depends are not universally regarded as absolute. Some mathematicians have argued that there too there is an element of choice and convention. In fact many mathematicians will admit in private that they think they create something, a good example or a good idea. In its most extreme form, this humanist or constructivist outlook rejects the idea of mathematicians as passive discoverers of a remote reality and instead asserts that mathematical phenomena are created by humans alone and do not otherwise exist.

Distinguishing between the two points of view is a little like peeling an onion—there are layers and layers of examples and counterexamples. Calculus as a technique of calculation was invented but the related mathematical phenomena of slopes and areas under a curve correspond to real things. A theorem may be discovered but its proof is usually invented. Group theory may be concerned with the properties of abstract, invented concepts but it also seems to be the language in which some important realities about the universe are revealed to mathematical physicists. The distinction between invented and discovered mathematics verges on being a subjective one, or at least a psychological one. Einstein is reported to have felt that he invented the concept of relativistic spacetime, after the fact, but that he felt he was discovering an aspect of reality while he was doing the work. It is a feeling familiar to many mathematicians: "we are all Platonists in the trenches," as one put it. But the debate continues wherever mathematicians gather. "Do you invent or do you discover?"

spatial ideas. Of course these two sides keep crossing and interacting.

Science or Art?

The notion that mathematics is closely related to physical reality has had many champions. John von Neumann, father to both the theory of games and the modern computer, has written that "mathematics is not an empirical science . . . and yet its development is very closely linked with the natural sciences." It is undeniable, he says, "that some of the best inspirations in mathematics—in those parts of it which are as pure mathematics as one can imagine—have come from the natural sciences." Soviet mathematicians have argued along similar lines. A. D. Alexandrov, for example, says that it is the high level of abstraction peculiar to mathematics that gave birth to notions of its independence from the material world, but that "the vitality of mathematics arises from the fact that its concepts and results, for all their abstractness, originate . . . in the actual world."

Not all mathematicians accept the idea that their creations are intimately dependent on physical reality, of course. Some prefer to think in terms of man-made intellectual structures built upon axioms that are essentially arbitrary—which just happens, in some cases, to have enormous applicability to phenomena in the real world. Others, steeped in modern philosophy, point out that physical reality as mirrored in the intricacies of quantum theory is none too firm a hitching post in any case—let alone mathematical "things made by God." But the real thrust of those whose vision of the nature of mathematics de-emphasizes the importance of the physical connection is not epistemological but rather aesthetic, concerned with criteria internal to mathematics and bound up with the process by which new mathematics is created.

The great French mathematician Henri Poincaré wrote about "the feeling of mathematical beauty, of the harmony of numbers and forms, of geometric elegance. This is a true aesthetic feeling that all real mathematicians know." He went on to describe the creative process in mathematics in terms astoundingly like those now used by psychologists studying the specialization of the two halves of the brain. Poincaré distinguished "two mechanisms or, if you wish, the working methods of the two egos": the one logical, capable of the intensive work upon a problem that usually precedes an intuitive breakthrough and the calculations that follow it, which he identified with the conscious mind and which psychologists now describe as left-brain functions; the other closely linked to an aesthetic sense and capable of recognizing that pattern, among all the possibilities that present themselves, that is both beautiful and important. The recognition of the pattern that solves the problem, Poincaré says, cannot be willed but comes of its own accord in what seems like a sudden flash of intuition from the unconscious mind; psychologists now attribute pattern-recognition to right-brain activity. Much remains to be ascertained about the creative process, but clearly there begins to be a physiological rationale for the insistence of mathematicians that aesthetics, a sense of the beautiful and the elegant, is an important element in mathematical success.

One who has championed the aesthetic aspects of mathematics forcefully is the English number theorist Godfrey Hardy, whose proudest boast was that he had never done anything useful in the sense of practical applications. Hardy described mathematicians as makers of patterns of ideas; he asserted that for them, as for other artists, "beauty and seriousness [are] the criteria by which [their] patterns should be judged." Beauty, he says, "is the first test: there is no permanent place in the world for ugly mathematics." And he summed up his life's work in this way:

"The case for my life, then, or for that of any one else who has been a mathematician in the same sense in which I have been one, is this: that I have added something to knowledge, and helped others to add more; and that these somethings have a value which differs in degree only, and not in kind, from that of the creations of the great mathematicians, or of any of the other artists, great or small, who have left some kind of memorial behind them."

Another who has described and defended mathematics as a creative art is the American algebraist Paul Halmos. "It is, I think, undeniable that a great part of mathematics was born, and lives in respect and admiration, for no other reason than that it is interesting—it is interesting in itself . . . I like the idea of things being done for their own sake," he says. "Is there really something wrong with saying that mathematics is a glorious creation of the human spirit and deserves to live even in the absence of any practical application?" Halmos compares mathematics to music, to literature, and especially to painting:

"The origin of painting is physical reality, and so is the origin of mathematics—but the painter is not a camera and the mathematician is not an engineer . . . In painting and in mathematics there are some objective standards of good—the painter speaks of structure, line, shape, and texture, where the mathematician speaks of truth, validity, novelty, generality—but they are relatively the easiest to satisfy. Both painters and mathematicians debate among themselves whether these objective standards should even be told to the young—the beginner may misunderstand and overemphasize them and at the same time lose sight of the more important subjective standards of goodness." Mathematics, he argues, "is a creative art because mathematicians create beautiful new concepts; it is a creative art because mathematicians live, act, and think like artists; and it is a creative art because mathematicians regard it so."

If mathematics is the most intellectual of the arts, however, it is also strikingly like a science, particularly in its insistence that there is only one version of truth. So useful have the logical structures and ideas of mathematics been as a language for physics, so intimately interwoven has been their evolution, that many scientists have remarked on what physicist Eugene Wigner calls "the unreasonable power of mathematics." Let us rejoin the discussion as it considers this dual character of mathematics.

BERS: Objectively, I certainly feel that mathematics is part of science. There is no doubt.

INQUIRER: Yet some of the words you were using earlier about elegance, and emotional reaction, are not necessarily objective.

BERS: Evolution has made our minds such that what is elegant and beautiful is what is useful and powerful. And the history of science seems to confirm this.

SULLIVAN: I feel mathematics is like this tree that starts from very basic things like space and number, but it has these wonderful branches and flowers that go beyond. I mean, it's too fantastic—the same way that music is too fantastic. It's sort of unbelievable: you start concentrating on one theorem, some really fantastic theorem, and you can't really hold it. It's so amazing.

There is this aspect I mentioned earlier, of lying on a couch thinking, of pure thought which is kind of denser in mathematics than in art. Somehow it is sort of distilled in mathematics: [pure thought] is almost all there is.

BERS: There is also the absolute standard of being right. The requirement of being correct, and also that anyone can check whether you are right, exists only in mathematics. It does not exist in—I almost said in the other arts. This is unique. In mathematics you have complete freedom with a complete lack of arbitrariness.

SULLIVAN: Two physicists can argue about some point, [and they] argue and argue and argue. You can have two mathematicians doing exactly the same thing, and then suddenly one of them will say, "You're right." One of them will completely see the point and it will be right, because these points can be decided. We could sit here and argue about whether there is a counterexample to some theorem or other, but if you change the statement and have an argument, it can be decided.

Beauty and Power

INQUIRER: How does one distinguish good mathematics? What are the criteria?

PUCKETTE: I would go back to [an earlier] description of sudden joy to say what, to a pure mathematician at least, is important and unimportant. [I think] others feel the way I do that a theorem or a result is only as useful as it is beautiful. Or else perhaps sometimes beauty and importance coincide.

BERS: But this begs the question.

SULLIVAN: No it doesn't beg the question to my mind. Because I sort of appreciate [certain difficult and complex theorems]. But I actually like or feel more satisfied by results that are very simple, that may even be trivial to prove, if they explain something or have a lot of applications.

INQUIRER: Can you give an example?

SULLIVAN: Look at two planes. Generally they would intersect in a line, but they might coincide. You consider a plane and a line—the line might cut a plane or lie in the plane. You observe this pattern and there's hardly anything to prove—its obvious. But as you pursue this pattern in the study of spaces and manifolds and so on, it has great universality, [it is] very profound, has many ramifications, yet comes from a simple thing in linear algebra. I like that idea and I like to see all the things that rush out of it. . . . This is a very down to earth, naive apprehension of something, different from writing down a complicated function and observing that it satisfies certain equations and existence theorems. And it almost gives me more joy, is almost more important, a simple thing like this. You watch this mathematician Thom [René Thom, a French geometer] work; he uses ideas like this over and over again until he just overcomes complicated problems. It's very powerful.

BERS: Simplicity. I think you've hit here on a very important point, simplicity. I think mathematicians generally agree that simplicity and beauty are important, and there is no trouble in recognizing them when you see them.

SULLIVAN: I agree with what Bers has said, that what is striking and beautiful in mathematics is pretty universally agreed upon. There are other

words, such as importance, that we could be discussing here.

INQUIRER: Has your taste for what is beautiful changed over your career?

SULLIVAN: Well, I now like things to be simpler, more geometric, to be more explained by examples; I have been slowly sliding over from the idea that one can understand structure to wanting to see lots of examples passing in review.

BERS: Certainly historically the conception of what is beautiful has changed. And in general when an older man said something was not beautiful, he was wrong. Poincaré did not like Lebesgue integrals and space-filling curves, things like that.

SULLIVAN: I don't like them either.

BERS: Well, you're wrong.

SULLIVAN: You know, that only proves that there is a subtle balance between richness and complicatedness. You like a subject to be rich, but not too complicated. On that particular day, Poincaré may have felt that the phenomena in question were simply too complicated. Later it turned out to fall out of the general theory naturally.

PUCKETTE: So it was just the way he [Poincaré] was looking at it that made it seem disconnected.

INQUIRER: Do you find it surprising that mathematics is so useful in the physical sciences?

SULLIVAN: I hate to keep repeating this, but mathematics is built on the concepts of number and space—what could be more useful? I don't find it surprising at all that mathematics is to the point for physical reality.

BERS: The fact is that in the days before calculus and for a long time thereafter much of mathematics was created to facilitate applications in physics. And this may be the reason why before mathematics can become really successful in biology or psychology, mathematics itself will have to be changed. New mathematics will be created. At least it is not inconceivable.

SULLIVAN: It is also true that a lot of people working in biology, even in physics, don't really know that much mathematics.

BERS: But when they say "to know something," it is different than when I say to know something. I remember a lecture here at Columbia on algebraic topology and its applications to physics. T. D. Lee [a Columbia physicist] was in the audience and he said, "I don't believe that algebraic topology will be useful in physics, but if it should turn out that I am wrong, then every theoretical physicist will have to take out two months and learn it." And they would do it. They would learn a few examples and the rules for how to compute. That's all they need.

SULLIVAN: No, what I was saying is that many scientists don't even know mathematics in the sense of taking two months out. There are lots of nice examples around, many theories are explained by one or two nice examples, and if you have the culture of knowing these examples, you might be able to draw on this stuff and use it. I have the feeling that a lot of mathematics can be applied that exists now.

Isolation and Frustration

The nearly universal recognition that mathematics is a powerful scientific tool might be thought very gratifying to mathematicians. In fact, the identification with science is more often a source of frustration, because it is essentially the only thing most people know about their subject. Listen to the anguish with which Halmos says, "It saddens me that educated people don't even know that my subject exists. There is something that they call mathematics, but they neither know how the professionals use that word, nor can they even conceive why anybody should do it."

It is useless to debate whether this gap between mathematicians and the rest of the world is due to some deep-seated fear of mathematics or to the failure of more than a very few mathematicians to make the effort to communicate something of what is going on in their subject to a broader audience. The formidable abstractness of many of the ideas of mathematics and the fussy preciseness that makes many mathematicians insist on using their technical jargon even with nonspecialists certainly add to the problem. It is further complicated by pedagogy: until the university, mathematics is usually taught by people who do not really understand it themselves on more than a very superficial level. Certainly intellectual capability is not really the main barrier to a wider apprehension of at least many mathematical ideas. In experimental programs in which practicing mathematicians have taught very young ghetto children advanced algebra and similar subjects, the rapidity with which the students absorbed concepts far advanced beyond those normally taught at their grade level, the enthusiasm for the subject, and the rapport between students and mathematicians have astounded professional educators. Nonetheless, such efforts and successes in bridging the barrier are the exception, not the rule. Mathematics is one of the few subjects that a student can study through high school and even a few years into college without coming into contact with any results invented since 1800. Those of us who do not major in mathematics or a few areas of physics can pass entirely through the educational system and never encounter any of the revolutionary ideas of twentieth century mathematics. And many mathematicians see nothing wrong with this state of affairs.

The gap extends beyond a general poverty of knowledge of mathematical ideas to a lack of familiarity with even the trappings of mathematical culture. Most educated people have heard of physicists such as Einstein, Heisenberg, and Fermi and have some rough idea of their work; more would make it a point of pride to be familiar with at least the names of the major composers, painters, and writers not only of the past but of the present. Yet how many can name a couple of first-rank mathematicians in this century or identify even a single concept associated with such great geniuses of the past as Gauss, Cauchy, or Riemann?

All this tends to leave mathematicians isolated, dependent only upon themselves and their colleagues for appreciation and recognition. Isolation is not the only stress placed upon would-be practitioners. As a mathematician pointed out in a plea for understanding addressed to a widely read scientific journal, there is also the loneliness of total involvement in a problem over days or weeks to the exclusion of nearly everything else; there is a risk of frustration when such enormous efforts end, as they most often do, in failure; there is the likelihood of a lifetime of insignificance, since nearly all the really major innovations in mathematics are the work of the exceptional genius, not the average contributor; and there is the near certainty of early obsolescence. With such a catalogue of discouragements, it may seem remarkable that anyone would want to become a mathematician. What is the nature of the experience, and what are its rewards?

The Joy of Understanding

BERS: I think the thing which makes mathematics a pleasant occupation are those few minutes when suddenly something falls into place and you understand. Now a great mathematician may have such moments very often. Gauss, as his diaries show, had days when he had two or three important insights in the same day. Ordinary mortals have it very seldom. Some people have it only once or twice in their lifetime. But the quality of this experience—those who have it know it—is really joy comparable to no other joy. The first time you learn something, you also have this joy. So—this has been observed by many people—the work consists in preparing yourself for this moment of understanding, which comes as a result of an unconscious process.

PUCKETTE: Most of my mathematical experience has been rigged, so far. I have been taught but not gone off on any research efforts where the outcome was uncertain. Most of the experience given to me has been moments of joy, simply because it is in fact possible to bring them to me. You stare at a problem on a competition or exam for 30 minutes or so and suddenly the whole thing flies together. The attraction [of mathematics] is that it's great fun.

SULLIVAN: There are always rare moments of understanding that are very nice . . . I remember one experience. I was already a graduate student and I was trying to learn some of Milnor's work [John Milnor, a mathematician at the Institute for Advanced Study in Princeton]. I remember going back and trying to think it through one more time. Suddenly I got the picture that he was actually trying to present in his whole book, a sort of geometrical picture that involved this idea of transversality which I've described before. From that, the whole book just sort of fell away. That was the point from which I reproduced the whole book, even though before it was all in my head as a big complicated thing. The whole thing just fell away and for the first time I realized that I really could understand some nontrivial mathematics. Before that I never really felt the master of something; I could do it forwards and backwards, but this was sort of a geometrical idea that was very strong. It was a very vivid experience.

This is part of the [problem of] lack of confidence about being able to understand mathematics. It's not so easy, mathematics. The idea that it is possible to really understand something very well and in a very simple way was a kind of thought process that I just didn't know. Before everything had been like history; I mean, how do you understand history? You know it, talk about it, go on and on and on; but you can't just suddenly see it coming out of a point. That to me was a big step. And the idea that you can have ideas like this, new ideas, not just understanding other people's ideas—that was really getting somewhere.

BERS: I remember why I decided to study mathematics. When I was in high school, I liked mathematics, but I did very little reading because there were few books about mathematics to read where I lived in Latvia. But I once constructed a one-to-one correspondence between an infinite set and a subset. I thought something must be wrong. I showed it to my geometry teacher who said, "This is the stupidest question I ever heard." [Today such examples are taught in beginning courses in set theory.] So I went away and felt very bad. I also tried to read one book which we had in the library which said the basic concept of mathematics is sets, but didn't explain what they were. I was lost. I applied to an engineering school. Then I saw in a bookstore—I was a little over 17—a small book on set theory by Kamke, and I said "Aha, I will learn what a set is." So I read it and it really hit me, and I felt, this is what I want to study.

The second such experience was when I first discovered something that I considered nontrivial. It was when I was working on gas dynamics, solving partial differential equations. It's too technical to explain; however, I remember how it was—a fantastic feeling, which one is lucky to have five or six times during a lifetime.

PUCKETTE: I suppose the first thing of a mathematical nature that I was really interested in was in kindergarten—no, this is true—where I learned the first 5 or 6 powers of 2. Just by adding 2 and 2 to get 4, 4 and 4 to get 8, and so on. I don't know why I decided to do this.

I got to where I couldn't add very well after a while, but there were always second and third graders who I could ask for the next number. I don't remember what it was about it that fascinated or excited me. I couldn't have added 2 and 3 if you had asked me, so I certainly wasn't hit by any sense of structure (or at least none that I can remember now). But there was something about it that just fascinated me, and continued to do so for several months.

SULLIVAN: Although there is a point about what Professor Bers was saying about the joy of your own great moments of lucidity and discovery, mixed very sparsely amid years of confusion, there's also a more daily relationship with mathematics when you understand what someone else is doing. I think of it as a learning process. Oftentimes you are learning something new, but often

it is something old, so it is not your own discovery. But there's a lot of joy in just daily thinking about mathematics. I mean, it's very rich. It's actually easier than you make it sound.

This is why there is often very little scholarship and sense of the past. A good advisor can sort of plop you down on that square there and you can start thinking about it; and because mathematics is very rich and current, you can *find* things. It's not that hard to do mathematics. I was amazed [to discover that] it's harder to understand mathematics than to do it. Of course it's hard to find something really good.

This is one of the great arguments: You see people around like this Thurston [William Thurston, a Princeton mathematician] who is sort of a geometrical magician and you say, "Well gee, why should I be trying to work on this? If he spends ten minutes on these problems he'll go so much farther than I." But this doesn't disturb one because there is such a vast range of problems that you can start almost anywhere, and there are nice things to see. It's like having a fantastic landscape and countryside [on which] you can go anywhere you like.

It's a pleasant *and* painful process. There's this dull pain all the time you have to think and concentrate and try to understand. But there are more frequent levels of understanding—a sort of superficial understanding when you can just say something empirically, then a little better understanding when you start seeing relationships, then [the best level] when you find a totally new area, which happens very rarely.

For me the attraction of turning to mathematics is . . . that in mathematics it is possible to actually make progress in a train of thought. The levels of understanding are conservative; I mean, every year I feel I change.

PUCKETTE: I would say my attraction to mathematics has been rather manipulated, so far. I've never come yet to the point where I can sit down and actually see a frontier that I can push back a little bit. I unconsciously spend a moment thinking about the Poincaré conjecture, the Fermat conjecture, and so on. I'll probably never even hope to see any of these solved. But it's great fun.

It's not obvious to me now why I'm interested in studying mathematics. But I know that I *am* very interested in studying mathematics.

BERS: Mathematics is growing so rapidly now that it is an effort just to understand some things that have come along. At some point one has to reconcile oneself that one will never understand too many things. There are very few mathematicians that have a real overview of all of mathematics. And at some point one has to understand that one will die without knowing many things one would like to know. I envy the people who are getting their education now because they will learn much more than I did.

Most of us have to accustom ourselves to the fact that there is only a certain level that we can reach. There always will be people, and one can name them, who will be definitely better than you, or go faster. It is somehow like a big cathedral, mathematics. You don't expect that you will do the overall design. But you can still be a good worker.

SULLIVAN: One of the things I like about mathematics is that you should be able to enjoy a discovery that has just been made as much as if you made it yourself.

BERS: And also the enjoyment of others. Most professional mathematicians spend a large part of their time teaching. Teaching calculus, for example, I find a very enjoyable occupation, because I get to communicate very great ideas. And mathematicians are like a small village: they gossip shamelessly; they know each other. There are too many nowadays really, but they are still a small village, partly because they are all alone. A chemist works with plastics or an electrical engineer with transistors; people have some feel for what these are, but what does a mathematician do? Nobody understands. So there is a certain amount of loneliness. The advantage is that you are doing something that in a way is very real and imperishable. And impersonal. And—I don't claim that mathematicians are more honest than other people—but in your work you have to be honest, because if you fool yourself you are lost. And this means something.

Some of the mathematical writings of Archimedes are written in the form of letters. Obviously there was communication with other mathematicians from the very beginning. At first often letters. And now, especially in a center like where we are, one can communicate with many people. Social intercourse was always necessary for mathematics. After all, the idea of a proof must have developed from the idea of discourse. To prove something was to convince somebody.

This [discourse] is one of the secondary attractions of mathematics. Of course when you study the works of a great old man, you really are in a sense in a very intimate intellectual intercourse. Secondly, on a more mundane level, you have friends all over the world. I mean, we know people, and some of them quite closely at least on the intellectual level, in Japan, in Red China, in Russia, and all over the world. When you meet them, you are able to talk about mathematics very easily, to communicate across these boundaries, and also across the age barriers. In what other profession can you see a 20-year-old kid lecturing at the blackboard and old venerable people sitting there and taking notes. This is a wonderful thing.

SULLIVAN: There are only risks and hazards if you think that the objective is to make great discoveries in your own name. If you just want to wander out in mathematics and manipulate it, eat it, feel it, try to understand it, communicate it and so on, there's a tremendous amount to do that is enjoyable. Painful too, because it's frustrating when you don't understand things. But there is a lot to do that is enjoyable. This process can go on as long as you can stay awake.

Pattern and Form

However natural eating and breathing mathematics may be for a practitioner, it is not part of the normal diet of most of us. But we nonetheless live in a world in which mathematical concepts and generalizations based on them increasingly determine our outlook. Plato, in a lecture that puzzled his contemporaries in ancient Greece, expressed a vision of a universe organized on mathematical principles which is identified as the Good. A modern interpretation of that idea, according to the functional analyst Felix Browder, might begin with a vision of mathematics as "the science of significant form . . . the ultimate and transparent form of all human knowledge." He argues that the eighteenth century vision of a rational, mechanistic universe was influenced in no little way by the Newtonian synthesis of mathematics and a Copernican cosmos. Who would argue that the Einsteinian synthesis expressed in the theory of general relativity has not altered the prevailing world view in our own century?

A similar point of view was expressed by the mathematician turned philosopher Alfred North Whitehead: "The notion of the importance of pattern is as old as civilization. Every art is founded on the study of pattern. The cohesion of social systems depends on the maintenance of patterns of behavior, and advances in civilization depend on the fortunate modification of such behavior patterns. Thus the infusion of patterns into natural occurrences and the stability of such patterns, and the modification of such patterns is the necessary condition for the realization of the Good. Mathematics is the most powerful technique for the understanding of pattern, and for the analysis of the relation of patterns.

"Here, we reach the fundamental justification for the topic of Plato's lecture. Having regard to the immensity of its subject matter, mathematics, even modern mathematics, is a science in its babyhood. If civilization continues to advance, in the next two thousand years the overwhelming novelty in human thought will be the dominance of mathematical understanding."

Let us explore the idea of mathematics as culture and as a formative influence on culture further in the thoughts of our captive mathematicians.

SULLIVAN: There is a famous remark about the texture of mathematics that the things we work on today could be explained very simply to Euclid or somebody like that. There is a great permanence of ideas; really great ideas are somehow very permanent. This is a kind of impact that doesn't really affect how we get our bread every day, but human knowledge is a big piece of culture, and good ideas just increase. There's not

much in existence that's really so good it will, like mathematics, last thousands of years.

BERS: It can suddenly become exceedingly important to humanity the moment we make contact with an extraterrestrial intelligence, if there is any. Mathematics is the only common language we will have. If we get a signal from somewhere, 2, 3, 5, 7, 11, 13 . . . [the sequence of prime numbers], then we will know, "This is it." We cannot conceive of an intelligence with a different kind of mathematics. This one thing would be unmistakable.

There is also a certain indirect influence between general ideas of mathematics and the way people think about other problems. I used to illustrate this with an analogy between Euclid's mathematics and the Declaration of Independence, which of course was written consciously as a mathematical proof, and the Lobachevsky or Hilbert point of view represented in the Gettysburg address; there is a self-evident axiom in the Declaration of Independence ("All men are created equal") and there is in the Gettysburg address a proposition to be tested by consistency proof.

SULLIVAN: So what you're saying is like what I was trying to say, that there is some increase or change in human thought, and the achievements of mathematics are a part of that. You don't have to postulate a hypothetical communication with outer space to get at the idea of an absolute, proven thought achievement.

BERS: Other great achievements, like music and painting, are easily enjoyed by a large number of people. We can hope that as education and leisure develop more people will enjoy them. But the number of people who really enjoy mathematics is very small. Thus far our attempts to communicate the beauty of our art to a wide audience have failed miserably.

SULLIVAN: We could have on television a curve tracing back and forth and sort of converging to a space-filling curve [see figure on p. 59]. Just in 5 or 10 seconds you could give everybody who saw it an intense feeling of geometrical joy, but without understanding the definitions or anything. And it would do this, I'm sure. I've seen an audience watch such a curve form. It's fantastic! There's a pattern happening there, an infinite process, and suddenly the whole screen is filled with a curve. It's an artistic thing.

INQUIRER: You're saying that there's something in the recognition of that pattern, something inherent in the way we look at space such that everybody has reactions to it whether one knows mathematics or not.

SULLIVAN: Sure. With a computer and television now you can do all kinds of things. It would be a dynamic piece of art.

A Space-filling Curve

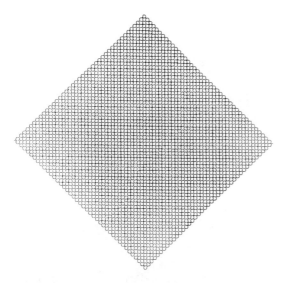

There are many varieties of space-filling curves that will trace over every point within a given area, gradually blackening the space. The partially-traced example given here is known as a Peano curve.

I think that mathematics could be part of the flowering of the human spirit in some fundamental way. I mean the fact that children can be very amused, like with what Puckette was doing with 2s, making little squares, doing various patterns. These are the same kind of things a mathematician enjoys, except often they are clothed in highly technical language.

There are all kinds of games which illustrate logic and deduction, and mystery stories are enjoyed by many people, so there's not anything special about mathematics that can't be enjoyed by the common man. It's part of everyone's brains. Actually I don't particularly feel that it's important that mathematics be enjoyed by a lot of people; that would be very nice, but it's more important that mathematicians work on good problems and pursue mathematics.

Clearly mathematicians take their subject seriously and believe it an important part of the human enterprise. This is underscored by a light-hearted exchange that occurred in the discussion when at one point Sullivan observed that mathematics is, for many mathematicians, a substitute passion or religion. To which Bers replied, "I didn't know it was a substitute." It is of course possible that mathematicians deceive themselves about their role in the scheme of things. But it is also possible that, in our ignorance of their world, we miss a fundamental and increasingly important aspect of our own.

References

A. D. Alexandrov, et. al., *Mathematics—Its Content, Methods, and Meanings*, Vol. 1, MIT Press, Cambridge, 1963.

Felix E. Browder, Is mathematics relevant? And if so, to what?, *University of Chicago Magazine*, 67:3 (Spring, 1975) pp. 11–16.

Paul R. Halmos, Mathematics as a creative art, *American Scientist*, 56 (April, 1968) pp. 375–389.

G. H. Hardy, *A Mathematician's Apology*, Cambridge University Press, New York, 1969.

John von Neumann, The mathematician, in R. B. Heywood, *The Works of the Mind*, University of Chicago Press, Chicago, 1947, pp. 180–196.

Henri Poincaré, Mathematical creation, *Scientific American*, 179 (August, 1948) pp. 54–57.

Alfred North Whitehead, Mathematics as an element in the history of thought, in J. R. Newman, *The World of Mathematics*, Vol. 1, Simon and Schuster, New York, 1956, pp. 402–416.

On the Present Incompleteness
of Mathematical Ecology

L. B. Slobodkin

Lawrence Basil Slobodkin received his doctorate in zoology in 1951 from Yale. He has been chief investigator for the U.S. Fish and Wildlife Service, a fisheries research biologist, a visiting investigator for Bingham Oceanographic Labs, and a professor of biology at S.U.N.Y., Stonybrook, since 1968. He has been a Guggenheim fellow and received the Russell award in 1961.

Newton, it can be argued, developed the calculus because he wished to explain the mechanical nature of the physical universe. Yet most of the major ideas of the calculus had been developed before Newton's time and often in contexts that had nothing to do with the motion of bodies. Was Newton just lucky? Did he simply force his physical observations to fit the available mathematics? Why should a methodology for computing the area of circles, first developed by Archimedes nearly 2,000 years before Newton, be so readily applied to the apparently unrelated problem of the motion of planets? Was humanity just lucky? Slobodkin suggests, at least by implication, that luck *may just be the appropriate word.*

Although this article was first published in 1965, the major threads of its arguments are as valid today as then. Slobodkin suggests that a mathematics appropriate to the description of phenomena in physics is simply not necessarily appropriate in biology. Further, he suggests that attempts to forcefully express a general theory of biological phenomena in terms of mathematics appropriate to phenomena in physics do grave damage to the "empirical truths" of biology. Newton was fortunate indeed to have lying around a set of mathematical ideas that could with relative ease be molded into the almost perfect vehicle for describing precisely those events of his interest. The biologists of the twentieth century have not been so lucky.

ALMOST ALL FIELDS of science are growing. The number of journals published per unit time; the number of Ph.D.'s and engineers produced; the dollars spent; facts learned; institutes; seminars; interdisciplinary, international, coordinated, crash, and other programs are all increasing at a dizzying rate. Publishers, symposium organizers, committee chairmen, editors, deans, and deanlets all compete for time with students and research.

To be a scientist in 1965 is a delightfully hectic and exciting business. Scientists are presumed to have certain intellectual abilities and standards which make them of value in supporting political, social, and religious movements and institutions so that each scientist must carefully budget his time, clarify his own opinions and, at all costs, maintain an honest intellectual perspective on the relative merit and state of programs and ideas, particularly in his own research area.

However, not all of the areas of science are growing at the same rate. The most rapidly growing areas are those in which there is essential una-

Source: L. B. Slobodkin, "On the Present Incompleteness of Mathematical Ecology," *American Scientist* 53 (1965): 347–357. Reprinted by permission of American Scientist. (References omitted.)

nimity on which problems are considered important and which techniques are appropriate to their solution. The more slowly growing areas are more difficult to characterize.

In my own area, ecology, there is an intermediate growth rate, despite a general sense of the practical urgency of certain ecological problems.

Every year, new ecological programs are starting at various points around the world. In calorimetry, the first work was done less than six years ago but the number of laboratories engaged has gone from one to more than ten in that time. Six years ago, life table data for animals were almost absent, but Alex Comfort, in revising his book on senescence in 1964, had simply to drop the project of summarizing the existing literature. New journals and review series are appearing on all the continents. The demand for teachers far outruns our supply.

However, while the field grows in a satisfactory fashion, the growth does not have the monolithic, Gargantuan aspect that characterizes the burgeoning of, say, cell biology. The number of good quantitative ecologists is in the thirties or forties for the entire world, rather than the thousands of biochemists and geneticists.

This relatively slow growth, combined with the lack of emergence of any one central problem which acts as a bandwagon for all of the field, implies that quantitative ecology is an unfinished or incomplete field in some different sense from genetics or nuclear physics. While all the ramifications of genetics and nuclear physics are not yet known, there is general consensus on the present broad theoretical format of these fields. While new facts are yet to be found and present theories may be overthrown, it is at least clear which ideas are most significant to test. Ecology, on the other hand, does not yet have any central theoretical formulation. I will try to explain, in part, the relatively slow and diffuse growth pattern of ecology and will then discuss some of the problems raised by sciences that share the incomplete character of ecology. I will then contend that there exist sciences whose present significance lies in the formulation of new thought patterns rather than in the prediction of events in terms of the more traditional mathematical and logical systems.

Initially, ecological theory had the avowed intent of quantifying natural history, but this is itself an ambiguous concept. To count all the animals on earth and then publish that number is a trivial kind of activity. It is, however, far from trivial to develop a theory which permits prediction of the total number of animals from a reasonably small group of measurements—in fact, it would be an intellectual triumph of major proportions.

The attempt to develop a quantitative theory of ecology, starting with the pioneer studies of Lotka, Voltera, D'Ancona, Kostitsyn, and others, was probably motivated by the conviction that underlying the endless special case descriptions of the interactions between organisms and their environments lay a relatively simple mathematical theory. Repeatedly, the analogy with one or another branch of physics appeared in their writing and still appears in current papers. Some of the questions that are asked also have about them an air of physics-like generality.

What is the pattern of population growth?

Is there a constant ecological efficiency? . . . or more naively

What determines the numbers of animals? . . . and so on.

These are eminently fair questions, but in the experimental and field analyses several things became apparent. For example, the simple models of population growth, beloved of the mathematician and ideally amenable to grandiose theory formation, simply do not hold. The lovely sigmoid pattern found in certain protozoa and bacteria does not generally happen in metazoans, and if it does happen, it happens for the wrong reasons. That is, an elegantly simple mathematical expression for sigmoid growth is

$$\frac{dN}{dT} = aN - bN^2$$

For bacteria, a and b have operationally clear meanings of a simple kind and N is an enumeration. For metazoans a similar shape may, under certain circumstances, arise, but the equation nevertheless doesn't apply since, among other things, N has no operational meaning—an old animal is not equivalent to a young one nor is a large one equivalent to a small one, etc. It is still possible to develop mathematical theories of population growth but they begin to take on the aspect of *coffer hypotheses*—long series of special constants and elaborations are introduced to make the mathematical theory fit some particular example or case—and on occasion, this, in itself, can become a fascinating exercise in the solution of practical problems, the use of computers, or in the development of applied mathematics. However, while special cases can be successfully analyzed, generalizations derived from them have not been remarkably productive.

One attempted solution, in the face of this difficulty, is to abandon all effort at maintaining the correspondence between mathematical theory and field observation and to develop rather elegant mathematical formulations which provide insight rather than prediction. Typically this type of analysis is designed to make an apparently paradoxical set of events intuitively acceptable. For example, numerous cases are known in which reproductive potential seems to have decreased during the course of evolution, in apparent contradiction to certain general evolutionary theorems. Various, plausible sounding, abstract systems have been constructed to demonstrate how this might have occurred. The difficulty here is in deciding how these hypothetical systems relate either to more conventional systems with predictive value or to any specific natural situation.

This is not equivalent to saying that only field observation can be used to explain field phenomena—in fact, it is almost certain at the moment that field observation by itself, in the absence of laboratory and theoretical study, is almost useless in providing explanations. The way in which the various kinds of study fit together is that theoretical and laboratory analyses can provide limits for the possible functions of various processes in the field—thereby permitting, and, in fact, making possible, decisions between various alternative hypotheses with respect to field data.

For example, populations of hydra in any particular area of a small lake tend to fluctuate rapidly. Laboratory populations of the same animal do not seem capable of increasing at the rate observed in the field, implying that the animals which appear at any point in the lake have in part

originated elsewhere. Simultaneous collections from various parts of the lake show that sudden increases in one place are fairly well correlated with disappearances elsewhere, as if the hydra migrated, but the observed rate of movement of hydra in the lake is inadequate to account for the migrations. Under deleterious conditions in the laboratory, hydra will secrete a gas bubble at the pedal disc, and float from the substrate, sinking when the bubble is either burst or lost. This of course provides an ideal mechanism for animals to leave one place in a lake and rapidly accumulate somewhere else. Crowding, as such, triggers bubble formation. In this case, the laboratory study and the field study lean on each other. Both of these grew out of a laboratory study on population dynamics in hydra which was undertaken to determine the efficiency with which hydra can transform food into flesh that can be consumed by a predator, and more particularly to see if this efficiency is the same as that of Daphnia. (Incidentally it is, and this also poses a problem in its own right.) The Daphnia experiments in turn grew out of an attempt to see if the mathematically elegant logistic equation really applies to metazoans (which it does not).

The sequence of studies indicated above is typical of many of the various studies that have been made in quantitative ecology. We start with a high standard of mathematical elegance which generates plausible sounding statements. At some point, these statements are experimentally or observationally tested. Typically, they are refuted in a limited sense (as for example, while Daphnia populations do not grow according to the logistic equation, I can concisely describe how they do grow by saying "It is like the logistic equation, if the logistic equation would take cognizance of time lags and differences in both needs and contributions of different kinds of animals"), but the empirical studies themselves are sufficiently fascinating to generate their own hypotheses and further empirical work. Finally, we find that we are talking about some very specific mechanism, like the bubble formation of hydra, which essentially brings us to another ecological generality. That is, on the basis of laboratory studies with Daphnia, fungus flies, mice, and other organisms, it is fair to say that every population has some mechanism of escaping from its environment as that environment begins to become crowded. The physiological basis of the escape mechanism varies from species to species but its ecological role seems constant. We could predict therefore that hydra would have some escape mechanism but we could not have predicted that it would involve making a bubble.

In short, we are talking about a research area that generates its own problems and generalizations and, in that sense, is a delightful thing to work with; but notice how we have departed from the original dream of a physics-like theory with high mathematical elegance. The critical incompleteness of quantitative ecology lies in its mathematical aspect, which is extremely odd since most of the subareas of ecology start from a mathematical formulation as clear as that of any physical problem. Despite the long time, the competent minds, and the plethora of data, progress in the mathematics of mathematical ecology has not been as satisfactory as one might have hoped in, say, 1945. I suspect that the explanation for this lies partly in the illegitimacy of the analogy with physics.

The world of the physicist, even with the current rash of new particles and particle-like objects, consists of not more than one hundred different entities, each one of which is characterizable by a set of state measurements of not more than 20 or 30 variables. While the possible modes of interaction of this many components may well overtax even a large computer, it is nevertheless the case that a mathematical model is in one sense feasible, even if it may not be a numerical model.

The relation between physical phenomena and the mathematics of physical theory involves the generation by experimental observational data of a kind of mathematics, or of logic, such that a one-to-one correspondence can be established between the admissible statements of the mathematics and conceivable observations in nature.

The complexity and richness of this type of theory is intimately related to the relation between the number of predictions that arise, the number of manipulative operations permitted, and the number of assumptions and definitions that were required to construct the theory. In general, "better" theories are those in which a small planting of assumptions and definitions and rules yields a rich harvest of testable consequences (as Mark Twain almost said). A theoretical advance consists in demonstrating that one or more of the rules or definitions that had been used to predict a given class of phenomena are in some sense redundant. Occasionally, a theoretician is willing to abandon the attempt to predict a class of phenomena, restriciting himself to a subclass, if, in return for this restriction, he can discard a fairly large share of his rules and assumptions.

A "bad" theory, in the eyes of a physicist, on the other hand, has a relatively very large number of rules and assumptions for the amount of predictive power. This criterion of the quality of a theory is essentially an aesthetic one—which has been adopted by mathematicians as almost their sole criterion of quality. Ecologists who collaborate with mathematicians are familiar with the frustrating event of having the mathematicians produce elegant looking theories for slightly simpler problems than the ecologists had in mind.

There do exist respectable sciences that have essentially no theory at all in the physicists' sense. Mineralogy and, to an even greater extent, taxonomy are primarily concerned with framing assumptions—for in essence a definition is an assumption, and the naming of a species is a definition. Nevertheless, the distinction is made between good taxonomy and bad taxonomy and perhaps more significantly between good taxonomists and bad taxonomists. That is, the normal criteria of scientific quality, which we use as biologists, are not the same as those of the physicist and mathematician.

Perhaps the key to understanding the incompleteness of the more mathematical aspects of quantitative ecology is to assume that the differences in the criteria of quality that do, in fact, exist between mathematics and physics on one hand and biology on the other are not merely a matter of the comparative tastes and personalities of biologists as opposed to those of physicists but are in some intrinsic. (Note the diminishing self-confidence of the biophysical converts to biology.) It is almost as if a theory can only contain a certain amount of complexity. If it is composed of simple elements it can generate complex theorems and if it is composed of intrinsically complex elements it can only generate relatively simple theorems, in the sense of being very closely related to the definitions and assumptions.

Is there any reason why biological systems might choose to be of the second sort rather than the first sort—why—specifically, they might "choose" to use complex special mechanisms to solve certain problems? This is a rather peculiar problem and must be examined carefully.

The physical world involves a small number of particles and their very rich family of interactions, and this fact is the key to the relative success of the physicists' standard of elegance as actually applied. The biological world incorporates these particles and their interactions in large packages and each package seems to have a relatively small number of rather specific things that it can do, which differ to a large degree from those that any other species can do.

Not all of the responses of a biological system are specific—that is, to certain classes of general environmental changes, populations respond by altering the rates of rather generalized processes, reproduce faster, change their life expectancy distributions or feeding rate, etc. It is with this class of phenomena that quantitative ecology, in its narrow sense of a quasi-physical theory, has its greatest success. For example, Hairston and his co-workers have been able to demonstrate that rather slight environmental changes, producing relatively slight changes in the life expectancy of an intermediate host, can effectively produce a major reduction in schistosome populations, while direct killing of the intermediate host would not work in the absence of habitat alteration. This kind of result only arises from the theory of quantitative ecology and has in fact already shown itself of major practical and intellectual significance.

But, as the theory is developed for any population, a point is reached at which the organism plays what might best be described as a trick—pulls out a new tool of a very specific kind which has some very specific function relevant to the environment of that particular species. For example, it has recently been shown that a species of rotifer, *Brachionus calyciflorus,* when in the presence of predatory rotifers, either *A. splanchna sieboldi, A. girodi, A. brightwelli,* or *A. predenta,* as a response to a specific chemical secreted by the predator, develops enlarged spines which make them inedible! No respectable mathematical theory can be expected to forecast anything like that nor should it be expected to. It is, however, a legitimate question of ecological theory to ask: When will an organism or species evolve a trick and when will it not?

In fact a partial response to this question can be formulated in terms of an evolutionary argument, too long to recapitulate here. The problem of the development of specific mechanisms to face specific problems seems to depend on the clarity with which the organism can recognize the problem, the degree to which the problem would alter biological rates if the specific mechanism were not available, and the frequency with which the problem arises—analogous to a degree to the problem of when is it worthwhile to own five or six screwdrivers, each with a specific function, rather then one with fair competence to handle a spectrum of jobs.

The incompleteness of ecology seems to be based on empirical facts, and must be explained in empirical terms. A possible general explanation is suggested by Von Neumann's discussion of the relation between brain-like digital computers and actual brains. He pointed out that the number of digits carried in a number in many kinds of digital computers is well in excess of the number of significant figures in most empirical measurements. This is necessary since most computer programs involve a sequential series of steps which quickly accumulate rounding errors. He then considered the neuron as a possible element of a computer-like system and concluded that the precision of neuronal response is so low that, if neuronal systems functioned in the same fashion as these computer elements, the precision of the final response would be excessively low. He concluded that there exists some other type of theory which would properly describe events in a brain and that this type of theory is lacking in arithmetical and logical "depth." That is, it is lacking in long chains of operations or arguments. The degree to which this concept can be related to ecological events is not completely self-evident. It seems clear, however, that the response of organisms to environmental change is of the same order of precision as that of individual neurons, certainly not higher. It is also clear that accumulation of variance with time in any property of a population generally does not occur and would be disastrous if it did occur.

I have suggested elsewhere the possibility that the process of evolutionary adaptation consists of a hierarchical system of relatively simple feedback units in which many elements in the system are assumed to have essentially direct access to the environment, thereby minimizing the length of sequential processes. This scheme may in fact be incorrect but it does demonstrate the possibility of making formulations explicitly for biological problems, without attempting to force the biology into a pre-existing mathematical mold.

This does not deny that, on occasion, insight derived from mathematics may prove extremely useful, nor does it deny the likelihood that biological insights may provide raw material for new developments in mathematics. I am strongly convinced, however, that, to insist on the theory of biology conforming to aesthetic standards derived from extant mathematics is illegitimate and is, in fact, an imposition of metaphysical criteria on the empirical world. Empirical sciences must develop their own standards of quality and cannot take refuge from the necessity of thought in the shadow of Newton or Euclid.

The above statement, whose partial validity cannot be seriously questioned, has certain very important implications. Specifically, it implies that scientific research quality can not legitimately be evaluated by its degree of conformity to any preconception of its mathematical form.

I can now return to the initial question: Why do certain areas of research tend to develop more rapidly than others? Several components enter into the growth rate of a science, each to an uncertain degree. One of the most obvious and legitimate is the need of various social agencies for certain clearly visualizable information which can only be produced as the result of scientific research.

Several enlightened governments, during and since the Second World War, have apparently come to the conclusion that the specific demands that a government may want to make of its scientific establishment cannot generally be foreseen in detail. It can be predicted that, from time to time, questions will arise which will require specific scientific answers. It is therefore generally valuable to treat the scientific establishment as a resource or machine which must be kept in functional order. This seems to be most effectively done by supporting a certain amount of research which is, frankly, not related to immediate goals, but might be of consequence in the future. Either the questions asked may later prove important or the kind of intellectual and physical activity involved in the research might be applicable to other research projects which, in turn, might have practical significance.

This kind of support, like all government support, requires decisions as to the appropriate recipients of funds. As indicated above, decisions based on utility as opposed to lack of utility are straighforward. Within the class of low immediate utility projects the decision process changes its character and becomes more difficult. The goal of the supporting agencies and their referees is the laudable one of supporting "good" as opposed to "bad" science, "important" as opposed to "unimportant" science.

The idea of good science tends to become confounded with either the capacity of the field in question to generate an elegant theory in the sense that Newtonian physics or Mendelian genetics generates an elegant theory or the hope that it will do so in the near future, in the sense that modern nuclear physics may generate an elegant theory in the near future. It seems likely, however, that the concept of elegance, narrowly defined, is irrelevant to certain areas of the empirical world. Obsession with elegance will tend to concentrate effort on only limited portions of reality. There are indications that this is now happening.

A disenchanted friend of mine described modern experimental physics as "a dance performed around a bubble chamber" and, to an equal degree, biology threatens to become a study in DNA engineering. Various individuals, schools, and agencies have been issuing proclamations defining the "important problems" of biology and the more fundamentalistic of these have actually eliminated those fields they consider unimportant from various departments, curricula, and even universities.

The differences in relative growth of scientific areas are, therefore, seen to have several components. Some of these components are completely legitimate results of social needs, or at least of what are assumed to be social needs. Others are a legitimate consequence of particular advances being to some extent self-accelerating. I have been calling attention here to a less legitimate process of differential growth in which preconceptions of the form scientific theory ought to take, by persons in authority, act to alter the growth pattern of different areas. This is a new problem which is probably not yet ineradicable; but it is a frightening and terribly twentieth century trend, perhaps ultimately even more dangerous than the strange meanings that have been recently given to words like freedom and peace.

The greatest intellectual contribution made by science to mankind is the idea that human senses, suitably extended by various stratagems and devices, are capable of providing valid information about the world. Furthermore, this information requires the construction of appropriate theoretical frameworks before predictions and insights can be gained. The theoretical framework cannot be imposed *a priori*. To say that all of biology should have an elegant mathematical framework is as much of an imposition of metaphysics on observation as it was to say that the only suitable astronomic theories must involve cycles and epicycles, or that genetic data must conform to the principles of Marxian dialectics.

Traditionally, science consisted of an "account of the present undertakings, studies and labours of the ingenious in many considerable parts of the world." This passage was published on the title page of each volume of the *Philosophical Transactions of the Royal Society of London* until 1775. It was then eliminated, as if, by then, science needed no definition. Perhaps it is significant that shortly before the Royal Society found it no longer necessary to define science it did seem vital to protect the public from persons who would use science for self-aggrandizement. Starting in 1761, an "Advertisement" was printed in each volume of the *Transactions*, in effect warning the public against considering publication of an idea in a scientific journal as providing the imprimatur of the scientific establishment for the validity of the idea. This Advertisement appeared for the last time in 1936.

Long before 1936, science had become a reasonably lucrative profession. To pretend that science is a kind of genteel intellectual game had not been possible for many years. Perhaps this is why the Advertisement was dropped from the *Transactions*, but I do not actually know.

The fact that science has become an adjunct of national policy does not, in itself, necessarily eliminate the possibility of new and radical concepts arising from science. This possibility will be eliminated, however, as soon as the central authorities of scientific administration no longer feel embarrassed in closing whole areas of research as "unimportant."

Any system of intellectual constructs which is espoused by the agents of secular power seems to generate its own metaphysical orthodoxy. Science fought its way free of government-sponsored religion only to threaten now to become the new established church.

I hope that I have demonstrated, at least in part, that the world is so made that elegant systems (in one traditional sense) are in principle unable to deal with some of its more fascinating and delightful aspects. New forms of thought as well as new subjects for thought must arise in the future as they have in the past, giving rise to new standards of elegance. To say that a region of the world is but poorly described by existing kinds of theory is an affirmation of the possibility of intellectual advance, not a denial.

As for the future of ecology? I can only deny the usefulness of all shibboleths. Our future lies in full utilization of our intellect. Just as astronomers will not accept a map of the cosmos which places the sun at either the center or the edge, we must act as if we are neither at the beginning nor the end of our scientific progress. All of this may have been obvious in the seventeenth century but, in the twentieth, it may be worth restating.

Preface to *The Common Sense of the Exact Sciences*

Bertrand Russell

Bertrand Russell's life has been summarized in the introduction to the article.

Bertrand Russell needs no introduction. With that formality aside, we may now proceed to introduce this remarkable figure and this delightful essay. Born in 1872, Russell was the second son of the then viscount Amberly; his grandfather was an earl, the third son of the Duke of Bedford. Bertrand was a link in a chain of socially and politically influential Russells stretching back to the time of the Tudors. His parents died when he was still rather young and his early education, at the hands of tutors, took place under the direction of his grandfather. Russell entered Cambridge University in 1890, won a first in the Trypos, and was elected to the Apostles, an informal but highly selective society formed of the intellectual luminaries of the university. His election brought him into contact with A. N. Whitehead, T. M. Keynes, Lytton Strachly, and a number of others who were or would become prominent in the intellectual life of the early twentieth century.

From 1895 to 1910, Russell continued his association with Cambridge through fellowships, and in 1910 he was appointed to a special lectureship in logic and the philosophy of mathematics. While his earliest mathematical interests were in geometry he soon found himself drawn to the logical foundations of mathematics, and it was in this area that he was to make his most significant contributions.

It was Russell's belief that all of mathematics could be derived by the operation of formal logic on a relatively few fundamental assumptions. To realize this end, he began a formal work that through a number of revisions and forms, and in collaboration with A. N. Whitehead, became the Principia Mathematica. *This work is the most successful attempt ever to derive all mathematics from a single set of general principles.*

In the process of developing the ideas that became the Principia *Russell discovered a number of formal paradoxes that derive from the theory of sets. The most famous of these bears his name, Russell's Paradox.*

Briefly, Russell's Paradox observes that most collections (sets) are not members of themselves. For example, the set of all presidents of the United States is not a president, it is a group of presidents. However, some collections are indeed members of themselves. For example, the set of all sets that have more than three elements has more than three elements and hence is an element of itself. The difficulty arises when one considers the collection of all sets that are not elements of themselves. Call this collection S. Now one may ask, "Is S one of the things in S?" If the answer is no, then S is not in S and thus S is one of those collections not inside itself. This means that S meets the criterion for being a member of S. Briefly, if S is not in S, then S is in S, an obvious contradiction. The same difficulty is encountered if one begins by assuming that S is one of the elements in S.

Having found the paradox, Russell immediately began discussing ways to avoid or circumvent it, among these his theory of types. However, none of these devices have proven completely satisfactory and Russell's Paradox haunts the world of mathematics to this day.

Source: Bertrand Russell, Preface to *The Common Sense of the Exact Sciences*, by W. K. Clifford (Alfred A. Knopf, 1946), pp. *v–x*.

In 1916 legal action was taken by England against Russell with charges related to his speaking and writing against the war then daily slaughtering thousands in the trenches of Europe. Russell's pacifism caused him to be removed from his position at Cambridge University and ultimately led to a brief imprisonment. He maintained his vigorous, indeed impassioned, advocacy of world disarmament and universal political freedom until the end of his long and amazingly productive life.

By 1925 Russell had largely abandoned his formal investigations in mathematics. There are a number of plausible reasons for this divergence, but his subsequent writings do suggest that he was somewhat disenchanted with a discipline that he had in his youth viewed as the perfect and unassailable refuge of the rational mind. His own investigations had demonstrated that all known methodologies for formulating modern mathematics are in some sense imperfect. They all require some tolerance for ambiguity and irresolvable paradox. For Russell, who believed passionately that rational thought and behavior must be made the basis of all human endeavor, it must have been profoundly discouraging to discover that paradox lies at the foundation of that most rational of all human activities, mathematics. He died in 1970 at the age of 98.

This essay is a preface, written in 1945, for a republication of The Common Sense of the Exact Sciences *by W. K. Clifford. It suggests the impression this book made on a much younger Russell when he first read it. By implication this brief essay suggests a great deal about Russell the man and his view of the nature and development of mathematics.*

THE COPY OF this book which I still possess was given to me by my tutor when I was fifteen years of age. I read it at once, with passionate interest and with an intoxicating delight in intellectual clarification. From that day until I came to write this Preface, I had not looked at the book. Now, having re-read it after fifty-seven years, many of them devoted to the subjects of which it treats, I find that it deserved all the adolescent enthusiasm that I bestowed upon it when I first read it.

Clifford possessed an art of clarity such as belongs only to a very few great men—not the pseudo-clarity of the popularizer, which is achieved by ignoring or glossing over the difficult points, but the clarity that comes of profound and orderly understanding, by virtue of which principles become luminous and deductions look easy. When I first became acquainted with Clifford, it was only three years since I had been struggling with Euclid's theory of proportion—a subject that is now considered too difficult for schoolboys, but which in those days had to be mastered by every budding mathematician. As Euclid treats it, it is

a puzzling subject, not only because it is inherently complicated, but because Euclid never mentions his perfectly adequate reasons for not adopting the much simpler arithmetical procedure, of which the fallacies are not obvious until they are pointed out. Clifford, by telling just what is necessary and no more, makes the whole theory as clear as noonday. In this and in other matters the book is invaluable to the schoolboy who, though interested by mathematics, is bewildered, as any intelligent boy must be if he is badly taught.

The later parts of the book, as explained in the original Preface, owe much to Karl Pearson, since Clifford's early death left the manuscript incomplete. Karl Pearson, however, had so fully assimilated Clifford's way of looking at mathematics that he was able to carry out his task without producing in the reader any awareness of discontinuity. The book can therefore be treated as a whole, and there is no need to struggle to separate the editor's work from the author's.

The subject of which the book treats—the basis of pure mathematics in logic and of applied mathematics in observation—is one in which immense progress has been made since the time when Clifford wrote, but knowledge of subsequent work only increases the reader's admiration for his prophetic insight. All that is said on the relation of geometry to physics is entirely in harmony with Einstein's theory of gravitation, which was published thirty-six years after Clifford's death. The Book's explicit rejection of "matter" and "force" as concepts to be used in physics is due to Karl Pearson, but has some sanction in Clifford's notes and is clearly in line with his thinking. In this respect, as in many others, Clifford was ahead of almost all the best thinking of his time.

Non-Euclidean geometry, in which two straight lines may enclose a space, or a triangle may have all its angles zero, was a subject which, though inaugurated by Lobachevsky in 1829, had only just begun to attract the notice of most geometers in Clifford's day. It was a very exciting and rather disturbing subject, since it showed that many things which, since Greek times, had been thought capable of mathematical proof could in fact be established only by observation. Clifford himself did important work on this subject, and read a paper on a branch of it to the British Association in 1873. But the work remained unpublished, and might have been forgotten if it had not been mentioned and carried further by a German mathematician, Felix Klein, in his *Lectures on Non-Euclidean Geometry,* in which he states that he felt himself more intimately related to Clifford than to any other geometer. At the time when I first read *The Common Sense of the Exact Sciences,* I had only lately heard of the possibility of geometries that contradicted Euclid; what I read in this book did much to diminish the bewilderment that I had been feeling. In spite of all the work that has since been done, hardly anything that Clifford (or Karl Pearson) says on this subject could be bettered by a writer at the present day. Some other geometrical topics, however—for instance, the mention of quaternions, for which apparently the editor is responsible—would be omitted by most modern authors, since they have not proved as important or as illuminating as seemed likely at one time.

The opening chapter, on Number, although it says admirably what, in the seventies, seemed best worth saying, cannot tell the reader what is now known to be most important, since in this subject the great advances made by Dedekind, Cantor, and Frege came in the decade immediately following Clifford's death. He was, moreover, a geometer rather than an analyst, and it was in geometry that his mathematical intuition appeared at its best.

A taste for mathematics, like a taste for music, can be generated in some people, but not in others. My brother, to the end of his life, could not distinguish *God Save the King* from *Rule, Britannia!* For him even the most admirable book on harmony and counterpoint would have been totally useless. In like manner there are people for whom such books as Clifford's serve no purpose; they are the people who have no wish to understand the matters of which it treats. But I think that these could be much fewer than bad instruction makes them seem. Pupils who have not an unusually strong natural bent towards mathematics are led to hate the subject by two shortcomings on the part of their teachers. The first is that mathematics is not exhibited as the basis of all our scientific knowledge, both theoretical and practical: the pupil is not convincingly shown that what we can understand of the world, and what we can do with machines, we can understand and do by virtue of mathematics. The second defect is that the difficulties are not approached gradually, as they should be, and are not minimized by being connected with easily apprehended central principles, so that the edifice of mathematics is made to look like a collection of detached hovels rather than a single temple embodying a unitary plan. It is especially in regard to this second defect that Clifford's book is valuable.

Clifford's book may not only still be read with great profit by young people interested in mathematics, but should also be studied with diligent admiration by all who are engaged in trying to make difficult ideas intelligible. New ideas almost always appear first in an unnecessarily complicated form, and are therefore thought harder to master than they are subsequently found to be. Plato thought the years from twenty to thirty not too long for acquiring a knowledge of the mathematics that had been discovered in his day, most of which in our time any promising student achieves by the age of thirteen. This acceleration is due to the labors of many men who have done something of what Clifford did in this book. As the total amount of human knowledge increases and the journey from childish ignorance to the frontier of discovery lengthens, it becomes more and more important to hasten the process and to make the journey as easy as possible. In each generation some of this work has to be done afresh, since some old subjects turn out to be unimportant and some new ones important. Plato and Euclid thought the construction of the regular solids the most important problem in geometry; nowadays this is a mere bypath. The earliest extant treatise on arithmetic, that of Ahmes the Egyptian, of about 1700 B.C., is largely concerned to show how to exhibit fractions as sums of other fractions having 1 for their numerators, a matter that has since become totally without interest. The discarding of such useless traditional problems is one part of what must be done if instruction is to be sufficiently rapid.

The other thing that must be done—and here Clifford is supremely excellent—is to discover the point of view from which a subject is most easily surveyed. A wood in which the trees are planted in rows looks regular when viewed along a row from one end of it, but may appear completely higgledy-piggledy when viewed on a slant. The same sort of thing is true of a mathematical subject: if you approach it from the wrong angle, each step will be difficult, you will be entangled in thickets, and you will get no view of the whole; but if you start at the right point and advance in the right direction, the obstacles disappear and progress is easy. Clifford's survey of elementary Euclidean geometry, beginning with the two axioms that things can be moved without change of shape, and that the size of things can be increased or dimished by a change of scale without change of shape, is just what is needed to make geometry easy to a beginner without undue sacrifice of logical rigor. And the same merits remain when he comes, later, to treat of conic sections.

Clifford was much more than a mathematician: he was a philosopher, of considerable merit in what concerned the foundations of mathematical knowledge. Moreover, he saw all knowledge, even the most abstract, as part of the general life of mankind, and as concerned in the endeavor to make human existence less petty, less superstitious, and less miserable. He lived at a time when optimism was not so difficult as it has since become, and when hope for the future seemed justified by the history of the previous two hundred years. It was possible, without any blind act of faith, to believe that the human species would become progressively more humane, more tolerant, and more enlightened, with the consequence that war and disease and poverty, and the other major evils of our existence, would continually diminish. In this beneficent process rational knowledge was to be the chief agent, and mathematics, as the most completely rational kind of knowledge, was to be in the van. This faith was Clifford's, and it was mine when I first read his book; in turning over its pages again, the ghosts of old hopes rise up to mock me. Over large parts of the earth's surface the most civilized individuals have suffered persecution, there has been a deliberate lowering of the standard of comfort, and in the course of combating these evils we have been compelled to destroy many ancient cities and reduce whole countries, many of them friendly countries, to the verge of starvation.

In the world in which we find ourselves it is difficult to believe in the influence of reason on human affairs, or in the importance to mankind of theoretical knowledge. *Practical* knowledge, yes, since it enables us to kill our enemies; but it was not on this account that Clifford valued knowledge, or that Klein, a German, went out of his way to praise him. Difficult as it is to maintain the beliefs that inspired the best men of the nineteenth century, there is, I still think, every ground for regarding the old virtues of tolerance and enlightenment as the basis for the hopes that are possible. If the men of that time were too optimistic, it is easy for us to be too pessimistic, for bad periods are no more eternal than good ones, though while they last they may seem so. I hope that, in reading this book, readers may imbibe something of its author's belief in the possiblity of excellent things, and that this may help them to acquire some of the strength that is needed to fight against the evils of the age in which we are compelled to live.

part two

Real Mathematics

BUDDHISM WAS EXPORTED from India to China several centuries before the beginning of the Christian era. One of the dedicated band of Buddhist missionaries who was instrumental in that introduction, on first hearing sutras chanted in Chinese (as opposed to Sanskrit, for example), remarked that the experience was just like swallowing rice that had been chewed by someone else. That observation has since become synonymous in Chinese with the blandness of vicarious experience. For most mathematicians the experience of reading about mathematics is very much like that of the Buddhist missionary. For them there is no effective substitute for reading real mathematics, and almost all expository essays on the subject of mathematics are but a very pale imitation of the genuine article.

This part presents a selection of readings that treat the development and the underlying ideas of actual topics in mathematics. The subjects range from the elementary to some of the most famous of currently unsolved mathematical problems. The aim of each essay is to provide insight into the nature of mathematics and how mathematics is developed by mathematicians.

Most readers of this or any other mathematics book are concerned whether the topics are accessible to the layperson. It would be ingenuous of any author to suppose that every topic in modern mathematics can be made accessible to a general audience in an eight- or ten-page article. In fact many topics cannot be clearly described for even an audience of mathematicians in so little space. However, a surprisingly large number of the most recent developments in mathematics can be described in ways that make their gross dimensions clear to the interested general reader. More often than not, it is the timidity of the mathematician or possibly his or her indifference to general public acceptance that leads to the attitude that the nature and ideas of modern mathematics are simply beyond public accessibility.

The essays in this part are all quite readable if the reader is willing to make a modest investment of time and thought. The key word is investment. *It would be deceptive to suggest that one can read an article on the Riemann hypothesis as easily as one can read a paperback spy novel. There is no claim that difficult and complicated ideas can be made elementary. Indeed, to sense the reality of mathematics one must make some effort to chew its ideas oneself; otherwise one is in the position of swallowing rice chewed by someone else.*

Each article's introduction includes definitions and descriptions of a few of the key ideas assumed but not treated in the essay. Since mathematical ideas are somewhat cumulative, if the reader wishes to read the essays in a random order it may be necessary to read more than one of the introductions in order to understand all terms used in a given article. We have tried to ease the reader's browsing by giving references to other relevant introductions in this volume.

The Early History of Fermat's Last Theorem

Paulo Ribenboim

Paulo Ribenboim was born in Brazil and did postgraduate work in Nancy, France, and Bonn, Germany. He held academic positions in Brazil, at the University of Illinois, and at the University of Paris. He is currently professor of mathematics at Queen's University in Ontario, Canada.

This essay is among the most revealing of any in this volume. It is tempting to suggest that those nonmathematicians who really wish to understand the essential nature of mathematics and how it is created ought to begin with this discussion. Readers who feel that the previous statement is excessive should consider the following facts. First, the essay discusses one of the most famous unsolved problems of mathematics. Second, the problem is easily stated and can be understood by anyone who has completed two weeks of high school algebra. Third, the problem has attracted the attention of virtually every famous mathematical personality of the past 300 years. Fourth, the history of the problem has all the drama of a really good soap opera, including missing proofs, plagiarism, bitter feuds, brilliant insights, mindless stupidity, and all those other wonderful gossipy historical tidbits that capture and maintain attention. It is simply fascinating.

Finally, a bit of advice. The reader is urged not to be discouraged by the mathematical details; instead, one should read right through them. The details are not essential to the flow of the narrative, and the broad outlines of the development of the problem will be clear even if the mathematical niceties are obscure. The one exception to this is the statement of the problem itself. Briefly, there is an infinite number of triples of positive integers x, y, z, *that satisfy the equation*

$$x^2 + y^2 = z^2.$$

For example,

$$3^2 + 4^2 = 9 + 16 = 25 = 5^2$$

also

$$5^2 + 12^2 = 25 + 144 = 169 = 13^2$$

and so on. The French mathematician Fermat left a note in a manuscript in which he claimed to have a proof of the fact that 2 is the only exponent for which this is true. That is

$$x^n + y^n = z^n$$

has a solution in positive integers x, y, z, *only when* n = 2. *Thus it would be impossible, if the theorem is true, to find positive integers* x, y, *and* z *such that*

$$x^3 + y^3 = z^3$$

or

$$x^{11,463} + y^{11,463} = z^{11,463}$$

or any other n. *It is an amazingly simple question but one whose solution eludes the world of mathematics to this very hour.*

Source: Paulo Ribenboim, "The Early History of Fermat's Last Theorem," in *Thirteen Lectures on Fermat's Last Theorem* (Springer-Verlag, 1979), pp. 1–9, 13–16. Reprinted by permission of Springer-Verlag. (References omitted.)

The Problem

Pierre de Fermat (1601–1665) was a French judge who lived in Toulouse. He was a universal spirit, cultivating poetry, Greek philology, law, but mainly mathematics. His special interest concerned the solutions of equations in integers.

For example, Fermat studied equations of the type

$$X^2 - dY^2 = \pm 1,$$

where d is a positive square-free integer (that is, without square factors different from 1) and he discovered the existence of infinitely many solutions. He has also discovered which natural numbers n may be written as the sum of two squares, namely those with the following property: every prime factor p of n which is congruent to 3 modulo 4 must divide n to an even power.

In the margin of his copy of Bachet's edition of the complete works of Diophantus, Fermat wrote:

It is impossible to separate a cube into two cubes, or a biquadrate into two biquadrates, or in general any power higher than the second into powers of like degree; I have discovered a truly remarkable proof which this margin is too small to contain.

This copy is now lost, but the remark appears in the 1670 edition of the works of Fermat, edited in Toulouse by his son Samuel de Fermat. It is stated in Dickson's *History of the Theory of Numbers*, volume II, that Fermat's assertion was made about 1637. Tannery (1883) mentions a letter from Fermat to Mersenne (for Sainte-Croix) in which he wishes to find two cubes whose sum is a cube, and two biquadrates whose sum is a biquadrate. This letter appears, with the data June 1638, in volume 7 of *Correspondance du Père Marin Mersenne* (1962); see also Itard (1948). The same problem was proposed to Frènicle de Bessy (1640) in a letter to Mersenne, and to Wallis and Brouncker in a letter to Digby, written in 1657, but there is no mention of the remarkable proof he had supposedly found.

In modern language, Fermat's statement means:

The equation $X^n + Y^n = Z^n$, *where* n *is a natural number larger than 2, has no solution in integers all different from 0.*

No proof of this statement was ever found among Fermat's papers. He did, however, write a proof that the equations $X^4 - Y^4 = Z^2$ and $X^4 + Y^4 = Z^4$ have no solutions in integers all different from 0. In fact, this is one of two proofs by Fermat in number theory which have been preserved.[1] With very few exceptions, all Fermat's other assertions have now been confirmed. So this problem is usually called Fermat's last theorem, despite the fact that it has never been proved.

Fermat's most notable erroneous belief concerns the numbers $F_n = 2^{2^n} + 1$, which he thought were always prime. But Euler showed that F_5 is not a prime. Sierpiński and Schinzel pointed out some other false assertions made by Fermat.

Mathematicians have debated whether Fermat indeed possessed the proof of the theorem. Perhaps, at one point, he mistakenly believed he had found such a proof. Despite Fermat's honesty and frankness in acknowledging imperfect conclusions, it is very difficult to understand today how the most distinguished mathematicians could have failed to rediscover a proof, if one had existed.

To illustrate Fermat's candor, we quote from his letter of October 18, 1640, to Frénicle de Bessy:

Mais je vous advoue tout net (car par advance je vous advertis que comme je suis pas capable de m'attribuer plus que je ne sçay, je dis avec même franchise ce que je ne sçay pas) que je n'ay peu encore démonstrer l'exclusion de tous diviseurs en cette belle proposition que je vous avois envoyée, et que vous m'avez confirmée touchant les nombres, 3, 5, 17, 257, 65537 & c. Car bien que je réduise l'exclusion à la plupart des nombres, et jue j'aye même des raisons probables pur le reste, je n'ay peu encore démonstrer nécessairement la vérité de cette proposition, de laquelle pourtant je ne doute non plus à cette heure que je faisois auparavant. Si vous en avez la preuve assurée, vous m'obligerez de me la communiquer: car après cela rien ne m'arrestera en ces matières.[2]

Again, in a letter to Pascal from August 29, 1654, Fermat proposes the same problem:

Au reste, il n'est rien à l'avenir que je ne vous communique avec toute franchise. Songez cependant, si vous la trouvez à propos, à cette proposition: les puissances carrées de 2, augmentées de l'unité, sont toujours des nombres premiers: $2^2 + 1 = 5, 2^{2^2} + 1 = 17,$ $2^{2^3} + 1 = 257, 2^{2^4} + 1 = 65537$, sont premiers, et ainsi à l'infini. C'est une proposition de la verité de laquelle je vous répond. La démonstration en est trés malaisée, et je vous avoue que je n'ai pu encore la trouver pleinement; je ne vous la proposerois pas pour la chercher si j'en étois venu à bout.[3]

Incidentally Pascal has written to Fermat stating:

Je vous tiens pour le plus grand géomètre de toute l'Europe.[4]

It is also highly improbable that Fermat would have claimed to have proved his last theorem, just because he succeeded in proving it for a few small exponents.

In contrast, Gauss believed that Fermat's assertions were mostly extrapolations from particular cases. In 1807, Gauss wrote: "Higher arithmetic has this special feature that many of its most beautiful theorems may be easily discovered by induction, while any proof can be only obtained with the utmost difficulty. Thus, it was one of the great merits of Euler to have proved several of Fermat's theorems which he obtained, it appears, by induction."

Even though he himself gave a proof for the case of cubes, Gauss did not hold the problem in such high esteem. On March 21, 1816, he wrote to Olbers about the recent mathematical contest of the Paris Academy oṅ Fermat's last theorem:

I am very much obliged for your news concerning the Paris prize. But I confess that Fermat's theorem as an isolated proposition has very little interest for me, because I could easily lay down a multitude of such propositions, which one could neither prove nor dispose of.

In trying to prove Fermat's theorem for every positive integer $n \geq 3$, I make the following easy observation. If the theorem holds for an integer m and $n = lm$ is a multiple of m, then it holds also for n. For, if x, y, z are non-zero integers and $x^n + y^n = z^n$ then $(x^l)^m + (y^l)^m = (z^l)^m$ contradict-

ing the hypothesis. Since every integer $n \geq 3$ is a multiple of 4 or of a prime $p \neq 2$, it suffices to prove Fermat's conjecture for $n = 4$ and for every prime $p \neq 2$. However, I shall occasionally also mention some proofs for exponents of the form $2p$, or p^n where p is an odd prime.

The statement of Fermat's last theorem is often subdivided further into two cases:

The *first case* holds for the exponent p when there do not exist integers x, y, z such that $p \nmid xyz$ and $x^p + y^p = z^p$.

The *second case* holds for the exponent p when there do not exist integers x, y, z, all different from 0, such that $p|xyz$, $\gcd(x, y, z) = 1$ and $x^p + y^p = z^p$.

Early Attempts

It was already known in antiquity that a sum of two squares of integers may well be the square of another integer. Pythagoras was supposed to have proven that the lengths a, b, c of the sides of a right-angle triangle satisfy the relation

$$a^2 + b^2 = c^2;$$

so the above fact just means the existence of such triangles with sides measured by integers.

But the situation is already very different for cubes, biquadrates and so on. Fermat's proof for the case of biquadrates is very ingenious and proceeds by the method which he called *infinite descent*. Roughly, it goes as follows: Suppose a certain equation $f(X, Y, Z) = 0$ has integral solutions a, b, c, with $c > 0$, the method just consists in finding another solution in integers a', b', c' with $0 < c' < c$. Repeating this procedure a number of times, one would reach a solution a'', b'', c'', with $0 < c'' < 1$, which is absurd. This method of infinite descent is nothing but the well-ordering principle of the natural numbers.

Little by little Fermat's problem aroused the interest of mathematicians and a dazzling array of the best minds turned to it.

Euler considered the case of cubes. Without loss of generality, one may assume $x^3 + y^3 = z^3$ where x, y, z are pairwise relatively prime integers, x, y are odd, so $x = a - b$, $y = a + b$. Then $x + y = 2a$, $x^2 - xy + y^2 = a^2 + 3b^2$

and $z^3 = x^3 + y^3 = 2a(a^2 + 3b^2)$, where the integers $2a$, $a^2 + 3b^2$ are either relatively prime or have their greatest common divisor equal to 3. Euler was led to studying odd cubes $a^2 + 3b^2$ (with a, b relatively prime), and forms of their divisors; he concluded the proof by the method of infinite descent. The properties of the numbers $a^2 + 3b^2$ which are required had to be derived from a detailed study of divisibility, and therefore were omitted from the proof published in Euler's book on algebra (1822). This proof, with the same gap, was reproduced by Legendre. Later, mathematicians intrigued by the missing steps were able without much difficulty, to reconstruct the proof on a sound basis. In today's language, numbers of the form $a^2 + 3b^2$ are norms of algebraic integers of the quadratic extension $\mathbb{Q}(\sqrt{-3})$ of the rational field $\mathbb{Q}$ and the required properties can be deduced from the unique factorization theorem, which is valid in that field.

Gauss gave another proof for the case of cubes. His proof was not "rational" since it involved complex numbers, namely those generated by the cube root of unity $\zeta = (-1 + \sqrt{-3})/2$, i.e., numbers from the quadratic field $\mathbb{Q}(\sqrt{-3})$. He consciously used the arithmetic properties of this field. The underlying idea was to call "integers" all numbers of the form $(a + b\sqrt{-3})/2$ where a, b are integers of the same parity; then to define divisibility and the prime integers, and to use the fact that every integer is, in a unique way, the product of powers of primes. Of course some new facts appeared. First the integers $\pm\zeta$, $\pm\zeta^2$ that divide 1 are "units" since $\zeta\zeta^2 = 1$ and therefore should not be taken into account so to speak, in questions of divisibility. Thus, all the properties have to be stated "up to units." Secondly, the unique factorization, which was taken for granted, was by no means immediate—in fact it turned out to be false in general. I shall return to this later.

Gauss's proof was an early incursion into the realm of number fields, i.e., those sets of complex numbers obtained from the roots of polynomials by the operations of addition, subtraction, multiplication, and division.

In the 1820s, a number of distinguished French and German mathematicians were trying intensively to prove Fermat's theorem.

In 1825, G. Lejeune Dirichlet read at the Académie des Sciences de Paris a paper where he attempted to prove the theorem for the exponent 5. In fact his proof was incomplete, as pointed out by Legendre, who provided an independent and complete proof. Dirichlet then completed his own proof, which was published in Crelle Journal, in 1828.

Dirichlet's proof is "rational," and involves numbers of the form $a^2 - 5b^2$. He carefully analyzed the nature of such numbers which are 5th powers when either a, b are odd, or a, b have different parity, and 5 does not divide a, 5 divides b, and a, b are relatively prime. Nowadays the properties he derived can be obtained from the arithmetic of the field $\mathbb{Q}(\sqrt{5})$. In this field too, every integer has a unique factorization. Moreover every unit is a power of $(1 + \sqrt{5})/2$, which is of crucial importance in the proof. Of course, for Dirichlet this knowledge took the form of numerical manipulations which lead to the same result.

In 1832 Dirichlet settled the theorem for the exponent 14.

The next important advance was due to Lamé, who, in 1839, proved the theorem for $n = 7$. Soon after, Lebesgue simplified Lamé's proof considerably by a clever use of the identity,

$$(X + Y + Z)^7 - (X^7 + Y^7 + Z^7) =$$
$$7(X + Y)(X + Z)(Y + Z)$$
$$\times [(X^2 + Y^2 + Z^2 + XY + XZ + YZ)^2 + XYZ(X + Y + Z)]$$

already considered by Lamé.

While these special cases of small exponents were being studied, a very remarkable theorem was proved by Sophie Germain, a French mathematician.

Previously Barlow, and then Abel, had indicated interesting relations that x, y, z must satisfy if $x^p + y^p = z^p$ (and x, y, z are not zero). Through clever manipulations, Sophie Germain proved:

If p *is an odd prime such that* 2p + 1 *is also a prime then the first case of Fermat's theorem holds for* p.

These results were communicated by letter to Legendre and Cauchy since the regulations of the

Academy prevented women from presenting the discoveries in person.

There are many primes p for which $2p + 1$ is also prime, but it is still not known whether there are infinitely many such primes.

Following Sophie Germain's ideas, Legendre proved the following theorem: Let p, q be distinct odd primes, and assume the following two conditions:

1. p is never congruent modulo q to a pth power.
2. the congruence $X^p + Y^p + Z^p \equiv 0 \pmod{q}$ has no solution x, y, z, unless q divides xyz.

Then the first case of Fermat's theorem holds for p. With this result, Legendre extended Sophie Germain's theorem as follows:

If p is a prime such that 4p + 1, 8p + 1, 10 p + 1, 14p + 1, or 16p + 1 is also a prime then the first case of Fermat's theorem holds for the exponent p.

This was sufficient to establish the first case for all prime exponents $p < 100$.

Kummer's Monumental Theorem

By 1840, Cauchy and Lamé were working with values of polynomials at roots of unity, trying to prove Fermat's theorem for arbitrary exponents. Already in 1840 Cauchy published a long memoir on the theory of numbers, which however was not directly connected with Fermat's problem. In 1847, Lamé presented to the Academy a "proof" of the theorem and his paper was printed in full in Liouville's journal. However, Liouville noticed that the proof was not valid, since Lamé had tacitly assumed that the decomposition of certain polynomial expressions in the nth root of unity into irreducible factors was unique.

Lamé attributed his use of complex numbers to a suggestion from Liouville, while Cauchy claimed that he was about to achieve the same results, given more time. Indeed, during that same year, Cauchy had 18 communications printed by the Academy on complex numbers, or more specifically, on radical polynomials. He tried to prove what amounted to the Euclidean algorithm, and hence unique factorization for cyclotomic inte-

gers. Then, assuming unique factorization, he drew wrong conclusions. Eventually Cauchy recognized his mistake. In fact, his approach led to results which were later rediscovered by Kummer with more suitable terminology. A noteworthy proposition of Cauchy was the following one (*C. R. Acad. Sci. Paris*, 25, 1847, page 181), later also found by Genocchi and by Kummer:

If the first case of Fermat's theorem fails for the exponent p, then the sum

$$1^{p-4} + 2^{p-4} + \cdots + \left(\frac{p-1}{2}\right)^{p-4}$$

is a multiple of p.

By the year 1847, mathematicians were aware of both the subtlety and importance of the unique decomposition of cyclotomic integers into irreducible factors.

In Germany, Kummer devoted himself to the study of the arithmetic of cyclotomic fields. Already, in 1844, he recognized that the unique factorization theorem need not hold for the cyclotomic field $\mathbb{Q}(\zeta_p)$. The first such case occurs for $p = 23$. However, while trying to rescue the unique factorization he was led to the introduction of new "ideal numbers." Here is an excerpt of a letter from Kummer to Liouville (1847):

. . . Encouraged by my friend Mr. Lejeune Dirichlet, I take the liberty of sending you a few copies of a dissertation which I have written three years ago, at the occasion of the century jubileum of the University of Königsberg, as well as of another dissertation of my friend and student Mr. Kronecker, a young and distinguished geometer. In these memoirs, which I beg you to accept as a sign of my deep esteem, you will find developments concerning certain points in the theory of complex numbers composed of roots of unity, i.e., roots of the equation $r^n = 1$, which have been recently the subject of some discussions at your illustrious Academy, at the occasion of an attempt by Mr. Lamé to prove the last theorem of Fermat.

Concerning the elementary proposition for these complex numbers, that a *composite complex number may be decomposed into prime fac-*

tors *in only one way,* which you regret so justly in this proof, which is also lacking in some other points, I may assure you that *it does not hold in general* for complex numbers of the form

$$a_0 + a_1 r + a_2 r^2 + \cdots + a_{n-1} r^{n-1},$$

but it is possible to rescue it, by introducing a new kind of complex number, which I have called an *ideal complex number.* The results of my research on this matter have been communicated to the Academy of Berlin and printed in the *Sitzungsberichte* (March 1846); a memoir on the same subject will appear soon in the Crelle Journal. I have considered already long ago the applications of this theory to the proof of Fermat's theorem and I succeeded in deriving the impossibility of the equation $x^n + y^n = z^n$ from two properties of the prime number *n,* so that it remains only to find out whether these properties are shared by all prime numbers. In case these results seem worth some of your attention, you may find them published in the *Sitzungsberichte* of the Berlin Academy, this month.

The theorem which Kummer mentioned in this letter represented a notable advance over all his predecessors.

The ideal numbers correspond to today's *divisors.* Dedekind rephrased this concept, introducing the *ideals,* which are sets I of algebraic integers of the cyclotomic field such that $0 \in I$; if α, $\beta \in I$ then $\alpha + \beta$, $\alpha - \beta \in I$; if $\alpha \in I$ and β is any cyclotomic integer then $\alpha\beta \in I$. Ideals may be multiplied in a very natural way.

Each cyclotomic integer α determines a *principal ideal* consisting of all elements $\beta\alpha$, where $\beta \in A$, the set of cyclotomic integers.

If all ideals are principal there is unique factorization in the cyclotomic field, and conversely. For the cases when not all ideals are principal, Kummer wanted to "measure" to what extent some of the ideals were not principal. So he considered two nonzero ideals I, I' equivalent when I' consists of all multiples of the elements of I by some nonzero element α in the cyclotomic field. Thus, there is exactly one equivalence class when all ideals are principal. Kummer proved that

there are only finitely many equivalence classes of ideals in each cyclotomic field $\mathbb{Q}(\zeta_p)$.

Let h_p denote the number of such classes. If p does not divide h_p then p is said to be a *regular* prime. In this case, if the ideal I_p is a principal ideal then I is itself a principal ideal. But the main property used by Kummer is the following lemma:

If p *is a regular prime,* p $\neq$ 2, *if* ω *is a unit in the ring* A *of cyclotomic integers of* $\mathbb{Q}(\zeta_p)$, *and if there exists an ordinary integer* m *such that* $\omega -$ m$\in$A $(1 - \zeta)^{p-1}$, *then* ω *is the* p*th power of another unit.*

The proof of this lemma requires deep analytical methods.

Armed with this formidable weapon, Kummer proved that Fermat's last theorem holds for every exponent p which is a regular prime. This is the theorem which Kummer mentioned in his letter to Liouville. At first Kummer believed that there exist infinitely many regular primes. But, he later realized that this is far from evident—and in fact, it has, as yet, not been proved.

A well-known story concerning a wrong proof of Fermat's theorem, submitted by Kummer, originates with Hensel. Specifically, in his address to commemorate the first centennial of Kummer's birth, Hensel (1910) stated:

Although it is not well known, Kummer at one time believed he had found a complete proof of Fermat's theorem. (This is attested to by reliable witnesses including Mr. Gundelfinger who heard the story from the mathematician Grassmann.) Seeking the best critic for his proof, Kummer sent his manuscript to Dirichlet, author of the insuperably beautiful proof for the case $\lambda = 5$. After a few days, Dirichlet replied with the opinion that the proof was excellent and certainly correct, provided the numbers in α could not only be decomposed into indecomposable factors, as Kummer proved, but that this could be done in only one way. If, however, the second hypothesis couldn't be satisfied, most of the theorems for the arithmetic of numbers in α would be unproven and the proof of Kummer's theorem would fall apart. Unfortunately, it appeared to him that the numbers in α didn't actually possess this property in general.

This is confirmed in a letter, which is not dated (but likely from the summer of 1844), written by Eisenstein to Stern, a mathematician from Göttingen.

In a recent paper, Edwards (1975) analyzes this information, in the light of a letter from Liouville to Dirichlet and expresses doubts about the existence of such a "false proof" by Kummer. . . .

The Golden Medal and the Wolfskehl Prize

In 1816, and again in 1850, the Académie des Sciences de Paris offered a golden medal and a prize of 3,000 Francs to the mathematician who would solve Fermat's problem. The judges in 1856 were Cauchy, Liouville, Lamé, Bertrand, and Chasles.

Cauchy wrote the following report:

Eleven memoirs have been presented to the Secretary. But none has solved the proposed question. The Commissaries have nevertheless noted that the piece registered under number 2 contained a new solution of the problem in the special case developed by Fermat himself, namely when the exponent is equal to 4.

Thus, after being many times put for a prize, the question remains at the point where M. Kummer left it. However, the mathematical sciences should congratulate themselves for the works which were undertaken by the geometers, with their desire to solve the question, specially by M. Kummer; and the Commissaries think that the Academy would make an honorable and useful decision if, by withdrawing the question from the competition, it would adjugate the medal to M. Kummer, for his beautiful researches on the complex numbers composed of roots of unity and integers.

In 1908 the very substantial Wolfskehl Prize, in the amount of 100,000 Mark, was offered with the same aim by the Königliche Gesellschaft der Wissenschaften, in Göttingen, Germany:

By the power conferred on us, by Dr. Paul Wolfskehl, deceased in Darmstadt, hereby we

fund a prize of one hundred thousand Marks, to be given to the person who will be the first to prove the great theorem of Fermat.

In his will, Doctor Wolfskehl observed that Fermat (*Oeuvres*, Paris, 1891, volume I, p. 291, observation 2) asserted mutatis mutandis that the equation $x^\lambda + y^\lambda = z^\lambda$ has no integral solutions for any odd prime number λ. This theorem has to be proved, either following the ideas of Fermat, or completing the researches of Kummer (*Crelle's Journal*, vol. XL, page 130; Abhandlungen der Akademie der Wissenschaften zu Berlin, 1857), for all exponents λ, for which it has some meaning [consult Hilbert, *Theorie der Algebraischen Zahlkörper*, 1894–1895, and *Enzyklopädie der Mathematischen Wissenschaften* (1900–1904), I C 4b, page 713].

The following rules will be followed:

The Königliche Gesellschaft der Wissenschaften in Göttingen will decide in entire freedom to whom the prize should be conferred. It will refuse to accept any manuscript written with the aim of entering the competition to obtain the Prize. It will only take in consideration those mathematical memoirs which have appeared in the form of a monograph in the periodicals, or which are for sale in the bookstores. The Society asks the authors of such memoirs to send at least five printed exemplars.

Works which are published in a language which is not understood by the scholarly specialists chosen for the jury will be excluded from the competition. The authors of such works will be allowed to replace them by translations, of guaranteed faithfulness.

The Society declines its responsibility for the examination of works not brought to its attention, as well as for the errors which might result from the fact that the author of a work, or part of a work, are unknown to the Society.

The Society keeps the right of decision in the case where various persons would have dealt with the solution of the problem, or for the case where the solution is the result of the combined efforts of several scholars, in particular in what concerns the partition of the Prize, at its own discretion.

The award of the Prize by the Society will

take place not earlier than two years after the publication of the memoir to be crowned. The interval of time is aimed to allow the German and foreign mathematicians to voice their opinion about the validity of the solution published.

As soon as the Prize will be conferred by the Society, the laureate will be informed by the secretary, on the name of the Society, and the result will be published everywhere the Prize would have been announced during the preceding year. The assignment of the Prize by the Society is not to be the subject of any further discussion.

The payment of the Prize will be made to the laureate, in the next three months after the award, by the Royal Cashier of Göttingen University, or, at the receiver's own risk, at any other place he will have designated.

The capital may be delivered against receipt, at the Society's will, either in cash, or by the transfer of financial values. The payment of the Prize will be considered as accomplished by the transmission of these financial values, even though their total value at the day's course would not attain 100,000 Mark.

If the Prize is not awarded by September 13, 2007, no ulterior claim will be accepted.

The competition for the Prize Wolfskehl is open, as of today, under the above conditions.

> Göttingen, June 27, 1908
> Die Königliche Gesellschaft
> der Wissenschaften.

A memorandum dated 1958 states that the Prize of 100,000 DM has been reduced to approximately 7,600 DM, in virtue of the inflation and financial changes.

Dr. F. Schlichting, from the Mathematics Institute of the University of Göttingen, was kind enough to provide me with the following information on the Wolfskehl Prize:

Göttingen, March 23, 1974.

Dear Sir:

Please excuse the delay in answering your letter. I enclose a copy of the original announcement, which gives the main regulations, and a note of the "Akademie" which is usually sent to persons who are applying for the prize, now worth a little bit more than 10,000 DM. There is no count of the total number of "solutions" submitted so far. In the first year (1907–1908) 621 solutions were registered in the files of the Akademie, and today they have stored about 3 meters of correspondence concerning the Fermat problem. In recent decades it was handled in the following way: the secretary of the Akademie divides the arriving manuscripts into (1) complete nonsense, which is sent back immediately, and into (2) material which looks like mathematics. The second part is given to the mathematical department and there, the work of reading, finding mistakes and answering is delegated to one of the scientific assistants (at German universities these are graduated individuals working for Ph.D. or habilitation and helping the professors with teaching and supervision)—at the moment I am the victim. There are about 3 to 4 letters to answer per month, and there is a lot of funny and curious material arriving, e.g., like the one sending the first half of his solution and promising the second if we would pay 1000 DM in advance; or another one, who promised me 10 per cent of his profits from publications, radio and TV interviews after he got famous, if only I would support him now; if not, he threatened to send it to a Russian mathematics department to deprive us of the glory of discovering him. From time to time someone appears in Göttingen and insists on personal discussion.

Nearly all "solutions" are written on a very elementary level (using the notions of high school mathematics and perhaps some undigested papers in number theory), but can nevertheless be very complicated to understand. Socially, the senders are often persons with a technical education but a failed career who try to find success with a proof of the Fermat problem. I gave some of the manuscripts to physicians who diagnosed heavy schizophrenia.

One condition of Wolfskehl's last will was that the Akademie had to publish the announcement of the prize yearly in the main mathematical periodicals. But already after the first years the periodicals refused to print the announcement, because they were overflowed by letters and crazy manuscripts. So far, the best effect has been had by another regulation of the prize: namely, that the interest from the original 100,000 Mark could be used by the Akademie. For example, in the 1910s the heads of the Göttingen mathematics department (Klein, Hilbert, Minkowski) used this money to invite Poincaré to give six lectures in Göttingen.

Since 1948 however the remainder of the money has not been touched.

I hope that you can use this information and would be glad to answer any further questions.

Yours sincerely,
F. Schlichting.

Notes

1. The other proof, partial but very interesting, was brought to light and reproduced by Hofmann (1943, pages 41–44). Fermat showed that the only solutions in integers of the system $x = 2y^2 - 1$, $x^2 = 2z^2 - 1$ are $x = 1$ and $x = 7$.
2. But I confess to you plainly (for I warn you in advance that since I am not capable of attributing to myself more than I know, I say with the same frankness what I do not know) that I have not yet been able to demonstrate the exclusion of all divisors in that elegant proposition I had sent you, and that you have confirmed for me touching the numbers 3, 5, 17, 257, 65537, etc. For even though I reduce the exclusion to the majority of numbers, and though I even have probable reasons for the rest, I have not yet been able to demonstrate necessarily the truth of this proposition, of which I yet doubt no more at this hour than I did before. If you have the certain proof of it, you would oblige me by communicating it to me: for after that nothing will stop me in these matters.
3. For the rest, there is nothing in the future that I will not communicate to you with all frankness. Think however, if you find it relevant, about this proposition: the square powers of 2, increased by one, are always prime numbers: $2^2 + 1 = 5$, $2^{2^2} + 1 = 17$, $2^{2^3} + 1 = 257$, $2^{2^4} + 1 = 65537$, are prime, and so on to infinity. It's a proposition for whose truth I can answer to you. Its demonstration is very awkward, and I confess to you that I have not yet been able to discover it fully; I would not propose it to you for research if I had come to the end of it.
4. I consider you the greatest geometer of all Europe.

π and *e*

E. C. Titchmarsh

Edward Charles Titchmarsh was born in England in 1899. He received his mathematical training at Oxford. Like many of the professional English mathematicians of his generation he never received a doctorate. Although he did make many original contributions to analysis, he is better known for his painstakingly careful organization of previously proved but randomly generated accomplishments of other professional mathematicians.

In the geometry of Euclid the relationship between the diameter of a circle and its circumference is expressed by the equation c = πd, *where* c *is the circumference,* d *is the diameter, and* π *is a constant. This fact—the existence of a fixed relationship between the diameter and circumference of a circle—was known to many ancient civilizations. Indeed, "I Kings 7:23" in the bible suggests that the value of* π *is three. Both the Egyptians and Babylonians had better approximations for* π *than the biblical value of three, but the Greeks were probably the first to discover that* π *is a number quite unlike any of the whole numbers or ratios that the ancients used in their mathematics. What more recent mathematical investigations have shown is that* π *is a transcendental. Briefly, a real number is called transcendental if it is not the root of any polynomial with integer coefficients. Irrational real numbers are those which, like* √2, *are not expressable as the ratio of any two integers. Although* √2 *is irrational, it is not transcendental since it is a root of the polynomial* x^2 – 2 *which has integer coefficients. A transcendental real number, on the other hand, is not the root of any polynomial with integer coefficients no matter how long or complicated the polynomial is. The fact that* π *is transcendental was first demonstrated by Lindemann in 1882 and was viewed, quite properly, as a significant mathematical achievement.*

The number e *may be viewed as a companion for* π *in the never-never land of the transcendental real numbers—a companion in the sense that, like* π, e *arises quite naturally in fairly elementary mathematics. It was used and various approximations were given long before the transcendental nature of* e *was discovered. There are many instances in the physical sciences in which the number* e *appears in some formula used to describe natural phenomena. As is the case with* π, e *seems to be linked to our attempts to explain and describe the universe of our experience.*

The Circumference of a Circle

Suppose that we want to measure the distance around a hoop, barrel or round object of any kind. One way would be to tie a string round it, so that the ends just meet, and then to pull the string out straight and measure that. Another way would be to place the hoop on the ground with a mark on it against a mark on the ground, and then roll it along until the mark on the hoop comes down again. The distance between the two points on the ground corresponding to the mark

Source: E. C. Titchmarsh, "π and *e*," in *Mathematics for the General Reader* (Doubleday, 1959). Reprinted by permission of Hutchison Publishing Group Limited.

on the hoop would be the length around the hoop.

Now consider the problem of the length of a circle in Cartesian geometry. To roll a purely ideal circle along an entirely conceptional straight line is not so easy. In fact it is not obvious that there is any definite number associated with a circle which can reasonably be called its length. A different method of approach to this problem is required. What we can do is to construct inside the circle polygons which follow the line of the circle round very closely. The length of each side of a polygon is naturally taken to be the distance between its endpoints. . . . The length of the perimeter of the polygon is then the sum of the lengths of its sides. We may then expect that the length of the perimeter of the polygon will be an approximation to the length of the circumference of the circle.

Let us consider a circle of radius 1. In Cartesian geometry such a circle is represented by the equation $x^2 + y^2 = 1$. First of all, inscribe in it a square represented by $ABCD$ in the figure. The

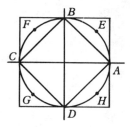

point A is $(1, 0)$ and the point B is $(0, 1)$. The length of AB, i.e., the distance between these two points, is $\sqrt{2}$. The length of the perimeter of the square is therefore $4\sqrt{2}$.

Next we bisect each arc AB, BC, CD, DA, by points E, F, G, H. On joining up AE, EB, etc. we obtain a regular octagon inscribed in the circle. The length of this octagon can be found, though it does not have such a simple expression as the length of the square. The octagon is already a good deal closer to the circle than the square was.

And so we can proceed, at each stage inserting new points on the circle mid-way between the old ones. We obtain regular inscribed polygons with

16, 32, 64, . . . and generally 2^n sides. Let us denote the length of the perimeter of the polygon with 2^n sides by l_n.

Now I think it is clear from the figure that each l_n is greater than the one before. This simply follows from the fact that the sum of two sides of any triangle is greater than the third, since what we do in passing from l_n to l_{n+1} is to replace each side of the polygon of 2^n sides by two sides of that with 2^{n+1} sides. Hence the numbers l_n form a sequence, each term of which is greater than the term before it. On the other hand, the numbers l_n do not increase beyond all bounds. The perimeter of each of the inscribed polygons which we have used is less than that of the square of which A, B, C, D are the mid-points of the sides. This is fairly obvious from the figure, and anyhow mathematicians can easily prove it. The length of the perimeter of this square is equal to 8, and so every number l_n is less than 8.

The sequence l_n is therefore convergent, and the number to which it converges is defined to be the length of the circumference of the circle. It is not a question of proving that this number is the length. It is so by definition—the length is not defined in any other way.

Half the length of a circle of radius 1 is a number which is always denoted by the Greek letter π (pi). Thus the limit of the numbers l_n in the above construction is 2π. In any circle, the circumference is proportional to the radius, so that the circumference of a circle of radius r is equal to $2\pi r$.

It is obvious from the values of the perimeters of the two squares which we drew inside and outside the circle, that π lies somewhere between $2\sqrt{2}$ and 4.

The Problem of Area

Possibly the idea of the area of a flat floor arose in connection with the problem of paving it with square tiles. One would want to know how many tiles were needed. Suppose that it is a rectangular floor, which could be exactly filled up with the tiles. If p of them go into it one way, and q the other way, then the total number required is $p \times q$. This number has nothing to do with the shape of the floor—two floors of different shapes with the same $p \times q$ are of equal importance from the tiling point of view. This number then deserves a special name, and it is called the *area*. The way in which we have obtained it clearly gives the rule for the area of a rectangle, area = length × breadth.

Even if the length and breadth are not exact multiples of a unit, as we have so far supposed, the same rule still gives a definite result, as long as the length and the breadth can be measured. This extends the definition of area to any rectangle.

We next require a rule for the area of a triangle. In Euclid's theory of triangles congruent triangles are regarded as being equal in all respects, so that, if they have areas, the areas must be equal. Now take any triangle ABC, and fit round it a rectangle as in the following figure.

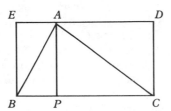

Here AP is perpendicular to BC. The triangles ABP and ABE are congruent and so of equal area. Similarly ACP and ACD are of equal area. Thus the triangle ABC must be half the area of the whole rectangle, i.e., half of $EB \times BC$, or half of $AP \times BC$. Hence we obtain the rule, area of triangle = half the base multiplied by the height.

Here we are using Euclidean geometry to give us hints as to how to proceed in certain cases, not as the logical base of our system. We must therefore really take the above rule as the definition of the area of a triangle. What the argument shows is that it is the only definition which is consistent with our ordinary geometrical ideas.

. . . The problem of area . . . has been introduced here in the case of triangles because we want to discuss circles, and because it is a fairly simple step from the triangle to the circle.

Area of a Circle

Besides having a perimeter with a definite length, a circle encloses a region with a definite area. This can be seen by using the same construction as before. Take the regular polygon with 2^n sides inscribed in the circle, and join each vertex of it to the center of the circle by a straight line. This divides the polygon into 2^n triangles. Now the area of each triangle is half the base multiplied by the height. Take as the base of each triangle the side which is one of the sides of the polygon. Then the sum of all the bases is the perimeter of the polygon, and so, when n is very large, is approximately equal to $2\pi r$ (if r is the radius). Also the height of each triangle is approximately r. Hence the area enclosed by the polygon approximates to πr^2 when n is large, and consequently the area enclosed by the circle is equal to πr^2.

The Value of π

Approximations to π are to be found in very ancient writings. In an Egyptian papyrus, written by Ahmes some time before 1700 B.C., and entitled "Directions for Obtaining the Knowledge of All Dark Things," the area of a circle is found by deducting from the diameter one ninth of its length and squaring the remainder (see F. Cajori, *A History of Mathematics*). If we take the radius to be 1, so that the diameter is 2 and the area π, this gives

$$\pi = \left(2 \times \frac{8}{9}\right)^2 = \left(\frac{16}{9}\right)^2 = \frac{256}{81}.$$

This is equal to 3.1604 . . . , a very fair approximation to π.

According to I Kings vii, 23, Hiram of Tyre made a molten sea, ten cubits from the one rim to the other; it was round all about, and a line of thirty cubits did compass it round about. According to this, the circumference of the "sea" was three times its diameter. If this were quite accurate, π would be equal to 3. No doubt Hiram, in his report to Solomon at any rate, ignored fractions of a cubit. If the molten sea was 9.6 cubits across, it would be about 30 cubits round, to the nearest cubit. If it was really ten cubits across, it must have been a good thirty-one cubits round.

The most celebrated approximation to π, 22/7, is due to Archimedes. He actually showed that π lies between 3 10/71 and 3 1/7. A still better rational approximation to π is 355/113. This is equal to 3.1415929 · · · , and it agrees with π to six places of decimals.

The numerical value of π to fifteen decimal places is

$$\pi = 3.14159\ 26535\ 89793 \cdots$$

It has been calculated to hundreds of decimal places, with what object it is difficult to say.

There are many striking formulae for π. In 1656, John Wallis, Savilian Professor of Geometry at Oxford, proved that

$$\pi = 2 \cdot \frac{2}{1} \cdot \frac{2}{3} \cdot \frac{4}{3} \cdot \frac{4}{5} \cdot \frac{6}{5} \cdot \frac{6}{7} \cdot \frac{8}{7} \cdot \frac{8}{9} \cdots$$

The expression on the right-hand side is an infinite product; that is, we are to multiply any finite number of factors, and take the limit of these "partial products" as the number of factors tends to infinity. This formula was the first in which π was expressed as the limit of a sequence of rational numbers. Perhaps the simplest such formula is the infinite series

$$\pi = 4\left(1 - \frac{1}{3} + \frac{1}{5} - \frac{1}{7} + \cdots\right)$$

published by Gregory in 1670. Another infinite series, this time for π^2, is

$$\pi^2 = 6\left(\frac{1}{1^2} + \frac{1}{2^2} + \frac{1}{3^2} + \cdots\right),$$

discovered independently by John Bernoulli and Euler.

Squaring the Circle

One type of problem which the ancient Greek geometers were fond of setting themselves was that of constructing a length with given properties. For example, they asked how to construct the side of a square which should be equal in area to a given triangle. "Construction" here had a special meaning. They were only allowed to use ruler and compasses; that is, a straight line through two given points could be constructed, and a circle with a given center and radius of a given length could be constructed. Anything else

must be made up by some combination of these processes. One might imagine the existence of other curves, but as they could not be so easily drawn in practice, it was not regarded as playing the game to use them in constructions.

The problem of the square equal in area to a given triangle was solved. Another problem which then suggested itself was that of constructing a square equal in area to a given circle; and of course it had to be done by Euclidean methods, i.e., with ruler and compasses only. The problem became known as that of squaring the circle. It was never solved, and we know now that it is *insoluble*. The proposed construction is an impossible one.

Let us see what this amounts to in terms of numbers. We may take the radius of the circle to be 1; its area is then π. The side of the proposed square would therefore have to be equal to $\sqrt{\pi}$.

It was proved by the German mathematician Lambert in 1761 that π is an irrational number. This is a very interesting discovery, but it does not prove that the problem of squaring the circle is impossible. Some irrational lengths, such as $\sqrt{2}$, can be constructed by Euclidean methods. But not every irrational length can be constructed by these methods. They lead to lengths of a special kind only, and it happens that $\sqrt{\pi}$ is not one of these. It was proved by another German mathematician, Lindemann, in 1882, that π is not merely irrational, but is what is called a *transcendental* number. This means that it is not a root of any algebraic equation with integer coefficients. Since every number which can be constructed by Euclidean methods is a root of such an equation, neither π nor $\sqrt{\pi}$ can be so constructed. Hence it is impossible to square the circle.

This of course does not mean that the proposed square does not exist. In fact we have shown above that it does. It merely means that it is impossible to construct it in the particular way used by the Greek geometers.

The Three Unsolved Problems of Antiquity

There were three famous problems which were proposed by the ancient geometers, but which were never solved. One was that of squaring the circle. The second was that of trisecting a given angle, i.e., dividing a given angle into three equal parts. The third was that of duplicating a cube, i.e., to construct a cube which should have twice the volume of a given cube. All the constructions, of course, had to be done by Euclidean methods.

The ancients failed to solve these problems, not because they were not clever enough, but because the problems themselves were insoluble. This is true in each case for the same sort of reason, viz., that the solution would involve a kind of irrational number which cannot be constructed by Euclidean methods. Of course, particular angles can be trisected. The trisection of a right angle involves the construction of an angle of 30°, which can be done quite easily. But in general the problem is an impossible one.

It seems that the fame of these problems is worldwide, but the fact that they are insoluble is not so well known. There must be many people toiling pathetically on in garrets, trying to solve them still. Circle-squarers, and particularly angle-trisectors, still exist. They send me their solutions sometimes. Often the nature of the problem has been misunderstood, and it is thought that a good approximation to the solution is what is wanted. Usually the constructions proposed are so intricate that anyone might have gone wrong in the course of making them up. I must admit that I never try to hunt out the mistakes in these complicated figures. But I can assure the circle-squarers, angle-trisectors and cube-duplicators that there is general agreement among mathematicians that they have set themselves an impossible task.

The Number e

An expression which occurs in many mathematical formulae is the product of all integers up to and including a given integer. If the last integer is n, this product is called "factorial n," and is written $n!$ (In the older books it used to be written $\lfloor n$, but the line under the letter made this inconvenient to print.) Thus

$$n! = 1 \times 2 \times 3 \times \cdots \times n.$$

For example $1! = 1$, $2! = 2$, $3! = 6$ and $4! = 24$.

The number e is defined to be one plus the sum of the reciprocals of all the factorials. In symbols

$$e = 1 + \frac{1}{1!} + \frac{1}{2!} + \frac{1}{3!} + \cdots$$

or

$$e = 1 + \sum_{n=1}^{\infty} \frac{1}{n!}.$$

When we say "the sum of the reciprocals of all the factorials" we are of course speaking of the sum of an infinite series; e is not to be found just by addition, but it is the limit of a sequence. . . . Since $n!$ increases very rapidly as n increases, $1/n!$ decreases very rapidly, and the reader can well imagine that the series just written down is convergent. This can be proved to be true, so that e is actually defined by the series. Numerical approximations to e can be found by taking the first few terms of the series and ignoring the remainder. An approximate value with fifteen decimal places is $e = 2.71828\ 18284\ 59045$.

. . .

. . . Here I shall only go as far as proving the following theorem: *e is an irrational number.*

In general, if a number is defined by a formula, for example as the sum of an infinite series, it is difficult to determine whether it is rational or irrational. The particular nature of the series which defines e makes it fairly easy to obtain the result in this case. The proof proceeds by *reductio ad absurdum.* That is, we assume for the sake of argument that the contrary of the proposed theorem is true, and show that the assumption leads to an absurdity or contradiction.

Suppose that e is a rational number; that is, that there are integers p and q such that $e = p/q$. Thus

$$\frac{p}{q} = 1 + \frac{1}{1!} + \frac{1}{2!} + \frac{1}{3!} + \cdots$$

Divide the series into two parts, the sum of the terms as far as $1/q!$ in the first part, and the remainder in the second part; thus

$$\frac{p}{q} = \left(1 + \frac{1}{1!} + \cdots + \frac{1}{q!}\right) + \left(\frac{1}{(q+1)!} + \frac{1}{(q+2)!} + \cdots\right).$$

Now multiply throughout by $q!$. In doing so, we treat the above expression as if it were a finite sum, and not an infinite series but it can be shown that in the case of a convergent series this is quite justifiable. The result is

$$p \times (q - 1)!$$

$$= (q! + \frac{q!}{1} + \frac{q!}{2} + \cdots + q + 1)$$

$$+ \frac{1}{q + 1} + \frac{1}{(q + 1)(q + 2)}$$

$$+ \frac{1}{(q + 1)(q + 2)(q + 3)} + \cdots.$$

The left-hand side is clearly an integer, and so is every term in the first bracket on the right-hand side. Hence the sum of the remaining terms is equal to the difference between two integers. This however is impossible; for the sum in question is clearly less than the corresponding sum in which each factor in each denominator is replaced by $q + 1$; and this is

$$\frac{1}{q + 1} + \frac{1}{(q + 1)^2} + \frac{1}{(q + 1)^3} + \cdots$$

or

$$\frac{1}{q + 1} \left\{ 1 + \frac{1}{(q + 1)} + \frac{1}{(q + 1)^2} + \cdots \right\}.$$

The series in the brace is simply an infinite geometrical progression, and its sum is

$$\frac{1}{1 - \frac{1}{q + 1}} = \frac{q + 1}{q}.$$

Hence the whole expression is equal to $1/q$. The corresponding sum in the previous expression has

therefore been proved on the one hand to be equal to an integer, and on the other hand to be less than $1/q$; and this is a contradiction if q is greater than 1. The assumption that e is equal to a rational number p/q is therefore false.

This is one of the simplest cases in which a number defined by such a formula can be proved to be irrational. The proof that π is irrational is considerably more difficult.

A proof that the number π is transcendental, and consequently that it is impossible to "square the circle," is given by Hobson, *Plane Trigonometry*, 4th Edn., pages 305–311. The first step in this proof consists of proving that the number e is transcendental. Anyone who had merely read this article might not suspect that there was any connection between the number e and the number π. But there is a connection, expressed by the formula $e^{i\pi} = -1$.

Proofs that π and e are transcendental are also given by Hardy and Wright, *An Introduction to the Theory of Numbers*, Chapter XI.

All this seems very remote from the original geometrical figure which gave rise to the problem of squaring the circle. It is not surprising that more than two thousand years should have elapsed between the time when this problem was proposed, and the time when it was proved to be insoluble.

Proofs of the impossibility of trisecting the angle and duplicating the cube are given by Courant and Robbins, *What Is Mathematics?* pp. 134–138.

Geometrical Constructions. The Algebra of Number Fields

Richard Courant and Herbert Robbins

Richard Courant was born in 1888 in Germany. He received his Ph.D. from Göttingen in 1910. He was associated with Göttingen from 1912 until 1933. With the rise of the Nazi regime he emigrated to the United States. From 1934 until his death in 1972, Courant worked to make New York University's Institute of Mathematical Sciences a center for mathematics as Göttingen had been before World War II.

Herbert E. Robbins was born in Pennsylvania and received his Ph.D. in mathematics from Harvard University in 1938. The recipient of a number of honors for scientific achievement, he is a professor of mathematical statistics at Columbia University and a member of the National Academy of Sciences.

As we learned in the previous essay by Titchmarsh on π and e, a number such as π is called transcendental *if it is not a root of any polynomial with whole number coefficients. It is usually most difficult to prove that a number is transcendental, and when π and e were shown to be so, the proofs were quite properly hailed as celebrated mathematical achievements. While all the details of these proofs cannot be given in a book intended for a general audience, some hint as to what was involved can be instructive. To provide such hints is one of the reasons Courant and Robbins's essay has been included in this anthology. The essay is an excerpt from the book* What Is Mathematics? *and in fact discusses much more than the transcendence of π and e.*

This essay suggests how geometrical and algebraic arguments may be used to prove the insolubility of the ancient Greek problem of trisecting the angle. It discusses the impossibility of producing a general formula for finding roots of equations greater than 5. All of this occurs in the context of geometrical constructions and comments on their meaning and interpretation in algebra. We have met both Courant and Robbins in Volume I. Courant wrote the essay on Gauss, and Robbins wrote the review of Ulam's book Adventures of a Mathematician.

Before reading the essay itself let's review a few terms. In elementary algebra it is shown that the roots of the general quadratic or second degree polynomial $ax^2 + bx + c$ are given by the formula $(-b \pm \sqrt{b^2 - 4ac})/2a$. A primitive form of this formula was known to many ancient civilizations. During the sixteenth and seventeenth centuries European mathematicians obtained formulas of the same type for the general cubic $ax^3 + bx^2 + cx + d$ and the general polynomial of degree 4 (quartic) $ax^4 + bx^3 + cx^2 + dx + e$. About 1820 the Norwegian mathematician Abel conclusively demonstrated that no such formula for the general polynomial of degree 5 can be produced. It is important to note that Abel demonstrated that it is logically *impossible to construct a formula for polynomials of degree 5 or more like the one for $ax^2 + bx + c$, not that it is difficult or has not yet been done—it* can't *be done.*

Source: Richard Courant and Herbert Robbins, "Geometrical Constructions. The Algebra of Number Fields," in *What Is Mathematics?* (Oxford University Press, 1941), pp. 104–107, 117–140. Reprinted by permission of Ernest D. Courant. (Exercise sections omitted.)

A system of numbers in which addition, multiplication, subtraction, and division (except by zero) of any two numbers can always be defined is called a field. *It is also important to note that even in a field (in fact, especially in a field) division by 0 is never allowed (defined). Thus, in a field, a divided by b is always defined except when b is 0. Notice that the integers* $\{ \ldots, -2, -1, 0, 1, 2, 3, \ldots \}$ *are* not *a field since division is not always possible; for example, 5 divided by 3 is not another integer but the fraction 5/3. The rational numbers (fractions), the real numbers, and the complex numbers are, however, all number fields.*

Introduction

Construction problems have always been a favorite subject in geometry. With ruler and compass alone a great variety of constructions may be performed, as the reader will remember from school: a line segment or an angle may be bisected, a line may be drawn from a point perpendicular to a given line, a regular hexagon may be inscribed in a circle, etc. In all these problems the ruler is used merely as a straightedge, an instrument for drawing a straight line but not for measuring or marking off distances. The traditional restriction to ruler and compass alone goes back to antiquity, although the Greeks themselves did not hesitate to use other instruments. . . .

Of all construction problems, that of constructing with ruler and compass a regular polygon of n sides has perhaps the greatest interest. For certain values of n—e.g., $n = 3, 4, 5, 6$—the solution has been known since antiquity, and forms an important part of school geometry. But for the regular heptagon ($n = 7$) the construction has been proved impossible. There are three other classical Greek problems for which a solution has been sought in vain: to trisect an arbitrary given angle, to double a given cube (i.e., to find the edge of a cube whose volume shall be twice that of a cube with a given segment as its edge) and to square the circle (i.e., to construct a square having the same area as a given circle). In all these problems, ruler and compass are the only instruments permitted.

Unsolved problems of this sort gave rise to one of the most remarkable and novel developments in mathematics, when, after centuries of futile search for solutions, the suspicion grew that these problems might be definitely unsolvable. Thus

mathematicians were challenged to investigate the question: *How is it possible to prove that certain problems cannot be solved?*

In algebra, it was the problem of solving equations of degree 5 and higher which led to this new way of thinking. During the sixteenth century mathematicians had learned that algebraic equations of degree 3 or 4 could be solved by a process similar to the elementary method for solving quadratic equations. All these methods have the following characteristic in common: the solutions or "roots" of the equation can be written as algebraic expressions obtained from the coefficients of the equation by a sequence of operations, each of which is either a rational operation—addition, subtraction, multiplication, or division—or the extraction of a square root, cube root, or fourth root. One says that algebraic equations up to the fourth degree can be solved "by radicals" (*radix* is the Latin word for *root*). Nothing seemed more natural than to extend this procedure to equations of degree 5 and higher, by using roots of higher order. All such attempts failed. Even distinguished mathematicians of the eighteenth century deceived themselves into thinking that they had found the solution. It was not until early in the nineteenth century that the Italian Ruffini (1765–1822) and the Norwegian genius N. H. Abel (1802–1829) conceived the then revolutionary idea of proving the *impossibility of the solution of the general algebraic equation of degree* n *by means of radicals*. One must clearly understand that the question is not whether any algebraic equation of degree n *possesses* solutions. This fact was first proved by Gauss in his doctoral thesis in 1799. So there is no doubt about the *existence* of the roots of an equation, especially since these roots can be found by suitable procedures to any degree of accuracy. The art of the numerical solution of equations is, of course, very important and highly developed. But the problem of Abel and Ruffini was quite different: can the solution be effected *by means of rational operations and radicals alone?* It was the desire to attain full clarity about this question that inspired the magnificent development of modern algebra and group theory started by Ruffini, Abel, and Galois (1811–1832).

The question of proving the impossibility of certain geometrical constructions provides one of the simplest examples of this trend in algebra. By the use of algebraic concepts we shall be able in this article to prove the impossibility of trisecting the angle, constructing the regular heptagon, or doubling the cube, by ruler and compass alone. (The problem of squaring the circle is much more difficult to dispose of; see p. 100.) Our point of departure will be not so much the negative question of the impossibility of certain constructions, but rather the positive question: How can all constructible problems be completely characterized? After we have answered this question, it will be an easy matter to show that the problems mentioned above do not fall into this category.

At the age of seventeen Gauss investigated the constructibility of regular "p-gons" (polygons with p sides), where p is a prime number. The construction was then known only for $p = 3$ and $p = 5$. Gauss discovered that the regular p-gon is constructible if and only if p is a prime "Fermat number,"

$$p = 2^{2^n} + 1.$$

The first Fermat numbers are 3, 5, 17, 257, 65537. So overwhelmed was young Gauss by his discovery that he at once gave up his intention of becoming a philologist and resolved to devote his life to mathematics and its applications. He always looked back on this first of his great feats with particular pride. After his death, a bronze statue of him was erected in Göttingen, and no more fitting honor could be devised than to shape the pedestal in the form of a regular 17-gon.

When dealing with a geometrical construction, one must never forget that the problem is not that of drawing figures in practice with a certain degree of accuracy, but of whether, by the use of straightedge and compass alone, the solution can be found theoretically, supposing our instruments to have perfect precision. What Gauss proved is that his constructions could be performed in principle. His theory does not concern the simplest way actually to perform them or the devices which could be used to simplify and to cut down the number of necessary steps. This is a question of much less theoretical importance. From a practical point of view, no such construction would give as satisfactory a result as could be obtained by the use of a good protractor. Failure properly to understand the theoretical character of the question of geometrical construction and stubbornness in refusing to take cognizance of well-established scientific facts are responsible for the persistence of an unending line of angle-trisector and circle-squarers. Those among them who are able to understand elementary mathematics might profit by studying this chapter.

Once more it should be emphasized that in some ways our concept of geometrical construction seems artificial. Ruler and compass are certainly the simplest instruments for drawing, but the restriction to these instruments is by no means inherent in geometry. As the Greek mathematicians recognized long ago, certain problems—for example that of doubling the cube—can be solved if, e.g., the use of a ruler in the form of a right angle is permitted; it is just as easy to invent instruments other than the compass by means of which one can draw ellipses, hyperbolas, and more complicated curves, and whose use enlarges considerably the domain of constructible figures. In the next sections, however, we shall adhere to the standard concept of geometrical constructions using only ruler and compass.

§1. Fundamental Geometrical Constructions

Construction of Fields and Square Root Extraction. To shape our general ideas we shall begin by examining a few of the classical constructions. The key to a more profound understanding lies in translating the geometrical problems into the language of algebra. Any geometrical construction problem is of the following type: a certain set of line segments, say a, b, c, . . ., is given, and one or more other segments x, y, . . ., are sought. It is always possible to formulate problems in this way, even when at first glance they have a quite different aspect. The required segments may appear as sides of a triangle to be constructed, as radii of circles, or as the rectangular coordinates of certain points . . . . For simplicity we shall suppose that only one segment x is required. The geometrical construction then amounts to solving an algebraic problem: first we must find a relationship (equation) between the required quantity x and the given quantities a, b, c, . . .; next we must find the unknown quantity x by solving this equation, and finally we must determine whether this solution can be obtained by algebraic processes that correspond to ruler and compass constructions. It is the principle of analytic geometry, the quantitative characterization of geometrical objects by real numbers, based on the introduction of the real number continuum, that provides the foundation for the whole theory.

First we observe that some of the simplest algebraic operations correspond to elementary geometrical constructions. If two segments are given with lengths a and b (as measured by a given "unit" segment), then it is very easy to construct $a + b$, $a - b$, ra (where r is any rational number), a/b, and ab.

To construct $a + b$ (Fig. 1) we draw a straight

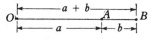

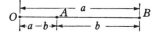

Figure 1   Construction of $a + b$ and $a - b$

line and on it mark off with the compass the distances $OA = a$ and $AB = b$. Then $OB = a + b$. Similarly, for $a - b$ we mark off $OA = a$ and $AB = b$, but this time with AB in the opposite direction from OA. Then $OB = a - b$. To construct $3a$ we simply add $a + a + a$; similarly we

can construct pa, where p is any integer. We construct $a/3$ by the following device (Fig. 2): we

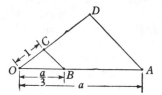

Figure 2   Construction of $a/3$

mark off $OA = a$ on one line, and draw any second line through O. On this line we mark off an arbitrary segment $OC = c$, and construct $OD = 3c$. We connect A and D, and draw a line through C parallel to AD, intersecting OA at B. The triangles OBC and OAD are similar; hence $OB/a = OB/OA = OC/OD = 1/3$, and $OB = a/3$. In the same way we can construct a/q, where q is any integer. By performing this operation on the segment pa, we can thus construct ra, where $r = p/q$ is any rational number.

To construct a/b (Fig. 3) we mark off $OB = b$

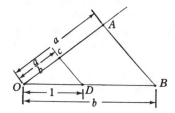

Figure 3   Construction of a/b

and $OA = a$ on the sides of any angle O, and on OB we mark off $OD = 1$. Through D we draw a line parallel to AB meeting OA in C. Then OC will have the length a/b. The construction of ab is shown in Figure 4, where AD is a line parallel to BC through A.

From these considerations it follows that *the "rational" algebraic processes*—addition, subtraction, multiplication, and division of known quantities—*can be performed by geometrical constructions*. From any given segments, measured by real numbers a, b, c, . . ., we can, by successive

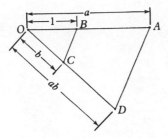

Figure 4   Construction of *ab*

application of these simple constructions, construct any quantity that is expressible in terms of *a*, *b*, *c*, . . ., in a rational way, i.e., by repeated application of addition, subtraction, multiplication and division. The totality of quantities that can be obtained in this way from *a*, *b*, *c*, . . ., constitute what is called a *number field*, a set of numbers such that any rational operations applied to two or more members of the set again yield a number of the set. We recall that the rational numbers, the real numbers, and the complex numbers form such fields. In the present case, the field is said to be *generated* by the given numbers *a*, *b*, *c*, ...

The decisive new construction which carries us beyond the field just obtained is the extraction of a square root: if a segment *a* is given, then $\sqrt{a}$ can also be constructed by using only ruler and compass. On a straight line we mark off $OA = a$ and $AB = 1$ (Fig. 5). We draw a circle with the

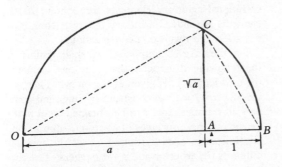

Figure 5   Construction of $\sqrt{a}$

segment *OB* as its diameter and construct the perpendicular to *OB* through *A*, which meets the circle in *C*. The triangle *OBC* has a right angle at

C, by the theorem of elementary geometry which states that an angle inscribed in a semicircle is a right angle. Hence, $\angle OCA = \angle ABC$, the right triangles *OAC* and *CAB* are similar, and we have for $x = AC$,

$$\frac{a}{x} = \frac{x}{1}, \quad x^2 = a, \quad x = \sqrt{a}.$$

Regular Polygons.   Let us now consider a few somewhat more elaborate construction problems. We begin with the *regular decagon*. Suppose that a regular decagon is inscribed in a circle with radius 1 (Fig. 6), and call its side *x*. Since *x* will

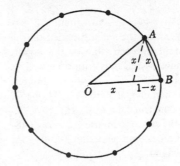

Figure 6   Regular decagon

subtend an angle of 36° at the center of the circle, the other two angles of the large triangle will each be 72°, and hence the dotted line which bisects angle *A* divides triangle *OAB* into two isosceles triangles, each with equal sides of length *x*. The radius of the circle is thus divided into two segments, *x* and $1 - x$. Since *OAB* is similar to the smaller isosceles triangle, we have $1/x = x/(1 - x)$. From this proportion we get the quadratic equation $x^2 + x - 1 = 0$, the solution of which is $x = (\sqrt{5} - 1)/2$. (The other solution of the equation is irrevelant, since it yields a negative *x*.) From this it is clear that *x* can be constructed geometrically. Having the length *x*, we may now construct the regular decagon by marking off this length ten times as a chord of the circle. The regular pentagon may now be constructed by joining alternate vertices of the regular decagon.

Instead of constructing $\sqrt{5}$ by the method of Figure 5 we can also obtain it as the hypotenuse of a right triangle whose other sides have lengths 1 and 2. We then obtain x by subtracting the unit length from $\sqrt{5}$ and bisecting the result.

The ratio $OB:AB$ of the preceding problem has been called the golden ratio, because the Greek mathematicians considered a rectangle whose two sides are in this ratio to be aesthetically the most pleasing. Its value, incidentally, is about 1.62.

Of all the regular polygons the hexagon (Fig. 7) is simplest to construct. We start with a circle of radius r; the length of the side of a regular hexagon inscribed in this circle will then be equal to r. The hexagon itself can be constructed by successively marking off from any point of the circle chords of length r until all six vertices are obtained.

From the regular n-gon we can obtain the regular $2n$-gon by bisecting the arc subtended on the circumscribed circle by each edge of the n-gon, using the additional points thus found as well as the original vertices for the required $2n$-gon. Starting with the diameter of a circle (a "2-gon"), we can therefore construct the 4, 8, 16, . . ., 2^n-gon. Similarly, we can obtain the 12-, 24-, 48-gon, etc., from the hexagon, and the 20-, 40-gon, etc., from the decagon. . . .

The results obtained thus far exhibit the following characteristic feature: *The sides of the 2^n-gon, the $5\cdot2^n$-gon, and the $3\cdot2^n$-gon, can all be found entirely by the processes of addition, subtraction, multiplication, division, and the extraction of square roots.* . . .

§2. Constructible Numbers and Number Fields

General Theory.   Our previous discussion indicates the general algebraic background of geometrical constructions. Every ruler and compass construction consists of a sequence of steps, each of which is one of the following: (1) connecting two points by a straight line, (2) finding the point of intersection of two lines, (3) drawing a circle with a given radius about a point, (4) finding the points of intersection of a circle with another circle or with a line. An element (point, line, or circle) is considered to be known if it was given at

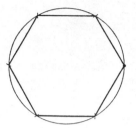

Figure 7   Regular hexagon

the outset or if it has been constructed in some previous step. For a theoretical analysis we may refer the whole construction to a coordinate system x, y. The given elements will then be represented by points or segments in the x, y plane. If only one segment is given at the outset, we may take this as the unit length, which fixes the point $x = 1$, $y = 0$. Sometimes there appear "arbitrary" elements: arbitrary lines are drawn, arbitrary points or radii are chosen. (An example of such an arbitrary element appears in constructing the midpoint of a segment; we draw two circles of equal but arbitrary radius from each endpoint of the segment, and join their intersections.) In such cases we may choose the element to be rational; i.e., arbitrary points may be chosen with rational coordinates x, y, arbitrary lines $ax + by + c = 0$ with rational coefficients a, b, c, arbitrary circles with centers having rational coordinates and with rational radii. We shall make such a choice of rational arbitrary elements throughout; if the elements are indeed arbitrary this restriction cannot affect the result of a construction.

For the sake of simplicity, we shall assume in the following discussion that only one element, the unit length 1, is given at the outset. Then according to §1 we can construct by ruler and compass all numbers that can be obtained from unity by the rational processes of addition, subtraction, multiplication and division, i.e., all the rational numbers r/s, where r and s are integers. The system of rational numbers is "closed" with respect to the rational operations; that is, the sum, difference, product, or quotient of any two rational numbers—excluding division by 0, as always—is again a rational number. Any set of numbers possessing this property of closure with respect to the four rational operations is called a *number field*.

Starting from the unit, we can thus construct the whole rational number field and hence all the rational points (i.e., points with both coordinates rational) in the x, y plane. We can reach new, irrational numbers by using the compass to construct, for example, the number $\sqrt{2}$ which . . . is not in the rational field. Having constructed $\sqrt{2}$ we may then, by the "rational" constructions of §1, find all numbers of the form

$$a + b\sqrt{2}, \tag{1}$$

where a, b are rational, and therefore are themselves constructible. We may likewise construct all numbers of the form

$$\frac{a + b\sqrt{2}}{c + d\sqrt{2}} \quad \text{or} \quad (a + b\sqrt{2})(c + d\sqrt{2}),$$

where a, b, c, d are rational. These numbers, however, may always be written in the form (1). For we have

$$\frac{a + b\sqrt{2}}{c + d\sqrt{2}} = \frac{a + b\sqrt{2}}{c + d\sqrt{2}} \cdot \frac{c - d\sqrt{2}}{c - d\sqrt{2}}$$

$$= \frac{ac - 2bd}{c^2 - 2d^2} + \frac{bc - ad}{c^2 - 2d^2}\sqrt{2} = p + q\sqrt{2},$$

where p, q are rational. (The denominator $c^2 - 2d^2$ cannot be zero, for if $c^2 - 2d^2 = 0$, then $\sqrt{2} = c/d$, contrary to the fact that $\sqrt{2}$ is irrational.) Likewise

$$(a + b\sqrt{2})(c + d\sqrt{2})$$
$$= (ac + 2bd) + (bc + ad)\sqrt{2} = r + s\sqrt{2},$$

where r, s are rational. Hence all that we reach by the construction of $\sqrt{2}$ is the set of numbers of the form (1), with arbitrary rational a, b.

These numbers (1) again form a field, as the preceding discussion shows. (That the sum and difference of two numbers of the form (1) are also of the form (1) is obvious.) This field is larger than the rational field, which is a part or *subfield* of it. But, of course, it is smaller than the field of *all* real numbers. Let us call the rational field F_0 and the new field of numbers of the form (1), F_1. The constructibility of every number in the "extension field" F_1 has been established. We may now extend the scope of our constructions, e.g., by taking a number of F_1, say $k = 1 + \sqrt{2}$, and

extracting the square root, thus obtaining the constructible number

$$\sqrt{1 + \sqrt{2}} = \sqrt{k},$$

and with it, according to §1, the field consisting of all the numbers

$$p + q\sqrt{k}, \tag{2}$$

where now p and q may be arbitrary numbers of F_1, i.e., of the form $a + b\sqrt{2}$, *with a, b*, in F_0, i.e., rational.

Now let us assume more generally that we are able to construct all the numbers of some number field F. We shall show that *the use of the ruler alone will never lead us out of the field* F. The equation of the straight line through two points whose coordinates a_1, b_1 and a_2, b_2 are in F is $(b_1 - b_2)x + (a_2 - a_1)y + (a_1b_2 - a_2b_1) = 0$; its coefficients are rational expressions formed from numbers in F, and therefore, by definition of a field, are themselves in F. Moreover, if we have two lines, $\alpha x + \beta y - \gamma = 0$ and $\alpha'x + \beta'y - \gamma' = 0$, with coefficients in F, then the coordinates of their point of intersection, found by solving these two simultaneous equations, are $x = (\gamma\beta' - \beta\gamma')/(\alpha\beta' - \beta\alpha')$, $y = (\alpha\gamma' - \gamma\alpha')/(\alpha\beta' - \beta\alpha')$. Since these are likewise numbers of F, it is clear that the use of the ruler alone cannot take us beyond the confines of the field F.

We can only break through the walls of F by using the compass. For this purpose we select an element k of F which is such that $\sqrt{k}$ is not in F. Then we can construct $\sqrt{k}$ and therefore all the numbers

$$a + b\sqrt{k}, \tag{3}$$

where a and b are rational, or even arbitrary elements of F. The sum and the difference of two numbers $a + b\sqrt{k}$ and $c + d\sqrt{k}$, their product, $(a + b\sqrt{k})(c + d\sqrt{k}) = (ac + kbd) + (ad + bc)\sqrt{k}$, and their quotient,

$$\frac{a + b\sqrt{k}}{c + d\sqrt{k}} = \frac{(a + b\sqrt{k})(c - d\sqrt{k})}{c^2 - kd^2}$$

$$= \frac{ac - kbd}{c^2 - kd^2} + \frac{bc - ad}{c^2 - kd^2}\sqrt{k},$$

are again of the form $p + q\sqrt{k}$ with p and q in F. (The denominator $c^2 - kd^2$ cannot vanish unless c and d are both zero; for otherwise we would have $\sqrt{k} = c/d$, a number in F, contrary to the assumption that $\sqrt{k}$ is not in F.) Hence the set of numbers of the form $a + b\sqrt{k}$ forms a field F'. The field F' contains the original field F, for we may, in particular, choose $b = 0$. F' is called an *extension field* of F, and F a *subfield* of F'.

As an example, let F be the field $a + b\sqrt{2}$ with rational a, b, and take $k = \sqrt{2}$. Then the numbers of the extension field F' are represented by $p + q\sqrt[4]{2}$, where p and q are in F, $p = a + b\sqrt{2}$, $q = a' + b'\sqrt{2}$, with rational a, b, a', b'. Any number in F' can be reduced to that form; for example

$$\frac{1}{\sqrt{2} + \sqrt[4]{2}} = \frac{\sqrt{2} - \sqrt[4]{2}}{(\sqrt{2} + \sqrt[4]{2})(\sqrt{2} - \sqrt[4]{2})}$$

$$= \frac{\sqrt{2} - \sqrt[4]{2}}{2 - \sqrt{2}}$$

$$= \frac{\sqrt{2}}{2 - \sqrt{2}} - \frac{\sqrt[4]{2}}{2 - \sqrt{2}}$$

$$= \frac{\sqrt{2}(2 + \sqrt{2})}{4 - 2} - \frac{(2 + \sqrt{2})}{4 - 2}\sqrt[4]{2}$$

$$= (1 + \sqrt{2}) - (1 + \tfrac{1}{2}\sqrt{2})\sqrt[4]{2}$$

We have seen that if we start with any field F of constructible numbers containing the number k, then by use of the ruler and a single application of the compass we can construct $\sqrt{k}$ and hence any number of the form $a + b\sqrt{k}$, where a, b, are in F.

We now show, conversely, that by a single application of the compass we can obtain *only* numbers of this form. For what the compass does in a construction is to define points (or their coordinates) as points of intersection of a circle with a straight line, or of two circles. A circle with center ξ, η and radius r has the equation $(x - \xi)^2 + (y - \eta)^2 = r^2$; hence, if ξ, η, r are in F, the equation of the circle can be written in the form

$$x^2 + y^2 + 2\alpha x + 2\beta y + \gamma = 0,$$

with the coefficients α, β, γ in F. A straight line,

$$ax + by + c = 0,$$

joining any two points whose coordinates are in F, has coefficients a, b, c in F, as we have seen on page 95. By eliminating y from these simultaneous equations, we obtain for the x-coordinate of a point of intersection of the circle and line a

quadratic equation of the form

$$Ax^2 + Bx + C = 0,$$

with coefficients A, B, C in F (explicitly: $A = a^2 + b^2$, $B = 2(ac + b^2\alpha - ab\beta)$, $C = c^2 - 2bc\beta + b^2\gamma$). The solution is given by the formula

$$x = \frac{-B \pm \sqrt{B^2 - 4AC}}{2A},$$

which is of the form $p + q\sqrt{k}$, with p, q, k in F. A similar formula holds for the y-coordinate of a point of intersection.

Again, if we have two circles,

$$x^2 + y^2 + 2\alpha x + 2\beta y + \gamma = 0,$$
$$x^2 + y^2 + 2\alpha' x + 2\beta' y + \gamma' = 0,$$

then by subtracting the second equation from the first we obtain the linear equation

$$2(\alpha - \alpha')x + 2(\beta - \beta')y + (\gamma - \gamma') = 0,$$

which may be solved with the equation of the first circle as before. In either case, the construction yields the x- and y- coordinates of either one or two new points, and these new quantities are of the form $p + q\sqrt{k}$, with p, q, k in F. In particular, of course, $\sqrt{k}$ may itself belong to F, e.g., when $k = 4$. Then the construction does not yield anything essentially new, and we remain in F. But in general this will not be the case.

Summarizing again: If certain quantities are given at the outset, then we can construct with a straightedge alone all the quantities in the field F generated by rational processes from the given quantities. Using the compass we can then extend the field F of constructible quantities to a wider extension field by selecting any number k of F, extracting the square root of k, and constructing the field F' consisting of the numbers $a + b\sqrt{k}$, where a and b are in F. F is called a subfield of F'; all quantities in F are also contained in F', since in the expression $a + b\sqrt{k}$ we may choose $b = 0$. (It is assumed that $\sqrt{k}$ is a new number not lying in F, since otherwise the process of adjunction of $\sqrt{k}$ would not lead to anything new, and F' would be identical with F.) We have shown that any step in a geometrical construction (drawing a line through two known points, drawing a circle with known center and radius, or marking the intersection of two known lines or circles) will either produce new quantities lying in the field already known to consist of constructible numbers, or, by the construction of a square root, will open up a new extension field of constructible numbers.

The totality of all constructible numbers can now be described with precision. We start with a given field F_0, defined by whatever quantities are given at the outset, e.g., the field of rational numbers if only a single segment, chosen as the unit, is given. Next, by the adjunction of $\sqrt{k_0}$, where k_0 is in F_0, but $\sqrt{k_0}$ is not, we construct an extension field F_1 of constructible numbers, consisting of all numbers of the form $a_0 + b_0\sqrt{k_0}$, where a_0 and b_0 may be any numbers of F_0. Then F_2, a new extension field of F_1, is defined by the numbers $a_1 + b_1\sqrt{k_1}$, where a_1 and b_1 are any numbers of F_1, and k_1 is some number of F_1 whose square root does not lie in F_1. Repeating this procedure, we shall reach a field F_n after n adjunctions of square roots. *Constructible numbers are those and only those which can be reached by such a sequence of extension fields; that is, which lie in a field F_n of the type described.* The size of the number n of necessary extensions does not matter; in a way it measures the degree of complexity of the problem.

The following example may illustrate the process. We want to reach the number

$$\sqrt{6 + \sqrt{\sqrt{\sqrt{1 + \sqrt{2}} + \sqrt{3}} + 5}}.$$

Let F_0 denote the rational field. Putting $k_0 = 2$, we obtain the field F_1, which contains the number $1 + \sqrt{2}$. We now take $k_1 = 1 + \sqrt{2}$ and $k_2 = 3$. As a matter of fact, 3 is the original field F_0, and a fortiori in the field F_2, so that it is perfectly permissible to take $k_2 = 3$. We then take $k_3 = \sqrt{1 + \sqrt{2}} + \sqrt{3}$, and finally $k_4 = (\sqrt{1 + \sqrt{2}} + \sqrt{3} + 5)^{1/2}$. The field F_5 thus constructed contains the desired number, for $\sqrt{6}$ is also in F_5, since $\sqrt{2}$ and $\sqrt{3}$, and therefore their product, are in F_3 and therefore also in F_5.

§3. The Unsolvability of the Three Greek Problems

Doubling the Cube.   Now we are well prepared to investigate the old problems of trisecting the angle, doubling the cube, and constructing the regular heptagon. We consider first the problem of doubling the cube. If the given cube has an edge of unit length, its volume will be the cubic unit; it is required that we find the edge x of a cube with twice this volume. The required edge x will therefore satisfy the simple cubic equation

$$x^3 - 2 = 0. \tag{1}$$

Our proof that this number x cannot be constructed by ruler and compass alone is indirect. We assume tentatively that a construction is possible. According to the preceding discussion this means that x lies in some field F_k obtained, as above, from the rational field by successive extensions through adjunction of square roots. As we shall show, this assumption leads to an absurd consequence.

We already know that x cannot lie in the rational field F_0, for $\sqrt[3]{2}$ is an irrational number. Hence x can only lie in some extension field F_k, where k is a positive integer. We may as well assume that k is the *least* positive integer such that x lies in some F_k. It follows that x can be written in the form

$$x = p + q\sqrt{w},$$

where p, q, and w belong to some F_{k-1}, but $\sqrt{w}$ does not. Now, by a simple but important type of algebraic reasoning, we shall show that if $x = p + q\sqrt{w}$ is a solution of the cubic equation (1), then $y = p - q\sqrt{w}$ is also a solution. Since x is in the field F_k, x^3 and $x^3 - 2$ are also in F_k, and we have

$$x^3 - 2 = a + b\sqrt{w}, \tag{2}$$

where a and b are in F_{k-1}. By an easy calculation we can show that $a = p^3 + 3pq^2w - 2$, $b = 3p^2q + q^3w$. If we put

$$y = p - q\sqrt{w},$$

then a substitution of $-q$ for q in these expressions for a and b shows that

$$y^3 - 2 = a - b\sqrt{w}. \tag{2'}$$

Now x was supposed to be a root of $x^3 - 2 = 0$, hence

$$a + b\sqrt{w} = 0. \tag{3}$$

This implies—and here is the key to the argument—that a and b must both be zero. If b were not zero, we would infer from (3) that $\sqrt{w} = -a/b$. But then $\sqrt{w}$ would be a number of the field F_{k-1} in which a and b lie, contrary to our assumption. Hence $b = 0$, and it follows immediately from (3) that $a = 0$ also.

Now that we have shown that $a = b = 0$, we immediately infer from (2') that $y = p - q\sqrt{w}$ is also a solution of the cubic equation (1), since $y^3 - 2$ is equal to zero. Furthermore, $y \neq x$, i.e., $x - y \neq 0$; for, $x - y = 2q\sqrt{w}$ can only vanish if $q = 0$; and if this were so then $x = p$ would lie in F_{k-1}, contrary to our assumption.

We have therefore shown that, if $x = p + q\sqrt{w}$ is a root of the cubic equation (1), then $y = p - q\sqrt{w}$ is a different root of this equation. This leads immediately to a contradiction. For there is only one real number x which is a cube root of 2, the other cube roots of 2 being imaginary; $y = p - q\sqrt{w}$ is obviously real, since p, q, and $\sqrt{w}$ were real.

Thus our basic assumption has led to an absurdity, and hence is proved to be wrong; a solution of (1) cannot lie in a field F_k, so that doubling the cube by ruler and compass is impossible.

A Theorem on Cubic Equations. Our concluding algebraic argument was especially adapted to the particular problem at hand. If we want to dispose of the two other Greek problems, it is desirable to proceed on a more general basis. All three problems depend algebraically on cubic equations. It is a fundamental fact concerning the cubic equation

$$z^3 + az^2 + bz + c = 0 \qquad (4)$$

that, if x_1, x_2, x_3 are the three roots of this equation, then

$$x_1 + x_2 + x_3 = -a.\textbf{*} \qquad (5)$$

*The polynomial $z^3 + az^2 + bz + c$ may be factored into the product $(z - x_1)(z - x_2)(z - x_3)$, where x_1, x_2, x_3, are the three roots of the equation (4). Hence, $z^3 + az^2 + bz + c = z^3 - (x_1 + x_2 + x_3)z^2 + (x_1x_2 + x_1x_3 + x_2x_3)z - x_1x_2x_3$, so that, since the coefficient of each power of z must be the same on both sides,

$$-a = x_1 + x_2 + x_3, \qquad b = x_1x_2 + x_1x_3 + x_2x_3,$$
$$-c = x_1x_2x_3.$$

Let us consider any cubic equation (4) where the coefficients a, b, c are rational numbers. It may be that one of the roots of the equation is rational; for example, the equation $x^3 - 1 = 0$ has the rational root 1, while the two other roots, given by the quadratic equation $x^2 + x + 1 = 0$, are necessarily imaginary. But we can easily prove the general theorem: *If a cubic equation with rational coefficients has no rational root, then none of its roots is constructible starting from the rational field F_0.*

Again we give the proof by an indirect method. Suppose x were a constructible root of (4). Then x would lie in the last field F_k of some chain of extension fields, $F_0, F_1, \cdots, F_k$, as above. We may assume that k is the *smallest* integer such that a root of the cubic equation (4) lies in an extension field F_k. Certainly k must be greater than zero, since in the statement of the theorem it is assumed that no root x lies in the rational field F_0. Hence x can be written in the form

$$x = p + q\sqrt{w},$$

where p, q, w are in the preceding field, F_{k-1}, but $\sqrt{w}$ is not. It follows, exactly as for the special equation, $z^3 - 2 = 0$, of the preceding article, that another number of F_k,

$$y = p - q\sqrt{w},$$

will also be a root of the equation (4). As before, we see that $q \neq 0$ and hence $x \neq y$.

From (5) we know that the third root u of equation (4) is given by $u = -a - x - y$. But since $x + y = 2p$, this means that

$$u = -a - 2p,$$

where $\sqrt{w}$ has disappeared, so that u is a number in the field F_{k-1}. This contradicts the hypothesis that k is the *smallest* number such that some F_k contains a root of (4). Hence the hypothesis is absurd, and no root of (4) can lie in such a field F_k. The general theorem is proved. On the basis of this theorem, a construction by ruler and compass alone is proved to be impossible if the algebraic equivalent of the problem is the solution of a cubic equation with no rational roots. This equivalence was at once obvious for the problem of doubling the cube, and will now be established for the other two Greek problems.

Trisecting the Angle.   We shall now prove that the trisection of the angle by ruler and compass alone is *in general* impossible. Of course, there are angles, such as 90° and 180°, for which the trisection can be performed. What we have to show is that the trisection cannot be effected by a procedure valid for *every* angle. For the proof, it is quite sufficient to exhibit only one angle that cannot be trisected, since a valid *general method* would have to cover every single example. Hence the non-existence of a general method will be proved if we can demonstrate, for example, that the angle 60° cannot be trisected by ruler and compass alone.

We can obtain an algebraic equivalent of this problem in different ways; the simplest is to consider an angle θ as given by its cosine: $\cos \theta = g$. Then the problem is equivalent to that of finding the quantity $x = \cos (\theta/3)$. By a simple trigonometrical formula, the cosine of $\theta/3$ is connected with that of θ by the equation

$$\cos \theta = g = 4 \cos^3 (\theta/3) - 3 \cos (\theta/3).$$

In other words, the problem of trisecting the angle θ with $\cos \theta = g$ amounts to constructing a solution of the cubic equation

$$4z^3 - 3z - g = 0. \qquad (6)$$

To show that this cannot in general be done, we take $\theta = 60°$, so that $g = \cos 60° = 1/2$. Equation (6) then becomes

$$8z^3 - 6z = 1. \qquad (7)$$

By virtue of the theorem proved in the preceding article, we need only show that this equation has no rational root. Let $v = 2z$. Then the equation becomes

$$v^3 - 3v = 1. \qquad (8)$$

If there were a rational number $v = r/s$ satisfying this equation, where r and s are integers without a common factor > 1, we should have $r^3 - 3s^2r = s^3$. From this it follows that $s^3 = r(r^2 - 3s^2)$ is divisible by r, which means that r and s have a common factor unless $r = \pm 1$. Likewise, s^2 is a factor of $r^3 = s^2(s + 3r)$, which means that r and s have a common factor unless $s = \pm 1$. Since we assumed that r and s had no common factor, we have shown that the only rational numbers which could possibly satisfy equation (8) are $+1$ or -1. By substituting $+1$ and -1 for v in equation (8) we see that neither value satisfies it. Hence (8), and consequently (7), has no rational root, and the impossibility of trisecting the angle is proved.

The theorem that the general angle cannot be trisected with ruler and compass alone is true only when the ruler is regarded as an instrument for drawing a straight line through any two given points and *nothing else*. In our general characterization of constructible numbers the use of the ruler was always limited to this operation only. By permitting other uses of the ruler the totality of possible constructions may be greatly extended. The following method for trisecting the angle, found in the works of Archimedes, is a good example.

Let an arbitrary angle x be given, as in Figure 8. Extend the base of the angle to the left, and swing a semicircle with O as center and arbitrary radius r. Mark two points A and B on the edge of the ruler such that $AB = r$. Keeping the point B on the semicircle, slide the ruler into the position where A lies on the extended base of the angle x, while the edge of the ruler passes through the intersection of the terminal side of the angle x with the semicircle about O. With the ruler in this position draw a straight line, making an angle y with the extended base of the original angle x. [It is an elementary exercise to show that y is $x/3$ and hence is the angle trisection.]

The Regular Heptagon.   We shall now consider the problem of finding the side x of a regular heptagon inscribed in the unit circle. The simplest way to dispose of this problem is by means

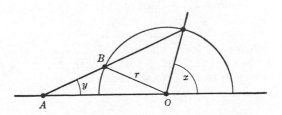

Figure 8   Archimedes' trisection of an angle

of complex numbers. We know that the vertices of the heptagon are given by the roots of the equation

$$z^7 - 1 = 0, \tag{9}$$

the coordinates x, y of the vertices being considered as the real and imaginary parts of complex numbers $z = x + yi$. One root of this equation is $z = 1$, and the others are the roots of the equation

$$(z^7 - 1)/(z - 1)$$
$$= z^6 + z^5 + z^4 + z^3 + z^2 + z + 1 = 0, \tag{10}$$

obtained from (9) by factoring out $z - 1$. Dividing (10) by z^3, we obtain the equation

$$z^3 + 1/z^3 + z^2 + 1/z^2$$
$$+ z + 1/z + 1 = 0. \tag{11}$$

By a simple algebraic transformation this may be written in the form

$$(z + 1/z)^3 - 3(z + 1/z) + (z + 1/z)^2$$
$$- 2 + (z + 1/z) + 1 = 0. \tag{12}$$

Denoting the quantity $z + 1/z$ by y, we find from (12) that

$$y^3 + y^2 - 2y - 1 = 0. \tag{13}$$

We know that z, the seventh root of unity, is given by

$$z = \cos \phi + i \sin \phi, \tag{14}$$

where $\phi = 360°/7$ is the angle subtended at the center of the circle by the edge of the regular heptagon; likewise we know . . . that $1/z = \cos \phi - i \sin \phi$, so that $y = z + 1/z = 2 \cos \phi$. If we can construct y, we can also construct $\cos \phi$, and conversely. Hence, if we can prove that y is not constructible, we shall at the same time show that z, and therefore the heptagon, is not constructible. Thus, considering the theorem of p. 98, it remains merely to show that the equation (13) has no rational roots. This, too, is proved indirectly. Assume that (13) has a rational root r/s, where r and s are integers having no common factor. Then we have

$$r^3 + r^2 s - 2rs^2 - s^3 = 0; \tag{15}$$

whence it is seen as above that r^3 has the factor s, and s^3 the factor r. Since r and s have no common factor, each must be ± 1; therefore y can have only the possible values $+1$ and -1, if it is to be rational. On substituting these numbers in the equation, we see that neither of them satisfies it. Hence y, and therefore the edge of the regular heptagon, is not constructible.

Remarks on the Problem of Squaring the Circle. We have been able to dispose of the problems of doubling the cube, trisecting the angle, and constructing the regular heptagon, by comparatively elementary methods. The problem of squaring the circle is much more difficult and requires the technique of advanced mathematical analysis. Since a circle with radius r has the area πr^2, the problem of constructing a square with area equal to that of a given circle whose radius is the unit length 1 amounts to the construction of a segment of length $\sqrt{\pi}$ as the edge of the required square. This segment will be constructible if and only if the number π is constructible. In the light of our general characterization of constructible numbers, we could show the impossibility of squaring the circle by showing that the number π cannot be contained in any field F_k that can be reached by the successive adjunction of square roots to the rational field F_0. Since all the members of any such field are algebraic numbers, i.e., numbers that satisfy algebraic equations with integer coefficients, it will be sufficient if the number π can be shown to be not algebraic, i.e., to be transcendental.

The technique necessary for proving that π is a transcendental number was created by Charles Hermite (1822–1905), who proved the number e to be transcendental. By a slight extension of Hermite's method F. Lindemann succeeded (1882) in proving the transcendence of π, and thus definitely settled the age-old question of squaring the circle. The proof is within the reach of the student of advanced analysis, but is beyond the scope of this [article].

Bicycle Tubes Inside Out

Herbert Taylor

Herbert Taylor was associated with the University of Southern California at the time this article was written.

This essay is rather in the nature of a time-out, a brief respite that requires no special terminology or any previous mathematical training; in fact the less formal mathematical education, the better. Taylor tries to get the reader to visualize a rather complicated and surprising transformation of a linked figure into an unlinked one. It is not a trivial task and the ideas underlying this apparently elementary puzzle come from topology, one of the most fertile and profound areas of modern mathematics. Readers who find that they are talented in this kind of visualization perhaps should study topology. There are a variety of challenging and as yet unsolved problems in topology just waiting for someone to visualize them in the right way.

THE OLD RUBBER sheet geometry discussed surfaces which could be bent, stretched, or twisted, while they were kept smooth and whole. One popular topological pastime is to try to visualize what a bicycle tube would look like turned inside out. As far as I know, these curiosities have no serious implications for mathematics, but they can be used to cultivate flexibility in visual thinking.

Let us start by moving the surface of Figure 1a to that of Figure 1b as an example. The reader is asked to visualize, or draw, a sequence of pictures moving Figure 1a to Figure 1b, without cutting, and without letting one part of the surface touch another part. Figure 1c is a possible sequence.

The next exercise involves cutting a temporary hole in the surface. Instead of merely turning a bicycle tube inside out, how about turning a more complicated surface inside out? It will soon be apparent that the mildly complicated Figure 2a could become very complicated, so, to simplify things we paint the inside black, and the outside gray. We are going to cut a small hole in the surface temporarily and put a rim on the hole to keep track of it.

Figure 2b shows a sequence for turning the surface inside out; shrinking the complicated part, and passing it through the hole.

After the hole is closed up, the black will cover the whole outside, whereas it formerly covered the whole inside. An advantage of the method of turning surfaces inside out, just pictured, is evident in Figure 3. This method makes it just as easy to see what happens to a sphere with many handles when it is turned inside out as to see what happens to the bicycle tube.

The last sequence will aim for a simple picture of what Figure 4 will look like, after one of the two linked surfaces is turned inside out.

These pictorial ideas are not new. They occurred to me 25 years ago, and perhaps to several people before that. The twister of Figure 5 was posed recently by Dennis L. Johnson, who is well-versed in the theory of knots. Now the reader is invited to finish up with a little light exercise, moving from Figure 5a to Figure 5b in the same fashion as 1a to 1b was done.

Source: Herbert Taylor, "Bicycle Tubes Inside Out," in David A. Klarner, ed. *The Mathematical Gardner,* 1981, pp. 75–78. Reprinted by permission of Wadsworth International Group.

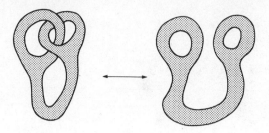

Figure 1a   Figure 1b

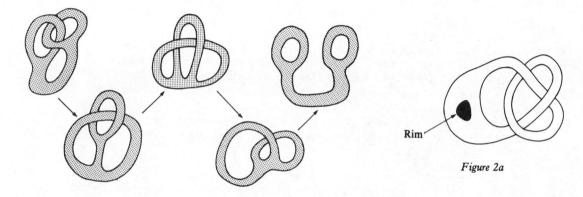

Figure 1c

Rim

Figure 2a

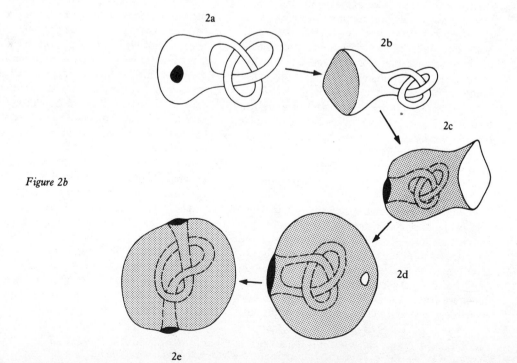

2a

2b

2c

Figure 2b

2d

2e

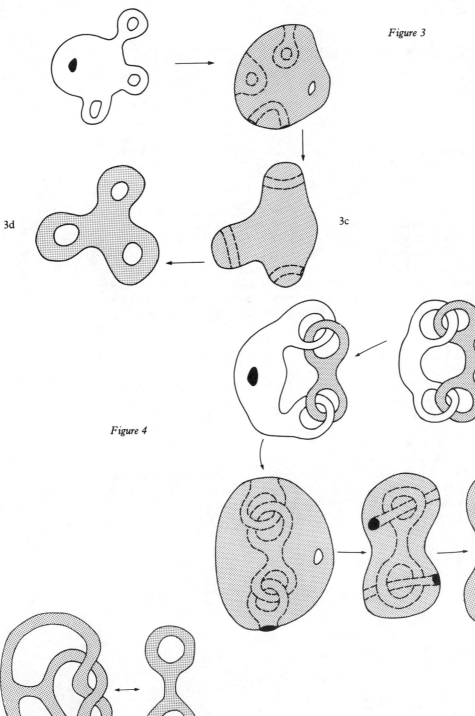

3a

3b

Figure 3

3d

3c

Figure 4

Figure 5a   *Figure 5b*

The Calculus According to Newton and Leibniz

C. H. Edwards, Jr.

Charles Henry Edwards, Jr., was born in Tennessee and did his undergraduate and graduate work at the University of Tennessee. A Sloan fellow and a member of the Institute for Advanced Study at Princeton, he is currently professor of mathematics at the University of Georgia.

If there is an event that marked the coming of age of mathematics in Western culture, it must surely be the essentially simultaneous development of the calculus by Newton and Leibniz in the seventeenth century. Before this remarkable synthesis mathematics had often been viewed as merely a strange but harmless pursuit, indulged in by those with an excess of leisure time. After the calculus, mathematics became virtually the only acceptable language for describing the physical universe. This view of mathematics and its association with the scientific method has come to dominate the Western view of how the world ought to be explained. This domination is so complete that it is virtually impossible for us to understand how earlier cultures explained what happened around them.

One might naturally suppose that an event so momentous must involve ideas so profound that average mortals can hardly hope to comprehend them. In fact, nothing could be further from the truth. The essential ideas of calculus—the derivative and the integral—are quite straightforward and had been known prior to either Newton or Leibniz. The contribution of Newton and Leibniz was to recognize that the idea of finding tangents (the derivative) and the idea of finding areas (the integral) are related and that this relation can be used to give a simple and unified description of both processes. When calculus is described in this way one might wonder what all the fuss is about.

Needless to say, the techniques of actually relating the two processes are nontrivial and may require extensive calculations. Nevertheless, the idea that the two processes are related is simple to state. Since there are an infinite number of ideas floating around, one must still stand in awe of Newton's and Leibniz's discovery that the two apparently unrelated processes of finding slopes and finding areas are in fact intimately related and that one process can be used to understand the other.

Hence, wondering what all the fuss is about is a fair response until the capacity of pre-scientific societies to control and predict physical nature is compared with the capacity of our modern society. From that perspective, one can understand why the invention of the calculus may be the single most important intellectual achievement of the seventeenth century.

Source: C. H. Edwards, Jr., excerpts from "The Calculus According to Newton" and "The Calculus According to Leibniz," in *The Historical Development of the Calculus* (Springer-Verlag, 1979), pp. 189–191, 231–234, 264–267. (Some references and exercise sections omitted.)

The Calculus According to Newton

The Discovery of the Calculus.   When we say that the calculus was discovered by Newton and Leibniz in the late seventeenth century, we do *not* mean simply that effective methods were then discovered for the solution of problems involving tangents and quadratures. For . . . such problems had been studied with some success since antiquity, and with conspicuous success during the half century preceding the time of Newton and Leibniz.

The previous solutions of tangent and area problems invariably involved the application of special methods to particular problems. As successful as were, for example, the different tangent methods of Fermat and Roberval, neither developed them into general algorithmic procedures. Between these special techniques for the solution of individual problems, and the general methods of the calculus for the solution of whole classes of related problems, we today may see only a moderate gap, but it was one that Fermat and Roberval and their early seventeenth century contemporaries saw no reason to attempt to bridge.

What is involved here is the difference between the mere discovery of an important fact, and the recognition that it *is* important—that is, that it provides the basis for further progress. In mathematics, the recognition of the significance of a concept ordinarily involves its embodiment in new terminology or notation that facilitates its application in further investigations. As Hadamard remarks, "The creation of a word or a notation for a class of ideas may be, and often is, a scientific fact of very great importance, because it means connecting these ideas together in our subsequent thought."[1]

For example, we have seen that Fermat constructed the difference $f(A + E) - f(A)$, noted that (for the polynomial functions he dealt with) it contained E as a factor, divided by E, and finally cancelled every term still containing E as a factor, thereby obtaining the quantity

$$\frac{f(A + E) - f(A)}{E}\bigg|_{E = 0}$$

Of course we now call this quantity the derivative, and denote it by $f'(A)$. But Fermat did not

call it anything, nor introduce any particular notation for it. If he had, the way would have been open for general applications, and he might have been (as he has been erroneously called) at least a co-discoverer of the differential calculus.

Perhaps the most clear-cut example in the history of calculus, between discovery and the recognition of significance, is provided by the "fundamental theorem of calculus," which explicitly states the inverse relationship between tangent and area problems (or, in modern terminology, between differentiation and integration). This relationship was implicit (if not conspicuous) in the results of the early seventeenth century area computations . . . e.g., the area under the curve $y = x^n$ over the interval $[0, x]$ is $x^{n+1}/(n + 1)$, while the slope of the tangent line to the curve $y = x^{n+1}/(n + 1)$ is x^n. Indeed, Barrow stated and proved a geometric theorem that clearly enunciated the inverse relationship between tangents and quadratures. However, he failed to recognize that his "fundamental theorem" provided the basis for "a new subject characterized by a distinctive method of procedure."[2] The contribution of Newton and Leibniz, for which they are properly credited as the discoverers of the calculus, was not merely that they recognized the "fundamental theorem of calculus" as a mathematical fact, but that they employed it to distill from the rich amalgam of earlier infinitesimal techniques a powerful algorithmic instrument for systematic calculation.

Isaac Newton (1642–1727).   Newton was born on Christmas Day in 1642. Nothing that is known about his youth and early education heralded the fact that his life and work would mark a new age in the intellectual history of mankind. He entered Cambridge in the summer of 1661 and received his B.A. early in 1665. Upon Barrow's retirement as Lucasian Professor in 1669, Newton was elected as his successor, and remained at Cambridge until 1696, when he left for London to serve as Warden of the Mint. Upon his death in 1727 he was buried in Westminster Abbey with such pomp that Voltaire remarked, "I have seen a professor of mathematics, only because he was great in his vocation, buried like a king who had done good to his subjects."

Apparently Newton did not begin his serious study of mathematics—beginning with Euclid's *Elements* and Descartes' *Geometrie*—until the summer of 1664. During the two years of 1665 and 1666 when Cambridge closed because of the plague, he returned to his country home in Lincolnshire, and there laid the foundations for the three towering achievements of his scientific career—the calculus, the nature of light, and the theory of gravitation. Of this *biennium mirabilissimum* he later wrote that "in those days I was in the prime of my age of invention and minded mathematics and philosophy more than at any time since."

Newton's *Principia Mathematica* of 1687 and *Opticks* of 1704 detailed his contributions to mechanics and optics. However, his contributions to pure mathematics (including the calculus) remained largely unpublished during his lifetime. Mathematical discoveries at that time were not usually announced by means of prompt journal publication, because journals devoted to mathematics did not yet exist, but were often communicated in the form of personal letters and privately circulated manuscripts (and even sometimes proposed as riddles). At his death Newton left behind a mass of approximately 5000 sheets of unpublished mathematical manuscripts, some of which had circulated amongst his contemporaries or served as a basis for his infrequent mathematical publications. This huge corpus of unpublished manuscript defied efforts directed towards its systematic organization for almost three centuries, until the appearance (in eight volumes from 1967) of the monumental Cambridge edition of *The Mathematical Papers of Isaac Newton*, edited by D. T. Whiteside. . . .

The Introduction of Fluxions. In October of 1666 Newton gathered together and organized the results of his calculus research during the previous two years into a manuscript later referred to as "The October 1666 Tract on Fluxions." This was the first of his formal papers on the calculus. Although unpublished until recently, apparently copies of the manuscript were seen by a few En-

glish mathematicians during Newton's lifetime and after his death.

Beginning in late 1665, Newton had studied the tangent problem by the method of combining the velocity components of a moving point in a suitable coordinate system. This approach was previously developed by Roberval, but this earlier work was probably unknown to Newton. This investigation of tangents by means of component motions provided both the motivation for the new method of fluxions, and the key to its geometric applications. . . .

The Calculus According to Leibniz

Gottfried Wilhelm Leibniz (1646–1716). In the century of Kepler, Galileo, Descartes, Pascal, and Newton, the most versatile genius of all was Gottfried Wilhelm Leibniz. He was born at Leipzig, entered the university there at the age of fifteen, and received his bachelor's degree at seventeen. He continued his studies in logic, philosophy and law, and at twenty completed a brilliant thesis on the historical approach to teaching law. When the University of Leipzig denied his application for a doctorate in law because of his youth, he transferred to the University of Altdorf in Nuremberg, and received his doctorate in philosophy there in 1667.

Upon the completion of his academic work, Leibniz entered the political and governmental service of the Elector of Mainz. His serious study of mathematics did not begin until 1672 (at the age of twenty-six) when he was sent to Paris on a diplomatic mission. The following four years that he spent in Paris were Leibniz' "prime age of invention" in mathematics (similar to Newton's 1664–66 period). During his stay in Paris he conceived the principal features of his own version of the calculus, an approach that he elaborated during the balance of his life, and which during the eighteenth century was dominant over Newton's approach. In 1676 he returned to Germany, and served for the next forty years as librarian and councillor to the Elector of Hanover. Although his professional career was devoted mainly to law and diplomacy, the breadth of his fundamental contributions—to diverse areas of mathematics, philosophy, and science—is probably not matched by the work of any subsequent scholar.

In regard to the calculating machine that he built during the Paris years, Leibniz remarked, "It is unworthy of excellent men to lose hours like slaves in the labor of calculation which could safely be relegated to anyone else if machines were used." A lifelong project was his search for a universal language or symbolic logic that would standardize and mechanize not only numerical computations but all processes of rational human thought, and would eliminate the mental labor of routine and repetitive steps. His goal was the creation of a system of notation and terminology that would codify and simplify the essential elements of logical reasoning so as to

furnish us with an Ariadne's thread, that is to say, with a certain sensible and palpable medium, which will guide the mind as do the lines drawn in geometry and the formulas for operations, which are laid down for the learner in arithmetic.[3]

Such a universal "characteristic" or language, he hoped, would provide all educated people—not just the fortunate few—with the powers of clear and correct reasoning.

Apparently the formulation of this far-reaching goal antedated Leibniz' serious interest in or detailed knowledge of mathematics. But, as Hofmann remarks, "A man who places such thoughts into the forefront of his mind has mathematics in his blood even if he is still ignorant of its detail."[4] Indeed, it was precisely (and only) in mathematics that Leibniz fully accomplished his goal. His infinitesimal calculus is the supreme example, in all of science and mathematics, of a system of notation and terminology so perfectly mated with its subject as to faithfully mirror the basic logical operations and processes of that subject. It is hardly an exaggeration to say that the calculus of Leibniz brings within the range of an ordinary student problems that once required the ingenuity of an Archimedes or a Newton. Perhaps the best measure of its triumph is the fact that today we can scarcely discuss the results of Leibniz' predecessors without restating them in his differential notation and terminology.

A few examples will indicate what Leibniz meant by symbolic notation as a "sensible and palpable medium, which will guide the mind" to correct conclusions. In the functional notation introduced much later by Lagrange, the chain rule says that, if $h(x) = f(g(x))$, then

$$h'(x) = f'(g(x))g'(x). \tag{1}$$

Nothing about the notation in Formula (1) suggests why it is true, nor how to prove it. But in differential notation, with $z = f(y)$ and $y = g(x)$, Formula (1) becomes

$$\frac{dz}{dx} = \frac{dz}{dy} \cdot \frac{dy}{dx}. \tag{2}$$

This formula, by contrast, conspicuously suggests its own validity, by cancellation of the right-hand side differential dy's as though they were real numbers. This symbolic cancellation of differentials also suggests a logical proof of the formula— by replacing the differentials dx, dy, dz by the finite increments Δx, Δy, Δz and proceeding to the limit.

The integral version of the chain rule is the formula for integration by substitution,

$$\int f(g(x))g'(x)\, dx = \int f(u)\, du. \tag{3}$$

The symbolic substitution $u = g(x)$, $du = g'(x)\, dx$ makes Formula (3) seem inevitable, whatever its proof may be. This amounts to the invariance of the differential form $f(u)\, du$ with respect to arbitrary changes of variable —one of Leibniz' most important discoveries.

Now consider a surface that is generated by revolving the curve $y = f(x)$ around the x-axis. Thinking of an infinitesimal segment ds of the curve as the hypotenuse of the "characteristic triangle" with sides dx and dy (see Fig. 1), the Pythagorean theorem gives

$$ds = \sqrt{(dx)^2 + (dy)^2} = \sqrt{1 + \left(\frac{dy}{dx}\right)^2}\, dx.$$

When this segment ds is revolved around the x-axis in a circle of radius y, it generates an infinitesimal area

$$dA = 2\pi y\, ds = 2\pi y \sqrt{1 + \left(\frac{dy}{dx}\right)^2}\, dx.$$

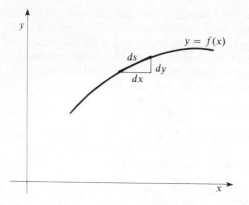

Figure 1

Adding up the infinitesimal areas, we obtain

$$A = \int dA = \int 2\pi y \sqrt{1 + \left(\frac{dy}{dx}\right)^2} \, dx. \qquad (4)$$

for the area of the surface. Thus we "discover" the correct Formula (4) by a quite routine and plausible manipulation of Leibniz' symbols. By contrast, its rigorous justification would require a detailed discussion and definition of the concept of surface area, followed by a proof (perhaps in terms of Riemann sums) that Formula (4) agrees with this definition.

These simple examples illustrate the principal features of the analytical or symbolic calculus of Leibniz—the central role of infinitesimal differences (differentials) and sums (integrals), and the inverse relationship between them; the characteristic triangle as a link between tangent (differential) and quadrature (integral) problems; the transformation of integrals by means of substitutions—and the manner in which this calculus does, indeed, guide the mind in the formal derivation of correct results.

In this [article] we outline the stages by which Leibniz gradually discovered and elaborated his calculus. The first crucial steps were taken during his Paris years, 1672–76, eight or ten years after Newton's formative period. However, Leibniz' first publication of the calculus was in 1684, twenty years prior to the publication of Newton's *De Quadratura* in 1704. In the final section . . . we discuss briefly the chief differences between the Newtonian and Leibnizian approaches to the calculus, and the unfortunate priority dispute between their respective followers that took place in the early eighteenth century.

In 1714, two years before his death, Leibniz composed the essay *Historia et origo calculi differentialis* (History and Origin of the Differential Calculus), opening with the lines (in the English translation of this extract provided by Weil):

It is most useful that the true origins of memorable inventions be known, especially of those which were conceived not by accident but by an effort of meditation. The use of this is not merely that history may give everyone his due and others be spurred by the expectation of similar praise, but also that the art of discovery may be promoted and its method become known through brilliant examples. One of the noblest inventions of our time has been a new kind of mathematical analysis, known as the differential calculus; but while its substance has been adequately explained, its source and original motivation have not been made public. It is almost forty years now that its author invented it. . . .[5]

English translations of the complete *Historia et origo*, and of a number of letters and manuscripts supplying additional details, are available in the volume of J. M. Child. . . .[6] In addition, Struik's source book contains English translations of three of Leibniz' earliest published papers on the calculus.[7]

The Beginning—Sums and Differences. In the *Historia et origo* and elsewhere, Leibniz always traced his inspiration for the calculus back to his early work with sequences of sums and differences of numbers. As a young student he had been interested in simple number properties, and in 1666 had published an essay entitled *De arte combinatoria* (On the Art of Combinations) that dealt with elementary properties of combinations and permutations.

Shortly after his arrival in Paris in 1672, he noticed an interesting fact about the sum of the differences of consecutive terms of a sequence of numbers. Given the sequence

$$a_0, a_1, a_2, \ldots, a_n$$

consider the sequence

$$d_1, d_2, \ldots, d_n$$

of differences, $d_i = a_i - a_{i-1}$. Then

$$
\begin{aligned}
&d_1 + d_2 + \ldots + d_n \\
&= (a_1 - a_0) + (a_2 - a_1) + \ldots + (a_n - a_{n-1}) \\
&= a_n - a_0.
\end{aligned} \tag{5}
$$

Thus the *sum of the consecutive differences equals the difference of the first and last terms of the original sequence*.

As an example, he observed that the "difference sequence" of the sequence of squares,

$$0, 1, 4, \ldots, n^2$$

is the sequence of consecutive odd numbers,

$$1, 3, 5, \ldots, 2n - 1,$$

because $i^2 - (i - 1)^2 = 2i - 1$. It follows that the sum of the first n odd numbers is n^2,

$$1 + 3 + 5 + \ldots + (2n - 1) = n^2. \tag{6}$$

The Meaning of Leibniz' Infinitesimals.   In his publications on the calculus, Leibniz stressed the routine and formal character of his rules for the calculation and manipulation of differentials, and asserted that the proper application of these rules of operation would invariably lead to correct and meaningful results, even if uncertainty remained as to the precise meaning of the infinitesimals that appeared in the computations. Indeed, it was the correctness of the results obtained that had been his guide in the formulation of his algorithms, and had confirmed his confidence in their operational validity.

Mathematical tradition generally attributes to Leibniz a belief in the actual existence of infinitesimal quantities—an infinitesimal quantity being one that is non-zero, yet smaller than every positive real number—and allegations to this effect are sometimes found in discussions of twentieth century "non-standard analysis." Nevertheless, Leibniz seems not to have committed himself on the question of the actual existence of infinitesimals, and he certainly expressed doubts on occasion. At any rate, he recognized that the question of the existence of infinitesimals is independent of the question as to whether computations with in-

finitesimals, carried out in accordance with the operational rules of the calculus, lead to correct solutions of problems. Consequently, whether or not infinitesimals actually exist, they can serve as "fictions useful to abbreviate and to speak universally." Leibniz gave a comprehensive statement of this point of view in an unpublished manuscript probably written sometime after 1700, in reply to criticisms of the calculus advanced in 1694 by the Dutch physician and geometer Bernard Nieuwentijdt:[8]

Whether infinite extensions [quantities] successively greater and greater, or infinitely small ones successively less and less, are legitimate considerations, is a matter that I own to be possibly open to question; but for him who would discuss these matters it is not necessary to fall back upon metaphysical controversies, such as the composition of the continuum, or to make geometrical matters depend thereon. . . . It will be sufficient if, when we speak of infinitely great (or more strictly unlimited), or of infinitely small quantities (i.e., the very least of those within our knowledge), it is understood that we mean quantities that are indefinitely great or indefinitely small, i.e., as great as you please, or as small as you please, so that the error that any one may assign may be less than a certain assigned quantity. Also, since in general it will appear that, when any small error is assigned, it can be shown that it should be less, it follows that the error is absolutely nothing. . . . If any one wishes to understand these [the infinitely great and infinitely small] as the ultimate things, or as truly infinite, it can be done, and that too without falling back upon a controversy about the reality of extensions, or of infinite continuums in general, or of the infinitely small, aye, even though he think that such things are utterly impossible; it will be sufficient simply to make use of them as a tool that has advantages for the purpose of the calculation, just as the algebraists retain imaginary roots with great profit. For they contain a handy means of reckoning, as can manifestly be verified in every case in a rigorous manner by the method already stated.

Thus Leibniz presents his calculus of infinitesimals as an abbreviated form of the rigorous Greek method of exhaustion, one whose more concise language is better adapted to the art of discovery. The basis for his argument is that, given an equality between two expressions involving differentials, that has been obtained by discarding higher-order differentials, it could have been established rigorously (and more tediously) by substituting for each differential the corresponding finite difference, and then proving that the difference between the resulting expressions could be made arbitrarily small by choosing the finite differences sufficiently small.

Finally, it should be mentioned that whereas Leibniz himself was somewhat circumspect regarding the actual existence of infinitesimals, this appropriate caution was generally not shared by his immediate followers (such as the Bernoulli brothers), who uncritically accepted infinitesimals as genuine mathematical entities. Indeed, this freedom from doubts about the foundations of the calculus probably promoted the rapid development of the subject and its applications.

Leibniz and Newton. . . . Leibniz' devotion to the advantages of appropriate notation was so wholehearted that one could ask whether he invented the calculus or merely a particularly felicitous system of notation for the calculus. Of course the answer is that he did both; indeed, his differential and integral notation so captured the essence of his calculus as to make notation and concept virtually inseparable. Newton, on the other hand, had little interest in notational matters; neither suggestive nor consistent notation was of great importance to him.

Leibniz' constant goal was the formulation of general methods and algorithms that could serve to unify the treatment of diverse problems. General methods are certainly implicit in all of Newton's work, but his greater enthusiasm for the solution of particular problems is evident. The difference is one of emphasis—Leibniz emphasizes general techniques that can be applied to specific problems, whereas Newton emphasizes concrete results that can be generalized.

In regard to the calculus itself, discrete infinitesimal differences of geometric variables played the central role in Leibniz' approach, while Newton's fundamental concept was the fluxion or time rate of change, based on intuitive ideas of continuous motion. As a consequence, Leibniz' notation and terminology effectively disguises the limit concept, which by contrast is fairly explicit in Newton's calculus.

For Leibniz, the separate differentials dx and dy are fundamental; their ratio dy/dx is "merely" a geometrically significant quotient. For Newton, however, especially in his later work, the derivative itself—as a ratio of fluxions or an "ultimate ratio of evanescent quantities"—is the heart of the matter. A second derivative is simply a fluxion of a fluxion, each fluxion involving only first-order infinitesimals, so Newton has no need of Leibniz' higher-order infinitesimals.

The integral of Newton is an indefinite integral, a fluent to be determined from its given fluxion; he solves area and volume problems by interpreting them as inverse rate of change problems. Leibniz' integral, by contrast, is an infinite sum of differentials. Of course, both ultimately compute their integrals by the process of antidifferentiation; the computational exploitation of the inverse relationship between quadrature and tangent problems was their key common contribution.

Whereas Leibniz had only a peripheral interest in infinite series (apart from their contribution to his early motivation), the expansion of functions in power series was for Newton an everyday working tool that he always regarded as an indispensable part of his "method" of analysis. For example, Newton was happy to evaluate an integral or solve a differential equation in terms of an infinite series for its solution, but Leibniz always preferred a "closed form" solution.

We have seen that Newton's formative work on the calculus dated from 1664–1666, while Leibniz' analogous period was 1672–1676. However, Leibniz' first publications on the calculus appeared in 1684 and 1686 (his *Acta Eruditorum* articles), whereas Newton, although he had shown manuscripts to colleagues in England, published nothing on the calculus until his *Principia* of 1687 and his *Opticks* of 1704 (with the *De Quadratura* as a mathematical appendix).

Beginning in the late 1690's Leibniz came under attack by followers of Newton who assumed that he had taken and used crucial suggestions (without acknowledging credit to Newton) from the letters of 1676, and that he had learned of Newton's work during his brief visits to London in 1673 and 1676 (although he and Newton never met). Eventually, inferences became public charges of plagiarism. Leibniz in 1711 appealed for redress from the Royal Society of London (of which he was a member and Newton the president). The Royal Society appointed a commission which ruled in 1712, in a decision that was evidently stage-managed by Newton, that Leibniz was essentially guilty as charged.

This unfortunate controversy had less to do with mathematics than with nationalistic rivalry between English and continental European mathematicians. Any serious study of the investigations of Newton and Leibniz makes it clear that their respective contributions were discovered independently.

An irony of the English "victory" in the Newton-Leibniz dispute was that English mathematicians, in steadfastly following Newton and refusing to adopt Leibniz' analytical methods, effectively closed themselves off from the mainstream of progress in mathematics for the next century. Although Newton's spectacular applications of mathematics to scientific problems inspired much of the eighteenth century progress in mathematics, these advances came mainly at the hands of continental mathematicians using the analytical machinery of Leibniz' calculus, rather than the methods of Newton.

Notes

1. J. Hadamard, Newton and the Infinitesimal Calculus, in *Newton Tercentenary Celebrations*. Cambridge: The Royal Society, 1947, p. 38.
2. C. B. Boyer, *The History of the Calculus and Its Conceptual Development*. New York: Dover (reprint), Chapter V, 1959, p. 187.
3. M. E. Baron, *The Origins of the Infinitesimal Calculus*. Oxford: Pergamon, 1969, Chapter 7, p. 9.
4. J. E. Hofmann, *Leibniz in Paris 1672–1676*. Cambridge University Press, 1974, p. 2.
5. A. Weil, Review of Hofmann (Reference 4 above). *Bull Am Math Soc* 81, 676–688, 1975.
6. J. M. Child, *The Early Mathematical Manuscripts of Leibniz*. Chicago: Open Court, 1920.
7. D. J. Struik, *A Source Book in Mathematics 1200–1800*. Cambridge, Mass.: Harvard University Press, 1969.
8. Child, *Early Mathematical Manuscripts*, pp. 149–150.

Non-Euclidean Geometry

Stephen F. Barker

Stephen Francis Barker was born in Ann Arbor, Michigan. He attended Swarthmore and then Harvard; his academic background is in philosophy. He has held academic positions at the University of Southern California, University of Virginia, Ohio State, and Johns Hopkins. He has been both a Santayana fellow at Harvard and a Guggenheim fellow.

The impact of the development of non-Euclidean geometry on the metaphysics of the nineteenth century has been noted elsewhere in this volume. While non-Euclidean geometry has not had the publicity of such other nineteenth-century events as organic evolution, nevertheless its long-term impact may well be almost as great. This essay is not, however, much concerned with the historical impact of the development of non-Euclidean geometry or even with historical facts. Instead Barker seeks to explain exactly what non-Euclidean geometry is and in what way it differs from the classical Euclidean geometry. This is not the complicated technical matter that the rather formidable title suggests; the ideas are taken directly from ordinary experiences related to how we understand and perceive the world around us. The carpenter's attention to making walls parallel is a common example of Euclid's idea of parallel lines. In the same way, the use of perspective in a painting and the apparent convergence of the rails as we look down a railroad track are things we have all experienced and are examples of another view of parallelism. Which view gives the true geometry of nature? It may be that at present we, unlike the Greeks, must conclude that both do.

We remind the reader that most high school geometry books give Playfair's axiom instead of Euclid's original fifth postulate. Playfair's axiom states, Through point P not on line ℓ there is one and only one parallel line. *Euclid's fifth postulate states,* If a line ℓ crosses lines m and n and makes the sum of the interior angles on the same side of the line less than two right angles, then the lines m and n, if extended indefinitely, must meet on the side on which the angles are less than the two right angles.

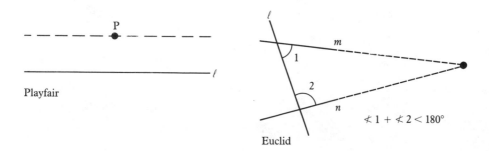

Playfair

Euclid

$\angle 1 + \angle 2 < 180°$

Source: Stephen F. Barker, "Non-Euclidean Geometry," in *Philosophy of Mathematics,* © 1964, pp. 32–55. Reprinted by permission of Prentice-Hall, Inc., Englewood Cliffs, N.J. (Some references omitted.)

Euclid's Fifth Postulate

Since Euclid's time, many people who have studied the *Elements* have been troubled by Euclid's fifth postulate. The fifth postulate seems anomalous. Even if our view is that the primary purpose of organizing geometry into a rigorous deductive system is just to exhibit in a perspicuous and elegant way the logical interrelations of the principles of the subject, still the fifth postulate looks out of place on account of its intricacy. It requires a much more complex sentence for its formulation than does any of the other postulates, and in its intricacy it closely resembles some of the theorems that Euclid proves (one of Euclid's theorems is the logical converse of the fifth postulate). We would have a more attractive system if we could eliminate the fifth postulate. Moreover, if we think as the Greeks did that the purpose of organizing geometry in rigorous deductive form is also that of establishing the truth of the theorems, then we shall especially want to have postulates that are as obviously and surely true as possible—for the degree of credibility which the theorems attain through being deduced from the postulates cannot be greater than the degree of credibility that the least credible postulate has in its own right. From this point of view, the fifth postulate seems anomalous because it does not have nearly as strong an air of obvious self-evidence as have the other four postulates. Being far more intricate than the others, it is less clearly true.

Down through the centuries, many different thinkers who were dissatisfied with the fifth postulate tried to find ways of eliminating it: ways of showing that it does not need to be regarded as a postulate. Ideally, they would have liked to show that the fifth postulate is not *independent* of the others; that is, that it can be proved as a theorem by reasoning which assumes the first four postulates alone (together with the axioms and definitions, of course). Or, failing this, they would have liked to show that at any rate Euclid's fifth postulate can be replaced by some other simpler and more self-evident principle which could serve as a new fifth postulate, so that Euclid's old fifth postulate could be deduced as a theorem and would no longer be needed as a postulate. Greek and Ar-

abic commentators on Euclid made a number of attempts to eliminate Euclid's fifth postulate by proving it as a theorem, but always their work failed to be satisfactory. In each case either the supposed proof contained some outright logical mistake, or else it covertly assumed some geometrical principle just as intricate as Euclid's fifth postulate itself.

Attempted proofs like these did succeed in bringing to light that there are various other geometrical principles any one of which could do the logical job that Euclid's fifth postulate does (the job, that is, of combining with the other four postulates to permit the deduction of theorems). For example, the principle that from a point not on a given line one and only one line can be drawn parallel to the given line is a principle which could do the job that Euclid's fifth postulate does (this principle, called Playfair's axiom, was substituted for Euclid's fifth postulate in a widely used eighteenth century version of Euclidean geometry; for this reason Euclid's fifth postulate itself sometimes is a bit misleadingly referred to as "the parallel postulate"). Also the principle that the sum of the angles of a triangle equals two right angles is another principle capable of doing the job that Euclid's fifth postulate does; and still another is the principle that given any three points not on a straight line there is just one circle that passes through them. These are three among the various principles, any one of which could be substituted for Euclid's fifth postulate without weakening the array of theorems that would be deducible. But there is no reason to hold that any of these alternative principles is significantly simpler than is Euclid's fifth postulate itself.

Sacchieri

The direct way of showing the fifth postulate to be not independent of the other postulates would be to construct a proof of the fifth postulate, using no premises except the other postulates (and the axioms and definitions). This was the approach tried without success by several Greek and Arabic commentators on Euclid. Another way of demonstrating the fifth postulate to be not independent of the others would be to employ the indirect method of reasoning called *reductio ad absurdum:* assume for the sake of argument that the fifth postulate is independent of the others and then show that this assumption leads to a contradiction and therefore must be false. This was the method which the Italian Sacchieri tried in the eighteenth century. To suppose that Euclid's fifth postulate is independent of the others is to suppose that it would be logically possible for all the others to be true but the fifth postulate false. This was Sacchieri's approach: to start with, he assumed that Euclid's first four postulates were true (he added to them the assumption that any straight line can be extended so as to be as long as you please—this assumption is suggested by Euclid's second postulate, but is not explicitly contained in it); and he assumed for the sake of argument that the fifth postulate was false. He then considered a line *AB* at whose endpoints perpendiculars of equal lengths, *AC* and *BD,* are erected.

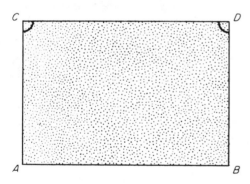

On the basis of his assumptions, he was able to prove that in every such quadrilateral, angle *ACD* must equal angle *BDC*. With regard to these angles, which he called "summit" angles, there arise three hypotheses: either (i) in all such quadrilaterals the summit angles are right angles; or (ii) in all such quadrilaterals the summit angles are obtuse angles; or (iii) in all such quadrilaterals the summit angles are acute angles. One and only one of these hypotheses must be correct, assuming that space is always the same, so that whatever is geometrically true of figures at one time and place

is always true of figures everywhere. On the basis of his assumptions, Sacchieri was able to show that Euclid's fifth postulate must be true if hypothesis (i) is; and since he was assuming the falsity of the fifth postulate, he set aside hypothesis (i). On the basis of his assumptions, he showed that hypothesis (ii) can be set aside also, for it is inconsistent with the assumption that a straight line can be extended to any desired length. This left only the third hypothesis. Sacchieri did his best to show that hypothesis (iii) was incompatible with his assumptions, and he believed that he was justified in setting it aside after finding that it led to some strange consequences. But he was unsuccessful in finding any strict logical impossibility that it led to. If he had succeeded in showing that (iii) was logically incompatible with his assumptions, that would have completed his proof: for then he would have obtained the contradiction which the *reductio ad absurdum* method seeks. The contradiction would have been that at least one of his three hypotheses must be true, yet that none of them would be true on his assumptions. This would have meant that his assumptions could not all be true together, and that in turn would have proved that the fifth postulate cannot be independent of the others. Sacchieri failed to achieve his purpose, but actually, without realizing it, he did succeed in doing something very different and highly important. For in trying to demonstrate the absurdity of hypothesis (iii), he deduced a variety of consequences from it, consequences which were parallel to, yet strangely unlike, the theorems of Euclidean geometry. Without understanding the significance of what he had done, Sacchieri had actually proved a number of the fundamental theorems of an entirely new type of geometry.

Lobachevskian Geometry

It was not until the nineteenth century that mathematicians came to understand the logical situation, and came to realize that Euclid's fifth postulate really is independent of his others, which means that there can be logically consistent systems of geometry that in place of Euclid's fifth postulate contain some contrary postulate instead.

During the earlier part of the nineteenth century three different mathematicians, without being in touch with one another, and all of them unaware of Sacchieri's work, independently developed a new type of geometry. The German mathematician Gauss, although he did not publish his thoughts on this matter, was probably the first to grasp the logical possibility of a geometry different from Euclid's; Gauss introduced the term "non-Euclidean geometry" to describe a type of geometry which is in effect that of Sacchieri's acute-angle hypothesis. The Russian mathematician Lobachevsky and the Hungarian Bolyai independently published accounts of this same type of geometry. Unlike Sacchieri, who had regarded his acute-angle hypothesis as absurd, these mathematicians were consciously developing what they regarded as a new type of logically consistent geometry.

The principles of this new geometry were strange and different from those of Euclidean geometry. In this new geometry, through a point not on a given line always more than one line can be drawn parallel to the given line. Also, the sum of the angles of a triangle is always less than two right angles, and the amount by which it is less is proportional to the area of the triangle; triangles having unequal areas can therefore never be similar. Moreover, the ratio of the circumference of a circle to its diameter is always greater than π, and the ratio is larger the larger is the area of the circle. But, strange as these principles were, they were not found to contradict one another.

Riemannian Geometry

Later in the nineteenth century the German mathematician Riemann, and independently Helmholtz, developed another type of geometry which in effect corresponded to Sacchieri's obtuse-angle hypothesis. In it both Euclid's fifth postulate and also the assumption that a straight line can be extended to any desired length are denied. In it, for each straight line there is a maximum length to which the line can be extended. Through two given points always more than one straight line can be drawn. The sum of the angles of a triangle always is greater than two right an-

gles, the excess being proportional to the area of the triangle. The ratio of the circumference of a circle to its diameter always is less than π and decreases as the area of the circle increases. Gauss's term "non-Euclidean geometry" came to be applied to the Riemannian as well as to the Lobachevskian type of geometry.

Actually, Riemann developed his conception not by means of the postulational approach, but by generalizing and extending a notion of "curvature" that Gauss had developed. Gauss, in studying surfaces and the equations describing them, had made use of the notion of a *geodesic*—the line lying within a surface that is the shortest distance between two points on the surface. He showed that the nature of the geodesics for a surface depends upon a property of the surface which he defined and called "curvature." In a plane surface of course all geodesics are straight lines, and the surface is said to have zero curvature. On a spherical surface, too, all geodesics are alike—they are all arcs of great circles; the spherical surface is said to have uniform positive curvature, the amount of curvature being inversely proportional to the size of the sphere. On the surface of an egg, however, the geodesics would not all be alike but would differ for pairs of points lying in different regions of the surface and also would differ, depending on the orientation of the points, even within the same region; an egg-shaped surface is said to have positive curvature varying from place to place on it. A saddle-backed surface is said to have negative curvature.

Now consider a blind map-maker who is imprisoned on a surface so that he can move only within this surface, never above or below it. From his point of view, a "straight line" could for practical purposes be identified with the shortest distance between two points. Then the "geometry" of the surface (what the sum of the angles of a "triangle" composed of three geodesics will be, and so forth) will depend on the curvature of the surface; any two regions of surface that are alike as regards the curvature there will be alike as regards their "geometry." Although the mathematical definition of curvature is not simple, curvature is something that can readily be visualized in connection with ordinary surfaces, and there is nothing paradoxical about it.

What Riemann did was to generalize Gauss's notion of curvature so that it could be applied also to three-dimensional space, enabling us to speak of the curvature of three-dimensional regions of space; meaning thereby the extent to which the "geometry" of a volume of space differs from Euclidean geometry. We can describe Euclidean geometry as envisaging a space all regions of which are of zero curvature. Lobachevskian geometry envisages a space all regions of which are alike in having some constant negative curvature. And Riemannian geometry envisages a space all regions of which are alike in having some constant positive curvature. Of course this opens up the possibility of envisaging any number of other kinds of space in which the curvature is not constant everywhere.

This way of speaking does sound paradoxical, however. When the layman hears talk of the "curvature" of space, he may imagine that he is supposed to visualize the curvature of three-dimensional space in just the same sort of way in which he can successfully visualize the curvature of surfaces within three-dimensional space. Perhaps the layman tries to imagine three-dimensional space somehow bent and twisted, perhaps in a fourth dimension. This sort of feat of imagination is as unnecessary as it is impossible. We must not suppose that mathematicians perform, or that they expect others to perform, any impossible feats of imagination. Both for two-dimensional surfaces and for three-dimensional volumes of space, the term "curvature" is basically defined by reference to mathematical properties of the equations describing the behavior of geodesics. The notion makes perfectly good sense both in the less abstract case of surfaces, where we can readily visualize its significance, and in the more abstract case of volumes of space, where we cannot visualize it as meaning any literal sort of bending or twisting of all three dimensions.

The Problem of Consistency

The development of Lobachevskian and of Riemannian geometries came as something of revolutionary intellectual significance. Earlier thinkers, and especially the philosopher Kant, had held that there was only one true geometry, whose laws were necessarily and immutably Euclidean. Was not that view clearly refuted by the appearance of these new types of geometry? But if mathematicians permit the development of alternative geometries whose laws contradict those of Euclidean geometry, what has become of the notion of truth in mathematics? Can it be that these conflicting geometries are equally true? Or is it that mathematicians no longer even seek the truth about space?

Many conservative-minded people were deeply puzzled by these questions and were deeply shocked by the working out of non-Euclidean geometries. They felt that Euclid's postulates and theorems were all true, and necessarily so; they felt that any non-Euclidean geometry must therefore contain what is necessarily false. And it seemed to them that a system of geometry must be logically inconsistent if it contains necessarily false postulates and theorems about space, such as that the sum of the angles of a triangle is less than, or greater than, two right angles. Yet no one ever succeeded in discovering either in Lobachevskian or in Riemannian geometry any pair of theorems that were strict logical contradictories of each other (that is, that contradicted each other by virtue of their logical form). Opponents of non-Euclidean geometry, although they tried hard, never were able to show that it violated the requirements of formal logical consistency. Yet these non-Euclidean systems had not positively been proved to be consistent either. The very important question whether they were consistent hung in the air for a time. The seriousness of this question was a powerful factor that forced mathematicians to seek still more rigorous logical procedures than those observed by Euclid. Another factor was their increasing awareness of logical weaknesses within Euclid's *Elements* itself.

Logical Gaps in Euclid's "Elements"

For more than two thousand years Euclid's *Elements* survived all challenges and stood as a supreme mathematical achievement. Euclid's standards of rigor were admired as the highest possible and the cogency of his proofs was thought unsurpassable. But gradually more and more small criticisms began to accumulate. During the nineteenth century mathematicians' standards of rigor grew sharply higher, and it came to be realized that Euclid's work, admirable as it is, does contain many logical gaps. There are many places in Euclid's proofs where his stated assumptions are not sufficient to make his conclusions follow merely by formal logic alone. An example of one such logical gap is found in Euclid's proof of his Proposition I. . . . In that proof Euclid prescribes that two circles are to be drawn, one with center at point A and the other with center at point B, the distance between A and B to serve as the radius of each. He then immediately goes on to speak of the point C at which these circles intersect one another. But what logical reason does Euclid have for saying that there must be one and only one such point C? What right has he to suppose that the circles must intersect one another at all; or that if they do, they do so only once? Euclid uses no postulate from which this follows; he has no postulate that assures the *continuity* of lines and circles. Thus there is a logical gap in his reasoning; from the premises that he actually states, it does not follow by formal logic alone that there need be just one such point C. To supply what is needed, one might introduce an added postulate saying that if a line (such as *ACE*, the circumference) belongs entirely to a figure (here the plane) which is divided into two parts (outside and inside the circle) and if the line has at least one point in common with each part, then it must also meet the boundary between the parts. In order to fill the logical gap in Euclid's proof of his Proposition I some such additional postulate would have to be added to his system.

Why is it that Euclid himself and most of his readers down through the centuries did not notice this logical gap? The reason surely is that the figure which accompanies Euclid's Proposition I made it seem perfectly clear to them that there must be such a point C; it was so obvious that they never thought of asking for proof of it. The reader who looks at the figure finds Euclid's reasoning perfectly convincing, for it is impossible to visualize the two circles lying in the same plane without meeting in some one point C. This situation occurs often in Euclid's proofs: in many

places his conclusions do not follow from his stated premises by formal logic alone, yet the reader finds the reasoning highly convincing because Euclid's book contains a diagram depicting the geometrical situation under discussion, a diagram which enables the reader to feel he sees that Euclid's conclusions must hold.

Is Euclid's reasoning *invalid* in cases where his conclusions fail to follow from the stated premises by pure logic alone? It would perhaps be overly severe to say that. Some philosophers and some logicians do occasionally speak as though they thought that no reasoning is really valid unless it is valid on account of its logical form alone; but that is an unduly extreme view. Many perfectly valid deductive arguments are not valid on account of their formal logical structure but rather on account of the particular meanings of nonlogical terms occurring in them; and it might be possible to regard Euclid's proofs in this light. However, these logical gaps nevertheless are very much to be deplored, even if they do not definitely mean that Euclid's reasoning is invalid. For these logical gaps are unintentional: it was simply because he was not aware of them that Euclid failed to close them—and the assumptions needed to close these gaps are not more trivial in content or in any way less worthy of being explicitly stated than are the postulates which Euclid explicitly sets forth. Euclid's goal when he set out to systematize geometry surely was to try to produce proofs that would be valid on account of their logical form alone (though he probably would not have described his goal in this way). Where his reasoning falls short of this, he is falling short of his intended goal, and his reasoning lacks the rigor which he and we would like it to have had.

Deductive Systems Abstractly Viewed

The desire to correct these gaps in Euclid's proofs was one reason for the development of a stricter style of systematic presentation for geometry. Another even stronger reason was that in systematizing non-Euclidean geometry, it had become absolutely imperative to avoid gaps in reasoning, in order to assure the strict reliability of proofs. The consistency of non-Euclidean geometry was in doubt, so it was imperative to ensure that no non-Euclidean theorem should be deduced that did not strictly follow from the axioms. And of course with non-Euclidean geometries it is out of the question, anyway, to have diagrams to which we can reliably appeal in eking out gaps in the assumptions—since anyone using a diagram is likely to interpret it in a Euclidean rather than in a non-Euclidean fashion. Euclidean geometry had got along for two millennia without complete rigor in its proofs because no one challenged its consistency and because its diagrams comfortably filled gaps in the reasoning. Non-Euclidean geometry could be given the benefit of the doubt in neither of these ways.

For these reasons there gradually developed late in the nineteenth century a more rigorous conception of how a deductive system should be organized so as to avoid the sort of logical gaps that affect Euclid's presentation. The goal is to present proofs which are valid solely on account of their logical form. In order to attain this goal, the presentation has to be made in such a way that it can be regarded from a very cold and abstract viewpoint. It is not that in thinking about a system we need *always* adopt this abstract point of view; but the system is to be presented so that whenever we wish to examine the validity of proofs it will be readily *possible* for us to regard the system in a very abstract light. This point of view will be abstract in two ways.

First, when we are adopting it we shall pay no attention to whether the axioms and theorems are *true*, for that may distract our attention from the logical interrelations between them. The danger in Euclidean geometry is that we are inclined to feel very confident that certain theorems are true, and so we may on that account make the mistake of imagining that they follow from premises which do not rigorously entail them; and in non-Euclidean geometry there is the opposite danger, that when we are inclined to feel that a certain theorem is absurdly false this may blind us to the fact that it does rigorously follow from its premises. The remedy is to pay no attention to whether the axioms or theorems are true, but to focus attention solely upon their deductive interrelations.

Moreover, the approach is abstract in a second and more radical sense: when we adopt this viewpoint we are to pay no attention to the *meanings* of the primitive terms occurring in the axioms. The meanings of the geometrical terms have nothing to do with the formal logical validity of the proofs of theorems. Yet it is all too easy to allow oneself unconsciously to make use of assumptions that one does not realize that one is using, when one keeps the meanings of the terms clearly in mind. This is what happened to Euclid. (Some modern writers overstate this point, saying that for the sake of rigor one must regard the primitive terms of the system as *meaningless*. That is an overstatement, for rigor certainly cannot require us to imagine terms to be meaningless when we know quite well that meanings are attached to them. The point is rather that for the sake of rigor when considering proofs, we must pay no attention to whatever we know concerning the accustomed meanings of the primitive terms of the system.)

Our goal is to construct the system so that every theorem will follow from the postulates by strict deductive logic—that is, on account of logical form alone. Our purpose in arranging the system so that it can be regarded from an abstract viewpoint is to ensure this goal. Thus, in principle, someone should be able to check the validity of each proof if he knows logic even if he does not understand the meanings of any of the terms of the system (and therefore, of course, has no basis for forming any opinion about the truth or falsity of any of the axioms or theorems). From this point of view, it is inappropriate to include in the system any definitions of the primitive terms; such definitions (such as Euclid's definition of a point as that which has no parts) have no influence whatever upon the validity of the proofs of the theorems and therefore are irrelevant to the system, when it is abstractly considered. Moreover, from this abstract viewpoint, the definitions of defined terms must be regarded merely as notational stipulations which allow us alternative ways of writing sentences. The definitions must be such as to show how any sentence of the system containing defined terms can be rewritten solely in the notation of the primitive terms of the system. Only when we are able to view the axioms, the primitive terms, and the definitions all in this abstract light can we be confident that our judgments about what logically follows from them are strict and rigorous.

Uninterpreted Geometry and Interpretations of It

It has become customary in recent decades to distinguish between what is called "pure geometry" and what is called "applied geometry." Pure geometry would be geometry studied from the abstract point of view we have been discussing, whereas applied geometry would be geometry studied from a point of view that does attribute specific meanings to the terms. However, this way of speaking is slightly unfortunate, since according to it Euclid's work would presumably have to be classified as applied rather than as pure geometry, making it sound as though Euclid was not really doing mathematics, but was doing something perhaps more like engineering—a misleading suggestion. Let us speak instead about an *uninterpreted* system as contrasted with an *interpreted* system of geometry. We can then say that Euclid's *Elements* is put forward as an interpeted system (since Euclid surely had some fairly definite meanings in mind for his terms). But in light of what we have previously been saying, we should think of a geometrical system as uninterpreted when we are seeking to make a rigorous study of its logical structure. Especially with non-Euclidean geometries, it is important to think of them as uninterpreted systems when we are studying the proofs of their theorems. When we regard a system as uninterpreted, we take no notice of what meanings, if any, its primitive terms possess, and we take no notice of whether its axioms and theorems are true, whether they are false, or of whether they are neither true nor false (as will happen if the terms in them possess no specific meanings—for sentences are incapable of truth or falsity if the terms occurring in them lack meanings).

When we want to regard a geometrical system as uninterpreted, the safest and clearest procedure is to express the axioms and theorems in sche-

matic form, replacing words like "point" and "line" by dummy letters, such as "P" and "L." Doing this helps us to avoid being influenced by the meanings that we normally associate with words like "point" and "line," and enables us to concentrate our attention upon the abstract logical structure of the system. To illustrate this approach, let us go back to Euclid's postulates . . . and let us consider the manner in which we might restate them if we wished to regard Euclid's system as uninterpreted (Euclid himself regarded it as an interpreted system, to be sure, but that need not prevent us from regarding it as an uninterpreted system).

Euclid's first postulate said that between any two points a straight line can be drawn. This amounts to saying that for any two distinct points there is a straight line to which each of them belongs. If we now restate this postulate in schematic form it can become:

1. For any two distinct P's, there is an S to which each of them bears the relation B.

Here, instead of speaking of points we speak of P's, instead of speaking of straight lines we speak of S's, and instead of speaking of one thing belonging to another we speak of one thing bearing the relation B to another.

Euclid's second posulate said that any finite straight line can be extended in a straight line. This amounts to saying that for any straight line having two endpoints, there is another straight line to which both these points belong, but on which only one of them is an endpoint. If we now restate this postulate in schematic form it can become:

2. For any S such that there are two distinct P's each bearing the relation E to it, there is another S to which each of those P's bears the relation B but to which only one of them bears the relation E.

Here, instead of speaking of one thing being an endpoint of another we speak merely of one thing bearing the relation E to another.

Continuing in this way, we could restate all Euclid's postulates and definitions in this schematic manner; moreover, we could foresee how anything that can be said using Euclid's notions could be restated in our schematic manner. This puts us in an excellent position for studying the formal logic of Euclid's system. It is now easy to keep our viewpoint abstract as we investigate questions about the deducibility of conclusions from the postulates or about the correctness of proposed proofs. In investigating such questions we employ only the schematic versions of the sentences concerned, for we are interested solely in deductions that are valid purely by virtue of their logical forms. Consequently, we pay no attention to what "*P*," "*S*," and the other dummy letters mean—which is easy to do, since these letters have no particular meanings.

But now, suppose we have been regarding a system as uninterpreted, and have formulated its postulates, definitions, and theorems in this abstract schematic manner. Suppose we were now to decide that we wished to change our point of view, and turn the uninterpreted system into an interpreted one by assigning meanings to all of its dummy letters. Consider the schematic postulates (1) and (2) that were just used as illustrations. These contain the dummy letters "*P*" and "*S*," representing unspecified kinds of things, and the dummy letters "*B*" and "*E*," representing unspecified relations between things. One way of assigning meaning to these dummy letters is of course to let "*P*" mean point (in some specific sense), let "*S*" mean straight line (in some specific sense), let "*B*" stand for the relation between a point and a line when the point belongs to the line, and let "*E*" stand for the relations between a point and a line when the point is at the end of the line. When we interpret their dummy letters in this way, (1) and (2) can turn into Euclid's first and second postulates. But what we now must notice is that there are also innumerable *other* ways in which these dummy letters could be given meanings so that (1) and (2) would turn into meaningful statements and thereby become true or false.

For example, we might interpret "*P*" to mean straight line, "*S*" to mean point, "*B*" to mean the relation between a line and a point when the line ends at the point, and "*E*" to mean the relation between a line and a point when the line includes the point. Under this scheme of interpretation, (1) and (2) become the statements:

For any two distinct straight lines, there is a point at which both of them end.

For any point such that there are two distinct straight lines each including it, there is another point where both these straight lines end, but which only one of them includes.

These are meaningful geometrical statements, but, as it happens, they are both false, if the terms "point" and "straight line" are used in a normal sense.

It is also possible for us to interpret (1) and (2) in ways that do not even pertain to space. For example, we could let "*S*" stand for intervals of time (such as the twentieth century, the year 1492, or Plato's lifetime). We could let "*P*" stand for instants of time (such as the vernal equinox of 1888, or the beginning of the twentieth century). We could let "*B*" mean the relation between an instant and an interval when the instant belongs to that interval. And we could let "*E*" stand for the relation between an instant and an interval when the instant is the earliest or latest instant of the interval. Under this scheme of interpretation, (1) and (2) become the statements:

For any two distinct instants, there is an interval to which each of them belongs.

For any interval such that there are two distinct instants each either the earliest or the latest instant of that interval, there is another interval to which each of these instants belongs, but of which only one of them is the earliest or latest.

Here again we obtain two meaningful statements, but this time they have nothing to do with space. And, as it happens, this scheme of interpretation gives us two statements both of which are true. Of course innumerable other still different ways of interpreting (1) and (2) could be found; some would give us true statements and some would give us false statements.

We say that we have given an interpretation of an entire uninterpreted system when we have selected a meaning for each of the dummy letters occurring in its schematic postulates and theorems. So long as they remain uninterpreted, the schematic sentences are neither true nor false; but when every dummy letter has been given a meaning then each postulate and theorem becomes a statement that is either true or false. Usually an uninterpreted system will turn out to be such that under many interpretations some or all of its postulates and theorems become false statements, while under some other interpretations its postulates and theorems all become true statements.

Inconsistency

The opponents of non-Euclidean geometries had hoped to be able to show them inconsistent. Let us consider what this means. Inconsistency, in the sense that concerns mathematicians, has nothing to do with the special meanings that the terms in the system may possess; inconsistency has to do only with the abstract logical structure of the system. To say that a system is inconsistent is to say that two theorems which logically contradict one another both are deducible from the axioms of the system (let us now call them axioms rather than postulates). For example, suppose there were a system from whose axioms we could deduce the theorem "For each S there is a P to which it bears the relation R," and from whose axioms we also could deduce the theorem "There is at least one S which bears the relation R to no P"; these two theorems contradict one another, and this means that the system to which they belong is inconsistent.

Why should we care whether a system is inconsistent? The traditional answer is that consistency is important because of its connection with truth. With an interpreted system, the discovery of inconsistency would show that not all the axioms of the system are true. With an uninterpreted system, the discovery of inconsistency would show that there could be no way of interpreting it so as to make all the axioms come out true—and a system which cannot come out true under any interpretation is comparatively uninteresting.

How may we discover whether a system is consistent? The direct way of demonstrating inconsistency is of course to find two theorems which contradict one another on account of their logical form and each of which follows rigorously from the axioms. Demonstrating consistency may be more complicated, however. At this stage we may

distinguish two somewhat different ways (later we shall consider a third). The first way would be to find an interpretation under which all the axioms (and consequently all the theorems) of the system do definitely come out true. The limitation of this first method is that it requires us to possess perfectly definite knowledge of the truth of the interpreted statements; only if there is no doubt about their truth can the proof of consistency be called a success. The second method of establishing consistency is to give a *relative* proof of consistency: we show that a given system is consistent provided some other, less suspect system is. This is done by showing that if there is any interpretation under which the latter system comes out true, then there must also be an interpretation under which the former system comes out true.

Using this second approach, mathematicians of the later nineteenth century made important progress with the question of the consistency of Lobachevskian and Riemannian geometries. They were able to establish that these non-Euclidean geometries must be consistent if Euclidean geometry is. To illustrate the idea behind this method, let us consider a way of dealing with Lobachevskian geometry that was informally suggested by the French mathematician Poincaré. Consider a sphere within which there is the following peculiarity: things inside uniformly shrink in size as they move away from the center, their shrinkage becoming proportionately greater and greater without limit as they approach the surface of the sphere. The inhabitants inside this sphere, along with their yardsticks, get smaller and smaller as they move outwards towards its surface, their steps get shorter and shorter, and they never reach it. In this sense, the interior of the sphere forms an infinite universe, from their point of view. Suppose they use the term "straight line" to mean the shortest distance between two points as measured with their yardsticks; and they interpret the other terms of geometry in appropriate corresponding ways, for instance, letting a "triangle" be a figure formed by three such "straight lines." The geometry of their universe is now Lobachevskian. The sum of the angles of a triangle will always be less than two right angles, the more so the larger the area of the triangle; through a point not on a given straight line more than one straight line can be drawn parallel to a given straight line; and so on. For example, if C is the center of the sphere, then a "triangle" drawn with vertices at points A, B, and D will have sides

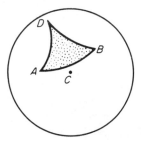

that curve because of the shrinkage of yardsticks (the sides of the "triangle" are to be the shortest paths from vertex to vertex, as measured with yardsticks; and to lay down the yardstick the fewest times one must follow a curved path that tends to minimize the effect of the shrinkage of the yardstick). This is why the sum of the angles of the "triangle" will be less than two right angles. Here we can discuss the matter only very informally, but the aim is to show that if Euclidean geometry is consistent then so must Lobachevskian geometry be. If Euclidean geometry is consistent, then this Euclidean "model" of a universe that has been described must be logically consistent; and if so, then the principles of Lobachevskian geometry which we have interpreted so as to hold in our "model," must be consistent too.

What about the consistency of Euclidean geometry itself? In earlier centuries it had always been taken for granted that the postulates of Euclidean geometry, considered as an interpreted system, all are true; and therefore that the system is of course consistent (if the postulates all are true, then the theorems deduced from them must all be true too, so no theorem can contradict another). But the rise of non-Euclidean geometries made this seem more doubtful; perhaps we cannot be so sure that the postulates and theorems of Euclidean geometry are all true. What then can be done to establish the consistency of the Euclidean system itself? Even if we are not sure of the

truth of Euclid's system, can we at least be confident of its consistency? To establish the consistency of Euclidean geometry relative to some other system of geometry would not be helpful, for any other system of geometry is at least as suspect as regards its consistency as is Euclidean geometry. What we can usefully do, however, is to establish the consistency of Euclidean geometry relative to our mathematical theory of real numbers. We take Euclidean geometry in its abstract, uninterpreted form and construct a numerical interpretation of it. Where Euclid spoke of points we now shall speak of triads of numbers (numbers of the kind called real numbers), where Euclid spoke of lines and figures we shall speak of certain sorts of sets of triads of numbers, and so on. Under our numerical interpretation the postulates and theorems of the system become statements about numbers, and these statements about numbers are true, if our accepted theory about numbers is correct. Thus we construct within number theory a "model" of Euclidean geometry, and the fact that we can do this means that Euclidean geometry must be consistent if our mathematics of real numbers is consistent. Our problem about the consistency of geometry is thus transformed into a problem about the consistency of the mathematical theory of real numbers.

Interpreted Geometry as Empirical

Non-Euclidean geometries have been developed and have been shown to be as logically consistent as Euclidean geometry. Does this decisively refute the traditional philosophical view which regarded geometrical knowledge as synthetic and a priori? The majority of writers of recent times who have dealt with the philosophy of geometry have held that it does. The existence of these non-Euclidean geometries as consistent mathematical disciplines has, it seems to them, decisively overthrown the traditional belief that the laws of the Euclidean geometry are necessarily true and that in them we have synthetic a priori knowledge of our world. Among these recent writers, the most widespread view nowadays has come to be the view that geometry can be regarded in just two ways. Uninterpreted geometry (or "pure" geometry), they hold, must be regarded as a study that involves purely analytic knowledge, for it considers only matters of pure logic—what follows from what. The knowledge deployed there is knowledge about logical deducibility, which rests on considerations of logical form. Interpreted geometry (or "applied" geometry) must be regarded as considering hypotheses about nature which may or may not be true. According to this view, when we give specific meanings to the primitive terms, changing our viewpoint from that of uninterpreted to that of interpreted geometry, then inevitably the sentences of geometry become empirical hypotheses about the world. And the only way of deciding whether they are true or false is inductively, through observation and experiment. Is our actual world Euclidean, or is it Lobachevskian, like the sphere imagined by Poincaré? According to this view, we must experiment to see; that is the only way.

Now, to have an interpreted system of geometry we must choose specific meanings for the undefined primitive terms occurring in the system. For purposes of our discussion, it will suffice if we focus our attention on the term "straight line"—not that this is the only primitive term (indeed, as we saw, there even are axiomatizations in which it is not a primitive term at all). But it is a key term so far as interpretation goes, because once we have decided what it is to mean, it becomes comparatively easy to settle on allied senses for the other terms.

Let us now consider some of the ways in which the term "straight line" might plausibly be interpreted. There is no one absolute sense in which the term *must* be interpreted; but for our present purposes we are not interested in interpretations that are too far removed from normal usage. Let us consider a few plausible senses that the term could be given. Here the point is to describe ways in which empirical significance might plausibly be attached to this term, so that sentences containing it will now express true-or-false assertions. What might somebody be claiming about a line, when he claims that it is straight?

There are several different sorts of procedure in ordinary life that we use for determining whether a line is straight, and with them go several different notions of what it is for a line to be straight. In connection with Poincaré's example, we considered the notion that the shortest distance between two points is what is to be meant by a straight line. According to this notion, to see whether a line is straight we investigate whether it is the shortest path between its endpoints. This method requires that we possess means of measuring distance, such as the yardstick (the procedure being to pick up the yardstick and lay it down each time so that one endpoint will rest just where the other endpoint previously rested). The method is straightforwardly applicable only where we may assume that the yardstick does not expand or contract as it is moved about. If the yardstick is made of metal and the temperature varies greatly, then the thermal expansion will introduce errors—unless we make compensating corrections.

Another notion of what it is for a line to be straight comes from the practice of the carpenter, who sights along his plank to see whether it is straight or crooked. Here the underlying idea is that light travels in straight lines. The carpenter, of course, would not rely upon this method if the plank were lying half in and half out of water; the method can be used straightforwardly only where the medium through which one looks is uniform so that it does not refract the light. Here then is another basic notion of what a straight line is: the path of a ray of light through a medium of uniform refractive index.

Another, though less practical, conception would be that a straight line is the path along which a stretched cord tends to lie as the tension on the cord increases without limit. Still another conception would be that a straight line is the path along which a moving body subject to no external forces will travel.

Several fairly plausible ways of interpreting the term "straight line" have now been mentioned. Now, what kind of assertions do the sentences of an uninterpreted geometry become when we interpret them in one or another of these ways? It is clear that all these suggested interpretations will turn the sentences of geometry into empirical statements. Through a point not on a line, how many lines can be drawn parallel to the given line (that is, in the same plane as the given line but never intersecting it)? Whichever of the interpretations so far proposed be adopted, this question becomes an empirical question, to be settled by observation and experiment. Under all these interpretations, it is an empirical question whether the universe is Euclidean, Lobachevskian, Riemannian, or something else.

On the basis of the world-view of classical Newtonian physics, one would expect Euclidean geometry to come out true and the others to come out false when interpreted in any of these suggested ways. The Newtonian world-view leads us to expect, for example, that through a point not on the path of a given light ray, one and only one ray of light can travel parallel to the given ray (through a medium of uniform refractive index). It leads us to expect that when from three given points a triangle is laid out by finding the pathways along which a measuring rod must be laid down the fewest times, then no matter how big the triangle may be, the sum of its angles always will equal two right angles. Whichever of the suggested conceptions of a straight line we choose to employ, classical physics would lead us to expect the Euclidean system to become a set of true statements when interpreted that way.

Einstein's theory of relativity overturned that classical Newtonian world-view, however. Einstein's theory, now well supported by experimental evidence, leads to a very different set of predictions. According to Einstein's theory we must expect that every two rays of light within the same plane will meet sooner or later, if their paths extend far enough. Also, Einstein's theory predicts that if you were to lay out very large triangles letting their sides be paths along which measuring rods needed to be laid down the fewest times, then you would find that the sum of the angles of such triangles is greater than two right angles, and gets larger the larger the area of the triangle. Thus, when geometry is understood in this way, its statements are empirical, and the physical world proves to be Riemannian rather than Euclidean in its structure. (Strictly speaking, Riemannian geometry has space whose curvature is constant, whereas the space of the physical world proves to be always curved but not curved to the same extent everywhere.)

Interpreted Geometry as A Priori

As we have seen, it certainly is possible to find ways of assigning meaning to the term "straight line" and to the other terms of geometry so that the axioms and theorems of geometry become empirical statements. Indeed, there are a variety of plausible ways in which this can be done (ways, that is, which are not sharply at odds with the normal usage of these terms). The ways we have so far considered turn many of the sentences of Euclidean geometry into untrue statements about the world, while making the sentences of Riemannian geometry come out true. To many philosophers this has seemed to settle the matter: space has been empirically proved to be Riemannian rather than Euclidean, they say; this is the ultimate, complete refutation of the outmoded Kantian philosophy of space. Such a view is hasty and unfair, however. Must an interpretation of a system of geometry turn its axioms into empirical statements? Is that the only possibility? Or is it also possible to interpret the axioms so that they become a priori statements?

Certainly there does remain a further style of interpretation of the term "straight line" and the other basic terms of geometry which needs to be considered—another way of understanding these terms which has deep roots in normal usage. This way of interpreting the term "straight line" does not tie its meaning strictly to any one type of experimental outcome, such as the path of a light ray or the path along which a yardstick is laid down the fewest times. According to this conception of a straight line, such observations do tend to indicate that a line is straight, but they are not conclusive on that score. According to this conception, it is an essential part of the meaning of "straight line" that a triangle whose sides are straight lines must have angles whose sum is equal to two right angles: if we find a triangle whose angles add up to more than this, that decisively shows that the sides of the figure are not really straight lines. According to this conception of geometrical terms, what we should say in describing the result of Einstein's theory of relativity is not that there are non-Euclidean triangles. Instead, we should say that, surprisingly enough, light rays do not travel in straight lines when passing through uneven gravitational fields; and that, surprisingly enough, yardsticks shrink in length and therefore have to be laid down oftener when used in strong gravitational fields. We already knew that light rays do not travel in straight lines through media of varying refractive index, and we knew that yardsticks expand and contract with varying temperature. What these findings of modern physics show, according to the conception we are discussing, is just that gravitational fields also can affect the paths of light rays and the lengths of yardsticks. New corrections must be introduced if we are to use light rays and yardsticks to determine straight lines through uneven gravitational fields. To be sure, these new corrections are of a special universal kind: different colors of light were differently refracted by the medium they pass through, and yardsticks of different materials are differently influenced by changes in temperature; whereas this new gravitational correction affects all light and yardsticks in just the same way. The universality of these corrections is not a decisive reason against our regarding them as corrections, however.

When we understand geometrical terms in this spirit, the sentences of geometry turn into a priori statements rather than empirical ones. The postulates and theorems of Euclidean geometry become necessarily true statements, while those of non-Euclidean geometry become necessarily false statements. It must have been this way of regarding geometrical terms that the German logician Frege had in mind when (following Kant's line of thought) he wrote:

. . . The truths of geometry govern all that is spatially intuitable, whether actual or product of our fancy. The wildest visions of delirium, the boldest inventions of legend and poetry, where animals speak and stars stand still, where men are turned to stone and trees turn into men, where the drowning haul themselves up out of swamps by their own topknots—all these remain, so long as they remain intuitable, still subject to the axioms of geometry.*

There is nothing absurd or definitely improper about this way of understanding geometry; it is a perfectly possible attitude to take. And this is enough to show that the view discussed in the previous section is too crude: the axioms and theorems of an interpreted geometry do not have to be empirical statements; they may be a priori ones.

Confusion about this matter often arises because people get the idea that if the postulates of some non-Euclidean geometry are true then the postulates of Euclidean geometry cannot all be true. They get the idea that Euclidean and non-Euclidean geometries are incompatible with one another and so cannot both be correct. This is a mistake. People who have this idea do not fully realize that the postulates of a geometry are capable of truth or falsity only when they are interpreted in some specific way; they do not fully realize that a pure, uninterpreted set of postulates is neither true nor false. It is misleading and confused to say, for instance, that the postulates of Riemannian geometry are true—for actually the Riemannian postulates are true under some interpretations and false under others. What we should say is that Riemannian geometry is true when, for instance, the term "straight line" is interpreted as meaning the path of a ray of light through a medium of uniform refractive index (and the other terms are interpreted in associated ways); or that Riemannian geometry is true when "straight line" is interpreted as meaning the path along which a measuring rod would have to be laid down the fewest times, assuming the temperature of the rod to be kept constant (and the other terms are interpreted in associated ways); or the like. It is equally misleading and confused to say simply that the postulates of Euclidean geometry are false—for the postulates of Euclidean geometry are true under some interpretations and false

*Gottlob Frege, *The Foundations of Arithmetic*, trans. J. L. Austin (Oxford: Basil Blackwell & Mott, 1953), p. 20e.

under others. What we should say is that the postulates of Euclidean geometry are false if we interpret "straight line" to mean the path of a ray of light through a medium of uniform refractive index, or to mean the path along which a measuring rod kept at constant temperature would have to be laid down the fewest times (and the other terms are interpreted in associated ways); but that the postulates of Euclidean geometry are true if we interpret "straight line" and the other terms in the fashion suggested in the preceding paragraphs, not tying their meaning strictly to any one physical phenomenon or procedure and treating it as an essential aspect of their meaning that the Euclidean principles must be satisfied.

Significance of the A Priori Interpretation

If it be granted that an a priori interpretation of geometry is possible that will make Euclidean axioms into necessary, a priori truths, two philosophical questions then arise. First, does this a priori interpretation constitute synthetic a priori knowledge in the traditional sense? And second, is this a priori interpretation preferable to empirical interpretations such as those mentioned earlier?

In dealing with the first question, let us consider the statement that the sum of the angles of a triangle equals two right angles. Let us construe this as an a priori truth—that is, a statement which we can know to be true without consulting experience, and which no new sensory observations could refute. Viewed in this spirit, is the statement synthetic or analytic? In dealing with this question it becomes of decisive importance to distinguish between the two different accounts given by Kant of the distinction between the analytic and the synthetic. Kant felt that his two accounts amounted to essentially the same thing; but they do not. Our example is synthetic, according to the second account of the distinction, for the statement is not true merely by virtue of its logical form, nor do we possess any definitions by appeal to which we can translate it into a statement true merely by virtue of its logical form. (Or, if you think that definitions are in our pos-

session by means of which this particular law could be translated into a statement true merely by virtue of its logical form, then we may retreat to a more basic thesis: under this a priori interpretation of geometry, *not all* the laws of Euclidean geometry can be translated into statements true merely by virtue of their logical form, for sufficient definitions for that purpose are not available.) Yet, according to the first account of the distinction, our example would qualify as an analytic statement: for nothing other than understanding of it is required in order to enable us to know that it is true. To see that this is so, consider the imaginary case of someone who contemplated this statement yet was doubtful of its truth. How should we describe his intellectual condition? Should we describe his condition by saying that perhaps he does understand the statement perfectly well, but his faculty of Rational Insight is beclouded? That really would be an unsatisfactory description of the case. If he doubts the statement, his doubt is by itself sufficient to show that he does not understand the statement (either he does not understand it at all, or he understands it in some manner other than the manner in which it is intended to be understood). If we meet someone who has such a doubt, our proper procedure in removing the doubt is not to urge him to blink the eye of his Reason and to focus it more intently; it is unlikly that such advice would be of any use. What would be of use is to offer hints about how we intend the sentence to be understood.

When geometrical terms are understood in the spirit suggested in the preceding section, it becomes a necessary a priori truth that the sum of the angles of a triangle must equal two right angles. But knowledge of this does not constitute an insight gained by Reason through some remarkable clairvoyant power—insight either into the ultimate nature of reality or into the ultimate structure of the human mind. On the contrary, this piece of knowledge reflects our determination to use geometrical terms in a certain manner. It reflects our determination not to *call* anything a triangle unless it has this character. Here the knowledge is based upon understanding of language, not upon insight into nature or into the mind. . . .

Finally, we must note a difficult remaining question. What is there to choose between understanding geometrical terms in a style that transforms geometrical sentences into empirical statements, and understanding geometrical terms in the style that transforms those same geometrical sentences into a priori statements? Both viewpoints are possible; but are both viewpoints equally plausible and advantageous? Here let us refer to an example mentioned earlier: in the sixteenth- and seventeenth-century dispute between those who said the earth moved and those who said it was at rest, neither viewpoint was absurd. Each viewpoint could accommodate the observed facts. Each viewpoint for its own justification could appeal to an actual tendency present in ordinary talk about motion. Some people would go so far as to say that the dispute was basically a verbal one and that both positions really were equally correct. Yet to say that would be misleading and would be unfair to the achievement of Copernicus, for there is reason to think that the Copernican view was superior to the Ptolemaic view—the tendency in ordinary talk about motion which the Copernican view emphasizes is a deeper tendency than is the one which the Ptolemaic view emphasizes. This is why the transition from the Ptolemaic to the Copernican view represented such an important intellectual advance: it enabled astronomers and physicists and everyone else to gain a clearer grasp of what, in a sense, they had all along meant by motion; and at the same time it led them to see that they had, in a sense, been mistaken in their heliocentric belief, and it thereby gave them a fresh and truer view of the solar system.

It may be the same with the twentieth-century choice between Euclidean and non-Euclidean geometry. Perhaps it could be held that those interpretations under which the sentences of geometry become empirical statements are interpretations which emphasize deeper and more important tendencies in our ordinary talk about space than does the sort of interpretation which makes the sentences of geometry into a priori statements. The layman is out of his depth here, but physicists at any rate seem markedly to prefer the point of view which interprets geometrical terms in ways that make the sentences of geometry into empirical statements. Physicists prefer to interpret Euclidean geometry so that it is false, rather than to say that gravity bends light rays and shrinks yardsticks. Physicists employ the geometry of Riemann in order to obtain a description of the universe which they find more manageable and more illuminating than is the description obtained by continuing to retain Euclidean principles.

We can at least say that this choice between interpreting geometry so that Euclidean laws of space may be retained or interpreting geometry so that Euclidean laws of space must be rejected, is an important linguistic choice of a kind that has occurred repeatedly in the history of thought. What is at stake is not a simple empirical question of truth and falsity, nor is the issue merely a verbal one; this is the kind of case where our problem is to decide which is the deeper of two conflicting tendencies, both present in our past use of the terms involved.

The Idea of Chance

Jacob Bronowski

Jacob Bronowski was born in Poland and educated in England. He received his Ph.D. in mathematics from Cambridge and held scientific positions in both the university and government. He was the author of a number of expository works on mathematics and science and is probably best known for his book, *The Ascent of Man*, which became the basis for a very popular series of television specials on science. Bronowski died in 1974.

The laws of probability have a rather curious, even shady beginning in Western civilization. It seems that some persons were involved in a game of chance. However, the game was interrupted (by a duel? by the authorities?) before it could be finished. The participants left but the pot remained, and the question was, how is the pot to be divided? Since the game had been going on for some time, some players were more favorably positioned to win than others; just giving each his money back would not do. For example, in a game of seven-card stud, the player with two aces and a king facing up after five cards would feel more secure than the player with a two, a four, and a jack showing. If the game were stopped at that point the player with the aces would be furious if merely offered his bet back. However, it is not impossible that the player with the two, four, and jack has two jacks in the face-down cards. Therefore the second player would violently object if he didn't get at least some of his bet back since there is a chance that he could have won.

The question of fairly dividing a poker pot when there are unequal chances of winning was put to Blaisé Pascal (1623–1662), who was one of the most notable mathematicians of his time. Pascal's solution to this and a variety of other gambling problems were communicated by letter to his friend Fermat, and their correspondence, later expanded and systematized by Huygens, was published by Huygens in 1657. From this modest beginning the ideas of probability and their application have had a continuous and expanding history currently manifest in such diverse ways as television program ratings and the reliability of ICBMs.

We have previously encountered Bronowski in Volume I, so neither he nor his superb expository skills require further comment. In this essay he discusses how the idea of chance may be systematized and expanded into a powerful tool for describing the world of experience.

I HAVE REPEATEDLY spoken of science as a language. This analogy seems to me so easy and helpful that I found it most natural to begin this book by comparing science with the English language. It seems to me natural to think of optics, for example, as a language to describe seeing and being seen. As a language, it is uncommon only in the single-minded pains which it takes to avoid other topics: to get rid of the confusion which might be caused by color blindness, for instance; and to avoid the more attractive topics of wishing and believing. Optics is the language in which seeing is seeing and nothing else—not even believing.

Source: Jacob Bronowski, "The Idea of Chance," in *The Common Sense of Science* (Cambridge, Mass.: Harvard University Press, 1953). Reprinted by permission of the publisher.

This analogy would not have occurred at all naturally to scientists in the last century. For a language is no more than a code for describing some chosen features of the world. Of course the purpose of language is to arrange with others how we shall act in the world. But in method it remains a description, which names the facts and mimics their arrangement. The nineteenth century would have thought this too modest a view of science. Its best minds did see science as a guide to action. But they were convinced that it helped them to act usefully because it does not merely describe the world: it explains it. And by an explanation they meant a model which follows nature exactly, link by link, along a chain of causes and effects. An animal is precisely a heat engine, they said; or a gas is a collection of small billiard balls; or the brain is a telegraph office. They believed that in the end there is only one scientific method: to set up a system of causes and effects. If science describes, they held, then it describes the cause by its effects; and if it predicts, it predicts the effect from its causes.

I have said at some length that this belief can no longer be sustained. Very well: we are to give up the universal search for causes. What are we to put in their place? For answer, we must go back to beginnings, and repeat something which cannot be said too often. The aim of science is to describe the world in orderly language, in such a way that we can if possible foresee the results of those alternative courses of action between which we are always choosing. The kind of order which our description has is entirely one of convenience. Our purpose is always to predict. Of course, it is most convenient if we can find an order by cause and effect; it makes our choice simple; but it is not essential.

What we are looking for, in science as much as in the day-to-day of our lives, is a system of prediction: a predictor, as it were. The principles which guide us in our predictions are in the end nothing more than steps in the calculation. And life is not an examination; we do not get marks for the steps; what matters is getting the right answer. So it is perfectly possible to base a system of prediction on no principle except trying to get the right answer. This is exactly what all plants and animals do. The bat avoids obstacles by

shouting at them that shrill cry just beyond my hearing, and then listens for the echo. Whatever system it has for translating the echo into a prediction it has found by evolution, and evolution has found it by trial and error. The radar set does all this more rationally. Yet the steps in its calculations are no better than the bat's; and they are no worse. For instance, the bat and evolution have long discovered that the best wavelengths for range-finding are the centimeter waves which the radar set also uses. A man catching a ball is a predictor, or a child flying a kite, or a cat at a mouse-hole. They remind us that the business of prediction, and of science is to get us to do roughly the right thing at roughly the right time.

There is of course nothing sacred about the causal form of natural laws. We are accustomed to this form, until it has become our standard of what every natural law ought to look like. If you halve the space which a gas fills, and keep other things constant, then you will double the pressure, we say. If you do such and such, the result will be so and so; and it will always be so and so. And we feel by long habit that it is this "always" which turns the prediction into a law. But of course there is no reason why laws should have this always, all-or-nothing form. If you self-cross the offspring of a pure white and a pure pink garden pea, said Mendel, then on an average one quarter of these grandchildren will be white, and three quarters will be pink. This is as good a law as any other; it says what will happen, in good quantitative terms, and what it says turns out to be true. It is not any less respectable for not making that parade of everytime certainty which the law of gases makes. And indeed, the gas law takes its air of finality only from the accumulation of just such chances as Mendel's law makes explicit.

It is important to seize this point. If I say that after a fine week it *always* rains on Sunday, then this is recognized and respected as a law. But if I say that after a fine week it rains on Sunday more often than not, then this somehow is felt to be an unsatisfactory statement; and it is taken for granted that I have not really got down to some underlying law which would chime with our habit of wanting science to say decisively either "always" or "never." Even if I say that after a fine week it rains on seven Sundays out of ten, you may accept this as a statistic, but it does not satisfy you as a law. Somehow it seems to lack the force of law.

Yet this is a mere prejudice. It is nice to have laws which say: this configuration of facts will always be followed by event A, ten times out of ten. But neither taste nor convenience really makes this a more essential form of law than one which says: This configuration of facts will be followed by event A seven times out of ten, and by event B three times out of ten. In form the first is a causal law and the second a statistical law. But in content and application, there is no reason to prefer one to the other. The laws of science have two functions, to be true and to be helpful; probably each of these functions includes the other. If the statistical law does both, that is all that can be asked of it. We may persuade ourselves that it is intellectually less satisfying than a causal law, and fails somehow to give us the same feeling of understanding the process of nature. But this is an illusion of habit. No law ever gave wider satisfaction than the law of gravitation. Yet we have seen that the explanation it gave of the workings of nature was false, and the understanding we got from it mistaken. What it really did, and did superbly, was to predict the movements of the heavenly bodies to an excellent approximation.

There is, however, a limitation within every law which does not contain the word "always." Bluntly, when I say that a configuration of facts will be followed sometimes by event A and at other times by B, I cannot be certain whether at the next trial A or B will turn up. I may know that A is to turn up seven times and B three times out of ten; but that brings me no nearer at all to knowing which is to turn up on the one occasion I have my eye on next time. Mendel's law is all very fine when you grow peas by the acre; but it does not tell you, and cannot, whether the single second generation seed in your windowbox will flower white or pink. Mendel himself ran into this trouble when he tested his law, because he had to do his experimental work in a rather small monastery garden.

So far, this is obvious enough. It is obvious that if we did know what is to happen precisely next

time, then we would at once have not a statistical law, but a law of certainty into which we could write the word "always." But this limitation carries with it a less obvious one. If we are not sure whether A or B will turn up next time, then neither can we be sure which will turn up the time after, or the time after that. We know that A is to turn up seven times and B three; but this can never mean that every set of ten trials will give us exactly seven As and three Bs. In fact, it is not possible to write down an irregular string of As and Bs in such a way that every set of ten successive letters which we pick out from it, beginning where we like, is made up precisely of seven of one and three of the other. And of course it is quite impossible to write them down so that any choice of ten letters picked here and there will contain just seven As.

Then what do I mean by saying that we expect A to turn up seven times to every three times which B turns up? I mean that among all the sets of ten trials which we can choose from an extended series, picking as we like, the greatest number will contain seven As and three Bs. This is the same thing as saying that if we have enough trials, the proportion of As to Bs will tend to the ratio seven to three. But of course, no run of trials, however extended, is necessarily long enough. In no run of trials can we be sure of reaching precisely the balance of seven to three.

Then how do I know that the law is in fact seven As and three Bs? What do I mean by saying that the ratio tends to this in a long trial, when I never know if the trial is long enough? And more, when I know that at the very moment when we have reached precisely this ratio, the next single trial must upset it—because it must add either a whole A or a whole B, and cannot add seven tenths of one and three tenths of the other. I mean this. After ten trials, we may have eight As and only two Bs; it is not at all improbable. It is not very improbable that we may have nine As, and it is not even excessively improbable that we may have ten. But it is very improbable that, after a hundred trials, we shall have as many as eighty As. It is excessively improbable that after a thousand trials we shall have as many as eight hundred As; indeed it is very improbable that at this stage the proportion of As departs from seven out of ten by as much as five percent. And if after a hundred thousand trials we should get a proportion which differs from our law by as much as one percent, then we should have to face the fact that the law itself is almost certainly in error.

Let me quote a practical example. One of the French *encyclopédistes* of the eighteenth century, the great naturalist Buffon, was a man of wide interests. His interest in geology and evolution got him into trouble with the Sorbonne, which made him formally recant his belief that the earth has changed since Genesis. His interest in the laws of chance was less perilous, and it prompted him in 1733 to ask an interesting question. If a needle is thrown at random on a sheet of paper ruled with lines whose distance apart is exactly equal to the length of the needle, how often can it be expected to fall on a line and how often into a blank space? The answer is rather odd: it should fall on a line a little less than two times out of three—precisely, it should fall on a line two times out of π, where π is the familiar ratio of the circumference of a circle to its diameter, which has the value 3.14159265. . . . How near can we get to this answer in actual trials? This depends of course on the care with which we rule the lines and do the throwing; but, after that, it depends only on our patience. In 1901 a minor Italian mathematician, Mario Lazzerini, having taken due care, demonstrated his patience by making well over 3,000 throws. The value he got for π at one stage was right to the sixth place of decimals, which is an error of only a hundred thousandth part of one percent.

This is the method to which modern science is moving. It uses no principle but that of forecasting with as much assurance as possible, but with no more than is possible. That is, it idealizes the future from the outset, not as completely determined, but as determined within a defined area of uncertainty. Let me illustrate the kind of uncertainty. We know that the children of two blue-eyed parents will certainly have blue eyes; at least, no exception has ever been found. By contrast, we cannot be certain that all the children of two brown-eyed parents will have brown eyes. And we cannot be certain of it even if they have already had ten children with brown eyes. The

reason is that we can never discount a run of luck of the kind which Dr. Johnson once observed when a friend of his was breeding horses. "He has had," said Dr. Johnson, "sixteen fillies without one colt, which is an accident beyond all computation of chances." But what we can do is to compute the *odds* against such a run; this is not as hard as Johnson supposed. And from this we can compute the likelihood that the next child will have brown eyes. That is, we can make a forecast which states our degree of uncertainty in a precise form. Oddly enough, it is just here that Mendel's own account of his work is at fault. He assumed in effect that once a couple has had ten brown-eyed children the chance that they may yet have blue-eyed children is negligible. But it was not.

This area of uncertainty shrinks very quickly in its proportion if we make our forecasts not about one family but about many. I do not know whether this or that couple will have a child next year; I do not even know whether I shall. But it is easy to estimate the number of children who will be born to the whole population, and to give limits of uncertainty to our estimate. The motives which lead to marriage, the trifles which cause a car to crash, the chanciness of today's sunshine or tomorrow's egg, are local, private, and incalculable. Yet, as Kant saw long ago, their totals over the country in a year are remarkably steady; and even their ranges of uncertainty can be predicted.

This is the revolutionary thought in modern science. It replaces the concept of the *inevitable effect* by that of the *probable trend*. Its technique is to separate so far as possible the steady trend from local fluctuations. The less the trend has been overlaid by fluctuations in the past, the greater is the confidence with which we look along the trend into the future. We are not isolating a cause. We are tracing a pattern of nature in its whole setting. We are aware of the uncertainties which that large, flexible setting induces in our pattern. But the world cannot be isolated from itself: the uncertainty *is* the world. The future does not already exist; it can only be predicted. We must be content to map the places into which it may move, and to assign a greater or less likelihood to this or that of its areas of uncertainty.

These are the ideas of chance in science today.

They are new ideas: they give chance a kind of order: they recreate it as the life within reality. These ideas have come to science from many sources. Some were invented by Renaissance brokers; some by seventeenth-century gamblers; some by mathematicians who were interested in aiming-errors and in the flow of gases and more recently in radioactivity. The most fruitful have come from biology within little more than the last fifty years. I need not stress again how successful they have been in the last few years, for example in physics: Nagasaki is a monument to that. But we have not yet begun to feel their importance outside science altogether. For example, they make it plain that problems like Free Will or Determinism are simply misunderstandings of history. History is neither determined nor random. At any moment, it moves forward into an area whose general shape is known but whose boundaries are uncertain in a calculable way. A society moves under material pressure like a stream of gas; and on the average, its individuals obey the pressure; but at any instant, any individual may, like an atom of gas, be moving across or against the stream. The will on the one hand and the compulsion on the other exist and play within these boundaries. In these ideas, the concept of chance has lost its old dry pointlessness and has taken on a new depth and power; it has come to life. Some of these ideas have begun to influence the arts: they can be met vaguely in the novels of the young French writers. In time they will liberate our literature from the pessimism which comes from our divided loyalties: our reverence for machines and, at odds with it, our nostalgia for personality. I am young enough to believe that this union, the union as it were of chance with fate, will give us all a new optimism.

Let me make this point more explicit. It was assumed in the classical sciences of the last century that such a phenomenon as radioactivity, or the inheritance of a blood group, or loss of nerve, or the rise in prices in a time of scarcity, is each the result of many influences; and that step by step these could be taken apart and the phenomenon traced to all its causes. In each case, what was happening could be treated as a laboratory experiment. It could be isolated from those events in the world which had no bearing on it, and lay as it were beyond the box of the laboratory. And within this box, the causes could be studied one by one, much as we study how the volume of a gas changes when the pressure is varied while we keep the temperature the same, and then when the temperature is varied while we keep the pressure the same.

But this picture of the phenomenon in isolation from the rest of the world and from the observer turns out to be false. There comes a time when it will not do any longer even as an approximation. Then it turns out that time and space, which Newton thought absolute, cannot be given physical meaning without the observer. The laboratory cannot exist in a void, and the experiment cannot be put in a box. And as we refine our measurements, the limitations of the observer look larger and larger. The liquid on whose surface the microscope is trained leaps and shivers under the lens, until we can see the Brownian movement of its molecules. The stately flow of the gas is shot through and through with the random darting of its particles. Enlarge the pointer on the dial a millionfold, and the instrument can no longer be read, because the turbulent movement of its atoms shifts the point from instant to instant. The experimental errors are woven into the very substance of the world.

And while all this was going on in the laboratory, nature and society outside were of course thronged with a million larger examples. Everything in the plant and the living body, in earthquakes and the weather, in animal society and human workshops and the prices on the ticker tape, is beyond the control of the neatly designed experiment. There had been a moment in history, an imaginary moment but no less important for that, when the weights falling from the Leaning Tower had been a key to open the secret of the stars. Ever since, the mute laboratory worker had gone on in the faith that his little box would sort out the sun-spot cycle and the coming of the Black Death and the Wall Street crash. The world is a machine, and he would repeat the triumph of Newton and make a model which would act out its fate minute by minute. Adam Smith and Jeremy Bentham and Mill, Hartley and Mesmer and Freud, Zola and Proust and Theodore Dreiser, each in his own way worked a lifetime in that hope.

But there were also men who were faced with particular problems which they could not wait three centuries to take to pieces. They were not always respectable scientific problems. The gambling friends of Pascal and Euler were impatient men. The insurance brokers in Florence and Amsterdam and London did not care about theory; they wanted empirical results. And then, most interesting, at the end of the last century Francis Galton and later Karl Pearson began to look at human characters: size and weight and configuration and growth. They formed no tidy theories like Lombroso's theory of criminal types. They seemed even to have a harsh suspicion of Mendel's theory of inheritance. Rather they looked back to work like that of Laplace and Gauss, who had first considered what errors must be regarded as unavoidable even in astronomical observation. Thus they came to formulate the notion of the chance distribution of a set of characters in a population. And from their work in turn has developed the whole theory of statistical differences, which I believe to be the basis of science for the future.

Let me quote an example from my own experience. In 1945 I went to Japan, and since I did not speak Japanese there were sent with my party several full-blooded young Japanese who had been brought up in America. It struck me when we set out that they were on the whole smaller men than the white Americans in the party. When we got to Japan, it struck me forcibly that the Japanese we had brought with us were themselves taller on the whole than the native Japanese. Here were two differences provided by nature and by society which could not be treated by laboratory experiment. Nor were they invariable differences. Although on the average the group of white Americans were taller than the group of Japanese Americans, and these in turn taller than the native Japanese, there were men in each group who overlapped into the others. Indeed, the smallest man I set eyes on was a white American, and there was one tall Japanese American. Nevertheless, I was willing to formulate two personal hypotheses: that the Japanese are by heredity smaller than white Americans, and that Japa-

nese brought up in America are taller than home-grown Japanese, presumably because America provides them with different foods or a different environment.

How do we test such hypotheses? The problem is just like those which Pearson tackled, and the method is due to him and to a brewer with a statistical bent who called himself *Student*. We find the average of each of our three types; and at the same time we calculate from the individuals in each group a measure of the variation round its average which this group itself seems to display. Since in the nature of things we observe only a few members in each group, neither our averages nor our measures of variation are free from error. But in each case, the variation allows us to estimate what is the largest error we are likely to make in measuring these averages. That is, we surround each average as we have measured it by an area of uncertainty. If these three areas of uncertainty do not overlap, then we know with some confidence that my hypotheses were justified. But if two of the areas overlap, then we cannot be sure that the difference between the two averages round which they have been drawn is a real one. We have failed to establish a systematic difference between these two groups, because the random fluctuations within each group, as we have observed them on this occasion, are large enough to swamp the possible difference.

This is the essential content of the statistical method. It has many applications, and they differ one from another in the detail of application. But the underlying thought is the same. Essentially the thought depends not on unlimited accuracy in measuring a character, but on judging the accuracy by a measure of the inherent variation from individual to individual which we cannot escape. We look for a trend or systematic difference. The line of this trend will itself be blurred by the unsteady hand of chance or random fluctuation. We cannot get rid of this random scrawl. But we can from it determine a measure of random variation, and use that to draw round the trend an area of uncertainty. If the area is small enough by standards which are agreed between us, then the trend is established, and we know the limits within which it is likely to lie. If the area is too large, and the limits too wide, we have not been able to establish a trend. It may exist, but in this set of observations it has been swamped by the random fluctuations.

Let me take another practical instance. We believe that streptomycin is effective in helping to cure tuberculosis. We base this belief on experiment. But in every experiment, patients are themselves in many stages of the disease; they inevitably receive different doses and respond in different degrees; the whole picture is overlaid by unavoidable variation. Can we extract any positive results in so variable a field? Yes, if we choose our statistical technique intelligently. For example, suppose we have measures of the health of each patient from time to time during treatment. Then we can test the hypothesis that on the whole patients get better as treatment goes on. The first step is to find, by taking straightforward averages after each month of treatment, what seems to be the average improvement in each month. This allows us to draw a line of improvement on our graph. The patients are still widely scattered round this line. But we can measure the scatter or random variation round the line of improvement, and we can compare it with the scatter of all results when we neglect the systematic trend or line. And this will be our criterion for judging whether the line of improvement is a real effect or not. We shall see by how much the total scatter is reduced when we compare it with the scatter round our line. If the reduction is substantial by standards on which statisticians are agreed, then we say that we have found a meaningful effect of the treatment; we call it significant. We shall still need further analysis to assure ourselves that what makes the treatment work is the streptomycin. But if the hypothesis that there is a trend with treatment turns out not to reduce the random scatter in the condition of patients, then we have not established an effect at all; the result fails to reach significance.

This approach is very simple in conception. At bottom, it divides the phenomenon which we observe in a hundred instances round us into two parts. I have called the parts systematic and random, or trend and fluctuation, or effect and chance. But under all these names, there runs essentially the same conception: that we can isolate the effect only to a certain accuracy. To determine whether the effect is real, we have therefore to compare its area of uncertainty with the accuracy to which we can isolate it. We have to judge the effect by the fluctuation to which our estimate is liable. If the effect stands out plainly above the fluctuation, then we have a significant result. We have established an effect, and although the unavoidable fluctuation still surrounds it with an area of uncertainty, we can apply our finding with this small margin or tolerance. But if the effect turns out not to be large when compared with the inherent fluctuation, then we have not established its significance. Even if it exists, its area of uncertainty is too large to be useful. Our only hope then is to do more experiments, since each experiment reduces the area of uncertainty.

The idea of chance as I have explained it here is not difficult. But it is new and unfamiliar. We are not used to handling it. So it does not seem to have the incisiveness of the simple laws of cause and effect. We seem to be in a land of sometimes and perhaps, and we had hoped to go on living with always and with certainty. We may see, again and again, that smokers contract cancer of the lung more often than non-smokers; but we go on feeling (as we nervously console ourselves with a cigarette) that the connection has not been "proved."

Yet I believe that the difficulty is only one of habit. We shall become accustomed to the new ideas just as soon as we are willing and as we have to. And we are having to. On all sides science is crowding into fields of knowledge, which cannot be isolated in the laboratory, and asking us to come to conclusions in matters where we cannot hope to trace a causal mechanism. It may seem to be overtaxing our notion of science to hope that we shall find some common method of tackling the problems of physics and economics, of evolution and soil chemistry, of medicine and meteorology, of psychology and aerial bombardment. We have grown accustomed to thinking of science itself as divided into smaller and smaller pieces of specialization, an atomic universe of knowledge of its own, which no one and nothing can again hope to master. But this may well be an illusion. The different branches of science may seem so far apart only because we lack the common method on which they grow and which holds them together organically. Look back to the state of knowledge in the year 1600: the branches of science and of speculation seemed as diverse and as specialized, and no one could have foreseen that they would all fall into place as soon as Descartes and Hobbes introduced the unifying concept of cause and effect.

The statistical concept of chance may come as dramatically to unify the scattered pieces of science in the future. What Hobbes and Newton did was to change the whole concept of natural law: instead of basing it on the analogy of the human will, they built it on cause and on force. But this analogy with human effort is now breaking down. We are on the threshold of another scientific revolution. The concept of natural law is changing. The laws of chance seem at first glance to be lawless. But I have shown in this [article] that they can be formulated with as much rigor as the laws of cause. Certainly they can be seen already to cover an infinitely wider field of human experience in nature and in society. And it may be that they will give to that field the unity which the last fifty years have lacked. If they do, they will give us all also a new confidence. We have been swept by a great wave of pessimism, which rises from our own feeling of helplessness in the recognition that none of us understands the deep workings of the world. As science and knowledge have been broken into pieces, there has come upon us all a loss of nerve. That happened to the old classical culture of the Mediterranean in the seventeenth century. The future lay with the driving and purposeful optimists of the north, who seized the notion of cause and purpose, and with it conquered nature and the world together. We are looking for another such universal concept to unify and to enlighten our world. Chance has a helpless ring in our ears. But the laws of chance are lively, vigorous, and human; and they may give us again that forward look which in the last half century has so tragically lowered its eyes.

Hilbert's 10th Problem

Martin Davis and Reuben Hersh

Martin Davis was born in New York and received his doctorate in mathematics at Princeton in 1950. He has taught at the University of Illinois, the Institute for Advanced Study, University of California at Davis, Ohio State, Rensselaer Polytechnic, Hartford University, Institute of Mathematical Sciences at NYU, and Yeshiva University. He has been awarded the Chauvenet award and the Ford award by the Mathematical Association of America and the Steele prize by the American Mathematical Society.

Reuben Hersh was born in New York, did his undergraduate work at Harvard, and received his Ph.D. from New York University in 1962. Before that he had served as an assistant editor for *Scientific American*. He has been at the University of New Mexico since 1970. He has received the Chauvenet prize from the Mathematical Association of America.

The text of David Hilbert's famous address to the International Congress in 1900 is printed in Part Three of Volume I. Appended to Volume I is a list of his twenty-three problems with some indication as to the current state of progress on each. This essay by Davis and Hersh is a most readable tour of the 10th problem and its solution in the negative. The authors do an excellent job of covering all aspects of the question, and it would be pointless to try to embellish their efforts here. There is, however, one point worth noting. The innocent statement of the 10th problem rather quickly leads its investigators into the underbrush of the foundations of mathematics. Notice that the example of the process for which there is a green-light machine but not a green-light/red-light machine is in some sense self-referential. The process of showing there is no such machine is another example of that type of situation, "It is in the list only if it isn't," which so often leads to unsolvable or meaningless problems in mathematics. It is this type of result that makes even nonintuitionists just a bit uneasy and lends some force to the intuitionists' claims that modern mathematics allows too much.

Can a procedure be devised that will indicate if there are solutions to a Diophantine equation (an equation where whole-number solutions are sought)? This question on a famous list has now been answered.

"We hear within us the perpetual call: there is the problem. Seek its solution. You can find it by pure reason, for in mathematics there is no *ignorabimus* [We shall not know]." So did David Hilbert address the Second International Congress of Mathematicians in Paris on August 8, 1900, greeting the new century by presenting a list of 23 major problems to challenge future mathematicians. Some of Hilbert's problems are still unsolved. Others have inspired generations of mathematical investigators and have led to major new mathematical theories. The most recently conquered of Hilbert's problems is the 10th, which was solved in 1970 by the 22-year-old Russian mathematician Yuri Matyasevich.

David Hilbert was born in Königsberg in 1862 and was professor at the University of Göttingen from 1895 until his death in 1943. After the death of Henri Poincaré in 1912 he was generally regarded as being the foremost mathematician of his time. He made fundamental contributions in several fields, but he is perhaps best remembered for his development of the abstract method as a powerful tool in mathematics.

Hilbert's 10th problem is easily described. It has to do with the simplest and most basic mathematical activity: solving equations. The equations to be solved are polynomial equations, that is, equations such as $x^2 - 3xy = 5$, which are formed by adding and multiplying constants and variables and by using whole-number exponents. Moreover, Hilbert specified that the equations must use only integers, that is, positive or negative whole numbers. No irrational or imaginary numbers or even fractions are allowed in either the equations or their solutions. Problems of this type are called Diophantine equations after Diophantus of Alexandria, who wrote a book on the subject in the third century.

Hilbert's 10th problem is: Give a mechanical procedure by which any Diophantine equation can be tested to see if solutions exist. In Hilbert's words: "Given a Diophantine equation with any number of unknown quantities and with rational integral numerical coefficients: to devise a process according to which it can be determined by a finite number of operations whether the equation is solvable in rational integers." Hilbert does not ask for a process to find the solutions but merely for a process to determine if the equation has solutions. The process should be a clear-cut formal procedure that could be programmed for a computing machine and that would be guaranteed to work in all cases. Such a process is known as an algorithm.

If Hilbert's problem is simply stated, Matyasevich's solution is even more simply stated: No such process can ever be devised; such an algorithm does not exist. Worded in this way, the answer sounds disappointingly negative. Matyasevich's result, however, constitutes an important and useful addition to the understanding of properties of numbers.

Matyasevich's work extended a series of researches by three Americans: one of us (Davis), Julia Robinson and Hilary Putnam. Their work

in turn was based on earlier investigations by several founders of modern logic and computability theory: Alan Turing, Emil Post, Alonzo Church, Stephen Kleene and the same Kurt Gödel who is famous for his work on the consistency of axiomatic systems (Hilbert's second problem) and on the continuum hypothesis of Cantor (Hilbert's first problem).

Let us start on Hilbert's 10th problem by looking at a few Diophantine equations. The term "Diophantine equation" is slightly misleading, because it is not so much the nature of the equation that is crucial as the nature of the admissible solutions. For example, the equation $x^2 + y^2 - 2 = 0$ has infinitely many solutions if one does not think of it as a Diophantine equation. The solutions are represented by the graph of the equation, which is a circle in the plane formed by the x axis and the y axis. The center of the circle is at the coordinates $x = 0, y = 0$. That point is called the origin; it is abbreviated (0,0). The radius of the circle is $\sqrt{2}$ (see Fig. 1). The coordinates of any point on the circle satisfy the equation, and there are an infinite number of such points. If we consider the problem as a Diophantine equation, however, there are only four solutions: (1) $x = 1, y = 1$; (2) $x = -1, y = 1$; (3) $x = 1, y = -1$, and (4) $x = -1, y = -1$.

Suppose the equation is changed to $x^2 + y^2 - 3 = 0$. There are still an infinite number of solutions if it is treated as an ordinary equation but no solutions at all if it is treated as a Diophantine equation. The reason is that now the graph is a circle with radius equal to $\sqrt{3}$, and no points on this curve have both coordinates simultaneously equal to whole numbers.

A famous family of Diophantine equations has the form $x^n + y^n = z^n$, where n may equal 2, 3, 4 or any larger integer. If n is equal to 2, the equation is satisfied by the lengths of the sides of any right triangle and is called the Pythagorean theorem. One such solution is the set of numbers $x = 3, y = 4, z = 5$. If n is equal to or greater than 3, the equation is what is known as Fermat's equation. The 17th-century French mathematician Pierre de Fermat thought he had proved that these equations have no positive whole-number solutions. In the margin of his copy of Diophan-

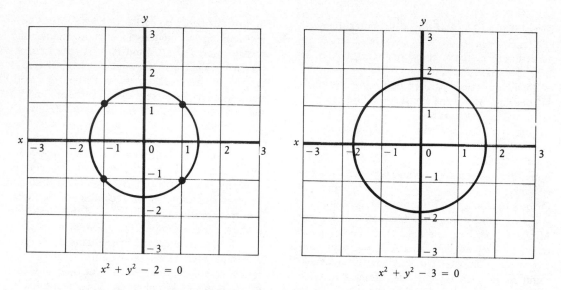

$$x^2 + y^2 - 2 = 0 \qquad\qquad x^2 + y^2 - 3 = 0$$

Figure 1   Graphs of two equations illustrate the difference between an ordinary equation and a Diophantine equation, for which one is interested only in whole-number solutions; this difference is central to Hilbert's 10th problem. The equations in point are $x^2 + y^2 - 2 = 0$ *(left)* and $x^2 + y^2 - 3 = 0$ *(right)*; both are represented by circles with their center at the origin, that is, at the point with coordinates $x = 0, y = 0$. In the case of $x^2 + y^2 - 2 = 0$ the circle has a radius of $\sqrt{2}$. If the equation is treated as an ordinary equation, there are infinitely many solutions. If, however, it is treated as a Diophantine equation, there are only four solutions: (1) $x = 1, y = 1$, (2) $x = -1, y = 1$, (3) $x = 1, y = -1$, and (4) $x = -1, y = -1$. These solutions are represented by dots where the graph crosses the four points with those coordinates on the Cartesian grid. In the case of $x^2 + y^2 - 3 = 0$, the circle has a radius of $\sqrt{3}$. As an ordinary equation it has an infinite number of solutions; as a Diophantine equation, however, it has none at all.

tus' book he wrote that he had found a "marvelous proof" that was unfortunately too long to be written down in that space. The proof (if indeed Fermat had one) has never been found. Known as Fermat's last theorem, it is probably the oldest and most famous unsolved problem in mathematics. These examples show that Diophantine equations are easy to write down but hard to solve. They are hard to solve because we are so exclusive about the kind of numbers we accept as solutions.

For first-degree equations, that is, equations in which unknowns are not multiplied together and all exponents are equal to 1, such as $7x + 4y - 3z - 99t + 13u - 10 = 0$, the existence of solutions can be determined by a technique of division known since ancient times as Euclid's algorithm. For second-degree equations with two unknowns, such as $3x^2 - 5y^2 + 7 = 0$ or $x^2 - xy - y^2 = 1$, a theory developed early in the 19th century by the great Karl Friedrich Gauss enables one to determine whether there are any solutions. Recent work by the young British mathematician Alan Baker has shed considerable light on equations greater than the second degree that have two unknowns. For equations greater than the first degree that have more than two unknowns, there exist only some special cases that can be handled by special tricks, and a vast sea of ignorance.

Why is it so difficult to find a process such as the one Hilbert called for? The most direct approach would be to simply test all possible sets of values of the unknowns, one after another, until a solution is found. For example, if the equation has two unknowns, one could make a list of all pairs of integers. Then one would simply go through the list trying one pair after another to see if it satisfies the equation. This is certainly a clear-cut, mechanical procedure that a machine could carry out. What will be the result?

If the equation is the first one we mentioned, $x^2 + y^2 - 2 = 0$, one would test $(0,0)$, $(0,1)$, $(1,0)$, $(0, -1)$, $(-1,0)$ and reject them all. The next candidate, $(1,1)$, is a solution. We were lucky: only six pairs had to be considered. If, on the other hand, the equation were $x^2 + y^2 = 20{,}000$, one would have to test thousands of pairs of numbers before a solution was found. Still, it is clear that if a solution exists, it will be found in a finite number of steps.

On the other hand, what about the second equation: $x^2 + y^2 - 3 = 0$? One can try pairs of integers from now till eternity, and all that will ever be known is that a solution has not been found yet. One would never know whether or not the next pair tried would be a solution. For this particular example it is possible to prove there are no solutions. But the proof requires a new idea; it cannot be obtained merely by successively substituting integers into the equation.

A device that carries out a process of the kind suggested by Hilbert should accept as an input the coefficients of an arbitrary Diophantine equation. As an output it should turn on a green light if the equation has a solution and a red light if it has none. Such a machine might be called a Hilbert machine. By way of contrast a device that simply searches for solutions by successive trials *ad infinitum* could be described as a green-light machine. If the equation has a solution, the green light goes on after a finite number of steps. If the equation has no solution, the computation simply goes on forever; unlike the Hilbert machine, the green-light machine has no way of knowing when to give up (see Fig. 2).

It is easy to build a green-light machine for Diophantine equations. The question is, can we do better and build a Hilbert machine, that is, a green-light-red-light machine that will always stop after a finite number of steps and give a definite yes or no answer? What Matyasevich proved is that this can never be done. Even if we allow the machine unlimited memory storage and unlimited computing time, no program can ever be written and no machine can ever be built that will do what Hilbert wanted. A Hilbert machine does not exist.

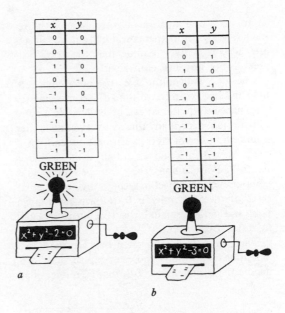

Figure 2 Pairs of integers can be individually tested by green-light machines to see if they are solutions to Diophantine equations. Trial and error comes up with a solution for the equation $x^2 + y^2 - 2 = 0$ on the sixth try (Fig. 2a). Green-light machine testing equation $x^2 + y^2 - 3 = 0$ has no way of knowing when to give up, however, because there are no whole-number solutions (Fig. 2b). All it knows is that it has found no solutions yet.

Hilbert continued in his address of 1900: "Occasionally it happens that we seek the solution under insufficient hypotheses or in an incorrect sense, and for this reason do not succeed. The problem then arises: to show the impossibility of the solution under the given hypotheses, or in the sense contemplated." That is exactly what has happened with the 10th problem.

In order to explain how we know that no Hilbert machine exists, we have to discuss some simple ideas about computability. Suppose S stands for a set of integers. S is "listable" if a green-light machine can be built that will do the following job: accept any integer as an input, and as an output turn on a green light after a finite number of steps if and only if the input (the integer) belongs to S. For example, the set of even numbers is listable. In this case the machine would divide the input by 2 and turn on a green light if the remainder is 0. In mathematical literature such sets are called recursively enumerable; the word "listable" is our informal equivalent.

The set S is "computable" if a green-light-red-light machine (similar to the Hilbert machine for Diophantine equations) can be built to do a more difficult job: accept any integer as input and, after a finite number of steps, turn on a green light if the integer is in S and a red light if the integer is not in S. For example, the set of even numbers is computable. The machine would divide the input by 2; if the remainder is 0, it turns on a green light and if the remainder is 1, it turns on a red light (see Figs. 3 and 4).

There is a close connection between these two definitions. For the purposes of explanation, let $\overline{S}$ denote the complement of S, that is, the set of all

Figure 4   Red light goes on on the green-light-red-light machine if the machine can determine that the input is not a member of the set. Suppose the input x is the whole number 23; 2 goes into 23 with a remainder of 1, signifying that 23 is not a member of S. Complement of set S is $\overline{S}$, the set of odd numbers; 23 is a member of $\overline{S}$. Since a green-light-red-light machine can be built to sort members of S from members of $\overline{S}$, the set S is called computable.

Figure 3   Green-light-red-light machine is an imaginary device that tests numbers to determine if they are members of a given set. Hilbert's 10th problem asks if a green-light-red-light "Hilbert machine" can be built to test Diophantine equations to see whether or not they have solutions. In the case of testing numbers for membership in a set, green light goes on if the machine can determine in a finite number of steps that a given input is a member of the set. Say that S is the set of all even numbers. To test inputs one can devise an algorithm for dividing each input x by 2. If the remainder of the division is 0 (written Rem $x/2 = 0$), machine would turn on its green light, signifying that x is a member of S.

integers that do not belong to S. If in the two examples S is the set of even integers, then $\overline{S}$ is the set of odd integers. We can prove that if S is computable, S and $\overline{S}$ are both listable. To put that statement another way: If a green-light-red-light machine exists for S, then there exists a green-light machine for S and a green-light machine for $\overline{S}$. The proof is simple. To build a green-light machine for S, just unscrew the red bulb of the green-light-red-light machine. To build a green-light machine for $\overline{S}$, unscrew the green bulb of the Hilbert machine and put it into the socket that held the red bulb. (See Fig. 5.)

The converse is also true: If S and $\overline{S}$ are listable, then S is computable. The equivalent of this statement is: If a green-light machine exists for each of S and $\overline{S}$, then a green-light-red-light machine can be built for S. This is easily done. In the green-light machine for $\overline{S}$, replace the green bulb with a red bulb. Then hook up the two machines in parallel, so that the input goes into both

Figure 5 Green-light-red-light machine for the set S can be transformed into a green-light machine for S (that is, a machine that simply lights up when the input is a member of S) plus a green-light machine for $\overline{S}$, the complement of S. The proof is simple. To build a green-light machine for S, unscrew the red lamp of the green-light-red-light machine. To build a green-light machine for $\overline{S}$, unscrew the green lamp of the green-light-red-light machine and put it into the socket that held the red lamp. This fact can be stated in another way. If a set (such as S) is computable, then both the set and its complement (such as $\overline{S}$) are listable, that is, the members of S (in this case the set of even numbers) can be listed separately and sorted from the members of $\overline{S}$ (the set of odd numbers).

simultaneously. The result is clearly a green-light-red-light machine. (See Fig. 6.)

Knowing all of this, we can now state one of the crucial facts in computability theory, one that plays a central role in the solution of Hilbert's 10th problem: There is a set K that is listable but not computable! That is, there exists a green-light machine for K, but it is impossible to build a green-light machine for $\overline{K}$, the complement of K.

To prove this seemingly strange fact, let each green-light machine be specified by a detailed "customer's manual" in the English language. The customer's manual describes exactly how the machine is constructed. The customer's manuals can be set in order and numbered sequentially 1, 2, 3, and so on. In that way all green-light machines are numbered; M_1 is the first machine, M_2 is the second, and so on. There is a subtle point

hidden here. Such an ordered list of customer's manuals would not be possible for green-light-red-light machines. The difficulty is that one cannot tell from the manual whether the red light or the green light will turn on for any input to the corresponding machine.

The set K is defined as the set of numbers n such that the nth machine lights up when it receives n itself as an input. In other words, the number 1 belongs to K if and only if M_1 turns on its green light when "1" is entered into its input. The number 2 belongs to K if and only if M_2 eventually lights up when "2" is entered into its input, and so on (see Fig. 7).

In order to build a green-light machine for K we need, along with the library of customer's manuals, a little man who can read them and carry out their instructions. He should perhaps be

Figure 6 Green-light machine for each of S and $\overline{S}$ can be used to construct a green-light-red-light machine for the set S. This statement is the converse of the one for Figure 5. In the green-light machine for $\overline{S}$ replace the green lamp with a red lamp. Then hook the machines in parallel so that the input goes into both simultaneously. The result is clearly a green-light-red-light machine. This assertion can be stated differently: If both a set and its complement are listable, then the set is computable.

Figure 7   The set K is listable, that is, a green-light machine for K exists. Let all conceivable green-light machines be numbered: M_1 is the first machine, M_2 is the second machine, M_3 is the third machine, and so forth up to the nth machine. K is defined as the set of numbers n such that the nth machine lights up when it receives n itself as an input. In the illustration a little man has entered the number 3,781 as an input to $M_{3,781}$ and the green light has turned on, indicating that the whole number 3,781 is a member of set K.

a wise old man, but he must be an obedient man who does exactly what he is told. We give the little man a number, say 3,781. The little man looks into customer's manual No. 3,781. Reading the manual, he is able to build the green-light machine $M_{3,781}$. Once this is done, he inserts the integer 3,781 as input into green-light machine $M_{3,781}$. If the green light goes on, the number 3,781 belongs to K. Thus we have a green-light machine for K.

What about $\overline{K}$? How can we be sure there is no green-light machine for it? Well, suppose there were such a machine. Then since $\overline{K}$ is the complement of K, this machine should light up for any input, say for 297, if and only if M_{297} does *not* light up for 297. (If M_{297} lit up, it would mean that the integer 297 belongs to K and not to $\overline{K}$.) Thus the machine for $\overline{K}$ certainly is not the same as M_{297} (see Fig. 8). By the same token, however, it is not the same as M_n for any other value of n. The same argument would apply to any other

number just as well as to 297, and it shows that no green-light machine for $\overline{K}$ appears anywhere in the library of customer's manuals. Since every possible green-light machine eventually turns up in our list, it follows that no green-light machine for $\overline{K}$ can possibly exist. That is to say, $\overline{K}$ is not listable.

The result is certainly remarkable. It deserves contemplation and appreciation. We know perfectly well what the set K is; in principle we can produce as much of it as we wish with a computer printout. Nevertheless, there can never be a formal procedure (an algorithm or a machine program) for sorting K from $\overline{K}$. Thus here is an example of a precisely stated problem that can never be solved by mechanical means.

This discussion has of course been informal and nonrigorous. It is possible, however, to reformulate all the ideas and arguments with precise mathematical definitions and proofs. In fact, they have been formulated in a branch of mathematical

Figure 8   The set $\overline{K}$ is not computable, that is, no green-light machine exists for $\overline{K}$, the complement of K. Suppose there were such a green-light machine for $\overline{K}$. Since $\overline{K}$ is the complement of K, this machine should light up for any input, say for 297, if and only if M_{297} does not light up for 297. Thus the machine for $\overline{K}$ is certainly not the same as M_{297}. By the same token, it is not the same as M_n for any other value of n. Thus no green-light machine exists for $\overline{K}$, meaning that $\overline{K}$ is not listable. A listable set whose complement is not listable is not computable; no green-light-red-light machine can be built for it. Thus there is no algorithm for sorting K from $\overline{K}$.

logic called recursive function theory, established in the 1930's by Gödel, Church, Post, Kleene and Turing.

Now, what has all this to do with Diophantine equations? Simply this. Matyasevich has proved that every listable set has a corresponding Diophantine equation. More precisely, if S is a listable set, then there is a corresponding polynomial P, with integer coefficients and variables $x, y_1, y_2, \ldots, y_n$, which is denoted by $P_s(x, y_1, y_2, \ldots, y_n)$. Any integer, such as 17, belongs to set S if and only if the Diophantine equation $P(17, y_1, y_2, \ldots, y_n) = 0$ has a solution.

It might be thought that for some sets we would have to resort to inconceivably complicated polynomials, but this is not the case. The degree

of P need not exceed the fourth power; the number of variables $y_1, y_2, \ldots, y_n$ need not exceed 14. (No one knows yet if both of these bounds can be achieved simultaneously.)

This result of Matyasevich's quickly leads to the conclusion that no Hilbert machine can exist. Recall the listable set K constructed a few paragraphs above. According to Matyasevich, there is a Diophantine equation, $P_K(x, y_1, y_2, \ldots, y_n) = 0$, associated with this set. If it were possible to build a Hilbert machine, that is, a green-light-red-light machine for testing Diophantine equations to see if they have solutions, then for any integer x we could determine whether or not there existed integers $y_1, y_2, \ldots, y_n$ such that the equation has a solution. In so determining, however, we would also be determining whether or not x belongs to K. In other words, a Hilbert machine applied to the Diophantine equation that describes K could be used as a green-light-red-light machine for K. We have proved, however, that K is not computable, so that no green-light-red-light machine can exist for K. The only way out of this dilemma is to conclude that there is no Hilbert machine. In other words, Hilbert's 10th problem is unsolvable!

The fact that a Diophantine equation is associated with every listable set is a positive result that is of great interest in itself, quite aside from its application to Hilbert's 10th problem. A particularly important and interesting set of integers is the set of prime numbers. A prime number is one that is factorable (divisible) only by 1 and by itself. Some examples are 2, 3, 5, 7, 11, 13 and 17. That they are listable is rather obvious. An algorithm for listing them has come down from the Greeks with the name of "the sieve of Eratosthenes." Combining Matyasevich's result with a device developed by Putnam, we obtain a Diophantine equation $Q(y_1, y_2, \ldots, y_n) = z$ such that a positive number z is a prime if and only if this equation has a positive integer solution y_1, $y_2, \ldots, y_n$. (The exact form of the polynomial Q is a bit too complicated to fully write out here.)

Another remarkable result can be proved by combining Matyasevich's theorem with Gödel's work on undecidability. If there is any system of axioms whatsoever from which information can be deduced about Diophantine equations, one can always obtain a particular Diophantine equation that has the following properties: (1) the equation has no positive integer solutions and (2) the fact that it has no positive integer solutions cannot be logically deduced from the given set of axioms. Of course, once the Diophantine equation is obtained we can make up a new set of axioms from which one can prove that the Diophantine equation has no solution. But then this new set of axioms will give rise to another Diophantine equation for which the same can be asserted.

What went into the proof of Matyasevich's theorem? In addition to the results from classical and even ancient number theory that we have already mentioned, there is a key result known as the Chinese remainder theorem. It will be helpful to illustrate the Chinese remainder theorem by a numerical example.

Suppose one wishes to find a number whose remainders, when divided by the numbers 10, 3, 7 and 11, are respectively 4, 2, 3 and 1 (see Fig. 9). The Chinese remainder theorem assures us that there must be such a number. (In fact, in this case 584 is such a number.) All that is required for the Chinese remainder theorem to work is that no pair of the divisors used have any common factor (except, of course, 1). There can be any number of divisors, and the desired remainders can be any positive integers whatsoever.

In 1931 Gödel showed how to use the Chinese remainder theorem as a coding trick, in which an arbitrary finite sequence of numbers can be encoded as a single number. From the code number one recovers the sequence in the same way that 4, 2, 3 and 1 are obtained from 584 in the example—as remainders in successive divisions. The divisors can be chosen to be in arithmetic progression.

The first attempt to prove that a Hilbert machine cannot exist was made by one of us (Davis) in his doctoral dissertation in 1950. Gödel's technique of using the Chinese remainder theorem as a coding device was applied to associate a Diophantine equation, $P_s(k, x, z, y_1, y_2, \ldots, y_n) = 0$, with every listable set S. Unfortunately the relation between the set and the equation turned out to be more complicated than what was needed for Hilbert's 10th problem. Specifically, the relation was: A positive integer x belongs to the set S if and only if for some positive integer value of z it is possible to find a solution for every one of the Diophantine equations obtained by substituting $k = 1$, then $k = 2$ and so on up to z into the equation $P_s(k, x, z, y_1, y_2, \ldots, y_n) = 0$. Although the result seemed tantalizingly close to what was needed, it was only a beginning.

At about the same time Robinson began her own investigations of sets that can be defined by Diophantine equations. She developed various ingenious techniques for dealing with equations whose solutions behaved like exponentials (grew like a power). In 1960 she, Davis and Putnam collaborated in proving another result. They made use of both her work and Davis' result to show that to any listable set there corresponded a Diophantine equation of an "extended" kind, extended in the sense that variables in the equation

PROBLEM: To find the smallest number n that has the remainders of 4, 2, 3 and 1 when it is divided by 10, 3, 7 and 11.

SOLUTION: Let x be the number sought. "Rem" will be the abbreviation for "The remainder of. . . ." The problem can then be rewritten:

$$\text{Rem}\left(\frac{x}{10}\right) = 4 \qquad \text{Rem}\left(\frac{x}{7}\right) = 3$$

$$\text{Rem}\left(\frac{x}{3}\right) = 2 \qquad \text{Rem}\left(\frac{x}{11}\right) = 1$$

In order to find x four auxiliary problems for new unknowns y_1, y_2, y_3 and y_4 must be solved. In each case the numerator is obtained by multiplying three of the divisors together and using the fourth as the denominator. For example, in the first equation with y_1 the numerator 231 is equal to $3 \times 7 \times 11$, and 10 is put in the denominator:

$$\text{Rem}\left(\frac{231y_1}{10}\right) = 4, y_1 < 10 \qquad \text{Rem}\left(\frac{330y_3}{7}\right) = 3, y_3 < 7$$

$$\text{Rem}\left(\frac{770y_2}{3}\right) = 2, y_2 < 3 \qquad \text{Rem}\left(\frac{210y_4}{11}\right) = 1, y_4 < 11$$

The set of smallest integers that are solutions to these auxiliary equations is $y_1 = 4$, $y_2 = 1$, $y_3 = 3$ and $y_4 = 1$.

To get x (the orginal number sought) the numerators of the four auxiliary equations are added together:

$$
\begin{aligned}
x &= (231y_1) + (770y_2) + (330y_3) + (210y_4)\\
&= (231 \times 4) + (770 \times 1) + (330 \times 3) + (210 \times 1)\\
&= 924 + 770 + 990 + 210\\
&= 2{,}894
\end{aligned}
$$

Thus 2,894 is one value of x. A smaller number can be obtained if the product of all four divisors is subtracted from this solution:

$$2{,}894 - (10 \times 3 \times 7 \times 11) = 2{,}894 - 2{,}310 = 584.$$

Therefore 584 is the smallest solution to the problem.

Figure 9   Chinese remainder theorem is used in the solution to Hilbert's 10th problem. In this case the theorem is employed to find a number whose remainders, when divided by the numbers 10, 3, 7 and 11, are respectively 4, 2, 3 and 1. Integer 584 is the smallest solution.

were allowed to occur as exponents. An example of such an equation is $2^t + x^2 + z^3$. Davis, Robinson and Putnam combined their work with some of Robinson's earlier results and discovered the following: If even one Diophantine equation could be found whose solutions behaved exponentially in an appropriate sense, then it would be possible to describe every listable set by a Diophantine equation. This would in turn show that Hilbert's 10th problem is unsolvable.

It took a decade to find a Diophantine equation whose solutions grow exponentially in the appropriate sense. In 1970 Matyasevich found such an equation by using what are known as the Fibonacci numbers (see Fig. 10). These celebrated numbers were discovered in A.D. 1202 by Leonardo of Pisa, who was also known as Fibonacci.

He found them by computing the total number of pairs of descendants of one pair of rabbits if the original pair and each offspring pair reproduced itself once a month. The Fibonacci series is obtained by starting with 1 and 1 and successively adding the preceding two numbers to get the next: the first Fibonacci number is 1, the second is 1, the third is $1 + 1 = 2$, the fourth is $1 + 2 = 3$, the fifth is $2 + 3 = 5$ and so on. The property that is important for Hilbert's 10th problem is that the Fibonacci numbers grow exponentially. That is, the nth Fibonacci number is approximately proportional to the nth power of a certain fixed real number.

If one could find a Diophantine equation whose solutions relate n to the nth Fibonacci number, it would be the desired example of a Diophantine

1. 1
2.   1
3. $1 + 1 = 2$
4. $1 + 2 = 3$
5. $2 + 3 = 5$
6. $3 + 5 = 8$
7. $5 + 8 = 13$
8. $8 + 13 = 21$
9. $13 + 21 = 34$
10. $21 + 34 = 55$
11. $34 + 55 = 89$
12. $55 + 89 = 144$
13. $89 + 144 = 233$
.
.
.
n

$$\approx \frac{1}{\sqrt{5}} \left(\frac{1 + \sqrt{5}}{2} \right)^n$$

Figure 10   Fibonacci numbers were discovered in A.D. 1202 by Leonardo of Pisa, known as Fibonacci. The sequence is obtained by starting with 1 and 1 and successively adding the last two numbers to get the next one. The sequence grows exponentially: the nth number in the sequence is approximately proportional to the nth power of the real number $[(1 + \sqrt{5})/2]$.

equation whose solutions behave exponentially. The solution of Hilbert's 10th problem would follow from this example. What Matyasevich did was to construct such a Diophantine equation (see Fig. 11). Once he had shown that the set of Fibonacci numbers is associated in this way with a Diophantine equation, it followed immediately from the theorem of Davis, Robinson and Putnam that for every listable set there is an associated Diophantine equation, including in particular the set K, which is not computable. And so ends the story of Hilbert's 10th problem.

$$\text{I. } u + w - v - 2 = 0$$
$$\text{II. } l - 2v - 2a - 1 = 0$$
$$\text{III. } l^2 - lz - z^2 - 1 = 0$$
$$\text{IV. } g - bl^2 = 0$$
$$\text{V. } g^2 - gh - h^2 - 1 = 0$$
$$\text{VI. } m - c(2h + g) - 3 = 0$$
$$\text{VII. } m - fl - 2 = 0$$
$$\text{VIII. } x^2 - mxy + y^2 - 1 = 0$$
$$\text{IX. } (d - 1)l + u - x - 1 = 0$$
$$\text{X. } x - v - (2h + g)(e - 1) = 0$$

Figure 11   Matyasevich's solution to Hilbert's 10th problem involves a Diophantine equation that is obtained by squaring each of these 10 equations and then adding them together and setting the resulting complicated polynomial equal to zero. In these equations the values u and v in the solutions are related in such a way that v is the $(2n)$th Fibonacci number. From the solution it followed that for every listable set there is an associated Diophantine equation. Since there exist listable sets whose complements are not listable, then not every listable set can have a green-light-red-light machine. Since having a green-light-red-light machine for a set is equivalent to having a Hilbert machine for Diophantine equations, Matyasevich's result means that no Hilbert machine can be built to test Diophantine equations.

The Riemann Hypothesis

Philip J. Davis and Reuben Hersh

Philip J. Davis obtained his Ph.D. from Harvard in 1950 in applied mathematics. He was chief of the numerical analysis section of the National Bureau of Standards in Washington, D.C., from 1951 to 1963 during which time he was named as a Guggenheim fellow. He has been professor of applied mathematics at Brown University since 1963. Davis received the Washington Academy of Science award in 1960 and the Chauvenet prize in 1963.

Reuben Hersh is introduced in the previous article.

One of the most famous living mathematicians—a Fields medalist and one who individually solved one of Hilbert's twenty-three problems—was once overheard to say that if he could resolve Riemann's hypothesis he would consider himself to be truly successful. Such is the attraction and fascination that this seemingly isolated and rather arcane problem has for the modern mathematical community. Davis and Hersh in this essay sketch the broad outlines of this problem and suggest some of the consequences its solution would have for number theory.

Briefly, the Riemann hypothesis asserts that the zeros of the Riemann zeta function $\zeta(z)$ = $1 + 1/2^z + 1/3^z + 1/4^z + \ldots$ all have the real part 1/2. In this expression the variable z is a complex number, $z = a + bi$ where a and b are real and $i = \sqrt{-1}$ or $i^2 = 1$. In this form a is called the real part and bi the imaginary part of z. (Imaginary numbers have been around since at least the fifteenth century and are as valid as any other system of numbers.) The zeros of $\zeta(z) = 1 + 1/2^z + 1/3^z + \ldots$ are those complex numbers $z_0 = a_0 + b_0i$ such that if z in the general formula is replaced by the specific number z_0, then the sum of the terms is zero, i.e.,

$$1 + \frac{1}{2^{z_0}} + \frac{1}{3^{z_0}} + \frac{1}{4^{z_0}} + \ldots = 0$$

That an infinite number of terms may have a finite sum may strike the novice as strange, but mathematics observes that

$$1 - \frac{1}{2} - \frac{1}{4} - \frac{1}{8} - \frac{1}{16} - \ldots = 0$$

because

$$1 - \frac{1}{2} = \frac{1}{2}$$

$$1 - \frac{1}{2} - \frac{1}{4} = \frac{1}{4}$$

$$1 - \frac{1}{2} - \frac{1}{4} - \frac{1}{8} = \frac{1}{8}$$

and

$$1 - \frac{1}{2} - \frac{1}{4} - \frac{1}{8} - \ldots - \frac{1}{2^n} = \frac{1}{2^n}.$$

Source: Philip J. Davis and Reuben Hersh, "The Riemann Hypothesis," in *The Mathematical Experience* (Boston: Birkhäuser, 1981), pp. 363–369. Reprinted by permission of Birkhäuser.

As a result we know that the sum $1 - 1/2 - 1/4 - \ldots$ *is less than any number greater than zero but never less than zero itself, hence, it must equal zero. In somewhat the same way it can be shown that for some complex numbers* $z_0 = a_0 + b_0 i$, *the sum* $1 + 1/2^{z_0} + 1/3^{z_0} + \ldots = 0$. *The Riemann hypothesis asserts that all such* z_0 *must have the form* $z_0 = 1/2 + b_0 i$, *i.e., the real part of* z_0 *must be* $1/2$.

In 1859 Riemann published a paper in which he made six assumptions or conjectures among which was this now-famous one. Assuming these six, Riemann then proved the prime number theorem. Since Riemann's paper first appeared, five of his six conjectures have been proven true. Only this one still eludes resolution by the mathematical community, and a successful solution would instantaneously catapult its fortunate creator to the summit of the mathematical world.

WE TAKE AS our first example the most revered and uncontroversial branch of pure mathematics—number theory.

Within number theory, we take as our case study the problem of the distribution of the primes. . . . The attraction of this problem is that we are able to *see* what is going on long before we can *prove* it. For instance, . . . for x less than 10,000,000,000 the number of primes less than or equal to x, when multiplied by log x, fall in a near-perfect straight line when graphed against x.

When one is confronted with such evidence as this, it is impossible not to be impressed by the weight of the argument. Exactly as in Popper's theory of scientific knowledge, one formulates a "bold conjecture"—very precise and informative, and therefore not likely to be true "by accident," so to speak. Then one subjects this conjecture to the test—by a numerical calculation, rather than by a physical experiment. The test fails to refute the conjecture. The conjecture thereby becomes greatly strengthened—proved, so to speak, in the sense of natural science though certainly not in the sense of deductive mathematics.

A more refined piece of natural scientific research into prime numbers was reported in a paper by I. J. Good and R. F. Churchhouse in 1967. They are interested in the Riemann zeta function. . . . The Riemann hypothesis concerns the "roots" of the zeta function—the complex numbers z at which the zeta function equals zero. Riemann conjectured that these roots all have real part = $1/2$. Geometrically, they lie on the line

"real part of $z = 1/2$"—i.e., a line parallel to the imaginary axis and $1/2$ unit to the right of it.

Now, this conjecture of Riemann is by universal agreement *the outstanding unsolved problem* in mathematics. One proof of the "prime number theorem" depends on the fact (which *has* been proved) that all the zeros are somewhere between the imaginary axis and the line $x = 1$. To prove that they all lie exactly on $x = 1/2$ would imply even more precise conclusions about the distribution of prime numbers. It was a major triumph of G. H. Hardy to prove that there are infinitely many zeros of the zeta function on the line $x = 1/2$. We still do not know if *all* of them are there.

It has been verified by calculations that the first 70,000,000 complex zeros of the zeta function are on $x = 1/2$. But, Good and Churchhouse say,

this is not a very good reason for believing that the hypothesis is true. For in the theory of the zeta function, and in the closely allied theory of the distribution of prime numbers, the iterated logarithm log log x is often involved in asymptotic formulae, and this function increases extremely slowly. The first zero off the line $r(s) = 1/2$, if there is one, might have an imaginary part whose iterated logarithm is, say, as large as 10, and, if so, it might never be practicable to find this zero by calculation.

(If log log $x = 10$, then x is approximately $10^{10,000}$.)

If this seems far-fetched, they mention another well-verified conjecture—known to be true in the first billion cases—which Littlewood proved is false *eventually*. Nevertheless, Good and Churchhouse write that the aim of their own work is to suggest a "reason" (their quotation marks) for believing Riemann's hypothesis.

Their work involves something called the Möbius function, which is written $\mu(x)$ (pronounced "mu of x"). To calculate $\mu(x)$, factor x into primes. If there is a repeated prime factor, as in $12 = 1 \cdot 2 \cdot 2 \cdot 3$ or $25 = 5 \cdot 5$, then $\mu(x)$ is defined to be zero. If all factors are distinct, count them. If there is an even number of factors, we set $\mu(x) = 1$; if there is an odd number, set $\mu(x) = -1$. For instance, $6 = 2 \cdot 3$ has an even number of factors, so $\mu(6) = 1$. On the other hand, $70 = 2 \cdot 5 \cdot 7$ so $\mu(70) = -1$.

Now add up the values of $\mu(n)$ for all n less than or equal to N. This sum of $+1$'s and -1's is a function of N, and it is called $M(N)$. It was proved a long time ago that the Riemann conjecture is equivalent to the following conjecture: $M(N)$ grows no faster than a constant multiple of $N^{1/2 + \epsilon}$ as N goes to infinity (here ϵ is arbitrary but greater than 0). Either conjecture implies the other; both, of course, are still unproven.

Good and Churchhouse give a "good reason" for believing the Riemann hypothesis by giving a "good reason" (not a proof!) that $M(N)$ has the required rate of growth.

Their "good reason" involves thinking of the values of the Möbius function as if they were random variables.

Why is this a good reason? The Möbius function is completely deterministic; once a number n is chosen, then there is no ambiguity at all as to whether it has any repeated factors—or, if it has no repeated factors, whether the number of factors is even or odd.

On the other hand, if we make a table of the values of the Möbius function, it "looks" random, in the sense that it seems to be utterly chaotic, with no discernible pattern or regularity, except for the fact that μ is "just as likely" to equal 1 or -1.

What is the chance that n has no repeated factor—i.e., that $\mu(n) \neq 0$? This will happen if n is not a multiple of 4 or a multiple of 9 or a multiple of 25 or any other square of a prime. Now, the probability that a number chosen at random is not

a multiple of 4 is 3/4, the probability that it is not a multiple of 9 is 8/9, the probability that it is not a multiple of 25 is 24/25, and so on. Moreover, these conditions are all independent—knowing that n is not a multiple of 4 tells us nothing about whether it is a multiple of 9. So according to the basic probabilistic law that the probability of occurrence of two independent events is the product of their separate probabilities, we conclude that the probability that $\mu(n)$ does not equal zero is the product

$$\frac{3}{4} \cdot \frac{8}{9} \cdot \frac{24}{25} \cdot \frac{48}{49} \cdot \cdots$$

Even though this product has an infinite number of factors, it can be evaluated analytically, and it is known that it is equal to $6/\pi^2$.

Therefore, the probability that $\mu(n) = 1$ is $3/\pi^2$, and the probability that $\mu(n) = -1$ is the same. The "expected value" of μ is, of course, zero; on the average, the $+1$'s and the -1's should just about cancel.

Now suppose we choose a very large number of integers at random and independently. Then, for each of these choices, we would have $\mu = 0$ with probability $1 - 6/\pi^2$, $\mu = 1$ with probability $3/\pi^2$, and $\mu = -1$ with probability $3/\pi^2$. If we should then add up all the values of μ, we would get a number which might be very large, if most of our choices happened to have $\mu = 1$, say. On the other hand, it would be unlikely that our choices gave $\mu = 1$ very much more often than $\mu = -1$. In fact, a theorem in probability (Hausdorff's inequality) says that, if we pick N numbers in this way, then, with probability 1, the sum grows no faster than a constant times $N^{1/2 + \epsilon}$ as N goes to infinity.

This conclusion is exactly what we need to prove the Riemann conjecture! However, we have changed the terms in our summation. For the Riemann conjecture, we should have added the values of μ for the numbers from 1 to N. Instead, we took N numbers at random.

What justifies this? It is justified by our feeling or impression that the table of values of μ is "chaotic," "random," "unpredictable." By that token, the first N values of μ are nothing special, they are a "random sample."

If we grant this much, then it follows that the

Riemann hypothesis is true *with probability one*. This conclusion seems at the same time both compelling and nonsensical. Compelling because of the striking way in which probabilistic reasoning gives *precisely* the needed rate of growth for $M(N)$: nonsensical because the truth of the Riemann hypothesis is surely not a random variable which may hold only "with probability one."

The author of the authoritative work on the zeta function, H. M. Edwards, calls this type of heuristic reasoning "quite absurd." (Edwards refers, not to Good and Churchhouse, but to a 1931 paper of Denjoy which uses similar but less detailed probabilistic arguments.)

To check their probabilistic reasoning, Good and Churchhouse did some numerical work. They tabulated the values of the sum of $\mu(n)$ for n ranging over intervals of length 1,000. They found statistically excellent confirmation of their random model.

In a separate calculation, they found that the total number of zeros of $\mu(n)$ for n between 0 and 33,000,000 is 12,938,407. The "expected number" is $33,000,000 \cdot (1 - 6/\pi^2)$, which works out to 12,938,405.6. They call this "an astonishingly close fit, better than we deserved." A nonrigorous argument has predicted a mathematical result to 8 place accuracy.

In physics or chemistry, experimental agreement with theory to 8 place accuracy would be regarded as a very strong confirmation of the theory. Here, also, it is impossible to believe that such agreement is accidental. The principle by which the calculation was made *must* be right.

When we respond in this way to heuristic evidence, we are in a certain sense committed to the realist or Platonist philosophy. We are asserting that the regularity which has been predicted and confirmed is not illusory—that there is *something there* which is lawful and regular.

It is easy to make up an example of a sequence of statements which are true for $n = 1, 2$, up to 1,000,000,000,000 and false from then on (for instance, the statement "n is not divisible by both 2^{12} and 5^{12}"). So the fact that a conjecture about the natural numbers is true for the first 2,000,000,000 cases certainly does not prove it will be true for the 2,000,000,001st case. But for conjectures such as those about the distribution of primes, no one believes that the behavior we observe in our sample will suddenly change to something radically different in another sample, taken farther out toward infinity.

Only with some confidence in the orderliness or "rationality" of the number system is it possible to do successful research. "God is subtle, but not malicious," said Einstein. This faith, which a physicist needs in order to believe he can understand the universe, is also needed by a mathematician trying to understand his mental universe of number and form. Perhaps this is what Dieudonné means when he calls realism "convenient." It is more than convenient; it is indispensable.

The point to notice in this discussion is that none of it makes any sense from a constructivist *or* formalist point of view. The constructivist says that the Riemann hypothesis will become true or false only when a constructive proof one way or the other is given. It makes no sense to discuss whether it is *already* true or false, apart from any proof. The formalist says that the Riemann hypothesis makes no sense except as a conjecture that a certain statement can be derived from certain axioms. Again, there is no acceptance of truth or falsity in mathematics apart from what is proved or disproved.

It is interesting to ask, in a context such as this, why we still feel the need for a proof, or what additional conviction would be carried if a proof should be forthcoming which was, say, 200 or 300 pages long, full of arduous calculations where even the most persistent may sometimes lose their way.

It seems clear that we want a proof because we are convinced that all the properties of the natural numbers *can* be deduced from a single set of axioms, and if something is true and we *can't* deduce it in this way, this is a sign of a lack of understanding on our part. We believe, in other words, that a proof would be a way of understanding *why* the Riemann conjecture is true; which is something more than just knowing from convincing heuristic reasoning that it *is* true.

But then a proof which is so complex and nonperspicuous that it sheds no light on the matter would fail to serve this purpose.

Why would we still want a proof, even a hopelessly complex and nonperspicuous one? Suppose a proof were published which took 500 pages to write. How would it be decided that the proof was correct? Suppose it were so decided by a sufficient number of experts. Would we be overjoyed because we would now know definitely that Riemann's conjecture is true?

Perhaps, though, there is another purpose to proof—as a testing ground for the stamina and ingenuity of the mathematician. We admire the conqueror of Everest, not because the top of Everest is a place we want to be, but just because it is so hard to get there.

The Four-Color Problem

Kenneth Appel and Wolfgang Haken

Kenneth Appel was born in Brooklyn and received his doctorate from the University of Michigan in 1959. He has been associated with the University of Illinois since 1961.

Wolfgang Haken was born in Germany in 1928. He received his doctorate in 1953 from the University of Kiel in Germany. Since a two-year stay at the Institute for Advanced Study at Princeton from 1963 to 1965 he has been associated with the University of Illinois.

In 1978 the postage meters of the University of Illinois bore for a time the inscription "Four Colors Suffice"—a rather modest and somewhat belated tribute to the monumental effort that had been conducted at the University of Illinois to resolve the four-color problem. The problem, its history, and the effort required for its solution are all carefully outlined in this essay.

Appel and Haken are the mathematicians who devised and orchestrated the herculean task of listing and reducing the large number of configurations needed to produce the proof. This effort has not, surprisingly enough, been greeted with universal acclaim in the mathematics community. The complaints are based on the fact that all details of "real" proofs in mathematics can be read and confirmed in a reasonable amount of time by other mathematicians. These authors' proof obviously does not meet this requirement. The number and variety of cases that must be checked for this proof could not be done by hand in a single lifetime, much less a few evenings sandwiched in between grading examinations and writing snide comments on dissertations.

As Appel and Haken quite modestly suggest toward the end of this essay, the type of proof they have devised may be the first of a completely new type of mathematical result. Such new theorems will have their gross outline and direction guided by human hands, but their endless details will be checked and rechecked only by computer. However distressing such a prospect may be to those purists who demand that all mathematics worthy of the name must be so succinct as to allow engraving on tablets of stone, to many the author's vista is a most exciting one. Truth, it would seem, is truth. If we must restrict our body of mathematics to that portable by an atherosclerotic professor emeritus in oversized type, we may well miss much of value and use along the way.

IN 1976, THE Four-Color Problem was solved: every map drawn on a sheet of paper can be colored with only four colors in such a way that countries sharing a common border receive different colors. This result was of interest to the mathematical community since many mathematicians had tried in vain for over a hundred years to prove this simple-sounding statement. Yet among mathematicians who were not aware of the developments leading to the proof, the outcome had rather dismaying aspects, for the proof made unprecedented use of computer computation; the correctness of the proof cannot be checked without the aid of a computer. Moreover, adding to

Source: Kenneth Appel and Wolfgang Haken, "The Four-Color Problem," in *Mathematics Today: Twelve Informal Essays* (Springer-Verlag, 1978), pp. 153–180. Copyright by Springer. (References omitted.)

Announcement of Success

FOUR COLORS
SUFFICE

the strangeness of the proof, some of the crucial ideas were perfected by computer experiments. One can never rule out the chance that a short proof of the Four-Color Theorem might some day be found, perhaps by the proverbial bright high-school student. But it is also conceivable that no such proof is possible. In this case a new and interesting type of theorem has appeared, one which has no proof of the traditional type.

Early History

Despite the novel aspects of the proof, both the Four-Color Problem and its proof have deep roots in mathematics; to see this, one must examine the history of the problem. In 1852, Francis Guthrie (1831–1899), who had been a student in London with his brother Frederick, wrote to Frederick to point out that it seemed that the countries of every map could always be colored with only four colors in such a way that neighboring countries had different colors. By "neighboring" countries he must have meant countries adjacent along a borderline rather than at a single point (or even a finite number of points), for otherwise a map whose countries looked like the wedges of a pie (see Figure 1) would require as many colors as there were countries. By a "country" he certainly must have meant a connected region, for if a country is allowed to consist of more than one region it is not hard to construct an example of a map with five countries each of which is adjacent to each of the other four (see Figure 2). Francis asked Frederick if there was a way of proving mathematically whether or not this "Four-Color Conjecture" was true. Frederick Guthrie was still at University College, London, where both broth-

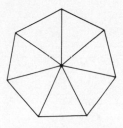

Figure 1   Why countries bordering at a single point are not called neighbors

ers had attended the lectures of Augustus De-Morgan (1806–1871), one of the major mathematicians of his time. Frederick, unable to answer his brother's question, asked DeMorgan, who could not find any method to determine the truth or falsity of the conjecture.

Guthrie and DeMorgan certainly realized that the map in Figure 3 requires four colors since each of the countries is adjacent to the other

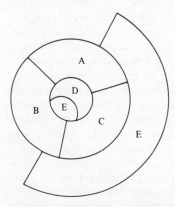

Figure 2   Why a country must consist of a single region

three. This means that a "Three-Color Conjecture" is false: three colors will not suffice to color all maps. Moreover, DeMorgan proved that it is not possible for five countries to be in such a position that each of them is adjacent to each of the other four. This result led him to believe that one

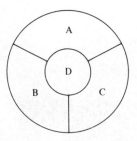

Figure 3   Why four colors are needed

would never need five different colors and thus that the Four-Color Conjecture was true. But the argument that five mutually adjacent countries cannot exist in a map does not constitute a proof of the Four-Color Conjecture. Many amateur mathematicians, not understanding this, have independently discovered proofs of DeMorgan's result and have then thought that they had proved

the Four-Color Conjecture. The difficulty is illustrated in Figure 4: among the six countries of this map there is no collection of four in which each member is adjacent to the other three; yet the map requires four colors—three for the countries

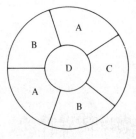

Figure 4   Why it is misleading to try to generalize from Figure 3

in the outer ring and a fourth for the country in the center.

Figure 4 shows that it is not legitimate to conclude that the number of colors required for a map is the same as the maximum of mutually adjacent countries. More powerful mathematical methods are required for a proof of the Four-Color Conjecture.

DeMorgan's Argument

Augustus DeMorgan, the first contributor to the theory of the Four-Color Conjecture, showed that no five regions in the plane can be mutually adjacent. The basic idea of his proof is to examine a hypothesized set of five regions which border one another, and derive an internal (geometric) contradiction. Start by assigning numbers to the regions as follows: Choose any region as Region 0, and any other as Region 1. From some point on the common boundary of Regions 0 and 1 proceed clockwise around the boundary of Region 0 until the boundary of a new region is encountered; call this Region 2. Number the next (new) region encountered with 3 and the last region with 4. Various possibilities are shown in the illustration.

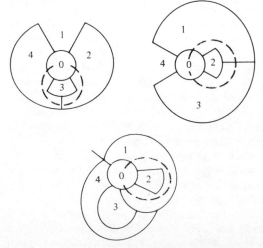

One is then easily able to show that either there is a closed curve (dashed line in the illustrations) which separates Region 1 from Region 3 or else one which separates Region 2 from Region 4. The two regions separated by this curve cannot border one another since, roughly, one is located inside the curve, the other outside it.

This argument depends on the fact that any closed curve in the plane which looks more or less like a circle bent out of shape (technically, any simple closed curve) has an interior and an exterior. That is, any other curve in the plane that contains a point in the interior and a point in the exterior must cross the given curve. (A precise statement of this idea is given in what is called the Jordan Curve Theorem. Although the idea seems almost obvious, it is not true for every surface; for example on the surface of a doughnut, a closed curve that loops through the hole does not have a distinct interior.) The contradiction that arises in DeMorgan's argument is based entirely on the ability of a simple closed curve to separate its interior from its exterior.

In 1878, the eminent mathematician Arthur Cayley (1821–1895), unable to determine the truth or falsity of the conjecture, proposed the problem to the London Mathematical Society. Within a year after Cayley's proposal, Arthur Bray Kempe (1849–1922), a London barrister and a member of the London Mathematical Society, published a paper that claimed to prove that the conjecture was true. Kempe's argument was extremely clever, and although his "proof" turned out not be complete it contained most of the basic ideas that eventually led to the correct proof one century later.

A map is called "normal" if none of its countries encloses other countries (see Figure 5) and no more than three countries meet at any point; for example, the maps in Figures 3 and 4 are normal. Figure 6 gives a larger example of part of a normal map (in cylindrical projection) that was constructed in 1977 by Edward F. Moore of the University of Wisconsin. (Figure 6 has further interesting properties that will be discussed later, but at this point it serves primarily as an example of a map that is not nearly as easy to color with only four colors as are the other examples.)

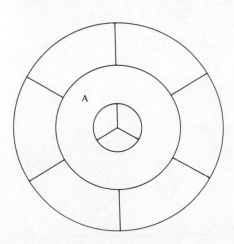

Figure 5   A non-normal map

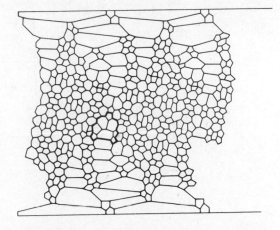

Figure 6   Part of Moore's example of a map with no "small" reducible configuration. (A reducible 12-ring configuration is indicated by heavy edges.)

Normal Maps

A normal map is one in which no more than three regions meet at any point, and in which no region entirely encircles another one. The states in the eastern half of the United States form a normal map, but the entire continental United States does not—because Utah, Colorado, Arizona and New Mexico all meet at a single point.

Since every map can be associated with a normal map which requires at least as many colors, it is sufficient to prove the Four-Color Conjecture for normal maps, for if it is true for these maps then it will be true for all maps. One then shows that any normal map (in a plane) satisfies the formula

$$4p_2 + 3p_3 + 2p_4 + p_5 - p_7 - 2p_8 - 3p_9 - \ldots - (N - 6)p_n = 12,$$

where p_n is the number of countries of the map that have exactly n neighbors and N is the largest number of neighbors that any country has. (Note that $n = 0$ and $n = 1$ cannot occur in a normal map since no enclaves or islands can occur in normal maps; thus the formula begins with p_2.) Now each p_n is either positive or zero and occurs in the formula with a positive sign only if n is less than 6. Thus for the formula to have a positive sum on the left (to match the positive number on the right) at least one of p_2, p_3, p_4, or p_5 must be positive. In other words, some country must have either two, three, four, or five neighbors.

It is easy to modify a non-normal map to produce a normal map which requires at least as many colors. Thus, if there were a map that required five colors, a so-called "five-chromatic map," then there would have to exist a normal five-chromatic map. Hence to prove the Four-Color Conjecture it would be sufficient to prove that a normal five-chromatic map is not possible. Kempe's argument, slightly modified shows that any normal map must have some country with five or fewer neighbors. Kempe noted that if there were a normal, five-chromatic map then there would have to be such a map with a smallest number of countries, a "minimal normal five-chromatic map." Then, proceeding by the classical method of *reductio ad absurdum*, he presented an argument that if a minimal normal five-chromatic map had a country with fewer than six neighbors—which, as he had just shown, every normal map must have—then there would have to be a normal map with fewer countries that was also five-chromatic. So, if the argument were totally correct up to this point, there could be no number that was the number of countries of a minimal five-chromatic map; hence no minimal five-chromatic map was possible. However, since this meant that there could not be any five-chromatic map at all, the proof would have been complete.

Eleven years later, in 1890, Percy John Heawood (1861–1955) pointed out that Kempe's argument that no minimal five-chromatic map could contain a country with five neighbors was flawed, and that the error did not appear easy to repair. Heawood, in trying to attack the problem, investigated a generalization of the original Four-Color Conjecture. The maps studied by Guthrie and Kempe were maps in a plane or on a sphere. Heawood also considered maps on more complicated

surfaces containing "handles" (Figure 7) and "twists" (Figure 8). He was able to obtain an el-

Figure 8   A "Mobius" strip with a twist

egant argument, applicable to all surfaces except the sphere and the plane, that provided an upper bound for the number of colors required to color maps on these surfaces. If the method he used had been applicable to the plane, it would have provided a proof of the Four-Color Conjecture.

Why Are Mathematicians Interested in the Problem?

Heawood continued to work on the problem for the next sixty years. During that time many other eminent mathematicians (as well as countless numbers of amateur mathematicians) devoted a great deal of effort to the Four-Color Conjecture. In fact, much of what is now known as Graph Theory—the geometry of wiring diagrams and airline routes—grew out of the work done in attempting to prove it. It is interesting to ask why so many mathematicians would spend so much time on what appeared to be a question of so little practical significance. To understand the answer to this question is to understand the motivation of pure mathematicians.

Toward the end of the nineteenth century, mathematicians were able to build many powerful theories that enabled them to settle many difficult questions. The feeling grew that any question that could be reasonably posed in the language of mathematics could be answered by the use of sufficiently powerful ideas. Moreover, most mathematicians felt that such questions could be answered in such a way that a competent

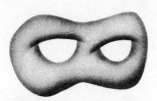

Figure 7   A "pretzel" surface with a handle

Kempe's Argument

The crux of Kempe's purported proof of the Four-Color Conjecture is that a minimal five-chromatic normal map (a smallest normal map that requires five colors) cannot contain any country with exactly two, three, four, or five neighbors. Since Kempe knew that every normal map must contain such a country, he concluded that there is no smallest normal map requiring five colors. Hence there can't be any map that requires five colors. To outline Kempe's argument, we will examine in detail how his proof went for countries with three or four neighbors.

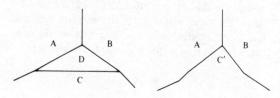

Suppose a minimal five-chromatic map had a country with exactly three neighbors (like country D in the figure above on the left). If that country is amalgamated with one of its neighbors (as in the figure on the right, where countries C and D are united to form country C′), then the resulting map has fewer countries than a minimal five-chromatic map. Hence it is colorable with four colors.

Now if all the countries except the amalgamated country (D) of the original map are assigned the colors of the corresponding countries in the map obtained by the amalgamation, the amalgamated country may be colored with the color not assigned to any of its three neighbors. Thus the original map must have been four-colorable, contradicting the assumption that it was five-chromatic. (Essentially the same argument suffices to show that no country in a minimal five-chromatic map can have exactly two neighbors.)

The corresponding argument for four neighbors is an idea of major importance in Kempe's work. Suppose that a minimal five-chromatic map had a country with exactly four neighbors. As before, one can amalgamate such a country and color the rest of the map with four colors, leaving the amalgamated country uncolored (as in the figure where the country with four neighbors is E). Now if the four neighbors of the uncolored country are colored with fewer than four distinct colors, a color may be chosen for the remaining country. Otherwise, the following argument of Kempe suffices.

Consider the colors of a pair of countries on opposite sides of the uncolored country (for example, the red of country A and the green of country C). Either there is a path of adjacent countries colored with those two colors leading

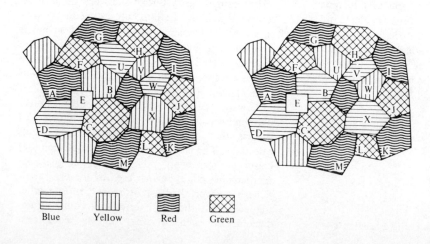

| Blue | Yellow | Red | Green |

from one of the countries to the other, or there is not. (In the figure above, the path consisting of countries A, F, G, H, I, J, K, L, M, C has only countries colored red and green and leads from A to C. On the other hand there is no path consisting of countries colored yellow and blue leading from B to D.) In honor of Kempe, such two-colored paths are now called Kempe chains.

If both pairs of opposing countries were joined by paths of the corresponding pairs of colors, the two paths would then have a country in common, which is certainly impossible. Thus there is some pair (B and D in our example) not joined by a Kempe chain. Choose one country (say B) of the pair and list all of the countries that are colored by one of the two selected colors (in our example

these would be yellow and blue, the colors of B and D) and are joined by a (yellow-blue) path to the chosen country. (In our example, countries, B, U, V, W, X form the list.) Now interchange the colors of the countries on the list. (The figure on the right results from the figure on the left by interchanging blue and yellow on countries B, U, V, W, X.) Now the uncolored country has neighbors of only three colors since the list of countries whose colors were interchanged cannot include more than one (in our case, B) of the four neighboring countries. Thus the uncolored country (E) may be colored with the fourth color (yellow), again leading to a contradiction with the hypothesis that the map required five colors.

---

mathematician could check the correctness of such an answer in a reasonable amount of time. The Four-Color Conjecture was certainly such a problem. Easily stated in the language of mathematics, it could be understood by any intelligent layman. If one could not settle this problem, then one had not developed the appropriate mathematical tools.

In the 1930's a small cloud appeared on the horizon. In logic, the branch of mathematics in which the idea of proof was most precisely stated, the work of Kurt Gödel and Alonzo Church led to some rather disturbing results. First, in what seemed like the most natural logical system, there are statements that are true but not provable in the system. Second, there must be theorems in the system with relatively short statements whose shortest proofs are too long to be written down in any reasonable length of time. In the 1950's it was discovered that the same difficulties affected branches of mathematics other than logic. Some mathematicians thought that since the Four-Color Conjecture had been studied without resolution for such a long time, it might be one of those problems for which neither a proof of correctness nor of incorrectness could be found. Others felt that if a proof existed it might be too long to write down. Still others felt that the disease of unsolvability could not spread to this area and that an

elegant mathematical argument must be possible either to prove or disprove the Conjecture.

We now know that a proof can be found. But we do not yet (and may never) know whether there is any proof that is elegant, concise, and completely verifiable by a (human) mathematical mind.

Unavoidable Sets and Reducible Configurations

So many areas of mathematics have been involved in various attempts to prove the Four-Color Conjecture that it would be impossible to discuss them all here. . . . We shall restrict our attention to the work that led directly to the proof.

Kempe had shown that in every normal map there is at least one country with either two, three, four, or five neighbors; there are no normal maps (on a plane) in which every country has six or more neighbors. This may be expressed by the statement that the set of "configurations" (see Figure 9) consisting of a country with two neighbors, a country with three neighbors, a country with four neighbors, and a country with five neighbors is *unavoidable* in the sense that every normal map must contain at least one of these

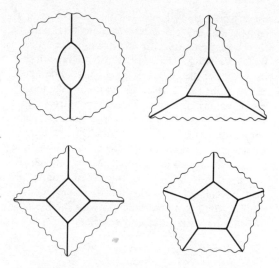

Figure 9   Kempe's small unavoidable set

four configurations. Unavoidability is one of the two important ideas that are basic to the theory. Throughout this essay when we say that a set of configurations is unavoidable we shall mean that every normal map must contain some configuration in the set.

The second important idea is *reducibility*. Intuitively, a configuration is reducible if there is a way of showing, solely by examining the configuration and the way in which chains of countries can be aligned, that the configuration cannot possibly appear in a minimal five-chromatic map. The methods of proving configurations reducible grew out of Kempe's proof that a country with four neighbors cannot occur in a minimal five-chromatic map. The use of the word "reducible" stems from the form of Kempe's argument; he proved that if a five-chromatic map contains a country with, say, four neighbors, then there is a five-chromatic map with a reduced number of countries. The reader who understands that argument has grasped the essential idea of reducibility proofs.

In the century since Kempe first introduced the idea of reducibility, certain standard methods for examining configurations to determine whether or not they are reducible have been developed. To use these methods to show that large configura-

tions are reducible requires examination of a large number of details and appears feasible only by computer. We may describe Kempe's attack on the Four-Color Conjecture as an attempt to find an unavoidable set of reducible configurations: finding such a set is sufficient for proving the Four-Color Conjecture.

From 1900 to 1970

In 1913, George David Birkhoff (1884–1944) of Harvard, one of the first eminent American mathematicians, examined Kempe's flawed proof and developed much of the basis for later arguments. Birkhoff, using Kempe's idea and some new techniques of his own, was able to show that certain larger configurations were reducible, for example, the configuration of Figure 10. Using these results

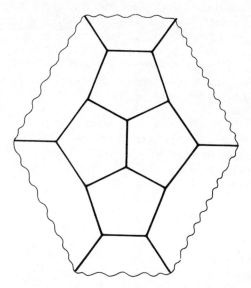

Figure 10   Birkhoff's reducible "diamond" configuration

and some similar ones of his own, Philip Franklin (1898–1965) of MIT proved that a five-chromatic map (one that, hypothetically, requires five colors) must contain at least 22 countries. The methods Birkhoff developed were used and improved by many mathematicians between 1913 and 1950. Although this fine work established that a large number of configurations were reducible, the set of all configurations that had been proved reducible in the forty years following Birkhoff's paper was not even close to being sufficient for a proof of the Four-Color Conjecture. In other words, these configurations did not even come close to forming an unavoidable set. Only a few mathematicians developed unavoidable sets of configurations; and they seemed to have little hope that their work would lead to an unavoidable set of reducible configurations. In fact, the primary use of reducible configurations during the first half of this century was to raise the so-called Birkhoff number of Franklin from 22 to 36 (i.e., to show that every map with fewer than 36 countries was four colorable). This was the best result prior to 1950.

Heinrich Heesch of the University of Hanover, who began his work on the Four-Color Conjecture in 1936, seems to have been the first mathematician (after Kempe) who publicly stated a belief that the Four-Color Conjecture could be proved by finding an unavoidable set of reducible configurations. In 1950 he conjectured that not only could such a set be found but that the configurations in the set would be of certain restricted sizes and about ten thousand in number. At that time it seemed extremely difficult to actually produce such a set (and to prove that each of its members was reducible). However, with the advent of high-speed digital computers, an attack on these problems became technically possible. The pessimism of earlier researchers, which appeared justified by the difficulties of hand computation, had to be reevaluated in the light of machines of ever-increasing speed and power. Heesch formalized the known methods of proving configurations reducible and observed that at least one of them (a straightforward generalization of the method used by Kempe) was, in principle, a sufficiently mechanical procedure to be done by computer.

Heesch's student Karl Dürre then wrote a computer program using this procedure to prove configurations reducible. Whenever such a program succeeds in proving a configuration reducible, the configuration is certainly reducible. However, a negative result shows only that the particular method of proving reducibility is not sufficient to prove the configuration reducible; it might be possible to prove it reducible by other methods. In some cases, when Dürre's program failed (to prove a configuration reducible) Heesch succeeded: he was able to show the configurations reducible by using data generated by the program and further calculations to implement a stronger technique which was, in principle, described by Birkhoff.

Dual Graphs and Reduction Obstacles

Heesch described reducible configurations in a somewhat more convenient way than did his predecessors. He began by recasting the original map into what mathematicians call a "dual" form. To do this, mark the capital in each country and then, whenever two countries are neighbors, join their capitals by a road across the common border (see Figure 11). Now delete everything except the capitals (called *vertices*) and the roads (called *arcs* or *edges*) you have added; what remains is known as the *dual graph* of the original map. It is possible, and often convenient, to redraw the dual so

Figure 11   The dual of Birkhoff's diamond

that all of the arcs are actually segments of straight lines. The edges of a graph divide the plane into regions which are usually called *faces*. If we begin with a normal map—which is all we ever consider here—all of these faces are triangles, because faces in the dual graph correspond to vertices of the original map, and in a normal map each vertex joins precisely three edges. In this case, the whole dual graph is called a *triangulation*. The number of edges that end at a particular vertex (in the dual graph) is called the *degree* of that vertex and is equal to the number of neighbors of the country (in the original map) that is represented by that vertex. A path of edges that starts and ends at the same vertex and does not cross itself separates the graph into two parts: its interior and its exterior. Such a path is called a *circuit*. Figure 11 shows the dual of the configuration of Figure 10, with the countries of Figure 10 lightly indicated; note that the ring of six surrounding countries in the original map is replaced by a circuit of six vertices and six edges in the dual configuration.

In the vocabulary of dual graphs, a configuration is a part of a triangulation consisting of a set of vertices plus all the edges joining them. The boundary circuit is called the *ring* of the configuration. The configuration of Figure 11 (which is drawn in dual form) is called a six-ring configuration since its ring contains six vertices; it corresponds exactly to the ring of six countries surrounding the original configuration.

While testing configurations for reducibility, Heesch observed a number of distinctive phenomena that provided clues to the likelihood of successful reduction. For instance, there were certain conditions involving the neighbors of vertices of the configuration under which no reducible configurations had ever been found. No reducible configuration had ever been found that contained, for example, at least two vertices, a vertex adjacent to four ring vertices, and no smaller configuration that was reducible. While no proof is known that reducible configurations with these "reduction obstacles" could not exist, it seemed prudent to assume that if one wanted reducible configurations one should avoid such configurations. Heesch found three major reduction obstacles (see Figure 12), including the one

described above, that were easily describable. No configuration containing one of them has yet been proved reducible.

Discharging

With Heesch's work the theory of reducible configurations seemed extremely well developed. While certain improvements in the attacks on reducibility have since been made, all of the ideas on reducibility that were needed for the proof of the Four-Color Theorem were understood in the late 1960's. Comparable progress had not been made in finding unavoidable sets of configurations. Heesch introduced a method that was analogous to moving charge in an electrical network to find an unavoidable set of configurations (not all reducible), but he had not treated the idea of unavoidability with the same enthusiasm as that of reducibility. The "method of discharging" that first appeared in rather rudimentary form in the work of Heesch has been crucial in all later work on unavoidable sets. In a much more sophisticated form it became the central element in the proof of the Four-Color Theorem, so we will explain it in some detail.

A triangulation that represents a minimal five-chromatic map, by the correct part of Kempe's work, cannot have any vertices with *fewer* than five neighbors. Thus, in what follows, we will, for convenience, use the word triangulation to mean those triangulations with no vertices of degree less than five. It follows from Kempe's work that if we assign the number $6 - k$ to every vertex of degree k (i.e., with k neighbors) then the sum of the assigned numbers (which we shall call charges) is exactly 12 (see Figure 13 for an example). (This somewhat surprising result depends both on the fact that the graph is drawn on a plane and that it is a triangulation.) The particular sum of 12 is not very important. What is extremely important in what follows is that for every planar triangulation this charge sum is positive. It is also important to notice that since vertices of degree k are assigned charge $6 - k$, vertices of degree greater than six (such vertices will be called *major* vertices) are assigned negative charge

Type 1

Type 2

Type 3

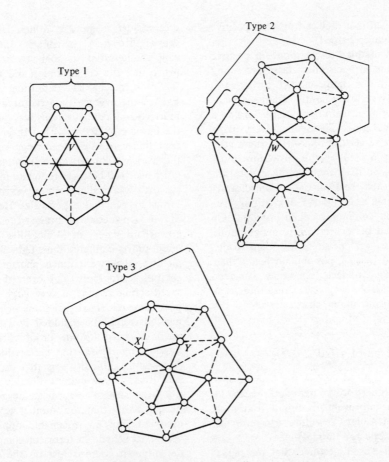

Figure 12   Examples of the three Heesch reduction obstacles

and only vertices of degree five are given positive charge. (Recall that by the convention mentioned above, we are not considering vertices of smaller degree.)

Now suppose that the charges in such a triangulation are moved around without losing or gaining charge in the entire system. In particular, positive charge is moved from some of the positively charged (degree-five) vertices to some of the negatively charged (major) vertices. While it is certainly not possible to change the sum of the charges by these operations, the vertices having positive charge may change; for example, some degree-five vertices may lose all positive charge (become discharged), while some major vertices

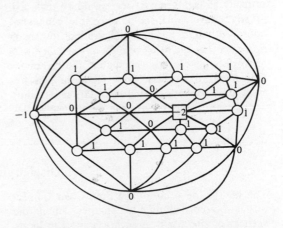

Figure 13   A small triangulation with the associated charges at the vertices

may gain so much that they end up with positive charge (become overcharged).

The purpose of this "discharging" of positive vertices is to find a precise procedure describing exactly how to move charge in such a way as to insure that every vertex of positive charge remaining in the resulting distribution must belong to a reducible configuration. Then, since every triangulation must have vertices of positive charge, the configurations signalled by this procedure must be unavoidable. So if all these configurations are also reducible, then the Four-Color Conjecture is proved. (A simple example of a discharging procedure, as it is commonly called, follows. Of course, if not all of the resulting configurations are reducible, no real progress has been made, since one would be in a position no better than that of Kempe. In fact, one may consider Kempe's unavoidable set as that resulting from the procedure of moving no charges at all.)

The Problem as of 1970

In 1970 Haken noticed certain methods of improving discharging procedures and began to hope that such improvements might lead to a proof of the Four-Color Conjecture. However the difficulties still appeared formidable.

First of all, it was conjectured that very large configurations (with rings of neighbors containing as many as eighteen vertices) would be included in any unavoidable set of reducible configurations. Although testing configurations of small ring size (say up to eleven) for reducibility was reasonably simple on a computer, the computer time involved increased by a factor of four for every unit increase in ring size. To make things worse, the computer storage requirements in-

creased just as quickly. When Dürre's program was applied to a particularly difficult fourteen-ring configuration it took twenty-six hours to prove that the configuration did not satisfy just the most mechanical definition of reducibility. Even if the average time required for examining fourteen-ring configurations was only 25 minutes, the factor of four to the fourth power in passing from fourteen- to eighteen-rings would imply that the average eighteen-ring configurations would require over 100 hours of time and much more storage than was available on any existing computer. It was known that experts like Heesch and Jean Mayer, a professor of French literature at Université Paul Valery in Montpellier, France, could often prove configurations reducible by elegant methods that were much shorter than existing computer programs, but even they seldom essayed configurations of very large ring size. The possibility remained that some of their ingenious methods might be included in a computer program to speed up the proof of reducibility of those configurations that were reducible.

A second difficulty was that no one knew for sure exactly how many reducible configurations would be needed to form an unavoidable set. It seemed likely that the number would be in the thousands but no reasonable upper bound had been established. In terms of computation time, the numbers seemed just on the border of the possible. Suppose, for example, that to show an eighteen-ring configuration reducible on a computer with enough storage were to take 100 hours. If there were a thousand eighteen-ring configurations in the unavoidable set, the time to prove them reducible would be 100,000 computer hours or over eleven years on an extremely large computer. For all practical purposes, if the set had been this large the proof would have at least re-

A Discharging Procedure

The key to the proof of the Four-Color Conjecture is the redistribution of "charges" among the vertices of the graph in such a way as to locate reducible configurations in the vicinity of positively charged vertices. We begin by assigning to

each vertex a charge equal to 6 less the degree of the vertex (see Figure 13). Thus degree-five vertices begin with charge of $+1$. Since the triangulations involved in the proof of the Four-Color Conjecture have no vertices of degree less than five, those of degree five are the only ones with positive initial charge.

In order to obtain a simple example of a discharging procedure, transfer 1/5 unit of charge from every vertex of degree five to each of its major neighbors, that is, to those neighbors of degree seven or greater. In the new charge distribution the inevitable presence of a vertex of positive charge implies that the triangulation must contain either the configuration consisting of two degree-five vertices joined by an edge or the configuration consisting of a degree-six vertex joined by an edge to a degree-five vertex:

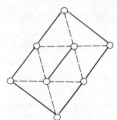 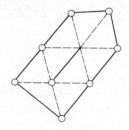

This may be verified by examining all possibilities. A vertex of degree five has positive charge (under the distribution resulting from the transfer) only if not all of its neighbors are major, i.e., if it has a neighbor of degree five or six. A vertex of degree six cannot have positive charge since, not being major, it never receives any. A vertex of degree seven can have positive charge only if it

has at least six neighbors of degree five; certainly at least two of these are adjacent. No vertex of degree greater than seven can have positive charge, since the charge supplied to it at the rate of 1/5 unit per degree-five neighbor cannot overcome its original negative charge. These two configurations (in addition to the configurations consisting of single vertices of degrees two, three, and four) form an unavoidable set. They are not reducible, however, for each of the two configurations contains reduction obstacles of Type 1. This particular discharging provides a simple proof of an unavoidability result which was obtained by P. Wernicke of the University of Göttingen in 1904. If, instead of using 1/5 in the example above, one used 1/4, then a proof of a result slightly stronger than a result of Franklin (1922) would be obtained. If 1/3 is used, an even better unavoidable set is obtained:

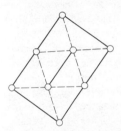 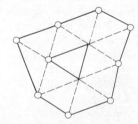

Finally, if 1/5 is replaced by 1/2, one obtains a situation close to the first approximation to our actual discharging procedure.

---

quired waiting for computers much faster than those currently available.

Even if the theorem could be proved by finding an unavoidable set of reducible configurations, the proof would not satisfy those who demanded mathematical elegance. There would certainly be no hope that a human being could personally check the reducibility of all of the configurations in the unavoidable set. On the other hand, by 1970 many experts on the Four-Color Conjecture had become very pessimistic about the possibility of a moderately short proof. Since the problem is so easily stated, a very large number of mathe-

maticians, amateur and professional, had tried to solve it. Some approaches offered quite reasonable (albeit unsuccessful) bases for attacks on the problem. Although these approaches often led to results of great importance for other areas of pure and applied mathematics, they have never come close to solving the Four-Color Problem.

Two types of standard "proofs" have appeared. The more usual type, often by amateurs, has either been based on a misunderstanding of the problem (for example, leading to a re-proof of the DeMorgan result mentioned earlier) or else contained an immediately recognizable error. The second type usually contains quite sophisticated ideas and is extremely difficult to analyze. Frank Bernhart, whose father Arthur Bernhart of the University of Oklahoma made very significant contributions to the theory of reducibility, has become expert at finding flaws in such arguments and has found an error in every one he has examined. At present, further proofs of moderate length have been announced but none have been presented in detail for expert scrutiny. It is certainly conceivable that one of these proofs is correct, but it is also reasonable to consider the possibility that no correct proof will ever be found except one based on an unavoidable set of reducible configurations. In that case it seems likely that any proof will require a computation that cannot be checked by hand. Thus it is possible that the Four-Color Theorem is an easily stated theorem that requires an argument quite different from those that have been previously used in mathematics, an argument that is not checkable by a human being alone.

Edward F. Moore of the University of Wisconsin, who created the map in Figure 6, developed powerful techniques for constructing maps that do not contain any small reducible configurations. The map in Figure 6, for instance, has no reducible configuration of ring size less than twelve. (It can be colored with four colors and does contain, as indicated, a reducible twelve-ring configuration.) While Moore's example shows that any unavoidable set of reducible configurations must contain at least one configuration of ring size twelve or greater, it appears very likely that thirteen-ring configurations are also necessary and a considerable computational effort will be required even for the best possible solution to the problem.

avoidable set of reducible configurations was to determine whether there was any hope of finding such a set with configurations of ring size sufficiently small that the computer time required for the reductions could be expected to be within reason. By the very nature of this question it was clear that we should not begin by examining the reducibility of all configurations considered, otherwise the time spent in making the estimate would exceed the expected time for the entire task.

Here the idea of reduction obstacles (see Figure 12) proved extremely useful. It is very easy to determine if a given configuration contains a reduction obstacle; and configurations without reduction obstacles, on the basis of known data, have a very good chance of being reducible. If there was a reasonable unavoidable set of configurations free of reduction obstacles, we felt that there would have to be an unavoidable set of roughly the same size containing only reducible configurations.

We decided, therefore, to study first certain kinds of discharging procedures to determine the types of sets of obstacle-free configurations that might arise. To gain understanding of what was needed even for this study, we limited this restricted problem to what are called "geographically good" configurations—those that avoided the first two of the three reduction obstacles of Heesch (see Figure 12). Geographically good configurations can be characterized very easily: no vertex inside the configuration can have more than three neighbors on the ring of the configuration, and if a vertex has precisely three such neighbors then these lie in consecutive order on the ring.

Geographically Good Configurations

When we began our work on the problem in 1972 we felt certain that the techniques we had available at that time would not lead to a nonmachine proof. We were even quite doubtful that they could lead to any proof at all before much more powerful computers were developed. Our first step in attacking the problem of finding an un-

Dialogue with a Computer

In the fall of 1972 we wrote a computer program which would carry out the particular type of discharging procedure that seemed most reasonable to us and which would give, as output, the configurations that resulted from the most important situations. Although a computer program could not be expected to proceed quite as cleverly as a human being, the immense speed of the computer

made it possible to accept certain inefficiencies. In any event, the program was written in such a way that its output could be easily checked by hand.

The first runs of the computer program in late 1972 gave us much valuable information. First, it seemed that, with the original type of procedure, geographically good configurations of reasonable size (ring size at most sixteen) would be found close to most vertices of ultimately positive charge. Second, the same configurations occurred sufficiently frequently that it might be expected that the list of different configurations might be reasonable in length. Third, as the procedure was originally organized, the computer output would be too large to handle; similar cases repeated the same argument too frequently. Fourth, there were clearly some flaws in both the type of procedure and in the details, since there were some vertices of ultimately positive charge in whose neighborhoods no geographically good configurations could be guaranteed. Fifth, the program obtained a tremendous amount of information in a few hours of computer time, so the idea of experimenting frequently was going to be feasible.

The program and the basic ideas of the discharging procedure had to be modified to overcome the problems indicated by the first runs. Since the basic program structure could be preserved, these changes were not too difficult to accomplish and a month later we made a second set of runs. Now that the gross problems indicated by the first runs were largely corrected, the program enabled us to pinpoint more subtle problems and the need for changes of detail. After some study, we found solutions for these problems and again modified the computer program.

This man-machine dialogue continued for another six months until it appeared that we had a feasible method of obtaining an unavoidable set of geographically good configurations. At this point we decided to prove formally that our method would provide a finite unavoidable set of geographically good configurations. To do this we were forced to put aside the experimental approach and describe the total procedure. It was necessary to prove that all cases had really been covered and that those cases that were not handled by the computer program really were as simple as they appeared. Much to our surprise this task proved extremely difficult and took over a year.

The problem stemmed from the necessity in pure mathematics to formulate general definitions of terms and to prove abstract statements about these terms. Special cases had to be examined in detail, often requiring rather complicated analyses, even if they seemed unlikely to arise in practice. The end result was a lengthy proof that an unavoidable set of geographically good configurations did exist, together with a procedure for constructing such a set with precise (but much larger than desirable) bounds on the sizes of the configurations in the set. The procedure itself was very important to us since we intended to use it in a possible attack on the Four-Color Conjecture. Soon thereafter, Walter Stromquist, at that time a graduate student at Harvard and a major contributor to reduction theory, gave a proof of the existence of unavoidable sets of geographically good configurations in a rather elegant way. But since Stromquist's proof did not provide a method of actually constructing the configurations in the set, it appeared unlikely that it would be immediately applicable to the Four-Color Conjecture itself.

Experiments and Modifications

In the fall of 1974, after completing the proof that our procedure would work for geographically good configurations, we discovered that we still had rather little knowledge of exactly how complicated it would be to actually carry out this procedure. To find out more we decided to try it out on a restricted problem, namely, triangulations that contained no pairs of adjacent degree-five vertices. Of course, this was a strong restriction, but the corresponding set of unavoidable geographically good configurations was quite small (47 configurations) and needed no configurations of ring size larger than sixteen. We tried to determine how much more complicated the general problem would be and decided that it might be fifty times as bad (this turned out to be a bit optimistic) and that there was good reason to proceed.

In early 1975 we modified the experimental program to yield obstacle-free configurations and forced it to search for arguments that employed configurations of small ring size. The resulting runs pointed out the need for new improvements in the procedure, but also yielded a very pleasant surprise: replacing geographically good configurations by obstacle-free ones did not seem to more than double the size of the unavoidable set.

At this point the program, which had by now absorbed our ideas and improvements for two years, began to surprise us. At the beginning we would check its arguments by hand so we could always predict the course it would follow in any situation; but now it suddenly started to act like a chess-playing machine. It would work out compound strategies based on all the tricks it had been "taught" and often these approaches were far more clever than those we would have tried. Thus it began to teach us things about how to proceed that we never expected. In a sense it had surpassed its creators in some aspects of the "intellectual" as well as the mechanical parts of the task.

Reducibility Programs

By the summer of 1975 it became clear that there was a good chance of mounting a successful attack on the Four-Color Conjecture. It seemed reasonably certain that we could find an unavoidable set of configurations that were all obstacle-free and likely to be reducible. Although it seemed very likely that such a set would contain some irreducible configurations, it seemed that there was a good chance that some small change of the procedure could be found to replace them with reducible configurations. Now, for the first time, we would need to test configurations for reducibility. Since we expected a set of configurations of ring size up to seventeen, it appeared that some sophisticated shortcut guessing would be needed in order to show configurations reducible. Since our methods, which would necessarily be somewhat restrictive, would not be certain to detect reducible configurations, we were also concerned about the probability of actually determining if a configuration was reducible by any of the known approaches.

We decided to begin writing an efficient program for testing the most mechanical form of reducibility. To do this we employed the assembler language for the IBM 360 computer at the University of Illinois. In late 1974 we were joined by John Koch, who was then a graduate student in computer science and is presently at Wilkes College. He decided to write a dissertation on reducibility for configurations of small ring size. (Frank Allaire, now of the University of Calgary, and Edward Swart, then at the University of Rhodesia, were then doing somewhat parallel work of which we were unaware.) By the fall of 1975, Koch had written programs to check the most mechanical definition of reducibility for configurations of ring size up to eleven and had begun his more general investigations. In the last half of 1975, programs for checking reducibility of twelve-, thirteen-, and fourteen-ring configurations were written by appropriately modifying Koch's work on eleven-ring configurations. These programs were improved to make use of the more general reduction procedure of Birkhoff and then we were almost ready to attack the main problem directly.

Discharging Procedure

Meanwhile, the work on the discharging procedure had gotten to the point where the changes needed to make improvements were structural changes rather than technical adjustments. Since each such change would have required a major modification in the program, we decided that the program should be discarded and that the final form of the discharging procedure could best be implemented by hand. Doing this would provide greater flexibility and would enable the procedure to be modified "locally" whenever it seemed desirable. In December 1975 we discovered that one of the rules that had been used to define the discharging procedures was too rigid. Relaxation of this rule resulted in a discharging procedure that was considerably more efficient. It now seemed possible that one might find an unavoidable set of reducible configurations of smaller ring size than would have been needed by the previous procedures. This meant that the required computer time might be less than previous estimates.

Soon after the discovery of the improved procedure we received a communication from Mayer pointing out that if the problem of "isolated five-vertices" were treated as a special problem rather than as a particular case of the general procedure, the unavoidable set could be greatly improved. (Mayer needed only fourteen configurations of ring size up to fourteen instead of our forty-seven configurations with ring sizes up to sixteen.) This led us to apply our new discharging procedure to this special case. Our general procedure for attacking the Four-Color Conjecture could not quite match the efficiency of Mayer's special procedure for this case: it yielded twenty-eight configurations of ring size up to thirteen. However, it appeared that the new procedure might cut the size of the resulting unavoidable set in half and limit the ring sizes of the configurations to fifteen or even fourteen.

Working Out the Proof

In January 1976 we began the construction of an unavoidable set of reducible configurations by means of our new discharging procedure. The final version of the discharging procedure had one further advantage for insuring the reducibility of the final configurations: the procedure was essentially self-modifying. It began by a first approximation to the final procedure. We considered each possible instance in which a major vertex was forced to become positive, and in each such case the neighborhood of the positive vertex was examined to find an obstacle-free configuration. If none was found, the neighborhood was called "critical," which means that the discharging procedure would have to be modified to avoid this problem. But even when an obstacle-free configuration was found, we could not yet guarantee a reducible configuration. The new reduction programs were used to try to find some obstacle-free configuration that was reducible. If none was found, the neighborhood was also called critical.

In classifying neighborhoods as critical, we did not distinguish between configurations with obstacles and those we could not show reducible by our programs.

This method of developing an unavoidable set of reducible configurations was only possible by another dialogue with the computer. To determine which neighborhoods were critical it was necessary to check for reducibility quickly, both in terms of computer time and in terms of real time. We were very fortunate in this dialogue, for it was seldom necessary to wait more than a few days for results, even though a considerable amount of computer time was often needed. Since this extensive man-machine interaction was absolutely essential for our success, we should explain the circumstances that made it all possible.

Although our arrangement for computer usage seemed quite natural to us at the time, we have since discovered that we were indeed extremely fortunate to be working at the University of Illinois, where a combination of a large computing establishment and an enlightened policy toward research use of computers gave us an opportunity that seemed unavailable at almost any other university or research establishment. When we approached the Computer Center and the University Research Board to ask for over a thousand hours of computer time, we could give no guarantee that the work would result in a proof of the Four-Color Conjecture. (We had no external support, although we had made applications; such support seems to depend on unanimity among the referees that an approach will succeed, and certainly no such unanimity is likely to exist with respect to a problem of this nature.) We were told by the Computer Center that since the University's computers were not fully utilized at all times by classwork and ordinary research, we could be included in a small group of computer users who were allowed to share the surplus computer time. We realize in retrospect that this policy was extraordinary and quite courageous; at many institutions the policy is to leave computers idle rather than take a chance that a project which uses a very large amount of time will be unsuccessful and will subject those who approve the request to bureaucratic difficulties. In any event, this policy provided as much time as we could use without disturbing the day-to-day flow of computer work at the University, and was essential to our success.

From January 1976 until June 1976 we worked to define the last details of the discharging procedure and simultaneously to create the unavoidable set of reducible configurations which it produced. Over a thousand hours of time on three computers was used and it was possible to do the reductions quickly enough (in real time) to keep pace with the development of the final discharging procedure (which was done by hand).

The discharging procedure involved about 500 special discharging situations (resulting from critical neighborhoods) that modified the first approximation of January 1976. It required analysis of about ten thousand neighborhoods of vertices of positive charge by hand and analysis of reducibility of over two thousand configurations by machine. While not all of this material became part of the final proof, a considerable part, including the proof of reducibility of about 1500 configurations, is essential. A person could carefully check the part of the discharging procedure that did not involve reducibility computations in a month or two, but it does not seem possible to check the reducibility computations themselves by hand. Indeed, the referees of the paper resulting from our work used our complete notes to check the discharging procedure, but they resorted to an independent computer program to check the correctness of the reducibility computations.

The Nature of Proof: Limits and Opportunities

The fundamental reason that the unavoidable set argument worked whereas other approaches to the Four-Color Conjecture did not is that all other approaches need somewhat stronger theoretical tools to make their methods apply. While these might be possible to create, there is no guarantee that they are actually possible; and if they are, there is no obvious way to go about finding them.

On the other hand, many mathematicians have believed that an unavoidable set of reducible configurations might exist, but that a smallest such

set was beyond the bounds of reasonable computation. This attitude appears justified when the problem is considered with respect to the tools available prior to 1960. After 1960, with the advent of faster computers, there were still strong reasons to believe that the computations would be infeasibly large, but there were certainly no theoretical difficulties to overcome other than the choice of a method for obtaining an unavoidable set. Thus by 1970 it became a problem of discovering whether efficient use of known techniques and technical (as opposed to theoretical) improvements would enable one to find an unavoidable set of reducible configurations.

Most mathematicians who were educated prior to the development of fast computers tend not to think of the computer as a routine tool to be used in conjunction with other older and more theoretical tools in advancing mathematical knowledge. Thus they intuitively feel that if an argument contains parts that are not verifiable by hand calculations it is on rather insecure ground. There is a tendency to feel that verification of computer results by independent computer programs is not as certain to be correct as independent hand checking of the proof of theorems proved in the standard way.

This point of view is reasonable for those theorems whose proofs are of moderate length and highly theoretical. When proofs are long and highly computational, it may be argued that even when hand checking is possible, the probability of human error is considerable higher than that of machine error; moreover, if the computations are sufficiently routine, the validity of programs themselves is easier to verify than the correctness of hand computations.

In any event, even if the Four-Color Theorem turns out to have a simpler proof, mathematicians might be well advised to consider more carefully other problems that might have solutions of this new type, requiring computation or analysis of a type not possible for humans alone. There is every reason to believe that there are a large number of such problems. After all, the argument that almost all known proofs are reasonably short can be answered by the argument that if one only employs tools which will yield short proofs that is all one is likely to get.

One might well ask whether this work has any practical value. The answer seems to be that the value is surely greater to mathematics than to cartography. The example of the Four-Color Theorem may help to clarify the possibilities and the limitations of the methods of pure mathematics and those of computation. It may be that a problem cannot be solved by either of these alone but can be solved by a combination of the two methods. There is a certain parallel in the early history of science. From the time of Plato until the late Middle Ages, mathematical methods were regarded as so superior to experimental methods that experimental physics was not considered (socially) acceptable among serious scientists. This severely handicapped the development of certain branches of physics. For instance, the laws of free fall of bodies under the influence of gravity were incorrectly stated by Aristotle, who tried to derive them theoretically, and the error was not corrected for about two thousand years until the simple observations and experiments of Galileo clarified the matter and initiated a rapid progress of mechanical dynamics. As soon as the importance of experimentation was recognized (and somewhat stronger limitations were recognized as applying to purely mathematical methods), a very fruitful development of physics was achieved through a combination of the two methods. Thus the fact that our result hints at somewhat more stringent limitations of purely mathematical methods than some mathematicians would like to see should be interpreted not as a negative result but rather as an indication of a direction for progress.

It may be argued that there is nothing of greater practical importance than obtaining an approximately correct idea of the powers and limitations of one's methods, since here misjudgments may have the most severe negative consequences. We hope that our result yields some progress in this direction and that this justifies the great effort in human resources which has been made in the attack on the Four-Color Problem in the years since 1852.

Group Theory and the Postulational Method

Carl H. Denbow and Victor Goedicke

Carl Herbert Denbow obtained his undergraduate, masters, and Ph.D. from the University of Chicago. His interest in the teaching of mathematics led him to be a coordinator for the International Teacher Development Program, chairman of an AID survey team in Cambodia, and director of the training program for the Peace Corps in Cameroon. He is currently a professor of mathematics at Ohio University.

Victor Alfred Goedicke was born in Wyoming and received his Ph.D. in astronomy in 1938 from the University of Michigan. His background in astronomy and mathematics enabled him to teach at Wesleyan, Brown, and Yale Universities. Since 1953 he has been a professor of mathematics and astronomy at Ohio University.

In 1832, the night before he was fatally wounded in a duel, Evariste Galois sat down and created Galois theory, a subject that has troubled and confused every generation of graduate students in mathematics from that day to this. That his achievement was a monument to the human intellect is self-evident. That Galois was much brighter than almost all who have since been doing or trying to do mathematics seems clear. This volume will not try to popularize Galois theory. However, on the way to his summit of mathematical invention this tragic if somewhat baroque figure did create a number of new mathematical systems which are quite easily approached and from which it is possible to gain a better insight into the nature of mathematics. Galois created the notion of abstract groups as he was producing his deep insights into the nature of polynomials and their roots. However, even this concept has become an important area of research in modern mathematics. In this essay Denbow and Goedicke introduce and develop the notion of group as an abstract mathematical system.

Since the whole point of this article is the inductive definition of the group concept, it would be inappropriate to spoil the reader's fun by giving a definition of group in this introduction. However, the essay ends with an exercise that the reader is asked to complete, and the four answers do form the needed definition. The reader who remains puzzled as to how to frame the answers will find the four desired properties listed in the editors' footnote at the end of the article. An algebraic system that satisfies these four properties is called a group.

Source: Carl H. Denbow and Victor Goedicke, "Group Theory and the Postulational Method," in *Readings for Mathematics: A Humanistic Approach,* 1972, Wadsworth Publishing Company. Originally from pp. 117–125 in *Foundations of Mathematics,* Carl H. Denbow and Victor Goedicke. Copyright © 1959 by Carl H. Denbow and Victor Goedicke. Reprinted by permission of Harper & Row, Publishers, Inc. (Problem sections omitted.)

The Search for Generality

Scientists and mathematicians are forever searching for more "inclusive" analyses of the things they study. They are never so happy as when they have discovered a relationship between two kinds of phenomena formerly considered independent. An excellent example of this is to be found in Newton's discovery of the law of universal gravitation, which showed that the forces with which objects at the surface of the earth are pulled downward are exactly the same kinds of forces as those which pull the moon toward the earth and the earth toward the sun, and, in fact, that all such forces throughout the universe are given by a single law so simple that any schoolboy can learn and understand it.* One of the great recent triumphs of physics is the creation of a theory which unifies the extensive data about the behavior of electromagnetic waves and the behavior of showers of atomic particles, whereas formerly a separate theory was required for each.

In the case of the scientists, this search for more inclusive theories is easy to understand. Experience tells us that a theory which works over a wide range of human experience is more likely to be useful than one which works over only a narrow range. If an astronomer studying energy generation has a theory which works for all the stars, he is more likely to be on the right track than an astronomer whose theory works only for the sun.

Mathematicians also search for more inclusive theories, and for somewhat similar reasons. If we can find a single theory which unifies several branches of mathematics, we have increased the power of mathematics accordingly, because we have simplified the structure of mathematical knowledge and facilitated the task of learning and applying it. It would be misleading, however, if we asserted that this was the only motivation for the discovery of these theories. In fact, the motivation is actually esthetic as well as utilitarian. To discover a kind of hidden master pattern in the structure of mathematical knowledge is an esthetic achievement, and the study of it should

give you esthetic pleasure as well as enlightenment. It is with this hope that we proceed to a discussion of one of the broad, inclusive branches of mathematics. It is called "group theory."

The Furniture Mover's Story

The theory of groups is rather recent in the history of mathematics. It was in fact the branch of mathematics developed by a French boy named Evariste Galois, who died in 1832 at the age of 20. The circumstances of his death are unusual. He died in a duel which, it is believed, was rigged by persons who felt it necessary to do away with him on political grounds. His behavior indicates that he knew that he was to die. He spent the entire night before the duel writing a kind of scientific testament, feverishly committing to paper the mathematical ideas which he would have liked to develop at his leisure and present to mankind in finished form. Then he went out to face his death, and mankind was deprived of one of its truly great minds.*

Our purpose in introducing the theory of groups is to simplify several areas of mathematics by demonstrating an underlying unity which they possess. (It is interesting to note that this underlying unity goes beyond mathematics, and that other examples of group theory are to be found in art, in the theory of crystal structure, in the theory of relativity, and in other unexpected areas.) But for your first introduction to group theory we have chosen an example which is very simple and direct, and nonmathematical in the ordinary sense. We hope that this illustration will show you that mathematics need not deal with numbers or quantities or geometry, and we hope further that it will show you how new kinds of mathematics can arise out of new ways of looking at familiar situations. And so we will ask you to follow us in a pathetic little story of a man whose wife was addicted to furniture moving.

Now of course most women move furniture around occasionally, in an effort to give the room

---

*"Every object in the universe is attracted by every other body in the universe with a force which is proportional to the product of the masses and inversely proportional to the square of the distance between them."

*For an interesting account of the life of Galois, see *Whom the Gods Love*, by Leopold Infeld, McGraw-Hill, 1948.

"that added something." But most women, after having experimented with the same unsuccessful arrrangement several times, will give it up. The wife of our hero, Mr. Adamson, was different. She could not resist the hope that if she tried a given arrangement just one more time she might be able to make it work out.

Imagine then an ordinary living room, containing among other things a sofa, a radio, and a table (Figure 1). At the end of each hard day's work,

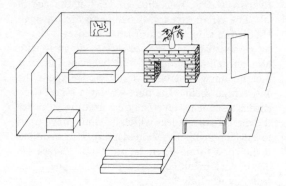

Figure 1   The Adamsons' living room

Mr. Adamson comes home to find that his wife has decided to try a new arrangement of these three objects. She makes her "orders of the day" explicit by writing a note, which is always in the same form. A typical example is $\begin{bmatrix} RST \\ TRS \end{bmatrix}$. Mr. Adamson knows all too well what this means. "Put the table where the radio now is, and put the radio where the sofa now is, and put the sofa where the table now is." Mr. Adamson has been the recipient of so many of these peremptory little messages that he has named them. He calls this one G, because it was first handed to him on green paper.

Mr. Adamson early learned that he is expected to replace the objects named in the top row by those in the bottom row, and not vice versa. The top symbols represent "before" and the bottom ones "after." He also noticed that there are several messages which look different but which contain the same instructions. For example, the message $\begin{bmatrix} SRT \\ RTS \end{bmatrix}$ contains exactly the same instructions as the one he originally received on green paper, so he calls this one G also. In fact, when he tries to tabulate all possible messages, he finds only six basically different ones. One of these he looks at with special longing; it is the message $\begin{bmatrix} RST \\ RST \end{bmatrix}$, which would require no work. Though he has never been granted this boon, he has included it for the sake of making his list complete, and has named it E (for easy). The message $\begin{bmatrix} RST \\ STR \end{bmatrix}$ he has named $\mathcal{J}$, because he can still remember the hot June day when he would have liked to go fishing instead of moving furniture. The remaining ones he named alphabetically; he used A for $\begin{bmatrix} RST \\ RTS \end{bmatrix}$ (in which the radio is not moved), and B for $\begin{bmatrix} RST \\ TSR \end{bmatrix}$, and C for $\begin{bmatrix} RST \\ SRT \end{bmatrix}$ (Table 1).

Table 1   The Six Messages

$E = \begin{bmatrix} RST \\ RST \end{bmatrix}$		$A = \begin{bmatrix} RST \\ RTS \end{bmatrix}$	
$C = \begin{bmatrix} RST \\ SRT \end{bmatrix}$		$\mathcal{J} = \begin{bmatrix} RST \\ STR \end{bmatrix}$	
$G = \begin{bmatrix} RST \\ TRS \end{bmatrix}$		$B = \begin{bmatrix} RST \\ TSR \end{bmatrix}$	

Now these names, G, $\mathcal{J}$, and the rest, are only names, and you may be inclined to think they are not very important. A name is only a name; it moves no furniture. But by now you should be suspicious of this agnostic attitude. We have seen that a set of language agreements is an important part of establishing a new system of thought, and that an apt naming system frequently clarifies our thinking and leads to new insights. (If this were not so, mathematics would still be a branch of English!) So let us see what will come out of this system of names which Mr. Adamson gave to his wife's repeated orders.

As Mr. Adamson now recalls it, his interest in the implications of this little game first occurred to him when his wife's aunt became ill. One night Mr. Adamson came home and found the inevitable message (this time it was *A*) accompanied by a note which said, "I am spending the night with poor Aunt Susan. Your dinner is in the refrigerator." Mr. Adamson was especially hot and tired that day, and decided to have a beer and read the paper before he moved the furniture, and, human nature being what it is, when the next evening came the furniture was still unmoved and another message (*B*) had arrived. Instead of actually moving the furniture twice, he decided to find out by means of pencil and paper what the final positions of the furniture should be after the two manipulations. He wrote an R, and S, and a T in three circles to indicate the original positions of the three pieces of furniture. Underneath he wrote the names of the furniture which would replace these after manipulation *A*, and under these a third set of letters to show the results of manipulation *B*. This "lazy man's method" of moving furniture is shown in Figure 2.

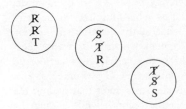

Figure 2

Mr. Adamson then inspected his list of the six possible manipulations to see which one would accomplish this all in one step, and discovered that *G* will do it. He abbreviated this information by writing "*A* + *B* = *G*." He proceeded happily to perform the rearrangement *G*, quite pleased with himself for having telescoped two days' messages into one. From this time onward (so depraved was his character) he shirked his work and let the messages pile up until his wife was due to return home, at which time he added the accumulated messages. He found that, no matter what

messages he had received, there was always one *single* manipulation which would produce the same furniture arrangement as the entire set of manipulations. (In the language of mathematics, he had discovered that his system of manipulations had the property of closure.)

After this discovery, he sought to avoid even the work of performing the additions (many of mankind's greatest achievements, he told himself, are the result of an effort to avoid work) by simply recording all his sums for future use, like an addition table. And finally (as often happens) this effort to avoid work was his undoing. His wife left him message *B* one Monday night, and left for Aunt Susan's; on Tuesday night she sent over message *A*; he recalled that he had already proved that *A* + *B* = *G*. He was just completing manipulation *G* on the furniture when his wife arrived and asked him, in icy tones, just what he thought he was doing. Flushed and unhappy, he worked out the separate messages on paper and found that message *B* followed by message *A* (which was the sequence his wife had ordered) gave a result different from that of message *A* followed by message *B*; in fact *A* + *B* = *G*, while *B* + *A* = *J*! In this way he discovered that addition of these messages is not commutative.

In the light of this discovery, Mr. Adamson saw the wisdom of working out a complete addition table. His results are shown in Table 2.

Table 2   Addition Table

First Term	Second Term					
	E	*A*	*C*	*J*	*G*	*B*
E	*E*	*A*	*C*	*J*	*G*	*B*
A	*A*	*E*	*J*	*C*	*B*	*G*
C	*C*	*G*	*E*	*B*	*A*	*J*
J	*J*	*B*	*A*	*G*	*E*	*C*
G	*G*	*C*	*B*	*E*	*J*	*A*
B	*B*	*J*	*G*	*A*	*C*	*E*

By this time he began to see that he was dealing with a kind of mathematics in which the things to be added were not *numbers*, but *operations*. He also saw that his addition table could be used for any situation in which the operations were similar to his furniture moving, whether the objects rearranged were pieces of furniture, or moons of Jupiter, or carbon atoms in a molecule. In other words, he was concerned with the study of certain operations rather than the nature of the objects being operated upon. (This same accusation has sometimes been leveled at surgeons.) The addition of these operations (or elements, as he sometimes called them) has some feature in common with the addition of numbers; for example, the element E plays a role similar to that of zero in number addition. (In number addition, 2 plus zero gives 2 again, 3 plus zero equals 3, and so forth; while in Mr. Adamson's addition of elements A plus E gives A again, B plus E equals B, and so forth.) From then on he always called E "the neutral element."

Mr. Adamson's next discovery came as a result of Aunt Susan's taking a turn for the worse. (Individual welfare frequently has to be sacrificed for the advancement of science.) There came a day when Mr. Adamson found himself with an accumulation of not two, but three messages, so that he had to perform the computation $B + \mathcal{J} + G$. He noted at once that his addition table permitted him to add only two elements at a time, and that this gave him a choice of procedure. If he added the $B + \mathcal{J}$ first, he would obtain A, and if he then, by consulting Table 2, performed the addition $A + G$, he would obtain B. By using parentheses he summarized these results as follows:

$$(B + \mathcal{J}) + G = A + G = B,$$

and since this is exactly the grouping which the problem required (after all, if he had been doing his job properly he would, at the end of the second day, have performed $B + \mathcal{J}$, and he would then on the third day have performed G), therefore B was undoubtedly the right answer. But Mr. Adamson was now firmly held in the grip of scientific curiosity, and he could not help wondering what *would* have happened *if* he had combined the elements $\mathcal{J}$ and G first. Having an experimental turn of mind, he tried it. He found from Table 2 that $\mathcal{J} + G = E$, so that

$$B + (\mathcal{J} + G) = B + E = B,$$

and found that, in this case at least, the order in which he carried out the simplification makes no difference. In other words, $(B + \mathcal{J}) + G =$ $B + (\mathcal{J} + G)$. Further experimentation showed him that this is always true. This result can be formulated as follows:

$$(x + y) + z = x + (y + z),$$

which is the same as the associative law of addition of numbers.

When Mr. Adamson had assembled his addition table, he noted with longing that there were several pairs which gave E as a sum, so that if his luck were good his wife might give him two successive messages which totaled E, and thus save him any work whatever. For example, $G + \mathcal{J} = E$; or in other words, $\mathcal{J}$ is the element which undoes element G, and leaves the original furniture arrangement as if no manipulation had been performed at all. For this reason we say that $\mathcal{J}$ is the "inverse" of G. Similarly, we note that G is the inverse of $\mathcal{J}$, since $\mathcal{J} + G$ also equals E. We note from Table 2 that A is its own inverse since $A + A = E$.

The more Mr. Adamson studied the table, the more he was impressed by the differences between addition of these elements and addition of numbers. He saw that writing $G + \mathcal{J} = E$ is something like writing $7 + (-7) = 0$; in words, $\mathcal{J}$ can be regarded as something like the negative of G. But then what of the equation $A + A = E$? Here is an element which is its own "negative"; if you add it to itself it gives zero! And what about the equation $G + G = \mathcal{J}$ and $\mathcal{J} + \mathcal{J} = G$? Here are two elements such that adding the first to itself gives the second, while adding the second to itself gives the first! He saw that he would have to be very careful to avoid carrying preconceptions from one system of mathematics to another.

Mr. Adamson often speculated about the further possibilities of this new system of mathematics. He knew, for example, that in the mathematics of numbers you can always solve an equation like $x + 3 = 7$, and that the solution is unique. That is, if $x + 3 = 7$, then there is one and only one number which x can be, namely 4. Now suppose that you wish to find an element to which you could add A to obtain $\mathcal{J}$; in other words, suppose you wish to solve the equation $X + A = \mathcal{J}$. Would such an equation always have a solution, and would the solution always be unique? These questions remained unsolved for many weeks, until his attention was forcibly directed to them in the following way. He had added the Monday and Tuesday messages and found that their sum was $\mathcal{J}$; then he received a note on Wednesday which read, "I have changed my mind; don't carry out the Tuesday instructions but only the Monday instructions." But by this time he had discarded the original messages, and he remembered only that the Tuesday message was A and the total of the two was $\mathcal{J}$! Necessity is the mother of invention, so he set up the equation $X + A = \mathcal{J}$, where X was the forgotten Monday message. Then he solved the equation by the simple expedient of locating the *column* headed A, and running his finger down it until he came to $\mathcal{J}$, then finding the number at the left end of this row, which turned out to be B. In other words, he found by a systematic search of Table 2 that $B + A = \mathcal{J}$; and B was therefore the answer to his problem. He noticed that the answer was unique (since $\mathcal{J}$ occurred only once in the column) and that in fact every such equation had one and only one solution, since every element occurs once and only once in each column and in each row.

But Mr. Adamson's curiosity had been aroused by the effort to solve equations in this system. He wondered if the equation could not be solved by some method neater than systematic search, just as equations in arithmetic or algebra can be solved. To solve the equation

$$x + 3 = 7,$$

he recalled, it is necessary to subtract 3 (or to add "minus" 3) on each side of the equation, giving

$$x + 3 + (-3) = 7 + (-3),$$

which, when simplified, yields

$$x = 4.$$

By analogy, we should expect to add the inverse of A to each side of the equation

$$X + A = \mathcal{J},$$

since the inverse is in a sense the negative of an element. Here we must remember that in our system pre-adding is different from post-adding; if for instance we pre-add A to B we get $A + B$, which is equal to G, but if we post-add A to B we get $B + A$, which is equal to $\mathcal{J}$. Let us post-add the inverse of A (which happens to be A itself) to both sides of the equation. (Obviously if we post-add on one side of an equation we must post-add on the other side.) This gives us

$$X + A + A = \mathcal{J} + A,$$

and since A is its own inverse, we can replace $A + A$ by E:

$$X + E = \mathcal{J} + A.$$

From the tables, we see that $X + E = X$, for every X, and $\mathcal{J} + A = B$. Making these substitutions, we obtain finally

$$X = B.$$

Thus Mr. Adamson found that equations can be solved by manipulation, just as in the algebra of numbers.

. . . [We] have omitted from the above selection something rather important: the definition of a group. However, the article contains all the information you need to create the definition yourself. Try to construct a definition of "group" that uses four characterizing axioms. It may be helpful to proceed as follows: A group G is a mathematical system consisting of a set, which we will also call G, and an operation defined for pairs of things in G. The operation denoted in the article by "$+$" satisfies the following axioms:

1. _____
2. _____
3. _____
4. _____

Editors' note: For any elements x, y, z in the set G in which "$+$" is defined for any two elements:

1. $x + y$ is always an element of G.

2. $(x + y) + z = x + (y + z)$.

3. $x + e = e + x$.

4. $x + (-x) = (-x) + x = e$ where $-x$ denotes the inverse of x.

part three

Foundations and Philosophy

IN THE LIFE of Niels Henrick Abel we find the essence of classic tragedy. Born in 1802 in an obscure Norwegian village Abel survived a childhood of dreary poverty. His father's ill-rewarded occupation as pastor and his large family combined as factors to guarantee that Abel would obtain no advantage in life except that provided by a sympathetic school master who recognized his genius and encouraged him to study mathematics. At age 16 Abel extended a famous result of Euler. Within the next four years he resolved in the negative the question of finding a formula for extracting roots of the general quintic (polynomial of degree 5), a problem whose solution had eluded mathematicians since the sixteenth century. Through all this, Abel, responsible for the support of his siblings since his father's death in 1820, endured poverty, lack of recognition, rejection of original works of monumental power and generality, and increasingly, failing health. He died of consumption in 1829, before his twenty-seventh birthday and just two days prior to the receipt of a letter appointing him to a professorship at Berlin University.

The history of mathematics contains few biographies more painful in the telling, and in the community of mathematicians Abel is widely regarded as the paradigm of the tragic mathematical hero. But consider. By the unwritten standards of that same community was Abel's life really the ultimate in misfortune? Suppose Abel were raised from his tuberculous pallet and established in a comfortable sinecure in Berlin. His minimal obligations easily fulfilled, this imaginary Abel turns to his real occupation, the purpose for which mathematical chairs are fabricated: the creation of new mathematics. But it is only a matter of time until our imaginary Abel's effulgent fountain of invention begins to sputter and then run dry. Consider then the octogenerian Abel, with all of his results generalized beyond recognition by 26-year-old Laplander, Hindustani, or even Texan mathematicians, with his major works now the stuff of examination questions and footnotes. "Who is that?" asks the new graduate student who sees the white-haired ancient. "Oh, that's old Abel," comes the reply. "Abel! You mean he's still alive?" In the mathematician's table of misfortune there are worse things than dying young at the summit of one's creative pilgrimage with yet higher peaks of achievement looming in the never-to-be-realized future. For no one can prove that they might not have been scaled.

The history of mathematics demonstrates that mathematics is a sport for the young. It does not deal kindly with those of advancing years, and in almost all cases the creative powers peak somewhere in the twenties or thirties only to decline quite rapidly with the onset of middle age. Those "over the hill" in mathematics, if they try to keep pace with the rising generation, create exactly the same depressing spectacle as the famous athlete past his prime flailing away with shattered nerves and shrunken muscles—a pantomime of ineptitude even more painful for the spectator than for the participant. Most mathematicians, quite naturally, accommodate themselves to their diminished capacities with reasonable grace and some good humor. There are a thousand dignified and relatively harmless ways in which those past their peak spend time. They serve on national committees and write textbooks, they develop an interest in teaching mathematics, they try to apply mathematics and become concerned about its social relevance, they organize meetings and accept positions in professional associations. Some, who are a bit more desperate than others, feign an interest in university administration and become department heads; and some, although this level of desperation is rare, even become deans. And then there are the truly desperate: those who take up the philosophy of mathematics.

The preceding view of mathematics includes some degree of exaggeration, but only some. To the majority of mathematicians, it makes no sense at all to talk about mathematics if one is capable of doing mathematics. Does the Yankee's thirty-game winning pitcher quit in midseason to do research on the physics of the screwball? It is absurd even to consider the idea. Thus in the exuberance of creative energy that possesses the mathematician during youth there is no time, no energy, no interest in such trifles as ultimate meaning, social value, practical application, or relevance to anything except other areas of mathematics. This may sound a bit selfish and slightly narrow-minded—it almost surely is. One can suppose that a wise, indeed kindly, providence has bestowed on a more reflective middle age a mandate of diminished creative zeal just so that the excess of youth can be put in proper perspective. For ultimately, if mathematics is to have any value, any meaning, indeed any future, then mathematics must be created in reference to that universe in which all of us, even mathematicians, continue to exist.

The Three Crises in Mathematics: Logicism, Intuitionism, and Formalism

Ernst Snapper

Ernst Snapper was born in the Netherlands in 1913. He received his Ph.D. from Princeton in 1941 and was immediately offered a position at Princeton, which he held from 1941 to 1945. Since then he has held special chairs at the University of Southern California, Miami University, Indiana University, and Dartmouth College.

This essay is as cogent and readable an introduction to the philosophy of modern mathematics as exists in the English language. While the main thrust of Snapper's essay is to explain the three approaches to mathematics noted in the title, it is clear that he also has another message. Briefly, it is that arguments about the philosophy of mathematics are arguments about philosophy. Mathematicians often feel that their special talents place them outside that arena in which other mortals contend. This conceit almost surely extends to matters of philosophy as well as politics, finance, and so on. Although no such survey exists or is contemplated, a poll of current mathematicians on their opinions of logicism, intuitionism, and formalism would be fascinating. It would be astonishing if as many as 10 percent of the sample were to connect these three different views of mathematics with their philosophical counterparts. This is due not so much to an ignorance of philosophy as to a refusal to admit that mathematics in any way partakes of the vague and arbitrary nature of philosophy.

What Snapper clearly reveals is that these three approaches to mathematics can be rephrased as views about the nature of abstract entities. These views in one guise or another date back to the ancient Greeks; debate as to which is the "correct" approach has been an ongoing philosophical entertainment for well over 2,000 years. Whether the mathematical aspect of this debate will add any new insights to those already offered by the philosophers remains to be seen. What is certain is that failure on the part of the mathematicians to admit the philosophical dimensions of their dispute will result in the mathematicians simply reinventing, in another language, a number of very old philosophical wheels. This seems at best a dubious use of mental resources, and Snapper's article probably ought to be required reading for anyone even mildly interested in the foundations of mathematics.

Source: Ernst Snapper, "The Three Crises in Mathematics: Logicism, Intuitionism, and Formalism," *Mathematics Magazine* 52 (Sept. 1979): 207–216. Reprinted by permission of the Mathematical Association of America. (Some references omitted.)

THE THREE SCHOOLS, mentioned in the title, all tried to give a firm foundation to mathematics. The three crises are the failures of these schools to complete their tasks. This article looks at these crises "through modern eyes," using whatever mathematics is available today and not just the mathematics which was available to the pioneers who created these schools. Hence, this article does not approach the three crises in a strictly historical way. This article also does not discuss the large volume of current, technical mathematics which has arisen out of the techniques introduced by the three schools in question. One reason is that such a discussion would take a book and not a short article. Another one is that all this technical mathematics has very little to do with the philosophy of mathematics, and in this article I want to stress those aspects of logicism, intuitionism, and formalism which show clearly that these schools are founded in philosophy.

Logicism

This school was started in about 1884 by the German philosopher, logician and mathematician, Gottlob Frege (1848–1925). The school was redis-

covered about eighteen years later by Bertrand Russell. Other early logicists were Peano and Russell's coauthor of *Principia Mathematica*, A. N. Whitehead. The purpose of logicism was to show that classical mathematics is part of logic. If the logicists had been able to carry out their program successfully, such questions as "Why is classical mathematics free of contradictions?" would have become "Why is logic free of contradictions?" This latter question is one on which philosophers have at least a thorough handle and one may say in general that the successful completion of the logicists' program would have given classical mathematics a firm foundation in terms of logic.

Clearly, in order to carry out this program of the logicists, one must first, somehow, define what "classical mathematics" is and what "logic" is. Otherwise, what are we supposed to show is part of what? It is precisely at these two definitions that we want to look through modern eyes, imagining that the pioneers of logicism had all of present-day mathematics available to them. We begin with classical mathematics.

In order to carry out their program, Russell and Whitehead created *Principia Mathematica* which was published in 1910. (The first volume of this classic can be bought for $3.45! Thank heaven, only modern books and not the classics

have become too expensive for the average reader.) *Principia*, as we will refer to *Principia Mathematica*, may be considered as a formal set theory. Although the formalization was not entirely complete, Russell and Whitehead thought that it was and planned to use it to show that mathematics can be reduced to logic. They showed that all classical mathematics, known in their time, can be derived from set theory and hence from the axioms of *Principia*. Consequently, what remained to be done was to show that all the axioms of *Principia* belong to logic.

Of course, instead of *Principia*, one can use any other formal set theory just as well. Since today the formal set theory developed by Zermelo and Fraenkel (ZF) is so much better known than *Principia*, we shall from now on refer to ZF instead of *Principia*. ZF has only nine axioms and, although several of them are actually axiom schemas, we shall refer to all of them as "axioms." The formulation of the logicists' program now becomes: Show that all nine axioms of ZF belong to logic.

This formulation of logicism is based on the thesis that classical mathematics can be defined as the set of theorems which can be proved within ZF. This definition of classical mathematics is far from perfect, as is discussed in [1]. However, the above formulation of logicism is satisfactory for the purpose of showing that this school was not able to carry out its program. We now turn to the definition of logic.

In order to understand logicism, it is very important to see clearly what the logicists meant by "logic." The reason is that, whatever they meant, they certainly meant more than classical logic. Nowadays, one can define classical logic as consisting of all those theorems which can be proven in first order languages (discussed below in the section on formalism) without the use of nonlogical axioms. We are hence restricting ourselves to first order logic and use the deduction rules and logical axioms of that logic. An example of such a theorem is the law of the excluded middle which says that, if p is a proposition, then either p or its negation $\neg p$ is true; in other words, the proposition $p \vee \neg p$ is always true where $\vee$ is the usual symbol for the inclusive "or."

If this definition of classical logic had also been the logicists' definition of logic, it would be a folly to think for even one second that all of ZF can be reduced to logic. However, the logicists' definition was more extensive. They had a general concept as to when a proposition belongs to logic, that is, when a proposition should be called a "logical proposition." They said: *A logical proposition is a proposition which has complete generality and is true in virtue of its form rather than its content.* Here, the word "proposition" is used as synonymous with "theorem."

For example, the above law of the excluded middle "$p \vee \neg p$" is a logical proposition. Namely, this law does not hold because of any special content of the proposition p; it does not matter whether p is a proposition of mathematics or physics or what have you. On the contrary, this law holds with "complete generality," that is, for any proposition p whatsoever. Why then does it hold? The logicists answer: "Because of its form." Here they mean by form "syntactical form," the form of $p \vee \neg p$ being given by the two connectives of everyday speech, the inclusive "or" and the negation "not" (denoted by $\vee$ and $\neg$, respectively).

On the one hand, it is not difficult to argue that all theorems of classical logic, as defined above, are logical propositions in the sense of logicism. On the other hand, there is no *a priori* reason to believe that there could not be logical propositions which lie outside of classical logic. This is why we said that the logicists' definition of logic is more extensive than the definition of classical logic. And now the logicists' task becomes clearer: It consists in showing that all nine axioms of ZF are logical propositions in the sense of logicism.

The only way to assess the success or failure of logicism in carrying out this task is by going through all nine axioms of ZF and determining for each of them whether it falls under the logicists' concept of a logical proposition. This would take a separate article and would be of interest only to readers who are thoroughly familiar with ZF. Hence, instead, we simply state that at least two of these axioms, namely, the axiom of infinity and the axiom of choice, cannot possibly be considered as logical propositions. For example, the axiom of infinity says that there exist infinite sets.

Why do we accept this axiom as being true? The reason is that everyone is familiar with so many infinite sets, say, the set of the natural numbers or the set of points in Euclidean 3-space. Hence, we accept this axiom on grounds of our everyday experience with sets, and this clearly shows that we accept it by virtue of its content and not by virtue of its syntactical form. In general, when an axiom claims the existence of objects with which we are familiar on grounds of our common everyday experience, it is pretty certain that this axiom is not a logical proposition in the sense of logicism.

And here then is the first crisis in mathematics: Since at least two out of the nine axioms of ZF are not logical propositions in the sense of logicism, it is fair to say that this school failed by about 20% in its effort to give mathematics a firm foundation. However, logicism has been of the greatest importance for the development of modern mathematical logic. In fact, it was logicism which started mathematical logic in a serious way. The two quantifiers, the "for all" quantifier $\forall$ and the "there exists" quantifier $\exists$ were introduced into logic by Frege, and the influence of *Principia* on the development of mathematical logic is history.

It is important to realize that logicism is founded in philosophy. For example, when the logicists tell us what they mean by a logical proposition (above), they use philosophical and not mathematical language. They have to use philosophical language for that purpose since mathematics simply cannot handle definitions of so wide a scope.

The philosophy of logicism is sometimes said to be based on the philosophical school called "realism." In medieval philosophy "realism" stood for the Platonic doctrine that abstract entities have an existence independent of the human mind. Mathematics is, of course, full of abstract entities such as numbers, functions, sets, etc., and according to Plato all such entities exist outside our mind. The mind can discover them but does not create them. This doctrine has the advantage that one can accept such a concept as "set" without worrying about how the mind can construct a set. According to realism, sets are there for us to discover, not to be constructed, and the same holds for all other abstract entities. In short, realism allows us to accept many more abstract entities in mathematics than a philosophy which had limited us to accepting only those entities the human mind can construct. Russell was a realist and accepted the abstract entities which occur in classical mathematics without questioning whether our own minds can construct them. This is the fundamental difference between logicism and intuitionism, since in intuitionism abstract entities are admitted only if they are man made.

Excellent expositions of logicism can be found in Russell's writing, for example [2], [3] and [4].

Intuitionism

This school was begun about 1908 by the Dutch mathematician, L. E. J. Brouwer (1881–1966). The intuitionists went about the foundations of mathematics in a radically different way from the logicists. The logicists never thought that there was anything wrong with classical mathematics; they simply wanted to show that classical mathematics is part of logic. The intuitionists, on the contrary, felt that there was plenty wrong with classical mathematics.

By 1908, several paradoxes had arisen in Cantor's set theory. Here, the word "paradox" is used as synonymous with "contradiction." Georg Cantor created set theory, starting around 1870, and he did his work "naively," meaning nonaxiomatically. Consequently, he formed sets with such abandon that he himself, Russell and others found several paradoxes within his theory. The logicists considered these paradoxes as common errors, caused by erring mathematicians and not by a faulty mathematics. The intuitionists, on the other hand, considered these paradoxes as clear indications that classical mathematics itself is far from perfect. They felt that mathematics had to be rebuilt from the bottom on up.

The "bottom," that is, the beginning of mathematics for the intuitionists, is their explanation of what the natural numbers 1, 2, 3, . . . are. (Observe that we do not include the number zero among the natural numbers.) According to intuitionistic philosophy, all human beings have a primordial intuition for the natural numbers within them. This means in the first place that we have an immediate certainty as to what is meant by the number 1 and, secondly, that the mental process which goes into the formation of the number 1 can be repeated. When we do repeat it, we obtain the concept of the number 2; when we repeat it again, the concept of the number 3; in this way, human beings can construct any *finite* initial segment 1, 2, . . . , *n* for any natural number *n*. This mental construction of one natural number after the other would never have been possible if we did not have an awareness of time within us. "After" refers to time and Brouwer agrees with the philosopher Immanuel Kant (1724–1804) that human beings have an immediate awareness of time. Kant used the word "intuition" for "immediate awareness" and this is where the name "intuitionism" comes from.

It is important to observe that the intuitionistic construction of natural numbers allows one to construct only arbitrarily long *finite* initial segments 1, 2, . . . , *n*. It does not allow us to construct that whole closed set of all the natural numbers which is so familiar from classical mathematics. It is equally important to observe that this construction is both "inductive" and "effective." It is inductive in the sense that, if one wants to construct, say, the number 3, one has to go through all the mental steps of first constructing the 1, then the 2, and finally the 3; one cannot just grab the number 3 out of the sky. It is effective in the sense that, once the construction of a natural number has been finished, that natural number has been constructed in its entirety. It stands before us as a completely finished mental construct, ready for our study of it. When someone says, "I have finished the mental construction of the number 3," it is like a bricklayer saying, "I have finished that wall," which he can say only after he has laid every stone in place.

We now turn to the intuitionistic definition of mathematics. According to intuitionistic philosophy, mathematics should be defined as a mental activity and not as a set of theorems (as was done above in the section on logicism). It is the activity which consists in carrying out, one after the other, those mental constructions which are inductive and effective in the sense in which the

intuitionistic construction of the natural numbers is inductive and effective. Intuitionism maintains that human beings are able to recognize whether a given mental construction has these two properties. We shall refer to a mental construction which has these two properties as a **construct** and hence the intuitionistic definition of mathematics says: *Mathematics is the mental activity which consists in carrying out constructs one after the other.*

A major consequence of this definition is that all of intuitionistic mathematics is effective or "constructive" as one usually says. We shall use the adjective "constructive" as synonymous with "effective" from now on. Namely, every construct is constructive, and intuitionistic mathematics is nothing but carrying out constructs over and over. For instance, if a real number *r* occurs in an intuitionistic proof or theorem, it never occurs there merely on grounds of an existence proof. It occurs there because it has been constructed from top to bottom. This implies for example that each decimal place in the decimal expansion of *r* can in principle be computed. In short, all intuitionistic proofs, theorems, definitions, etc., are entirely constructive.

Another major consequence of the intuitionistic definition of mathematics is that mathematics cannot be reduced to any other science such as, for instance, logic. This definition comprises too many mental processes for such a reduction. And here, then, we see a radical difference between logicism and intuitionism. In fact, the intuitionistic attitude toward logic is precisely the opposite from the logicists' attitude: According to the intuitionists, whatever valid logical processes there are, they are all constructs; hence, the valid part of classical logic is part of mathematics! Any law of classical logic which is not composed of constructs is for the intuitionist a meaningless combination of words. It was, of course, shocking that the classical law of the excluded middle turned out to be such a meaningless combination of words. This implies that this law cannot be used indiscriminately in intuitionistic mathematics; it can often be used, but not always.

Once the intuitionistic definition of mathematics has been understood and accepted, all there remains to be done is to do mathematics the intuitionistic way. Indeed, the intuitionists have developed intuitionistic arithmetic, algebra, analysis, set theory, etc. However, in each of these branches of mathematics, there occur classical theorems which are not composed of constructs and, hence, are meaningless combinations of words for the intuitionists. Consequently, one cannot say that the intuitionists have reconstructed all of classical mathematics. This does not bother the intuitionists since whatever parts of classical mathematics they cannot obtain are meaningless for them anyway. Intuitionism does not have as its purpose the justification of classical mathematics. Its purpose is to give a valid definition of mathematics and then to "wait and see" what mathematics comes out of it. Whatever classical mathematics cannot be done intuitionistically simply is not mathematics for the intuitionist. We observe here another fundamental difference between logicism and intuitionism: The logicists wanted to justify all of classical mathematics. (An excellent introduction to the actual techniques of intuitionism is [5].)

Let us now ask how successful the intuitionistic school has been in giving us a good foundation for mathematics, acceptable to the majority of mathematicians. Again, there is a sharp difference between the way this question has to be answered in the present case and in the case of logicism. Even hard-nosed logicists have to admit that their school so far has failed to give mathematics a firm foundation by about 20%. However, a hard-nosed intuitionist has every right in the world to claim that intuitionism has given mathematics an entirely satisfactory foundation. There is the meaningful definition of intuitionistic mathematics, discussed above; there is the intuitionistic philosophy which tells us why constructs can never give rise to contradictions and, hence, that intuitionistic mathematics is free of contradictions. In fact, not only this problem (of freedom from contradiction) but all other problems of a foundational nature as well receive perfectly satisfactory solutions in intuitionism.

Yet if one looks at intuitionism from the outside, namely, from the viewpoint of the classical mathematician, one has to say that intuitionism has failed to give mathematics an adequate foundation. In fact, the mathematical community has almost universally rejected intuitionism. Why has the mathematical community done this, in spite of many very attractive features of intuitionism, some of which have just been mentioned?

One reason is that classical mathematicians flatly refuse to do away with the many beautiful theorems that are meaningless combinations of words for the intuitionists. An example is the Brouwer fixed point theorem of topology which the intuitionists reject because the fixed point cannot be constructed, but can only be shown to exist on grounds of an existence proof. This, by the way, is the same Brouwer who created intuitionism; he is equally famous for his work in (nonintuitionistic) topology.

A second reason comes from theorems which can be proven both classically and intuitionistically. It often happens that the classical proof of such a theorem is short, elegant, and devilishly clever, but not constructive. The intuitionists will of course reject such a proof and replace it by their own constructive proof of the same theorem. However, this constructive proof frequently turns out to be about ten times as long as the classical proof and often seems, at least to the classical mathematician, to have lost all of its elegance. An example is the fundamental theorem of algebra which in classical mathematics is proved in about half a page, but takes about ten pages of proof in intuitionistic mathematics. Again, classical mathematicians refuse to believe that their clever proofs are meaningless whenever such proofs are not constructive.

Finally, there are the theorems which hold in intuitionism but are false in classical mathematics. An example is the intuitionistic theorem which says that every real-valued function which is defined for *all* real numbers is continuous. This theorem is not as strange as it sounds since it depends on the intuitionistic concept of a function: A real-valued function f is defined in intuitionism for all real numbers only if, for every real number r whose intuitionistic construction has been completed, the real number $f(r)$ can be constructed. Any obviously discontinuous function a classical mathematician may mention does not satisfy this constructive criterion. Even so, theorems such as this one seem so far out to classical mathematicians that they reject any mathematics which accepts them.

These three reasons for the rejection of intuitionism by classical mathematicians are neither rational nor scientific. Nor are they pragmatic reasons, based on a conviction that classical mathematics is better for applications to physics or other sciences than is intuitionism. They are all emotional reasons, grounded in a deep sense as to what mathematics is all about. (If one of the readers knows of a truly scientific rejection of intuitionism, the author would be grateful to hear about it.) We now have the second crisis in mathematics in front of us: It consists in the failure of the intuitionistic school to make intuitionism acceptable to at least the majority of mathematicians.

It is important to realize that, like logicism, intuitionism is rooted in philosophy. When, for instance, the intuitionists state their definition of mathematics, given earlier, they use strictly philosophical and not mathematical language. It would, in fact, be quite impossible for them to use mathematics for such a definition. The mental activity which is mathematics can be defined in philosophical terms but this definition must, by necessity, use some terms which do not belong to the activity it is trying to define.

Just as logicism is related to realism, intuitionism is related to the philosophy called "concep-

tualism." This is the philosophy which maintains that abstract entities exist only insofar as they are constructed by the human mind. This is very much the attitude of intuitionism which holds that the abstract entities which occur in mathematics, whether sequences or order-relations or what have you, are all mental constructions. This is precisely why one does not find in intuitionism the staggering collection of abstract entities which occur in classical mathematics and hence in logicism. The contrast between logicism and intuitionism is very similar to the contrast between realism and conceptualism.

A very good way to get into intuitionism is by studying [5], Chapter IV of [6], [7] and [8], in this order.

Formalism

This school was created in about 1910 by the German mathematician David Hilbert (1862–1943). True, one might say that there were already formalists in the nineteenth century since Frege argued against them in the second volume of his *Grundgesetze der Arithmetik;* the first volume of the

Grundgesetze appeared in 1893 and the second one in 1903. Nevertheless, the modern concept of formalism, which includes finitary reasoning, must be credited to Hilbert. Since modern books and courses in mathematical logic usually deal with formalism, this school is much better known today than either logicism or intuitionism. We will hence discuss only the highlights of formalism and begin by asking, "What is it that we formalize when we formalize something?"

The answer is that we formalize some given *axiomatized* theory. One should guard against confusing axiomatization and formalization. Euclid axiomatized geometry in about 300 B.C., but formalization started only about 2200 years later with the logicists and formalists. Examples of axiomatized theories are Euclidean plane geometry with the usual Euclidean axioms, arithmetic with the Peano axioms, ZF with its nine axioms, etc. The next question is: "How do we formalize a given axiomatized theory?"

Suppose then that some axiomatized theory T is given. Restricting ourselves to first order logic, "to formalize T" means to choose an appropriate first order language for T. The vocabulary of a first order language consists of five items, four of which are always the same and are not dependent on the given theory T. These four items are the following: (1) A list of denumerably many variables—who can talk about mathematics without using variables? (2) Symbols for the connectives of everyday speech, say $\neg$ for "not," $\wedge$ for "and," $\vee$ for the inclusive "or," $\rightarrow$ for "if then," and $\leftrightarrow$ for "if and only if"—who can talk about anything at all without using connectives? (3) The equality sign $=$; again, no one can talk about mathematics without using this sign. (4) The two quantifiers, the "for all" quantifier $\forall$ and the "there exist" quantifier $\exists$; the first one is used to say such things as *"all* complex numbers have a square root," the second one to say things like *"there exist* irrational numbers." One can do without some of the above symbols, but there is no reason to go into that. Instead, we turn to the fifth item.

Since T is an axiomatized theory, it has so-called "undefined terms." One has to choose an appropriate symbol for every undefined term of T and these symbols make up the fifth item. For instance, among the undefined terms of plane Euclidean geometry, occur "point," "line," and "incidence," and for each one of them an appropriate symbol must be entered into the vocabulary of the first order language. Among the undefined terms of arithmetic occur "zero," "addition," and "multiplication," and the symbols one chooses for them are of course 0, $+$, and $\times$, respectively. The easiest theory of all to formalize is ZF since this theory has only one undefined term, namely, the membership relation. One chooses, of course, the usual symbol $\in$ for that relation. These symbols, one for each undefined term of the axiomatized theory T, are often called the "parameters" of the first order language and hence the parameters make up the fifth item.

Since the parameters are the only symbols in the vocabulary of a first order language which depend on the given axiomatized theory T, one formalizes T simply by choosing these parameters. Once this choice has been made, the whole theory T has been completely formalized. One can now express in the resulting first order language L not only all axioms, definitions, and theorems of T, but more! One can also express in L all axioms of classical logic and, consequently, also all proofs one uses to prove theorems of T. In short, one can now proceed entirely with L, that is, entirely "formally."

But now a third question presents itself: "Why in the world would anyone want to formalize a given axiomatized theory?" After all, Euclid never saw a need to formalize his axiomatized geometry. It is important to ask this question, since even the great Peano had mistaken ideas about the real purpose of formalization. He published one of his most important discoveries in differential equations in a formalized language (very similar to a first order language) with the result that nobody read it until some charitable soul translated the article into common German.

Let us now try to answer the third question. If mathematicians do technical research in a certain branch of mathematics, say, plane Euclidean geometry, they are interested in discovering and proving the important theorems of the branch of mathematics. For that kind of technical work, formalization is usually not only no help but a definite hindrance. If, however, one asks such foundational questions as, for instance, "Why is this branch of mathematics free of contradictions?" then formalization is not just a help but an absolute necessity.

It was really Hilbert's stroke of genius to understand that formalization is the proper technique to tackle such foundational questions. What he taught us can be put roughly as follows. Suppose that T is an axiomatized theory which has been formalized in terms of the first order language L. This language has such a precise syntax that it itself can be studied as a *mathematical* object. One can ask for instance: "Can one possibly run into contradictions if one proceeds entirely formally within L, using only the axioms of T and those of classical logic, all of which have been expressed in L?" If one can prove mathematically that the answer to this question is "no," one has there a mathematical proof that the theory T is free of contradictions!

This is basically what the famous "Hilbert program" was all about. The idea was to formalize the various branches of mathematics and then to prove *mathematically* that each one of them is free of contradictions. In fact if, by means of this technique, the formalists could have just shown that ZF is free of contradictions, they would thereby already have shown that all of classical mathematics is free of contradictions, since classical mathematics can be done axiomatically in terms of the nine axioms of ZF. In short, the formalists tried to create a mathematical technique by means of which one could prove that mathematics is free of contradictions. This was the original purpose of formalism.

It is interesting to observe that both logicists and formalists formalized the various branches of mathematics, but for entirely different reasons. The logicists wanted to use such a formalization to show that the branch of mathematics in question belongs to logic; the formalists wanted to use it to prove mathematically that that branch is free of contradictions. Since both schools "formalized," they are sometimes confused.

Did the formalists complete their program successfully? No! In 1931, Kurt Gödel showed . . . that formalization cannot be considered as a mathematical technique by means of which one can prove that mathematics is free of contradic-

tions. The theorem in that paper which rang the death bell for the Hilbert program concerns axiomatized theories which are free of contradictions and whose axioms are strong enough so that arithmetic can be done in terms of them. Examples of theories whose axioms are that strong are, of course, Peano arithmetic and ZF. Suppose now that T is such a theory and that T has been formalized by means of the first order language L. Then Gödel's theorem says, in nontechnical language, "No sentence of L which can be interpreted as asserting that T is free of contradictions can be proven formally within the language L." Although the interpretation of this theorem is somewhat controversial, most mathematicians have concluded from it that the Hilbert program cannot be carried out: Mathematics is not able to prove its own freedom of contradictions. Here, then, is the third crisis in mathematics.

Of course, the tremendous importance of the formalist school for present-day mathematics is well known. It was in this school that modern mathematical logic and its various offshoots, such as model theory, recursive function theory, etc., really came into bloom.

Formalism, as logicism and intuitionism, is founded in philosophy, but the philosophical roots of formalism are somewhat more hidden than those of the other two schools. One can find them, though, by reflecting a little on the Hilbert program.

Let again T be an axiomatized theory which has been formalized in terms of the first order language L. In carrying out Hilbert's program, one has to talk about the language L as one object, and while doing this, one is not talking within that safe language L itself. On the contrary, one is talking about L in ordinary, everyday language, be it English or French or what have you. While using our natural language and not the formal language L, there is of course every danger that contradictions, in fact, any kind of error, may slip in. Hilbert said that the way to avoid this danger is by making absolutely certain that, while one is talking in one's natural language about L, one uses only reasonings which are absolutely safe and beyond any kind of suspicion. He called such reasonings "finitary reasonings," but had, of course, to give a definition of them. The most explicit definition of finitary reasoning known to the author was given by the French formalist Herbrand [9]. It says, if we replace "intuitionistic" by "finitary":

> By a finitary argument we understand an argument satisfying the following conditions: In it we never consider anything but a given finite number of objects and of functions; these functions are well defined, their definition allowing the computation of their values in an unequivical way; we never state that an object exists without giving the means of constructing it; we never consider the totality of all the objects x of an infinite collection; and when we say that an argument (or a theorem) is true for all these x, we mean that, for each x taken by itself, it is possible to repeat the general argument in question, which should be considered to be merely the prototype of these particular arguments.

Observe that this definition uses philosophical and not mathematical language. Even so, no one can claim to understand the Hilbert program without an understanding of what finitary reasoning amounts to. The philosophical roots of formalism come out into the open when the formalists define what they mean by finitary reasoning.

We have already compared logicism with realism, and intuitionism with conceptualism. The philosophy which is closest to formalism is "nominalism." This is the philosophy which claims that abstract entities have no existence of any kind, neither outside the human mind as maintained by realism, nor as mental constructions within the human mind as maintained by conceptualism. For nominalism, abstract entities are mere vocal utterances or written lines, mere names. This is where the word "nominalism" comes from, since in Latin *nominalis* means "belonging to a name." Similarly, when formalists try to prove that a certain axiomatized theory T is free of contradictions, they do not study the abstract entities which occur in T but, instead, study that first order language L which was used to formalize T. That is, they study how one can form sentences in L by the proper use of the vocabulary of L; how certain of these sentences can be proven by the proper use of those special sentences of L which were singled out as axioms; and, in particular, they try to show that no sentence of L can be proven and disproven at the same time, since they would thereby have established that the original theory T is free of contradictions. The important point is that this whole study of L is a strictly syntactical study, since no meanings or abstract entities are associated with the sentences of L. This language is investigated by considering the sentences of L as meaningless expressions which are manipulated according to explicit, syntactical rules, just as the pieces of a chess game are meaningless figures which are pushed around according to the rules of the game. For the strict formalist "to do mathematics" is "to manipulate the meaningless symbols of a first order language according to explicit, syntactical rules." Hence, the strict formalist does not work with abstract entities, such as infinite series or cardinals, but only with their meaningless names which are the appropriate expressions in a first order language. Both formalists and nominalists avoid the direct use of abstract entities, and this is why formalism should be compared with nominalism.

The fact that logicism, intuitionism, and formalism correspond to realism, conceptualism, and nominalism, respectively, was brought to light in Quine's article, "On What There Is" ([10], pages 183–196). Formalism can be learned from any modern book on mathematical logic. . . .

Epilogue

Where do the three crises in mathematics leave us? They leave us without a firm foundation for mathematics. After Gödel's paper appeared in 1931, mathematicians on the whole threw up their hands in frustration and turned away from the philosophy of mathematics. Nevertheless, the influence of the three schools discussed in this article has remained strong, since they have given us much new and beautiful mathematics. This mathematics concerns mainly set theory, intuitionism and its various constructivist modifications, and mathematical logic with its many offshoots. However, although this kind of mathematics is often referred to as "foundations of mathematics," one cannot claim to be advancing the philosophy of mathematics just because one is working in one of these areas. Modern mathematical logic, set theory, and intuitionism with its modifications are nowadays technical branches of mathematics, just as algebra or analysis, and unless we return directly to the philosophy of mathematics, we cannot expect to find a firm foundation for our science. It is evident that such a foundation is not necessary for technical mathematical research, but there are still those among us who yearn for it. The author believes that the key to the foundations of mathematics lies hidden somewhere among the philosophical roots of logicism, intuitionism, and formalism and this is why he has uncovered these roots, three times over. . . .

References

1. E. Snapper, What is mathematics? Amer. Math. Monthly, no. 7, 86 (1979) 551–557.
2. B. Russell, Principles of Mathematics, 1st ed. (1903) W. W. Norton, New York. Available in paperback.
3. B. Russell and A. N. Whitehead, Principia Mathematica, 1st ed. (1910) Cambridge Univ. Press, Cambridge, England. Available in paperback.
4. B. Russell, Introduction to Mathematical Philosophy, Simon and Schuster, New York, 1920. Available in paperback.
5. A. Heyting, Intuitionism, An Introduction, North-Holland, Amsterdam, Netherlands, 1966.
6. A. A. Fraenkel, Y. Bar-Hillel, and A. Levy, Foundations of Set Theory, North-Holland, Amsterdam, Netherlands, 1973.
7. M. Dummett, Elements of Intuitionism, Clarendon Press, Oxford, England, 1977.
8. A. S. Troelstra, Choice Sequences, Oxford Univ. Press, Oxford, England, 1977.
9. J. van Heijenoort, From Frege to Gödel, Harvard Univ. Press, Cambridge. Available in paperback.
10. P. Benacerraf and H. Putnam, Philosophy of Mathematics, Prentice-Hall, 1964.

Proofs and Refutations

Imre Lakatos

Imre Lakatos obtained his Ph.D. in 1961 from Cambridge and for the next thirteen years continued his investigation into a general philosophy of science. During much of this time he was associated with the London School of Economics. Lakatos died unexpectedly on February 2, 1974, before he had time to formally revise his brilliant essay "Proofs and Refutations."

Proof, it has been observed, is the essence of mathematics. Mathematics worthy of the name was first done by the ancient Greeks, it is argued, as they were the first to realize that statements of mathematical fact are empty without a demonstration. A statement becomes fact only after it is proven to be true. The distinction is brought out in Scottish law, which renders one of three judicial decisions in a case of law. In addition to "guilty" or "not guilty" the Scottish system includes the third category of "not proven." A statement may be true in God's eye but it isn't known to be true for humanity until it has been proved. All this seems reasonable enough until the crucial idea, the notion of proof, is examined more critically. Specifically, what is a proof and (more importantly) how can one be recognized?

Through the centuries since the Greeks first demanded formal demonstrations for establishing mathematical truth, the recognition of proof has been a serious problem. There have been a number of attempts to formalize the creation of proofs; among the most famous was that of Russell and Whitehead in Principia Mathematica. *Russell and Whitehead's attempt was reasonably successful in showing that the idea of proof can be formalized and that a systematic machinelike construction of proofs is possible. The difficulty with this approach is that it requires that the current language of mathematics, as formal and symbolic as it is, be translated into an even more formal language of specialized logic symbols. Virtually no one doing modern mathematics has the stomach for this and the question of proof recognition remains a difficult one.*

Almost every major mathematics journal in the world routinely publishes false theorems. The authors, referees, and editors often become convinced by the plausibility of an argument and miss the flaw that renders it invalid. Many of these errors are caught and appropriate corrections made. To argue that all have been detected would stretch credibility well past the breaking point. That not all false theorems have been detected brings us to this essay.

The setting for this article is an imaginary classroom in which a professor of mathematics generalizes a well-known theorem about figures in the plane and then gives a proof of the theorem. One of the students spots a flaw in the proof and the debate begins. Some tens of pages later, the patched-up proofs and their counterexamples roll on with no firm resolution yet in sight. This fictional classroom synthesizes an actual historical debate of many years' duration over the same theorems. When first published the subsequent objections required a republication, with terms redefined and arguments adjusted. But the new proof did not work either, and sixty-five years after the first proof's publication a really satisfactory resolution of the issue was still not available.

Source: Imre Lakatos, *Proofs and Refutations: The Logic of Mathematical Discovery* (Cambridge University Press, 1976), pp. 6–23. (References omitted.)

The point of this essay is that mathematics, as it is done by mathematicians, is anything but the systematic, orderly, and algorithmic process that it often pretends to be. In mathematics, as in most creative arts, the process of fabrication is organic, complex, beyond useful analysis, frequently irrational, and desperately human.

A Problem and a Conjecture

The dialogue takes place in an imaginary classroom. The class gets interested in a *PROBLEM:* is there a relation between the number of vertices V, the number of edges E and the number of faces F of polyhedra—particularly of *regular polyhedra*—analogous to the trivial relation between the number of vertices and edges of *polygons*, namely, that there are as many edges as vertices: $V = E$? This latter relation enables us to classify *polygons* according to the number of edges (or vertices): triangles, quadrangles, pentagons, etc. An analogous relation would help to classify *polyhedra*.

After much trial and error they notice that for all regular polyhedra $V - E + F = 2$.[1] Somebody *guesses* that this may apply for any polyhedron whatsoever. Others try to falsify this *conjecture*, try to test it in many different ways—it holds good. The results *corroborate* the conjecture, and suggest that it could be *proved*. It is at this point—after the stages *problem* and *conjecture*—that we enter the classroom.[2] The teacher is just going to offer a *proof*.

A Proof

TEACHER: In our last lesson we arrived at a conjecture concerning polyhedra, namely, that for all polyhedra $V - E + F = 2$, where V is the number of vertices, E the number of edges and F the number of faces. We tested it by various methods. But we haven't yet proved it. Has anybody found a proof?

PUPIL SIGMA: I for one have to admit that I have not yet been able to devise a strict proof of this theorem . . . . As however the truth of it

has been established in so many cases, there can be no doubt that it holds good for any solid. Thus the proposition seems to be satisfactorily demonstrated.[3] But if you have a proof, please do present it.

TEACHER: In fact I have one. It consists of the following thought-experiment. *Step 1:* Let us imagine the polyhedron to be hollow, with a surface made of thin rubber. If we cut out one of the faces, we can stretch the remaining surface flat on the blackboard, without tearing it. The faces and edges will be deformed, the edges may become curved, but V and E will not alter, so that if and only if $V - E + F = 2$ for the original polyhedron, $V - E + F = 1$ for this flat network—remember that we have removed one face. (Fig. 1

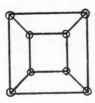 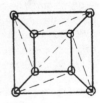

Figure 1   *Figure 2*

shows the flat network for the case of a cube.) *Step 2:* Now we triangulate our map—it does indeed look like a geographical map. We draw (possibly curvilinear) diagonals in those (possibly curvilinear) polygons which are not already (possibly curvilinear) triangles. By drawing each diagonal we increase both E and F by one, so that the total $V - E + F$ will not be altered (Fig. 2). *Step 3:* From the triangulated network we now remove the triangles one by one. To remove a triangle we either remove an edge—upon which one face and one edge disappear (Fig. 3a), or we remove two edges and a vertex—upon which one face, two edges and one vertex disappear (Fig. 3b). Thus if $V - E + F = 1$ before a triangle is removed, it remains so after the triangle is removed. At the end of this procedure we get a single triangle. For this $V - E + F = 1$ holds true. Thus we have proved our conjecture.[4]

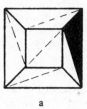 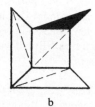

a   b

Figure 3

PUPIL DELTA: You should now call it a *theorem*. There is nothing conjectural about it any more.[5]

PUPIL ALPHA: I wonder. I see that this experiment can be performed for a cube or for a tetrahedron, but how am I to know that it can be performed for *any* polyhedron? For instance, you are sure, Sir, that *any polyhedron, after having a face removed, can be stretched flat on the blackboard?* I am dubious about your first step.

PUPIL BETA: Are you sure that *in triangulating the map one will always get a new face for any new edge?* I am dubious about your second step.

PUPIL GAMMA: Are you sure that *there are only two alternatives—the disappearance of one edge or else of two edges and a vertex—when one drops the triangles one by one? Are you even sure that one is left with a single triangle at the end of this process?* I am dubious about your third step.[6]

TEACHER: Of course I am not sure.

ALPHA: But then we are worse off than before! Instead of one conjecture we now have at least three! And this you call a "proof"!

TEACHER: I admit that the traditional name "proof" for this thought-experiment may rightly be considered a bit misleading. I do not think that it establishes the truth of the conjecture.

DELTA: What does it do then? What do you think a mathematical proof proves?

TEACHER: This is a subtle question which we shall try to answer later. Till then I propose to retain the time-honored technical term "proof" for a *thought-experiment— or "quasi-experiment"— which suggests a decomposition of the original conjecture into subconjectures or lemmas,* thus *embedding it* in a possibly quite distant body of knowledge. Our "proof," for instance, has embedded the original conjecture—about crystals, or, say, solids—in the theory of rubber sheets. Descartes or Euler, the fathers of the original conjecture, certainly did not even dream of this.[7]

Criticism of the Proof by Counterexamples Which Are Local but not Global

TEACHER: This decomposition of the conjecture suggested by the proof opens new vistas for testing. The decomposition deploys the conjecture on a wider front, so that our criticism has more targets. We now have at least three opportunities for counterexamples instead of one!

GAMMA: I have already expressed my dislike of your third lemma (viz., that in removing triangles from the network which resulted from the stretching and subsequent triangulation, we have only two possibilities: either we remove an edge or we remove two edges and a vertex). I suspect that other patterns may emerge when removing a triangle.

TEACHER: Suspicion is not criticism.

GAMMA: Then is a *counterexample* criticism?

TEACHER: Certainly. Conjectures ignore dislike and suspicion, but they cannot ignore counterexamples.

THETA (aside):   Conjectures are obviously very different from those who represent them.

GAMMA: I propose a trivial counterexample. Take the triangular network which results from performing the first two operations on a cube (Fig. 2). Now if I remove a triangle from the *inside* of this network, as one might take a piece out of a jigsaw puzzle, I remove one triangle without removing a single edge or vertex. So the third lemma is false—and not only in the case of the cube, but for *all* polyhedra except the tetrahedron, in the flat network of which all the triangles are boundary triangles. Your proof thus proves the Euler theorem for the tetrahedron. But we already *knew* that $V - E + F = 2$ for the tetrahedron, so why prove it?

TEACHER: You are right. But notice that the cube which is a counterexample to the third lemma is not also a counterexample to the main conjecture, since for the cube $V - E + F = 2$. You have shown the poverty of the argument—the proof—but not the falsity of our conjecture.

ALPHA: Will you scrap your proof then?

TEACHER: No. Criticism is not necessarily destruction. I shall improve my proof so that it will stand up to the criticism.

GAMMA: How?

TEACHER: Before showing how, let me introduce the following terminology. I shall call a *"local counterexample"* an example which refutes a lemma (without necessarily refuting the main conjecture), and I shall call a *"global counterexample"* an example which refutes the main conjecture itself. Thus your counterexample is local but not global. A local, but not global, counterexample is a criticism of the proof, but not of the conjecture.

GAMMA: So, the conjecture may be true, but your proof does not prove it.

TEACHER: But I can easily elaborate, and *improve the proof*, by replacing the false lemma by a slightly modified one, which your counterexample will not refute. I no longer contend that *the removal of any triangle follows one of the two patterns mentioned*, but merely that *at each stage of the removing operation the removal of any boundary triangle follows one of these patterns*. Coming back to my thought-experiment, all that I have to do is to insert a single word in my third step, to wit, that "from the triangulated network we now remove the *boundary* triangles one by one." You will agree that it only needed a trifling observation to put the proof right.[8]

GAMMA: I do not think your observation was so trifling; in fact it was quite ingenious. To make this clear I shall show that it is false. Take the flat network of the cube again and remove eight of the ten triangles in the order given in Fig. 4. At the

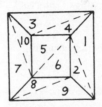

Figure 4

removal of the eighth triangle, which is certainly by then a boundary triangle, we removed two edges and no vertex—this changes $V - E + F$ by 1. And we are left with the two disconnected triangles 9 and 10.

TEACHER: Well, I might save face by saying that I meant by a boundary triangle a triangle whose removal does not disconnect the network. But intellectual honesty prevents me from making surreptitious changes in my position by sentences starting with "I meant . . ." so I admit that now I must *replace* the second version of the triangle-removing operation with a third version: that we remove the triangles one by one in such a way that $V - E + F$ does not alter.

KAPPA: I generously agree that the lemma corresponding to this operation is true: namely, that if we remove the triangles one by one in such a way that $V - E + F$ does not alter, then $V - E + F$ does not alter.

TEACHER: No. The lemma is that *the triangles in our network can be so numbered that in removing them in the right order $V - E + F$ will not alter till we reach the last triangle.*

KAPPA: But how should one construct this right order, if it exists at all?[9] Your original thought-experiment gave the instruction: remove the triangles in any order. Your modified thought-experiment gave the instruction: remove boundary triangles in any order. Now you say we should follow a definite order, but you do not say which and whether that order exists at all. Thus the thought-experiment breaks down. You improved the proof-analysis, i.e., the list of lemmas; but the thought-experiment which you called "the proof" has disappeared.

RHO: Only the third step has disappeared.

KAPPA: Moreover, did you *improve* the lemma? Your first two simple versions at least looked trivially true before they were refuted; your lengthy, patched up version does not even look plausible. Can you really believe that it will escape refutation?

TEACHER: "Plausible" or even "trivially true" propositions are usually soon refuted: sophisticated, implausible conjectures, matured in criticism, might hit on the truth.

OMEGA: And what happens if even your "sophisticated conjectures" are falsified and if this time you cannot replace them by unfalsified ones? Or, if you do *not* succeed in improving the argument further by local patching? You have succeeded in getting over a local counterexample which was not global by replacing the refuted lemma. What if you do not succeed next time?

TEACHER: Good question—it will be put on the agenda for tomorrow.

Criticism of the Conjecture by Global Counterexamples

ALPHA: I have a counterexample which will falsify your first lemma—but this will also be a counterexample to the main conjecture, i.e., this will be a global counterexample as well.

TEACHER: Indeed! Interesting. Let us see.

ALPHA: Imagine a solid bounded by a pair of nested cubes—a pair of cubes, one of which is inside, but does not touch the other (Fig. 5). This

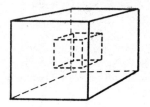

Figure 5

hollow cube falsifies your first lemma, because on removing a face from the inner cube, the polyhedron will not be stretchable on to a plane. Nor will it help to remove a face from the outer cube instead. Besides, for each cube $V - E + F = 2$, so that for the hollow cube $V - E + F = 4$.

TEACHER: Good show. Let us call it *Counterexample 1*.[10] Now what?

Rejection of the Conjecture. The Method of Surrender.

GAMMA: Sir, your composure baffles me. A single counterexample refutes a conjecture as effectively as ten. The conjecture and its proof have completely misfired. Hands up! You have to surrender. Scrap the false conjecture, forget about it and try a radically new approach.

TEACHER: I agree with you that the *conjecture* has received a severe criticism by Alpha's counterexample. But it is untrue that the *proof* has "completely misfired." If, for the time being, you agree to my earlier proposal to use the word "proof" for a "thought-experiment which leads to decomposition of the original conjecture into subconjectures," instead of using it in the sense of a "guarantee of certain truth," you need not draw this conclusion. My proof certainly proved Euler's conjecture in the first sense, but not necessarily in the second. You are interested only in proofs which "prove" what they have set out to prove. I am interested in proofs even if they do not accomplish their intended task. Columbus did not reach India but he discovered something quite interesting.

ALPHA: So according to your philosophy—while a local counterexample (if it is not global at the same time) is a criticism of the proof, but not of the conjecture—a global counterexample is a criticism of the conjecture, but not necessarily of the proof. You agree to surrender as regards the conjecture, but you defend the proof. But if the conjecture is false, what on earth does the proof prove?

GAMMA: Your analogy with Columbus breaks down. Accepting a global counterexample must mean total surrender.

Rejection of the Counterexample. The Method of Monster-Barring.

DELTA: But why accept the counterexample? We proved our conjecture—now it is a theorem. I admit that it clashes with this so-called "counterexample." One of them has to give way. But why should the theorem give way, when it has been proved? It is the "criticism" that should retreat. It is fake criticism. This pair of nested cubes is not a polyhedron at all. It is a *monster*, a pathological case, not a counterexample.

GAMMA: Why not? *A polyhedron is a solid whose surface consists of polygonal faces.* And my counterexample is a solid bounded by polygonal faces.

TEACHER: Let us call this definition *Def. 1.*[11]

DELTA: Your definition is incorrect. A polyhedron must be a *surface:* it has faces, edges, vertices, it can be deformed, stretched out on a blackboard, and has nothing to do with the concept of "solid." *A polyhedron is a surface consisting of a system of polygons.*

TEACHER: Call this *Def. 2.*[12]

DELTA: So really you showed us *two* polyhedra—*two* surfaces, one completely inside the other. A woman with a child in her womb is not a counterexample to the thesis that human beings have one head.

ALPHA: So! My counterexample has bred a new concept of polyhedron. Or do you dare to assert that by polyhedron you *always* meant a surface?

TEACHER: For the moment let us accept Delta's *Def. 2.* Can you refute our conjecture now if by polyhedron we mean a surface?

ALPHA: Certainly. Take two tetrahedra which have an edge in common (Fig. 6a). Or, take two tetrahedra which have a vertex in common (Fig. 6b). Both these twins are connected, both consti-

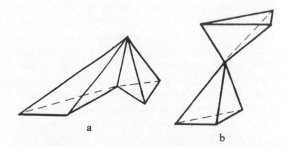

Figure 6

tute one single surface. And, you may check that for both $V - E + F = 3$.

TEACHER: *Counterexamples 2a and 2b.*[13]

DELTA: I admire your perverted imagination, but of course I did not mean that *any* system of polygons is a polyhedron. By polyhedron I meant *a system of polygons arranged in such a way that (1) exactly two polygons meet at every edge and (2) it is possible to get from the inside of any polygon to the inside of any other polygon by a route which never crosses any edge at a vertex.* Your first twins will be excluded by the first criterion in my definition, your second twins by the second criterion.

TEACHER: *Def. 3.*[14]

ALPHA: I admire your perverted ingenuity in inventing one definition after another as barricades against the falsification of your pet ideas. Why don't you just define a polyhedron as a system of polygons for which the equation $V - E + F = 2$ holds? This Perfect Definition . . .

KAPPA: *Def. P.*[15]

ALPHA: . . . would settle the dispute forever. There would be no need to investigate the subject any further.

DELTA: But there isn't a theorem in the world which couldn't be falsified by monsters.

TEACHER: I am sorry to interrupt you. As we have seen, refutation by counterexamples depends on the meaning of the terms in question. If a counterexample is to be an objective criticism, we have to agree on the meaning of our terms. We *may* achieve such an agreement by defining the term where communication broke down. I, for one, didn't define "polyhedron." I assume *familiarity* with the concept, i.e., the ability to distinguish a thing which is a polyhedron from a thing which is not a polyhedron—what some logicians call knowing the extension of the concept of polyhedron. It turned out that the extension of the concept wasn't at all obvious: *definitions are frequently proposed and argued about when counterex-*

amples emerge. I suggest that we now consider the rival definitions together, and leave until later the discussion of the differences in the results which will follow from choosing different definitions. Can anybody offer something which even the most restrictive definition would allow as a real counterexample?

KAPPA: Including *Def. P?*

TEACHER: Excluding *Def. P.*

GAMMA: I can. Look at this *Counterexample 3:* a star-polyhedron—I shall call it an *urchin* (Fig. 7). This consists of 12 star-pentagons (Fig. 8). It has 12 vertices, 30 edges, and 12 pentagonal faces—you may check it if you like by counting. Thus the Descartes-Euler thesis is not true at all, since for this polyhedron $V - E + F = -6$.[16]

Figure 7   Kepler's star-polyhedron, each face shaded in a different way to show which triangles belong to the same pentagonal face

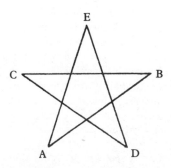

Figure 8

DELTA: Why do you think that your "urchin" is a polyhedron?

GAMMA: Do you not see? This is a polyhedron, whose faces are the twelve star-pentagons. It satisfies your last definition: it is "a system of polygons arranged in such a way that (1) exactly two polygons meet at every edge, and (2) it is possible to get from every polygon to every other polygon without ever crossing a vertex of the polyhedron."

DELTA: But then you do not even know what a polygon is! A star-pentagon is certainly not a polygon! *A polygon is a system of edges arranged in such a way that (1) exactly two edges meet at every vertex, and (2) the edges have no points in common except the vertices.*

TEACHER: Let us call this *Def. 4*.

GAMMA: I don't see why you include the second clause. The correct definition of the polygon should contain the first clause only.

TEACHER: *Def. 4'*.

GAMMA: The second clause has nothing to do with the essence of a polygon. Look: if I lift an edge a little, the star-pentagon is already a polygon even in your sense. You imagine a polygon to be drawn in chalk on the blackboard, but you should imagine it as a wooden structure: then it is clear that what you think to be a point in common is not really one point, but two different points lying one above the other. You are misled by your embedding the polygon in a plane–you should let its limbs stretch out in space![17]

DELTA: Would you mind telling me what is the *area* of a star-pentagon? Or would you say that some polygons have no area?

GAMMA: Was it not you yourself who said that a polyhedron has nothing to do with the idea of solidity? Why now suggest that the idea of polygon should be linked with the idea of area? We agreed that a polyhedron is a closed surface with edges and vertices—then why not agree that a

polygon is simply a closed curve with vertices? But if you stick to your idea I am willing to define the area of a star-polygon.[18]

TEACHER: Let us leave this dispute for a moment, and proceed as before. Consider the last two definitions together—*Def. 4* and *Def. 4'*. Can anyone give a counterexample to our conjecture that will comply with *both* definitions of polygons?

ALPHA: Here is one. Consider a *picture-frame* like this (Fig. 9). This is a polyhedron according

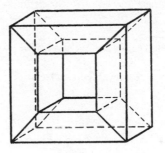

Figure 9

to any of the definitions hitherto proposed. Nonetheless you will find, on counting the vertices, edges and faces, that $V - E + F = 0$.

TEACHER: *Counterexample 4.*[19]

BETA: So that's the end of our conjecture. It really is a pity, since it held good for so many cases. But it seems that we have just wasted our time.

ALPHA: Delta, I am flabbergasted. You say nothing? Can't you define this new counterexample out of existence? I thought there was no hypothesis in the world which you could not save from falsification with a suitable linguistic trick. Are you giving up now? Do you agree at last that there exist non-Eulerian polyhedra? Incredible!

DELTA: You should really find a more appropriate name for your non-Eulerian pests and not mislead us all by calling them "polyhedra." But I am gradually losing interest in your monsters. I turn in disgust from your lamentable "polyhedra," for which Euler's beautiful theorem doesn't hold.[20] I look for order and harmony in mathematics, but you only propagate anarchy and chaos.[21] Our attitudes are irreconcilable.

ALPHA: You are a real old-fashioned Tory! You blame the wickedness of anarchists for the spoiling of your "order" and "harmony," and you "solve" the difficulties by verbal recommendations.

TEACHER: Let us hear the latest rescue-definition.

ALPHA: You mean the latest linguistic trick, the latest contraction of the concept of "polyhedron"! Delta dissolves real problems, instead of solving them.

DELTA: I do not *contract* concepts. It is you who *expand* them. For instance, this picture-frame is not a genuine polyhedron at all.

ALPHA: Why?

DELTA: Take an arbitrary point in the "tunnel"—the space bounded by the frame. Lay a plane through this point. You will find that any such plane has always *two* different cross-sections with the picture-frame, making two distinct, completely disconnected polygons! (Fig. 10).

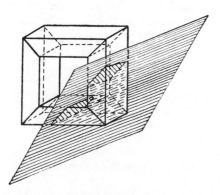

Figure 10

ALPHA: So what?

DELTA: *In the case of a genuine polyhedron, through any arbitrary point in space there will be at least one plane whose cross-section with the polyhedron will consist of one single polygon.* In the case of convex polyhedra *all* planes will comply with this requirement, wherever we take the point. In the case of *ordinary* concave polyhedra some planes will have more intersections, but there will always be some that have only one (Fig. 11 a and b). In the case of this picture-frame, if we take the point in the tunnel, all the planes will have two cross-sections. How then can you call this a polyhedron?

TEACHER: This looks like another definition, this time an *implicit* one. Call it *Def. 5*.[22]

ALPHA: A series of counterexamples, a matching series of definitions, definitions that are alleged to contain nothing new, but to be merely new revelations of the richness of that one old concept, which seems to have as many "hidden" clauses as there are counterexamples. *For all polyhedra $V - E + F = 2$ seems unshakable, an old and "eternal" truth. It is strange to think that once upon a time it was a wonderful guess, full of challenge and excitement. Now, because of your weird shifts of meaning, it has turned into a poor convention, a despicable piece of dogma. (He leaves the classroom.)*

DELTA: I cannot understand how an able man like Alpha can waste his talent on mere heckling. He seems engrossed in the production of monstrosities. But monstrosities never foster growth, either in the world of nature or in the world of thought. Evolution always follows an harmonious and orderly pattern.

GAMMA: Geneticists can easily refute that. Have you not heard that mutations producing monstrosities play a considerable role in macro-evolution? They call such monstrous mutants "hopeful monsters." It seems to me that Alpha's counterexamples, though monsters, are "hopeful monsters."[23]

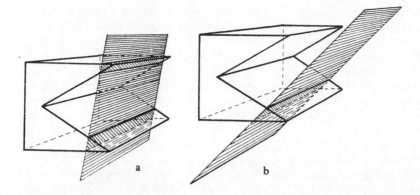

a   b

Figure 11

DELTA: Anyway, Alpha has given up the struggle. No more monsters now.

GAMMA: I have a new one. It complies with all the restrictions in Defs. 1, 2, 3, 4, and 5, but $V - E + F = 1$. This *Counterexample 5* is a simple cylinder. It has 3 faces (the top, the bottom and the jacket), 2 edges (two circles) and no vertices. It is a polyhedron according to your definition: (1) exactly two polygons at every edge and (2) it is possible to get from the inside of any polygon to the inside of any other polygon by a route which never crosses any edge at a vertex. And you have to accept the faces as genuine polygons, as they comply with your requirements: (1) exactly two edges meet at every vertex and (2) the edges have no points in common except the vertices.

DELTA: Alpha stretched concepts, but you tear them! Your "edges" are not edges! *An edge has two vertices!*

TEACHER: *Def. 6?*

GAMMA: But why deny the status of "edge" to edges with one or possibly zero vertices? You used to contract concepts, but now you mutilate them so that scarcely anything remains!

DELTA: But don't you see the futility of these so-called refutations? "Hitherto, when a new po-

lyhedron was invented, it was for some practical end; today they are invented expressly to put at fault the reasonings of our fathers, and one never will get from them anything more than that. Our subject is turned into a teratological museum where decent ordinary polyhedra may be happy if they can retain a very small corner.[24]

GAMMA: I think that if we want to learn about anything really deep, we have to study it not in its "normal," regular, usual form, but in its critical state, in fever, in passion. If you want to know the normal healthy body, study it when it is abnormal, when it is ill. If you want to know functions, study their singularities. If you want to know ordinary polyhedra, study their lunatic fringe. This is how one can carry mathematical analysis into the very heart of the subject.[25] But even if you were basically right, don't you see the futility of your *ad hoc* method? If you want to draw a borderline between counterexamples and monsters, you cannot do it in fits and starts.

TEACHER: I think we should refuse to accept Delta's strategy for dealing with global counterexamples, although we should congratulate him on his skillful execution of it. We could aptly label his method *the method of monster-barring*. Using this method one can eliminate any counterexample to the original conjecture by a sometimes deft but always *ad hoc* redefinition of the polyhedron, of its defining terms, or of the defining terms of its defining terms. We should somehow treat counterexamples with more respect, and not stubbornly exorcise them by dubbing them monsters. Delta's main mistake is perhaps his dogmatic bias in the interpretation of mathematical proof: he thinks that a proof necessarily proves what it has set out to prove. My interpretation of proof will allow for a *false* conjecture to be "proved," i.e., to be decomposed into subconjectures. If the conjecture is false, I certainly expect at least one of the subconjectures to be false. But the decomposition might still be interesting! I am not perturbed at finding a counterexample to a "proved" conjecture; I am even willing to set out to "prove" a false conjecture!

THETA: I don't follow you.

KAPPA: He just follows the New Testament: "Prove all things; hold fast that which is good" (1 Thessalonians 5: 21).

Notes

1. First noticed by Euler. His original problem was the classification of polyhedra, the difficulty of which was pointed out in the editorial summary: "While in plane geometry polygons (*figurae rectilineae*) could be classified very easily according to the number of their sides, which of course is always equal to the number of their angles, in stereometry the classification of polyhedra (*corpora hedris planis inclusa*) represents a much more difficult problem, since the number of faces alone is insufficient for this purpose."

   The key to Euler's result was just the invention of the concepts of *vertex* and *edge*: it was he who first pointed out that besides the number of faces the number of *points* and *lines* on the surface of the polyhedron determines its (topological) character. It is interesting that on the one hand he was eager to stress the novelty of his conceptual framework, and that he had to invent the term "*acies*" (edge) instead of the old "*latus*" (side), since *latus* was a polygonal concept while he wanted a

polyhedral one, on the other hand he still retained the term "*angulus solidus*" (solid angle) for his point-like vertices. It has been recently generally accepted that the priority of the result goes to Descartes. The ground for this claim is a manuscript of Descartes [c. 1639] copied by Leibniz in Paris from the original in 1675–6, and rediscovered and published by Foucher de Careil in 1860. The priority should not be granted to Descartes without a minor qualification. It is true that Descartes states that the number of plane angles equals $2\phi + 2\alpha - 4$ where by ϕ he means the number of faces and by α the number of solid angles. It is also true that he states that there are twice as many plane angles as edges (*latera*). The conjunction of these two statements of course yields the Euler formula. But Descartes did not see the point of doing so, since he still thought in terms of angles (plane and solid) and faces, and did not make a conscious revolutionary change to the concepts of 0-dimensional vertices, 1-dimensional edges and 2-dimensional faces as a necessary and sufficient basis for the full topological characterization of polyhedra.

2. Euler tested the conjecture quite thoroughly for consequences. He checked it for prisms, pyramids and so on. He could have added that the proposition that there are only five regular bodies is also a consequence of the conjecture. Another suspected consequence is the hitherto corroborated proposition that four colors are sufficient to color a map.

   The phase of *conjecturing* and *testing* in the case of $V - E + F = 2$ is discussed [by] Pólya. Pólya stopped here, and does not deal with the phase of *proving*—though of course he points out the need for a heuristic of "problems to prove." Our discussion starts where Pólya stops.

3. Euler. But later he proposed a proof.

4. This proof-idea stems from Cauchy.

5. Delta's view that this proof has established the "theorem" beyond doubt was shared by many mathematicians in the nineteenth century, e.g., Crelle, Matthiessen, Jonquières. To quote a characteristic passage: "After Cauchy's proof, it became absolutely indubitable

that the elegant relation $V + F = E + 2$ applies to all sorts of polyhedra, just as Euler stated in 1752. In 1811 all indecision should have disappeared."

6. The class is a rather advanced one. To Cauchy, Poinsot, and to many other excellent mathematicians of the nineteenth century these questions did not occur.

7. Thought-experiment (*deiknymi*) was the most ancient pattern of mathematical proof. It prevailed in pre-Euclidean Greek mathematics.

That conjectures (or theorems) precede proofs in the heuristic order was a commonplace for ancient mathematicians. This followed from the heuristic precedence of "*analysis*" over "*synthesis*." According to Proclos, ". . . it is . . . necessary to know beforehand what is sought." "They said that a theorem is that which is proposed with a view to the demonstration of the very thing proposed"—says Pappus. The Greeks did not think much of propositions which they happened to hit upon in the deductive direction without having previously guessed them. They called them *porisms*, corollaries, incidental results springing from the proof of a theorem or the solution of a problem, results not directly sought but appearing, as it were, by chance, without any additional labor, and constituting, as Proclus says, a sort of windfall (*ermaion*) or bonus (*kerdos*). We read in the editorial summary to Euler [1756–7] that arithmetical theorems "were discovered long before their truth has been confirmed by rigid demonstrations." Both the Editor and Euler use for this process of discovery the modern term "*induction*" instead of the ancient "*analysis*" (ibid.). The heuristic precedence of the result over the argument, of the theorem over the proof, has deep roots in mathematical folklore. Let us quote some variations on a familiar theme: Chrysippus is said to have written to Cleanthes: "Just send me the theorems, then I shall find the proofs." Gauss is said to have complained: "I have had my results for a long time; but I do not yet know how I am to arrive at them." And Riemann: "If only I had the theorems! Then I should find the proofs easily enough." Pólya stresses:

"You have to guess a mathematical theorem before you prove it."

The term "*quasi-experiment*" is from the above-mentioned editorial summary to Euler. According to the Editor: "As we must refer the numbers to the pure intellect alone, we can hardly understand how observations and *quasi-experiments* can be of use in investigating the nature of the numbers. Yet, in fact, as I shall show here with very good reasons, the properties of the numbers known today have been mostly discovered by observation. . . ."

8. Lhuilier, when correcting in a similar way a proof of Euler, says that he made only a "trifling observation." Euler himself, however, gave the proof up, since he noticed the trouble but could not make that "trifling observation."

9. Cauchy thought that the instruction to find at each stage a triangle which can be removed either by removing two edges and a vertex or one edge can be trivially carried out for any polyhedron. This is connected with his inability to imagine a polyhedron that is not homeomorphic with the sphere.

10. This *Counterexample 1* was first noticed by Lhuilier. But Gergonne, the Editor, added that he himself noticed this long before Lhuilier's paper. Not so Cauchy, who published his proof just a year before. And this counterexample was to be rediscovered twenty years later by Hessel. Both Lhuilier and Hessel were led to their discovery by mineralogical collections in which they noticed some double crystals, where the inner crystal is not translucent, but the outer is. Lhuilier acknowledges the stimulus of the crystal collection of his friend Professor Pictet. Hessel refers to lead sulphide cubes enclosed in translucent calcium fluoride crystals.

11. *Definition 1* occurs first in the eighteenth century; e.g.: "One gives the name *polyhedral solid*, or simply *polyhedron*, to any solid bounded by planes or plane faces." (Legendre). A similar definition is given by Euler. Euclid, while defining cube, octahedron, pyramid, prism, does not define the general term *polyhedron*, but occasionally uses it.

12. We find *Definition 2* implicitly in one of Jonquières' papers read to the French Academy against those who meant to refute Euler's theorem. These papers are a thesaurus of monster-barring techniques. He thunders against Lhuilier's monstrous pair of nested cubes: "Such a system is not really a polyhedron but a pair of distinct polyhedra, each independent of the other. . . . A polyhedron, at least from the classical point of view, deserves the name only if, before all else, a point can move continuously over its entire surface; here this is not the case. . . . This first exception of Lhuilier can therefore be discarded." This definition—as opposed to Definition 1—goes down very well with analytical topologists who are not interested at all in the theory of polyhedra as such but only as a handmaiden for the theory of surfaces.

13. *Counterexamples 2a* and *2b* were missed by Lhuilier and first discovered only by Hessel.

14. *Definition 3* first turns up to keep out twin-tetrahedra in Möbius. We find his cumbersome definition reproduced in some modern textbooks in the usual authoritarian "take it or leave it" way; the story of its monster-barring background—that would at least explain it—is not told.

15. *Definition P*, according to which Eulerianness would be a definitional characteristic of polyhedra, was in fact suggested by R. Baltzer: "Ordinary polyhedra are occasionally (following Hessel) called Eulerian polyhedra. It would be more appropriate to find a special name for non-genuine (*uneigentliche*) polyhedra." The reference to Hessel is unfair: Hessel used the term "Eulerian" simply as an abbreviation for polyhedra for which Euler's relation holds in contradistinction to the non-Eulerian ones. For *Def. P* see also the Schläfli quotation in footnote 16.

16. The "urchin" was first discussed by Kepler in his cosmological theory. The name "urchin" is Kepler's (*"cui nomen Echino feci"*). Fig. 7 is copied from his book which contains also another picture. Poinsot independently rediscovered it, and it was he who pointed out that the Euler formula did not apply to it. The now standard term "small stellated dodecahedron" is Cayley's. Schläfli admitted star-polyhedra in general, but nevertheless rejected our small stellated dodecahedron as a monster. According to him "this is not a genuine polyhedron, for it does not satisfy the condition $V - E + F = 2$."

17. The dispute whether polygon should be defined so as to include star-polygons or not (*Def. 4* or *Def. 4'*) is a very old one. The argument put forward in our dialogue—that star-polygons become ordinary polygons when embedded in a space of higher dimensions—is a modern topological argument, but one can put forward many others. Thus Poinsot defending his star-polyhedra argued for the admission of star-polygons with arguments taken from analytical geometry: ". . . all these distinctions (between 'ordinary' and 'star'-polygons) are more apparent than real, and they completely disappear in the analytical treatment, in which the various species of polygons are quite inseparable. To the edge of a regular polygon there corresponds an equation with real roots, which simultaneously yields the edges of a regular inscribed heptagon, without at the same time finding edges of heptagons of the second and third species. Conversely, given the edge of a regular heptagon, one may determine the radius of a circle in which it can be inscribed, but in so doing, one will find three different circles corresponding to the three species of heptagon which may be constructed on the given edge; similarly for other polygons. Thus we are justified in giving the name 'polygon' to these new starred figures." Schröder uses the Hankelian argument: "The extension to rational fractions of the power concept originally associated only with the integers has been very fruitful in Algebra; this suggests that we try to do the same thing in geometry whenever the opportunity presents itself. . . ." Then he shows that we may find a geometrical interpretation for the concept of p/q-sided polygons in the star-polygons.

18. Gamma's claim that he can define the area for star-polygons is not a bluff. Some of those

who defended the wider concept of polygon solved the problem by putting forward a wider concept of the area of polygon. There is an especially obvious way to do this in the case of regular star-polygons. We may take the area of a polygon as the sum of the areas of the isosceles triangles which join the center of the inscribed or circumscribed circle to the sides. In this case, of course, some "portions" of the star-polygon will count more than once. In the case of irregular polygons where we have not got any one distinguished point, we may still take any point as origin and treat negatively oriented triangles as having negative areas. It turns out—and this can certainly be expected from an "area"—that the area thus defined will not depend on the choice of the origin. Of course there is liable to be a dispute with those who think that one is not justified in calling the number yielded by this calculation an "area"; though the defenders of the Meister-Möbius definition called it *"the right definition"* which "alone is specifically justified." Essentialism has been a permanent feature of definitional quarrels.

19. We find *Counterexample 4* too in Lhuilier—Gergonne again added that he knew it. But Grunert did not know it fourteen years later (1827) nor did Poinsot forty-five years later (1858).

20. This is paraphrased from a letter of Hermite's written to Stieltjes: "I turn aside with a shudder of horror from this lamentable plague of functions which have no derivatives" (1893).

21. "Researches dealing with . . . functions violating laws which one hoped were universal, were regarded almost as the propagation of anarchy and chaos where past generations had sought order and harmony" (Saks). Saks refers here to the fierce battles between monster-barrers (like Hermite!) and refutationists that characterized in the last decades of the nineteenth century (and indeed in the beginning of the twentieth) the development of modern real function theory, "The branch of mathematics which deals with counterexamples" (Munroe). The similarly fierce battle that raged later between the opponents and protagonists of modern mathematical logic and set-theory was a direct continuation of this.

22. *Definition 5* was put forward by the indefatigable monster-barrer E. de Jonquières to get Lhuilier's polyhedron with a tunnel (picture-frame) out of the way: "Neither is this polyhedral complex a true polyhedron in the ordinary sense of the word, for if one takes any plane through an arbitrary point inside one of the tunnels which pass right through the solid, the resulting cross-section will be composed of two distinct polygons completely unconnected with each other; this can occur in an ordinary polyhedron for *certain* positions of the intersecting plane, namely in the case of some concave polyhedra, but not for all of them." One wonders whether de Jonquières has noticed that his *Def. 5* excludes also some concave spheroid polyhedra.

23. We must not forget that what appears today as a monster will be tomorrow the origin of a line of special adaptations. . . . I further emphasized the importance of rare but extremely consequential mutations affecting rates of decisive embryonic processes which might give rise to what one might term hopeful monsters, monsters which would start a new evolutionary line if fitting into some empty environmental niche." (Goldschmidt). My attention was drawn to this paper by Karl Popper.

24. Paraphrased from Poincaré. The original full text is this: "Logic sometimes makes monsters. Since half a century we have seen arise a crowd of bizarre functions which seem to try to resemble as little as possible the honest functions which serve some purpose. No longer continuity, or perhaps continuity, but no derivatives, etc. Nay more, from the logical point of view, it is these strange functions which are the most general, those one meets without seeking no longer appear except as a particular case. There remains for them only a very small corner. "Heretofore when a new function was invented, it was for some practical end; today they are invented expressly to put at fault the reasonings of our fathers, and

one never will get from them anything more than that.

"If logic were the sole guide of the teacher, it would be necessary to begin with the most general functions, that is to say with the most bizarre. It is the beginner that would have to be set grappling with this teratologic museum. . . ." Poincaré discusses the problem with respect to the situation in the theory of real functions—but that does not make any difference.

25. Paraphrased from Denjoy.

Mathematics and Computer Science: Coping with Finiteness

Donald E. Knuth

Donald Ervin Knuth received his Ph.D. in mathematics from the California Institute of Technology in 1963. He taught at Cal Tech from 1963 to 1968. From 1968 to the present he has been with the computer science department at Stanford. He has been a Guggenheim fellow and has received the G. M. Hopper award and the A. M. Turing award. He is a member of the National Academy of Science.

"A billion here, a billion there, pretty soon you're talking about real money!" is an often quoted statement made by a U.S. Senator to describe the budgetary process in Washington. To many people the dollar amounts used in funding government operations appear to be inconceivably large but clearly finite numbers. Even more awesome than the eleven- and twelve-digit governmental totals, however, are the astrophysicists' or molecular biologists' routinely used twenty- or even thirty-digit numbers; by comparison these render even the federal deficit insignificant. Surely these unimaginable quantities must represent the limit of human experience in quantification. Well, it just isn't so. On the first page of this essay Knuth creates, almost literally by the stroke of a pen, a finite quantity so large as to easily render any quantity even remotely descriptive of physical size insignificant. And he moves on from there.

The context of this discussion is the potential and limitations of the digital computer. The dramatic increase in capacity to compute presented by the development of computers has led to a rather common fallacy: that since computers can perform some tasks so well and so quickly there is virtually no feat of computation beyond their reach. Knuth points out that this assumption is false. There are impossibility proofs in computer science as surely as in mathematics, and there exist finite and easily described computational tasks that no computer will ever be able to perform. It is in this sense, as in some others, that Knuth suggests that even mathematicians must learn to cope with finiteness.

A WELL-KNOWN BOOK entitled *One, Two, Three, . . . Infinity* was published by Gamov about 30 years ago, and he began by telling a story about two Hungarian noblemen. It seems that the two gentlemen were out riding, and one suggested to the other that they play a game: Who can name the largest number. "Good," said the second man, "you go first." After several minutes of intense concentration, the first nobleman announced the largest number he could think of:

Source: Donald E. Knuth, "Mathematics and Computer Science: Coping with Finiteness," *Science* 194 (4271, December 17, 1976): 1235–1242. Copyright 1976 by the American Association for the Advancement of Science. (Some references omitted.) A lecture based on this material was presented at the AAAS annual meeting in Boston, 22 February 1976, in the session entitled "The Frontiers of the Natural Sciences" organized by R. M. Sinclair.

"Three." Now it was the other man's turn, and he thought furiously, but after about a quarter of an hour he gave up. "You win," he said.

In this article I will try to assess how much further we have come, by discussing how well we can now deal with large quantities. Although we have certainly narrowed the gap between three and infinity, recent results indicate that we will never actually be able to go very far in practice. My purpose is to explore relationships between the finite and the infinite, in the light of these developments.

Some Large Finite Numbers

Since the time of Greek philosophy, men have prided themselves on their ability to understand something about infinity; and it has become traditional in some circles to regard finite things as essentially trivial, too limited to be of any interest. It is hard to debunk such a notion, since there are no accepted standards for demonstrating that something is interesting, especially when something finite is compared with something transcendent. Yet I believe that the climate of thought is changing, since finite processes are proving to be such fascinating objects of study.

In the first place, it is important to understand that finite numbers can be extremely large. Let us start with some very familiar and fairly small numbers: the value of xn is $x + x + \cdots + x$, added n times. Similarly we can define a number I shall write as $x \uparrow n$, which means $xx \cdots x$ multiplied n times. For example, $10 \uparrow 10 = 10 \cdot 10 \cdot 10 \cdot 10 \cdot 10 \cdot 10 \cdot 10 \cdot 10 \cdot 10 \cdot 10 \cdot = 10{,}000{,}000{,}000$ is 10 billion; this is usually written 10^{10}, but it will be clear in a minute why I prefer to use an upward arrow. In fact, the next step uses two arrows

$$x \uparrow \uparrow n = x \uparrow (x \uparrow (\cdots \uparrow x) \cdots))$$

where we take powers n times. For example,

$$10 \uparrow \uparrow 10 = 10^{10^{10^{10^{10^{10^{10^{10^{10^{10}}}}}}}}}$$

$$= 1 \text{ followed by } 10^{10^{10^{10^{10^{10^{10^{10^{10}}}}}}}} \quad \text{zeros.}$$

This is a pretty big number; at least, if a monkey sits at a typewriter and types at random, the average number of trials before he types perfectly the entire text of Shakespeare's *Hamlet* would be much, much less than this: it is merely a 1 followed by about 40,000 zeros. The general rule is

$$\overset{k \text{ arrows}}{\overbrace{x \uparrow \uparrow \cdots \uparrow n}}$$

$$= \underbrace{x \overset{k-1}{\overbrace{\uparrow \cdots \uparrow}} (x \overset{k-1}{\overbrace{\uparrow \cdots \uparrow}} (\cdots \overset{k-1}{\overbrace{\uparrow \cdots \uparrow}} x) \cdots))}_{n \text{ times}}$$

Thus, one arrow is defined in terms of none, two in terms of one, three in terms of two, and so on.

In order to see how these arrow functions behave, let us look at a very small example

$$10 \uparrow \uparrow \uparrow \uparrow 3$$

This is equal to

$$10 \uparrow \uparrow \uparrow (10 \uparrow \uparrow \uparrow 10)$$

so we should first evaluate $10 \uparrow \uparrow \uparrow 10$. This is

$$10 \uparrow \uparrow (10 \uparrow \uparrow (10 \uparrow \uparrow (10 \uparrow \uparrow (10 \uparrow \uparrow (10 \uparrow \uparrow (10 \uparrow \uparrow (10 \uparrow \uparrow (10 \uparrow \uparrow 10)))))))))$$

and that is

$$10 \uparrow \uparrow (10 \uparrow \uparrow (10 \uparrow \uparrow (10 \uparrow \uparrow (10 \uparrow \uparrow (10 \uparrow \uparrow (10 \uparrow \uparrow (10 \uparrow \uparrow 10^{10^{10^{10^{10^{10^{10^{10^{10^{10}}}}}}}}})))))))$$

$$= 10 \uparrow \uparrow (10 \uparrow \uparrow (10 \uparrow \uparrow (10 \uparrow \uparrow (10 \uparrow \uparrow (10 \uparrow \uparrow (10 \uparrow \uparrow 10^{10^{\cdot^{\cdot^{\cdot^{10}}}}})))))$$

where the stack of 10's is $10 \uparrow \uparrow 10$ levels tall. We take the huge number at the right of this formula, which I cannot even write down without using the arrow notation, and repeat the double-arrow operation, getting an even huger number, and then we must do the same thing again and again. Let us call the final result $\mathscr{H}$. (It is such an immense number, we cannot use just an ordinary letter for it.)

Of course we are not done yet, we have only evaluated $10 \uparrow \uparrow \uparrow 10$; to complete the job we need to stick this gigantic number into the formula for $10 \uparrow \uparrow \uparrow \uparrow 3$, namely,

$$10 \uparrow \uparrow \uparrow \uparrow 3 = 10 \uparrow \uparrow \uparrow \mathscr{H}$$
$$= \underbrace{10 \uparrow \uparrow (10 \uparrow \uparrow (10 \uparrow \uparrow \cdots \uparrow \uparrow (10 \uparrow \uparrow 10)\cdots))}_{\mathscr{H} \text{ times}}$$

The three dots "$\cdot \cdot \cdot$" here suppress a lot of detail—maybe I should have used four dots. At any rate it seems to me that the magnitude of this number $10 \uparrow \uparrow \uparrow \uparrow 3$ is so large as to be beyond human comprehension.

On the other hand, it is very small as finite numbers go. We might have used $\mathscr{H}$ arrows instead of just four, but even that would not get us much further—almost all finite numbers are larger than this. I think this example helps open our eyes to the fact that some numbers are very large even if they are merely finite. Thus, mathematicians who stick mostly to working with finite numbers are not really limiting themselves too severely.

Realistic Numbers

This discussion has set the stage for the next point I want to make, namely that our total resources are not actually very large. Let us try to see how big the known universe is. Archimedes began such an investigation many years ago, in his famous discussion of the number of grains of sand that would completely fill the earth and sky; he did not have the benefit of modern astronomy, but his estimate was qualitatively the same as what we would say today. The distance to the farthest observable galaxies is thought to be at most about 10 billion light years. On the other hand, the fundamental nucleons that make up matter are about 10^{-12} centimeters in diameter. In order to get a generous upper bound on the size of the universe, let us imagine a cube that is 40 billion light years on each side, and fill it with tiny cubes that are smaller than protons and neutrons, say 10^{-13} cm on each side (see Fig. 1). The total number of little cubes comes to less than 10^{125}. We might say that this is an "astronomically large" number, but actually it has only 125 digits.

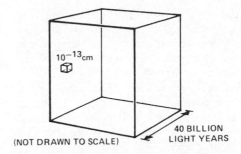

Figure 1   The known universe fits inside this box

Instead of talking only about large numbers of objects, let us also consider the time dimension. Here the numbers are much smaller; for example, if we take as a unit the amount of time that light rays take to travel 10^{-13} cm, the total number of time units since the dawn of the universe is only one fourth the number of little cubes along a single edge of the big cube in Fig. 1, assuming that the universe is 10 billion years old.

Coming down to earth, it is instructive to consider typical transportation speeds.

Snail	0.006	mile/hour
Man walking	4	mile/hour
U.S. automobile	55	mile/hour
Jet plane	600	mile/hour
Supersonic jet	1200	mile/hour

I would never think of walking from California to Boston, but the plane flight is only 150 times faster. Compare this to the situation with respect to the following computation speeds, given 10-digit numbers.

Man (pencil and paper)	0.2/sec
Man (abacus)	1/sec
Mechanical calculator	4/sec
Medium-speed computer	200,000/sec
Fast computer	200,000,000/sec

A medium-fast computer can add 1 million times faster than we can, and the fastest machines are 1000 times faster yet. Such a ratio of speeds is unprecedented in history: consider how much a mere factor of 10 in speed, provided by the auto-mobile, has changed our lives, and note that com-puters have increased our calculation speeds by six orders of magnitude; that is more than the ra-tio of the fastest airplane velocity to a snail's pace.

I do not mean to claim that computers do everything a million times faster than people can; mere mortals like us can do some things much better. For example, you and I can even recognize the face of a friend who has recently grown a moustache; and for tasks like filing, a computer may be only ten or so times faster than a good secretary. But when it comes to arithmetic, com-puters appear to be almost infinitely fast com-pared with people.

As a result, we have begun to think about com-putational problems that used to be unthinkable. Our appetite for calculation has caused us to deal with finite numbers much larger than those we considered before, and this has opened up a rich vein of challenging problems, just as exciting as the problems about infinity which have inspired mathematicians for so many centuries.

Of course, computers are not infinitely fast, and our expectations have become inflated even faster than our computational capabilities. We are forced to realize that there are limits beyond which we cannot go. The numbers we can deal with are not only finite, they are very finite, and we do not have the time or space to solve certain problems even with the aid of the fastest comput-ers. Thus, the theme of this article is coping with finiteness: What useful things can we say about these finite limitations? How have people learned to deal with the situation?

Advances in Technology and Techniques

During the last 15 years computer designers have made computing machines about 1000 times faster. Mathematicians and computer scientists have also discovered a variety of new techniques, by which many problems can now be solved enor-mously faster than they could before. I will pre-sent several examples of this; the first one, which is somehow symbolic of our advances in arithme-tic ability, is the following factorization of a very large number, completed in 1970 by Morrison and Brillhart.[1]

$$340,282,366,920,$$
$$938,463,463,374,607,431,768,211,457$$
$$= 5,704,689,200,685,129,054,721 \times$$
$$59,649,589,127,497,217$$

The point, of course, is not simply to compute the exact 39-digit product of these two large num-bers; that is trivial and takes only a few millionths of a second. The problem is to start with the big 39-digit number and to discover its prime factors. (The big number is $2^{128} + 1$, and its factors are of use, for example, in the design of codes of a type used for space communications.) The num-ber of microseconds per year is only 31,556,952,000,000, a 14-digit number, so even if we could test 1 million factors every second it would take about 2000 years to discover the smaller factor. The factorization actually took about 1 1/2 hours of computer time; it was achieved by a combination of sophisticated meth-ods representing a culmination of mathematical developments that began about 160 years earlier.

Latin Squares

Now let us look at another kind of example. Here is a so-called latin square of order 8, an arrange-ment of eight numbers in eight rows and eight columns so that each number appears in each row and each column.

```
1 2 3 4 5 6 7 8
2 1 4 3 6 5 8 7
3 4 1 2 7 8 5 6
4 3 2 1 8 7 6 5
5 6 7 8 1 2 3 4
6 5 8 7 2 1 4 3
7 8 5 6 3 4 1 2
8 7 6 5 4 3 2 1
```

On top of this square we can overlay another latin square of order 8, using italic numbers; again there is one italic digit of every kind in every row and in every column.

1 *1* 2 *2* 3 *3* 4 *4* 5 *5* 6 *6* 7 *7* 8 *8*
2 *3* 1 *4* 4 *1* 3 *2* 6 *7* 5 *8* 8 *5* 7 *6*
3 *5* 4 *6* 1 *7* 2 *8* 7 *1* 8 *2* 5 *3* 6 *4*
4 *7* 3 *8* 2 *5* 1 *6* 8 *3* 7 *4* 6 *1* 5 *2*
5 *4* 6 *3* 7 *2* 8 *1* 1 *8* 2 *7* 3 *6* 4 *5*
6 *2* 5 *1* 8 *4* 7 *3* 2 *6* 1 *5* 4 *8* 3 *7*
7 *8* 8 *7* 5 *6* 6 *5* 3 *4* 4 *3* 1 *2* 2 *1*
8 *6* 7 *5* 6 *8* 5 *7* 4 *2* 3 *1* 2 *4* 1 *3*

These two latin squares are called orthogonal, since the superposition shows that every pair of roman and italic numbers occurs exactly once. Thus we have roman 1 with italic *1* (in the upper left corner), roman 1 with italic *2* (near the lower right corner), and so on; all 8 × 8 possibilities appear. Latin squares and orthogonal latin squares are commonly used in the design of statistical experiments and for such things as crop rotation.

The great 18th-century mathematician Euler showed how to construct pairs of orthogonal latin squares of all sizes except for order 2, 6, 10, 14, 18, and so on, and he stated his belief that orthogonal latin squares of these missing orders do not exist. It is easy to verify this for order 2; and in 1900, an exhaustive analysis by a French mathematician showed that orthogonal latin squares of order 6 are indeed impossible. About 20 years later, an American mathematician published a proof that Euler was right in the remaining cases 10, 14, 18, . . . ; but unfortunately his "proof" had a serious flaw so the question was still not settled. Finally computers were invented, and an attempt was made to test Euler's conjecture in the smallest remaining case, order 10.

In 1952, a group of mathematicians at the University of California at Los Angeles (UCLA) decided to see if there were any latin squares orthogonal to the following one of order 10.

This particular square was selected more or less at random, using a procedure analogous to one discussed in the next example below; the probability that the above latin square will be generated[2] turns out to be about 10^{-26}, so I imagine that there are extremely many 10 × 10 latin squares, something like 10^{26} at least. However, the computer at UCLA ran for many hours trying to find an orthogonal mate for this square; finally, having produced no answers, it was shut off.[3] This was consistent with Euler's conjecture that no mates exist, but the investigators realized that several hundred more years of calculation would be required to show this exhaustively—and then they would have to try to find mates for the other 10^{26} or so initial squares.

The method used in this experiment was to look for a mate by filling in the entries row by row, one entry at a time in all possible ways, without violating the definition of orthogonal latin squares. Furthermore, they used the fact that the leftmost column of the orthogonal mate can be assumed to contain the digits 0 to 9 in order. Five years later Parker[4] discovered a far better way to look for orthogonal mates. His idea was to find all ways to put ten 0's into an orthogonal mate for a particular square; this means finding one entry in each row and each column so that no two entries contain the same digit. This is a much easier problem, and it turned out that there were roughly 100 ways to do it, using any cell in the first column. The remaining problem is to combine a solution for the 0's with a solution for the 1's and a solution for the 2's, and so forth, and again this is comparatively simple. Parker was able to deduce that there is exactly one latin square orthogonal to the one studied at UCLA, namely the italic digits in the following array.

0 1 2 3 4 5 6 7 8 9
1 8 3 2 5 4 7 6 9 0
2 9 5 6 3 0 8 4 7 1
3 7 0 9 8 6 1 5 2 4
4 6 7 5 2 9 0 8 1 3
5 0 9 4 7 8 3 1 6 2
6 5 4 7 1 3 2 9 0 8
7 4 1 8 0 2 9 3 5 6
8 3 6 0 9 1 5 2 4 7
9 2 8 1 6 7 4 0 3 5

0 *0* 1 2 2 8 3 5 4 9 5 4 6 7 7 3 8 6 9 *1*
1 *1* 8 7 3 4 2 9 5 3 4 6 7 5 6 0 9 2 0 8
2 *2* 9 5 5 6 6 4 3 8 0 7 8 0 4 *1* 7 9 1 3
3 *3* 7 6 0 9 9 0 8 4 6 5 1 8 5 2 2 1 4 7
4 *4* 6 8 7 1 5 7 2 5 9 3 0 6 8 9 1 0 3 2
5 *5* 0 *1* 9 7 4 8 7 0 8 2 3 9 1 4 6 3 2 6
6 *6* 5 9 4 0 7 2 1 7 3 1 2 3 9 8 0 4 8 5
7 *7* 4 3 1 5 8 1 0 2 2 0 9 4 3 6 5 8 6 9
8 *8* 3 0 6 2 0 3 9 6 1 9 5 1 2 7 4 5 7 4
9 *9* 2 4 8 3 1 6 6 1 7 8 4 2 0 5 3 7 5 *0*

And the total time for his program to be completed, on a slow computer in 1959, was less than 1 minute.

This example, together with the previous example about factoring, illustrates an important point: we should never expect that the first way we try to do something on a computer is the best way. Good programming is much more subtle than that; chances are that an expert can find a method that will go considerably faster than that of a novice, especially in combinatorial problems where there have been significant advances in techniques during recent years. By analyzing Parker's method statistically, I estimate that his approach runs about 100 billion times faster than the original method used by the extremely competent mathematicians who studied this problem at UCLA; that is 11 orders of magnitude faster, because of a better idea.

By now many sets of orthogonal latin squares of order 10 have been found, and orthogonal pairs are known to exist for all orders greater than 6. But computers were of little help in discovering these facts; the constructions were discovered by hand (by Parker himself in many cases), generalizing from patterns observed in the smaller cases.[5] For order 14 the problem is so much larger that even Parker's method would no longer be fast enough to search for all orthogonal mates by computer. This illustrates another point about combinatorial problems: the computation time often increases greatly when the size of the input to the problem has gone up only slightly.

Counting the Paths on a Grid

The next examples are all based on a single diagram, namely a grid of 100 squares; it is the diagram we would obtain if we drew boxes around the elements of a 10 × 10 latin square. (Incidentally, there are many possible examples that illustrate the points I wish to make, so it was necessary for me to find some way to narrow down the selection. Since a 10 × 10 array fits nicely on a page, I have decided to stick mostly to examples that are based somehow on this one diagram.)

First let us consider how many ways there are

to go along the lines of such a grid from the lower left corner to the upper right corner, without touching the same point twice. Problems like this have been studied by chemists and physicists concerned with the behavior of large molecules; it seems to be a difficult problem, and no way is known to calculate the exact number of such paths in a reasonable amount of time. However, it is possible to obtain approximate solutions which are correct with high probability.

The idea is to construct a "random" path from the starting point to the finishing point. First we must go up or to the right; by flipping a coin or rolling some dice we might decide to go right. Again there are two choices, and half the time we will go up. From here there are three possibilities, and we may choose from these at random, say to the right. And so on. Figure 2 shows the first ran-

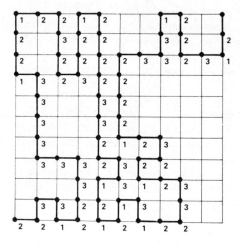

Figure 2   A "random" path from the lower left corner to the upper right corner of a 10 × 10 grid

dom path I generated in this way. At each choice point of Fig. 2, I have written the number of alternatives present when the path got that far. For example, the 1's at the edges mean that there is only one way to go, since the other way either is already occupied or leads into a trap.

The probability that this particular path would be obtained by such a random procedure is the product of all the individual probabilities at each choice point, namely

$$\frac{1}{2} \cdot \frac{1}{2} \cdot \frac{1}{3} \cdot \frac{1}{3} \quad \cdot \quad \cdot \quad \cdot \quad \frac{1}{3} \cdot \frac{1}{1} \cdot \frac{1}{2}$$
$$= 2^{-34}3^{-24}$$
$$= 1/4{,}852{,}102{,}490{,}441{,}335{,}701{,}504$$

about one chance in 5×10^{21}. So I am pretty sure that you have never seen this particular path before, and I doubt if I will ever generate it again.

In a similar vein, it is interesting to note that the great Mozart wrote a considerable amount of music that has never yet been performed. In one of his more playful moments, he specified 11 possibilities for each of the 16 bars of a waltz; the idea was that people from the audience should roll dice 16 times, obtaining a sequence of 16 numbers between 2 and 12 inclusive, and the performers would play the 16 bars corresponding to these respective rolls. The total number of ways to play Mozart's dice waltz is $2 \times 11^{14} = 759{,}499{,}667{,}966{,}482$; so it is safe to say that fewer than one out of every million of Mozart's melodies will ever be heard by human ear.

Actually I have a phonograph record that contains 36 randomly selected waltzes from Mozart's scheme, and after hearing the fifth one or so I began to feel that the rest all sounded about the same. We might suspect that a similar thing will happen in this random path problem; all random paths from lower left to upper right might tend to look approximately like the first few. Figure 3 shows the second path I generated by making random choices; note that this one has quite a different character, and the strange thing is that the probability of obtaining it is more than ten orders of magnitude larger than we saw before. But still the probability is "negligibly small."

The third path I generated in this way decided to get into a corner and to hug the edge. The fourth one had its own twist; and the fifth was reminiscent of the first. These paths are shown in Fig. 4; of course I am displaying here each path exactly as I obtained it, not suppressing any that were uninteresting or unexpected, because the experiment must be unbiased.

The difference between this game and Mozart's dice music is that we know of no way to generate a truly random path, in the sense that each path should occur with the same probability. Although

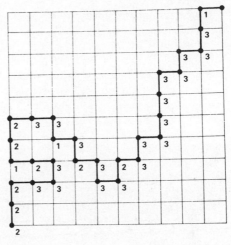

Figure 3   A second path, which would be obtained with probability $\approx 3 \times 10^{-12}$

we have seen that each path occurs with extremely small probability, virtually zero, the actual probabilities differ from each other by many orders of magnitude.

If we want to estimate the total number of possible paths, solely on the basis of these data, a theorem of statistics tells us that the best estimate is obtained by using the average value of the reciprocals of the probabilities observed. Thus, although three of these five paths had probabilities around 10^{-11}, suggesting that there are about 10^{11} possible paths, the much lower probabilities in the other two cases imply that it is much better to guess that there are about 10^{22} paths in all.

Based on the five experiments I have described, the best estimate of the average length of path will be about 70; and the best estimate of the chance that the point in the middle occurs somewhere on the path is that it almost always occurs, even though three-fifths of the experiments said the opposite. When large numbers like this are involved, we get into paradoxical situations, where the rules of statistics tell us that the best estimates are made by throwing away most of our data.

As you might expect, five experiments are not enough to determine the answers reliably. But by using a computer to generate several thousand random paths in the same way, I am fairly confi-

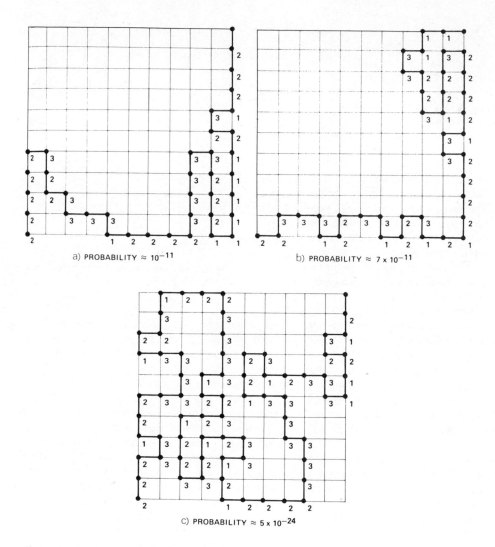

a) PROBABILITY ≈ 10^{-11}

b) PROBABILITY ≈ 7×10^{-11}

C) PROBABILITY ≈ 5×10^{-24}

Figure 4   Three more randomly generated paths, with their associated probabilities

dent that the total number of possible paths from lower left to upper right is $(1.6 \pm 0.3) \times 10^{24}$, and that the average length of path is 92 ± 5. Conflicting evidence was obtained about the chance of hitting the center, but it seems that 81 ± 10 percent of all paths do hit the center point. Of course, I have only generated an extremely small fraction of these paths, so I cannot really be sure; perhaps nobody will ever know the true answer.

The Shortest Paths

For the next examples we will add weights to the lines in the grid. The basic diagram is shown in Fig. 5, where a random digit has been placed beside each line; these digits may be thought of as the lengths of roads between adjacent points of intersection. Thus, there are three roads of length 4 on the bottom line, and the upper part of the diagram contains three adjacent roads of length 0.

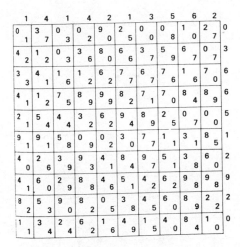

Figure 5   Network to be used in subsequent examples, based on 20 mathematical constants

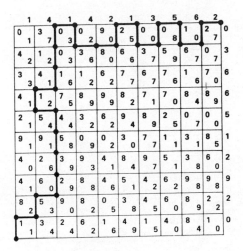

Figure 6   The shortest route from lower left to upper right in this network of roads

Actually I must admit that the sequences of numbers are not completely arbitrary; for example, the reader might recognize 1.414213562... in the top line as the square root of 2, and π appears down the second column. For our purposes these digits will be random enough.

The first problem we might ask about such a network of roads is: What is the shortest route from the lower left corner to the upper right corner? We have estimated that there are some 10^{24} possible paths, and we might want to know which of these is shortest, using the given lengths.

Fortunately we do not have to try all possible paths to find the shortest; there is a simple method due to Dijkstra[6] which can be used to solve this problem by hand in less than half an hour. The answer (see Fig. 6) is a curious sort of path, which might very well be missed if one does not use a systematic method; it is the only way to go from southwest to northeast in a path of length 43.

The idea underlying Dijkstra's method is rather simple. Suppose that at some stage we have found all positions at distance 20 or less, say, from the southwest corner. By looking at the roads connecting these points to the others it will be easy to see which points will be at distance 21, and so on. You can imagine a fluid spreading over the

diagram at the rate of one unit of length per minute.

Connecting Points in a Network

The next problem is somewhat harder. Suppose we want to construct electrical connections between all four of the corner points in Fig. 5: What is the shortest electrical network joining these four points, sticking to the lines and distances shown? Such a network is usually called a Steiner tree, and Fig. 7 shows the shortest possible one.

The number of possible Steiner trees connecting the four corners is much larger than the number of paths, but still I am sure that this is the shortest. In this case I do not know how to compute the shortest by hand, but a properly programmed computer can do it in a few seconds.

We say that we have a "good" algorithm for some problem if the time to solve it increases only as a polynomial in the size of the inputs; in other words, if doubling the size of the problem increases the solution time by at most a constant factor. There is a good algorithm to find Steiner trees connecting up to five points; it takes roughly n^3 steps, where n is the total number of points in the network of roads.[7] But if we want to connect larger numbers of points by Steiner trees, the

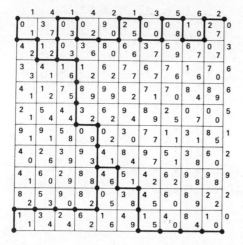

Figure 7   A shortest way to connect the four corners

computation rapidly gets larger; and when the number of points to be connected is, say, as large as $n/10$, no good algorithm is known.

On the other hand, when our job is to find the shortest way to connect up all n of the points in the network, a good algorithm is available, again one that is so good it can be performed by hand in half an hour.

A minimal connection of all points in a network is called a spanning tree, and in the particular network we are considering it is possible to prove that the number of possible spanning trees is really huge, more than 4×10^{52}; in fact, the exact number is 40,325,021,721,404,118,513,276,859, 513,497,679,249,183,623,593,590,784.

Yet we can find the best one, in a remarkably easy way discovered by Kruskal:[8] simply consider all the lines one by one in order of increasing length, starting with the shortest one, then the next shortest, and so on. In case of ties between lines of the same length, use either order. The rule is to include each line in the spanning tree if and only if it connects at least two points that are not connected by a path of previously selected lines. This is called the greedy algorithm because it is based on the idea of trying the best conceivable possibilities first. Such a policy does not always solve a combinatorial problem—we know that greed does not always pay off in the long

run—but in the case of spanning trees the idea works perfectly (see Fig. 8).

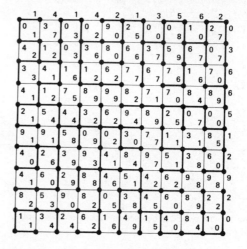

Figure 8   A minimum spanning tree

Maximum Matching

Another problem on this network for which a good algorithm is available is to choose 60 of the lines with the maximum possible sum, no two overlapping. We may think now of the points as people, instead of as cities, and the numbers now measure the amount of happiness generated between one person and his or her neighbor. The idea is to pair off the people so as to get the maximum total happiness. If men and women alternate in the diagram, with men at the corners, there will be 61 men and 60 women in all, so one man will have no partner; he makes a personal sacrifice for the greater good of the group as a whole. There are exactly 1,801,272,981,919,008 ways to do such a pairing, according to a mathematical theory worked out to solve a physical problem about crystals; Fig. 9 exhibits the best one.

It turns out that the circled man is the best to omit, and the others should pair up in this way. Once again we are able to find the optimum solution in 1 or 2 seconds on a computer if we use a suitable algorithm, even though the number of possible arrangements is far too large to examine exhaustively. In this case the algorithm is some-

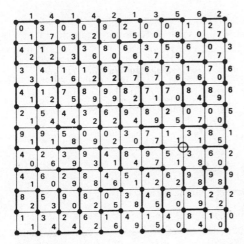

Figure 9   The best choice of 60 nonoverlapping lines in the diagram

what more subtle than the ones I have discussed earlier, but it is based on simple ideas. First we add a "dummy" woman who will be paired with the man who gets no real woman. The happiness rating is 0 between the dummy woman and every man. Then if we add or subtract some number from all the happiness ratings touching any particular person, the solution to the problem does not change. A clever way of adjusting these scores can be used so that all 61 of the ratings for the couples matched here are 9, and all the other ratings are 9 or less.

An Apparently Harder Problem

From these examples, one might get the idea that a good algorithm can be found for virtually any combinatorial problem. Unfortunately this does not appear to be true, although I did want to demonstrate that considerable progress has been made toward finding good methods. The next problem seems to be much harder: What is the shortest path from the lower left corner to the upper right corner that passes through all 121 points of the grid exactly once?

This is called the traveling salesman problem, because we might think of a salesman who wants to visit each city with minimum travel time. The

problem arises frequently in industry—for example, when the goal is to find the best order in which to do n jobs, based on the costs of changing from one job to another. But it has resisted all attacks; we know how to solve medium-sized problems, but the algorithms are not good in the technical sense since the running time goes up rapidly on large cases.

The traveling salesman's path shown in Fig. 10

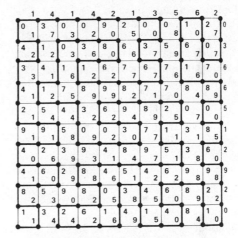

Figure 10   A shortest path from lower left to upper right, touching each point just once

is as short as possible, and it required several minutes of computer time to verify the fact. To my knowledge, this is the largest network for which the traveling salesman problem has yet been solved exactly. I used a method suggested in 1971 by Held and Karp,[9] based on a combination of ideas we have applied to other problems: it is possible to add or subtract numbers from all the lines which touch a particular point, without changing the shape of the minimum tour, and we can use the greedy algorithm to construct a minimum spanning tree for the changed distances. The minimum spanning tree is no longer than the shortest tour, since every tour is a spanning tree; but by properly modifying the distances we can make the minimum spanning tree very nearly a tour, so comparatively few possibilities need to be tried. I extended the Held and Karp method to take advantage of the fact that each point has at most four neighbors. In this way it was possible to verify at reasonable cost that this tour is optimum; but if I were faced with a larger problem, having say twice as many points to visit, there would be no known method to get the answer in a reasonable amount of time.[10]

In fact, it may well be possible in a few years to prove that no good algorithm exists for the traveling salesman problem. Since so many people have tried for so many years to find a good algorithm, without success, the trend is now to look for a proof that success in this endeavor is impossible. It is analogous to the question of solving polynomial equations: quadratic equations were resolved in ancient Mesopotamia, and the solution of cubic and quartic equations was found at the beginning of the Renaissance, but nobody was able to solve arbitrary equations of the fifth degree. Finally, during the first part of the 19th century, Abel and Galois proved conclusively that there is no way to solve fifth degree equations in general, using ordinary arithmetic. It is now believed that there is no good algorithm for the general traveling salesman problem, and we are awaiting another Abel or Galois to prove it.

In support of this belief, several important things have already been proved, notably that the traveling salesman problem is computationally equivalent to hundreds of other problems of general interest.[11] If there is a good algorithm for any one of these problems, which for technical reasons are called NP-complete problems, then there will be good algorithms for all the NP-complete problems. Thus, for example, a good algorithm for the traveling salesman problem would lead immediately to a good algorithm for many other difficult problems, such as the optimum scheduling of high school classes, the most efficient way to pack things into boxes, or the best Steiner trees connecting a large number of points. A good solution to any one of these problems will solve them all, so if any one of them is hard they all must be.

A Provably Harder Problem

In recent years, certain problems have, in fact, been shown to be intrinsically hard, in the sense

that there will never be a fast way to solve them. Probably the most interesting example of this type was developed in 1974 by A. Meyer and L. J. Stockmeyer. The problem is to decide whether or not certain logical statements about whole numbers $0, 1, 2, \ldots$ are true or false, even when the form of these statements is severely restricted.

Here are some examples of the sort of statements we must deal with:

$$048 \leq 1063$$

a statement which is clearly true.

$$\forall n\, \exists m (m < n + 1)$$

This is logical shorthand that can be translated as follows, for people who are not familiar with the new math: "For all numbers n there exists a number m such that m is less than $n + 1$." It is clearly a true statement, since we may take m equal to n.

$$\forall n \exists m (m + 1 < n)$$

"For all numbers n there exists a number m such that $m + 1$ is less than n." This statement is false, for if $n = 0$ there is no number less than zero; we are considering only statements about nonnegative numbers.

The next example is a little more complicated.

$$\forall x\, \forall y (y \geq x + 2 \rightarrow \exists z (x < z \land z < y))$$

"For all numbers x and all numbers y, if y is greater than or equal to $x + 2$ then there exists a number z such that x is less than z and z is less than y." In other words, if y is at least 2 more than x, there is a number z between x and y, and this is obviously true.

Finally we can also make statements about sets of numbers; for example

$$\forall S (\exists x (x \epsilon S) \rightarrow$$
$$\exists y (y \epsilon S \land \forall z (z \epsilon S \rightarrow y \leq z))$$

"For all sets S of numbers, if there exists a number x such that x is in S then there exists a number y such that y is in S and for all numbers z in S we have $y \leq z$." Informally, the statement says that every set of numbers which is not empty has a smallest element, and this is true.

The logical statements we shall be concerned with cannot be essentially any harder than these examples; they may not involve subtraction, multiplication, or division; they cannot even involve addition except addition of a constant. (They cannot involve the formula $x + y$.) Thus the statements must be very simple—much, much simpler than those used every day by mathematicians constructing proofs of theorems.

According to a well-known theorem of Büchi, it is possible to decide in a finite number of steps whether or not any statement of the simple kind we have described is true or false, even though these logical statements may concern infinitely many cases.

But the new theorem says that it is impossible actually to do this in the real world, even if we limit ourselves to statements that can be written in no more than 617 symbols: "No realistic algorithm will ever be able to decide truth or falsity for arbitrary given statements of length 617 or less."

In order to understand exactly what this theorem means, we have to know what it means to speak of a "realistic" algorithm. The theorem of Meyer and Stockmeyer is based on the fact that anything that can be done by computer can be done by constructing an electrical network, and so they envisage a setup like that shown in Fig. 11. At the top of such a device, one can insert any statement whose truth is to be tested. The logical language involved here makes use of 63 different symbols, including upper and lower case letters and a blank symbol, so we can place the statement (followed if necessary by blanks) into a sequence of 617 positions. Each position is converted into six electrical pulses, whose configuration of "on" and "off" identifies the corresponding character; thus, the letter X might be represented by the six pulses "off, on, on, off, off, on." The resulting 6×617 pulses now enter an electrical network or "black box" consisting of AND, OR, and NOT circuits; AND produces a signal that is "on" only when both inputs to AND are "on," OR produces a signal that is "on" when either or both of its inputs are "on," and NOT changes "on" to "off" and vice versa. At the bottom of the network, a pulse comes out which is "on" or "off" according to whether the given logical statement of length 617 was true or false.

According to Büchi's theorem, it is possible to construct such an electrical network with finitely many components, in a finite amount of time. But Meyer and Stockmeyer have proved that every such network must use at least 10^{125} components, and we have seen that this is much larger than the number of protons and neutrons in the entire known universe.

Thus it is hopeless to find an efficient algorithm for this finite problem. We have to face the fact that it can never be done—no matter how clever we may become, or how much money and energy is invested in the project.

What should we do in the face of such limitations? Whenever something has been proved impossible, there is an aspect of the human spirit that encourages us to find some way to do it anyway. In this particular case, we might try the following sneaky approach: We could build an electric circuit which gives the correct answer in all simple cases and which gives a random answer, true or false, in the other cases. Since the problem is so hard, nobody will be able to know the difference.

But this is obviously unsatisfactory. A better approach would be to distinguish between levels of truth; for example, the answer might be "true," "false," or "maybe." And we could give various shades of "maybe," saying perhaps that the statement is true in lots of cases.

Let us consider the traveling salesman problem again. It is reasonably likely that, some day, somebody will prove that no good algorithm exists for this problem. If so, that will be a truly great theorem; but what should we do when we actually need to solve such a problem?

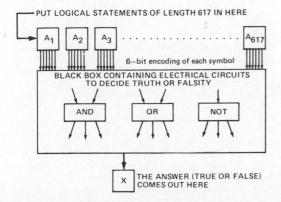

Figure 11   Electrical network to decide the correctness of logical statements containing 617 characters or less

The answer, of course, is to settle for a tour that is not known to be the shortest possible one, but is pretty close. It has recently been observed that we can quickly find a traveling salesman's tour that is guaranteed to be no worse than 50 percent longer than the shortest possible tour, if the distances satisfy the triangle inequality. And algorithms have recently been developed for other problems that give answers which are probably correct, where the degree of probability can be specified, but the answer is not certain.

In this way, computer scientists and mathematicians have been learning how to cope with our finite limitations.

Summary

By presenting these examples, I have tried to illustrate four main points.

1. Finite numbers can be really enormous, and the known universe is very small. Therefore the distinction between finite and infinite is not as relevant as the distinction between realistic and unrealistic.
2. In many cases there are subtle ways to solve very large problems quickly, in spite of the fact that they appear at first to require examination of too many possibilities.
3. There are also cases where we can prove that a fairly natural problem is intrinsically hard, far beyond our conceivable capabilities.
4. It takes a good deal of skill to decide whether a given problem is in the easy or hard class; but even if a problem does turn out to be hard there are useful and interesting ways to change it into one that can be done satisfactorily.

References and Notes

1. M. A. Morrison and J. Brillhart, *Math. Comput. 29*, 183 (1975).
2. M. Hall and D. E. Knuth, *Am. Math. Mon.* 72 (part 2, *Computers and Computing*), 21 (1965).
3. C. Tompkins, *Proc. Symp. Appl. Math. 6*, 195 (1956); L. J. Paige and C. Tompkins, *ibid. 10*, 71 (1960).
4. E. T. Parker, *ibid. 15*, 73 (1963).
5. For a complete survey see J. Dénes and A. D. Keedwell, *Latin Squares and Their Applications* (Academic Press, New York, 1974).
6. E. W. Dijkstra, *Numer. Math. 1*, 269 (1959).
7. First construct the matrix of distances between all pairs of points, then try all possible intermediate junction points.
8. J. B. Kruskal, Jr., *Proc. Am. Math. Soc. 7*, 48 (1956).
9. M. Held and R. M. Karp, *Math. Prog. 1*, 6 (1971).
10. It appears to be substantially easier to solve traveling salesmen problems when the distances are asymmetric, in the sense that the distance from x to y is uncorrelated with the distance from y to x. Such problems have been solved for up to 200 points by T. H. C. Smith, V. Srinivasan, and G. L. Thompson, *Ann. Discr. Math.*, in press.
11. R. M. Karp, in *Complexity of Computer Computations*, R. E. Miller and J. W. Thatcher, Eds. (Plenum, New York, 1972), p. 85. *See also* A. V. Aho, J. E. Hopcroft, J. D. Ullman, *The Design and Analysis of Computer Algorithms* (Addison-Wesley, Reading, Mass., 1974), chap. 10. For a popular account of related work, see G. B. Kolata, *Science 186*, 520 (1974).

The preparation and publication of this article was supported in part by NSF grant DCR 72–03752 A02, ONR contract NR 044–402, and the IBM Corporation. Some of the computations were done with the MACSYMA system, supported by the Defense Advanced Research Projects Agency under ONR contract N00014–75–C–0661; others were done on the SUMEX-AIM computer, supported by NIH RR00785; still others were done at the Université de Montréal, Centre des Recherches Mathématiques, where a preliminary version of this article was prepared under the auspices of the Chaire Aisenstadt.

Are Logic and Mathematics Identical?

Leon Henkin

Leon Henkin was born in Brooklyn and received his doctorate in 1947 from Princeton. Since 1953 he has been at Berkeley where he was chairman from 1959 to 1968. He has been a Fullbright and a Guggenheim fellow. He received the Chauvenet prize from the Mathematical Association of America in 1964.

According to the author the answer to the title's question is no. If a one-word answer were all that is required there would be no purpose in proceeding further. But there is, naturally, much more to this topic than a brief answer to that question. First, there is the context in which the question arose. Who made such an assertion and why? Second, there is the body of evidence on which the negative reply is based. How did this evidence evolve and who created it? Finally, it is reasonable to expect some comparison of the topics of logic and mathematics. What are the similarities and the differences? In fact, Henkin's essay answers all of these questions in an illuminating tour of the foundations of mathematics. The trip is well worth the effort.

IT WAS 24 years ago that I entered Columbia College as a freshman and discovered the subject of logic. I can recall well the particular circumstance which led to this discovery.

One day I was browsing in the library and came across a little volume by Bertrand Russell entitled *Mysticism and Logic*. At that time, barely 16, I fancied myself something of a mystic. Like many young people of that age I was filled with new emotions strongly felt. It was natural that any reflective attention should be largely occupied with these, and that this preoccupation should give a color and poignancy to experience which found sympathetic reflection in the writings of men of mystical bent.

Having heard that Russell was a logician I inferred from the title of his work that his purpose was to contrast mysticism with logic in order to exalt the latter at the expense of the former, and I determined to read the essay in order to refute it. But I discovered something quite different from what I had imagined. Indeed, contrasting aspects of mysticism and logic were delineated by Russell, but his thesis was that each had a proper and important place in the totality of human experience, and his interest was to define these and to exhibit their interdependence rather than to select one as superior to the other. I was disarmed, I was delighted with Russell's lucent and persuasive style, I began avidly to read his other works, and was soon caught up with logical concepts which have continued to occupy at least a portion of my attention ever since.

Bertrand Russell was a great popularizer of ideas, abstract as well as concrete. Probably many of you have been afforded an introduction to

Source: Leon Henkin, "Are Logic and Mathematics Identical?" *Science* 138 (November 16, 1962): 788–794. Copyright 1962 by the American Association for the Advancement of Science. (References omitted.) This article is adapted from an address given 5 September 1961 at the 5th Canadian Mathematical Congress, in Montreal. It is reprinted from the *Proceedings* of the congress, with permission.

mathematical logic through his writings, and perhaps some have even been led to the point of peeping into the formidable *Principia Mathematica* which he wrote with Alfred Whitehead about 1910. You will recall, then, the astonishing contention with which he shocked the mathematical world of that time—namely, that all of mathematics was nothing but logic. Mathematicians were generally puzzled by this radical thesis. Really, very few understood at all what Russell had in mind. Nevertheless, they vehemently opposed the idea.

This is readily understandable when you recall that a companion thesis of Russell's was that logic is purely tautological and has really no content whatever. Mathematicians, being adept at putting 2 and 2 together, quickly inferred that Russell meant to say that all mathematical propositions are completely devoid of content, and from this it was a simple matter to pass to the supposition that he held all mathematics to be entirely without value. *Aux armes, citoyens du monde mathématique!*

Half a century has elapsed since this gross misinterpretation of Russell's provocative enunciation. These 50 years have seen a great acceleration and broadening of logical research. And so it seems to me appropriate to seek a reassessment of Russell's thesis in the light of subsequent development.

Definitions and Proofs

In order to explain how Russell came to hold the view that all of mathematics is nothing but logic, it is necessary to go back and discuss two important complexes of ideas which had been developed in the decades before Russell came into the field. The first of these was a systematic reduction of all the concepts of mathematics to a small number of them. This process of reduction had indeed been going on for a very long time. As far back as the days of Descartes, for example, we can see at least an imperfect reduction of geometric notions to algebraic ones. Subsequently, with the development of set theory initiated by Georg Cantor, the reduction of the system of real numbers to that of

natural numbers marked another great step in this process. But perhaps the most daring of these efforts, the culminating one, was the attempt by a German mathematician, Gottlob Frege, to analyze the notion of natural number still further and reduce it to a concept which he considered to be of a purely logical nature.

Frege's work was almost entirely unnoticed in his own time (the last three decades of the 19th century), but when Bertrand Russell came upon Frege's work he realized its great significance and gave these ideas very wide currency through his own brilliant style of exposition. The ultimate elements into which the notion of natural number was analyzed by Frege and by Russell were entities which they called "propositional functions." To this day there persists a controversy among philosophers as to just what these objects are, but at any rate they are connected with certain linguistic expressions which are like sentences except for containing variables. Just as there is a certain *proposition* associated with (or expressed by) the sentence "U Thant is an astronaut," for example, so there is a *propositional function* associated with the expression "*x* is an astronaut." Since propositions had long been recognized as constituting one of the most basic portions of the domain of investigation of logicians, and since propositional functions are very closely related to propositions, it was natural to consider these, too, to be a proper part of the subject of logic. It is in this sense that Frege seemed able, by a series of definitions, to arrive at the notion of number, as well as at the other notions under study in various parts of mathematics, starting from purely logical notions.

The second important line of development which preceded Russell, and upon which he drew for his ideas, was the systematic study by mathematical means of the laws of logic which entered into mathematical proofs. This development was initiated by George Boole, working in England in the middle of the 19th century. He discovered that certain of the well-known laws of logic could be formulated with the aid of algebraic symbols such as the plus sign, the multiplication sign, and the equality sign and of variables. For example, Boole used the familiar equation $P \cdot Q = Q \cdot P$ to express the fact that sentences of the form "*P* and

Q" and "Q and P" must be both true or both false (whatever the sentences P and Q may be), while the generally unfamiliar algebraic equation $-(P \cdot Q) = (-P) + (-Q)$ indicates that the sentence "Not both P and Q" has the same truth value as "Either not P or not Q." Boole demonstrated that through the use of such algebraic notation one can effect a great saving in the effort needed to collate and apply basic laws of logic. Later his work was extended and deepened by the American C. S. Peirce and the German mathematician E. Schröder. And Russell himself, working within this tradition, found it a convenient basis for a systematic development of all mathematics from logic. By combining the symbolic formulation of logical laws with the reduction of mathematical concepts to a logical core, he was able to conceive of a unified development such as was attempted in the *Principia Mathematica*.

From Russell to Gödel

What was the *Principia* like? Well of course the work is still not completed (only three of four projected volumes having appeared); and since Bertrand Russell has most recently seemed to occupy himself with the political effects of certain physical research it may, perhaps, never be completed! Nevertheless, one can see clearly the intended scope of the work. Surprisingly, it reminds one of the present massive undertaking by the Bourbaki group in France. For even though the *Principia* and Bourbaki are very dissimilar in many ways, each attempts to present an encyclopedic account of contemporary mathematical research unified by a coherent point of view.

In the *Principia*, starting from certain axioms expressed in symbolic form which were intended to express basic laws of logic (axioms involving only what Russell conceived to be logical notions), the work systematically proceeds to derive the other laws of logic, to introduce by definition such mathematical notions as the concept of number and of geometric space, and finally to develop the main theorems concerning these concepts as part of a uniform and systemic development.

Viewed in retrospect, the contemporary logi-

cian is struck by the willingness of Russell and Whitehead to rest their case on what, for a mathematician, must be considered such flimsy evidence. The world of empirical science, of course, expects to achieve conviction on the basis of empirical evidence, but the quintessence of the mathematician's approach, especially of the mathematical logician's, is the demand always for *proof* before a thesis is accepted. Yet you see that whereas Russell was interested in establishing that in a certain sense all of mathematics could be obtained from his logical axioms and concepts, he never really set out to give a proof of this fact! All he did was to gather the basic ideas that had been developed in a nonformal and unsystematic way by mathematicians before him, and to say, in effect, "You see that I have been able to introduce all this loosely formulated work within the precise framework of my formal system. And it's pretty clear, isn't it, that I have all the tools available to formalize such further work as mathematicians are likely to do?"

In this respect one is reminded of the approach of that first great axiomatizer and geometer, Euclid. Euclid, too, conceived that all propositions of geometry—that is, all the true statements about triangles, circles, and those other figures in which he was interested—could be developed from the simple list of concepts and axioms he gave. But in his case, too, there was never any attempt to prove this fact other than by the empirical process of deriving a large number of geometric propositions from the axioms and then appealing to the good will of the audience, so to speak. "Well," we may imagine him saying, "look how much I have been able to deduce from my axioms. Aren't you pretty well convinced that *all* geometric facts follow from them?"

But of course there were mathematicians and logicians who were *not* convinced. And so the demand for proof was raised.

Actually, the proper formulation of the problem of whether a system of axioms is adequate to establish *all* of the true statements in some domain of investigation requires a mathematically precise formulation of the notion of "true sentence," and it was not until 1935 that Alfred Tarski, in a great pioneering work, made fully evident the form in which semantical notions must be analyzed for mathematical languages. Of course, it is a trivial matter to give the conditions under which any *particular* sentence is true. For example, in the theory of Euclidean geometry the sentence "All triangles have two equal angles" is true if, and only if, all triangles have two equal angles. However, Tarski made it clear that there is no way to utilize this simple technique in order to describe (in a finite number of words) conditions for the truth of all the infinitely many sentences of a language; for this purpose a very different form of definition, structural and recursive in character, is needed.

Even before Tarski's treatment of semantics, indeed as early as 1919, we find the first proof of what we call, in logic, "completeness." The mathematician Emil Post (in his doctoral dissertation published in that year), limiting his attention to a very small fragment of the system created by Whitehead and Russell, was able to show that for any sentence in that fragment which was "true under the intended interpretation of the symbols," one could indeed get a proof by means of the axioms and rules of inference which had been stated for the system. Subsequently, further efforts were made to extend the type of completeness proof which Post initiated, and it was hoped that ultimately the entire system of the *Principia* could be brought within the scope of proofs of this kind.

In 1930, Kurt Gödel contributed greatly to this development and to this hope when he succeeded in proving the completeness of a deductive system based upon a much larger portion of mathematical language than had been treated by Post. Gödel's proof deals with the so-called "first-order predicate logic," which treats of mathematical sentences containing variables of only one type. When such a sentence is interpreted as referring to some mathematical model, its variables are interpreted as ranging over the elements of the model; in particular, there are no variables ranging over sets of model elements, or over the integers (unless these happen to be the elements of the particular model). Now Gödel showed that if we have any system of axioms of this special kind, then whenever a sentence is true in every model satisfying these axioms there must be a proof of

finite length, leading from the axioms to this sentence, each line of the proof following from preceding lines by one of several explicitly listed rules of logic. This result of Gödel's is among the most basic and useful theorems we have in the whole subject of mathematical logic.

But the very next year, in 1931, the hope of further extension of this kind of completeness proof was definitely dashed by Gödel himself in what is certainly the deepest and most famous of all works in mathematical logic. Gödel was able to demonstrate that the system of *Principia Mathematica*, taken as a whole, was *incomplete*. That is, he showed explicitly how to construct a certain sentence, about natural numbers, which mathematicians could recognize as being true under the intended interpretation of the symbolism but which could not be proved from the axioms by the rules of inference which were part of that system.

Now, of course, if Gödel had done nothing more than this, one might simply conclude that Russell and Whitehead had been somewhat careless in formulating their axioms, that they had left out this true but unprovable sentence from among the axioms, and one might hope that by adding it as a new axiom a stronger system which was complete would be achieved. But Gödel's proof shows that this stronger system, too, would contain a sentence which is true but not provable; that, indeed, if this system were further strengthened, by the addition of this new true but unprovable sentence as an axiom, the resulting system would again be incomplete. And indeed, if a whole infinite sequence of sentences were to be obtained by successive applications of Gödel's method, and added simultaneously to the original axioms of *Principia*, the same process could still be applied to find *another* true sentence still unprovable.

Actually, Gödel described a very wide class of formal deductive systems to which his method applies. And most students of the subject have been convinced that any formal system of axioms and rules of inference which it would be reasonable to consider as a basis for a development of mathematics would fall in this class, and hence would suffer a form of incompleteness. From this viewpoint it appears that one of the basic elements on which Russell rested his thesis that all mathematics could be reduced to logic must be withdrawn and reconsidered.

Consistency and Decision Problems

I have been talking about completeness, which has to do with the adequacy of a formal system of axioms and rules of inference for proving true sentences. But I must mention, also, a second aim of the Russell-Whitehead *Principia* which also fared ill in the subsequent development of mathematical logic. Russell and Whitehead were very much concerned with the question of *consistency*. While they hoped to have a complete system, one containing proofs for all correct statements, they were also concerned that their system should *not* contain proofs of incorrect results. In particular, in a consistent system such as they sought, it would not be possible to prove both a sentence and its negation.

To understand their concern with the question of consistency it is necessary to recall the rude wakening which mathematicians sustained in 1897 in connection with Cantor's theory of transfinite numbers. For centuries before the time of Cantor mathematicians simply assumed that anyone who was properly educated in their subject could distinguish a correct proof from an incorrect one. Those who had trouble in making this distinction were simply "weeded out" in the course of their training and were turned from mathematics to lesser fields of study. And no one took up seriously the question of setting forth, in explicit and mathematical terms, exactly what was meant by a correct proof.

Now when Cantor began his development of set theory he concerned himself with both cardinal and ordinal numbers of transfinite type. (These numbers can be used for infinite sets in very much the same way that we use ordinary numbers for counting and ordering finite sets.) Many of the properties of transfinite numbers are identical to those of ordinary numbers, and in particular Cantor showed that, given any ordinal number b, we can obtain a larger number, $b + 1$. However, in 1897 an Italian mathematician, C. Burali-Forti,

demonstrated that there must be a *largest* ordinal number, by considering the set of all ordinal numbers in their natural order. Mathematicians were unable to find any point, either in the argument of Cantor or in that of Burali-Forti, which they intuitively felt rested on incorrect reasoning. Gradually it was realized that mathematicians had a genuine paradox on their hands, and that they would have to grapple at last with the question of just what was meant by a correct proof. Later, Russell himself produced an even simpler paradox in the intuitive theory of sets, based upon the set of all those sets which are not elements of themselves.

This background sketch will make clear why it was that Russell and Whitehead were concerned that no paradox should be demonstrable in their own system. And yet they themselves never attempted a *proof* that their system was consistent! The only evidence they adduced was that a large number of theorems had been obtained within their system without encountering paradox, and that all attempts to reproduce within the system of *Principia Mathematica* the Burali-Forti paradox, and such other paradoxes as were shown, had failed.

As with the question of completeness, mathematicians were not satisfied with an answer in this form, and there arose a demand that an actual proof of the consistency be given for the system of *Principia* (and for other systems then considered). The great and illustrious name of David Hilbert was associated with these efforts to achieve consistency proofs for various portions of mathematics, and under his stimulus and direction important advances were made toward this goal, both by himself and by his students. But as with the efforts to prove completeness, Hilbert's program came to founder upon the brilliant ideas of Kurt Gödel.

Indeed, in that same 1931 paper to which I have previously referred, Gödel was able to show that the questions of consistency and completeness were very closely linked to one another. He was able to show that *if* a system such as the *Principia* were truly consistent, then in fact it would not be possible to produce a sound proof of this fact! Now this result itself sounds paradoxical.

Nevertheless, when expressed with the technical apparatus which Gödel developed, it is in fact a precisely established and clearly meaningful mathematical result which has persuaded most, though admittedly not all, logicians that Hilbert's search for a consistency proof must remain unfulfilled.

I should like finally to mention a third aspect in which the original aim of mathematical logicians was frustrated. The questions of consistency and completeness clearly concerned the authors of *Principia Mathematica*, but the question of decision procedures seems not to have been treated to any serious extent by Russell and Whitehead. Nevertheless, this is an area of study which interested logicians as far back as the time of Leibniz. Indeed, Leibniz himself had a great dream: He dreamt that it might be possible to devise a systematic procedure for answering questions—not only mathematical questions but even questions of empirical science. Such a procedure was to obviate the need for inspiration and replace this with the automatic carrying out of routine procedure. Had Leibniz been conversant with today's high-speed computing machines he might have formulated his idea by asserting the possibility that one could write a program of such breadth and inclusiveness that any scientific question whatever could be placed on tape and, after the machine had been set to work on it for some finite length of time, a definitive reply would be forthcoming.

Logic after 1936

Leibniz's idea lay dormant for a long time, but it was natural to revive it in connection with the formal deductive systems which were developed by mathematical logicians in the early part of this century. Since these logicians had been interested in formulating mathematical ideas within a symbolic calculus and then manipulating the symbols according to predetermined rules in order to obtain further information about these mathematical concepts, it seemed natural to raise the question of whether one could not devise purely automatic rules of computation which would enable one to reach a decision as to the truth or falsity of any

given sentence of the calculus. And while the area of empirical science was pretty well excluded from the consideration of 20th-century logicians seeking such decision procedures, it was perhaps not beyond the hope of some that a system as inclusive as that of the *Principia* could some day be brought within the scope of such a procedure.

Efforts to find decision procedures for various fragments of the *Principia* were vigorous and many. The doctoral dissertation of Post, for example, contained some efforts in this direction, and further work was produced during the succeeding 15 years by logicians of many countries. Then in 1936 Alonzo Church, making use of the newly developed notion of recursive function, was able to demonstrate that for a certain fragment of mathematical language, in fact for that very first-order predicate logic which Gödel, in 1930, had showed to be complete, no decision procedure was possible. And so with decision procedures, as with proofs of completeness and consistency, efforts to establish a close rapport between logic and mathematics came to an unhappy end.

Well, I have brought you down to the year 1936. Probably most mathematicians have heard at least something of the development which I have sketched here. But somehow the education in logic of most mathematicians seems to have been terminated at about that point. The impression is fairly widespread that, with the discoveries of Gödel and Church, the ambitious program of mathematical logicians in effect ground to a halt, and that since then further work in logic has been a sort of helpless faltering by people, unwilling to accept the cruel facts of life, who are still seeking somehow to buttress the advancing frontiers of mathematical research by finding a nonexistent consistency proof.

And yet this image is very far indeed from reality. For in 1936, just at the time when, many suppose, the demise of mathematical logic had been completed, an international scholarly society known as the Association for Symbolic Logic was founded and began publication of the *Journal of Symbolic Logic*. In the ensuing 25 years this has greatly expanded to accommodate a growing volume of research. And at present there are four journals devoted exclusively to publishing material dealing with mathematical logic, while many articles on logic appear in a variety of mathematical journals of a less specialized nature.

In the space remaining I should like to mention very briefly some of the developments in mathematical logic since 1936.

Sets and Decision Methods

I have found it convenient for this exposition to divide research in mathematical logic into seven principal areas. And first I shall mention the area dealing with the foundations of the theory of sets.

To explain the connection of this field with logic it should be mentioned that those objects which Russell and Whitehead had called "propositional functions" are, in fact, largely indistinguishable from what are now called "sets" and "relations" by mathematicians. From a philosophical point of view there is perhaps still room for distinguishing these concepts from one another. But since, in fact, the treatment of propositional functions in *Principia Mathematica* is extensional (so that two functions which are true of exactly the same objects are never distinguished), for mathematical purposes this system is identical to one which treats of sets and relations.

Among systems of set theory which have been put forth by logicians as a basis for the development of mathematics, the principal ones are the theory of types used by Whitehead and Russell themselves, subsequently amplified by L. Chwistek and F. Ramsey, and an alternative line of development initiated by E. Zermelo, to which important contributions were subsequently made by A. Fraenkel and T. Skolem. Still another system, having certain characteristics in common with each of these two principal forms, was advanced and has been studied by W. Quine and, to some extent, by J. B. Rosser. Of these systems the Zermelo-type system has probably received most attention, along with an important variant form suggested and developed by J. von Neumann, P. Bernays, and Gödel.

Among the significant efforts expended on these systems were those directed toward establishing the status of propositions such as the axiom of choice and the continuum hypothesis of Cantor. Here the names of Gödel and A. Mostowski are especially prominent.

Gödel showed that a strong form of the axiom of choice and the generalized continuum hypothesis are simultaneously consistent with the more elementary axioms of set theory—under the assumption that the latter are consistent by themselves. Mostowski showed that the axiom of choice is independent of the more elementary axioms of set theory, provided that a form of these elementary axioms is selected which does not exclude the existence of nondenumerably many *"Urelemente"* (objects which are not sets). The independence of the axiom of choice from systems of axioms such as that used in Gödel's consistency proof, and the independence of the continuum hypothesis in any known system of set theory, remain open questions.

More recently the direction of research in the area of foundations of set theory seems to have shifted from that of formulating specific axiom systems and deriving theorems within them to consideration of the totality of different realizations of such axiom systems. It is perhaps J. Shepherdson who should be given credit for the decisive step in this shift of emphasis, although his work clearly owes much to Gödel's. Subsequent work by Tarski, R. Vaught, and R. Montague has carried this development much further.

An important tool in their work is the concept of the *rank* of a set, which may be defined inductively as the least ordinal number exceeding the rank of all elements of the set. This notion may be used to classify models of set theory according to the least ordinal number which is not the rank of some set of the model. Recently there have been some very interesting contributions by Azriel Lévy to these studies. His efforts have been directed toward successively strengthening the axioms of set theory so as to penetrate increasingly far into the realm of the transfinite.

A second area that I would delineate in contemporary logical research is that dealing with the decision problem. While it is true that the work of Church made it clear that there could be no *universal* decision procedure for mathematics, there has remained a strong interest in finding decision procedures for more modest portions of mathematical theory. Of special interest here is Tarski's decision method for elementary algebra and geometry, and an important extension of it which was made by Abraham Robinson. Wanda Szmielew has also given an important decision procedure—namely, one for the so-called "elementary theory" of Abelian groups. By contrast, the elementary theory of *all* groups was shown by Tarski to admit of no decision procedure. In fact, Szmielew and Tarski considered exactly the same set of sentences—roughly, all of those sentences which can be built up by the use of the group operation symbol, and variables ranging over the group elements, with the aid of the equality sign, as well as the usual logical connectives and quantifiers. If we ask whether any given sentence of this kind is true for all *Abelian* groups, it is possible to answer the question in an automatic way by using the method of Szmielew. But if we are interested in which of these sentences are true for *all* groups, then Tarski's proof shows that it is impossible to devise a machine method to separate the true from the false ones.

A result closely related to Tarski's is that of P. Novikov and W. Boone concerning the nonexistence of a decision method which would enable one to solve the word problem for the theory of groups, a problem for which a solution had long been sought by algebraists. In fact it is a simple matter to show that the Novikov-Boone result is equivalent to the nonexistence of a decision method for a certain *subset* of the sentences making up the elementary theory of groups—namely, all those sentences having a special, very simple, form. Hence, this result is stronger than Tarski's.

Recursive Functions

Now the key concept whose development was needed before negative solutions to decision problems could be achieved was the concept of a recursive function. Intuitively speaking this is simply a function from natural numbers to natural numbers which has the property that there is an automatic method for computing its value for any given argument. A satisfactory and explicit mathematical definition of this class of functions was first formulated by J. Herbrand and Gödel. But it remained for S. C. Kleene to develop the concept

to such an extent that it now underlies a very large and important part of logical research.

Much of the work with recursive functions has been along the line of classifying sets and functions, a classification similar to that involving projective and analytic sets in descriptive set theory. Kleene himself, his students Addison and Spector, and other logicians, including Post, Mostowski, J. Shoenfield, and G. Kreisel, have contributed largely to this development. Also to be mentioned are the applications which initially Kleene, and subsequently others, have attempted to make of the concept of recursive function by way of explicating the notion of "constructive" mathematical processes. In this connection several attempts have been made to link the notion of recursive function with the mathematical viewpoint known as intuitionism, a radical reinterpretation of mathematical language which was advanced by L. Brouwer and developed by A. Heyting.

Algebra, Logic, and Models

A fourth area of logical research deals with material which has recently been described as algebraic logic. This is actually a development which can be traced back to the very early work of Boole and Schröder. However, interest in the subject has shifted away from the formulation and derivation of algebraic equations which express laws of logic to the consideration of abstract structures which are defined by means of such equations. Thus, the theory of Boolean algebras, of relation algebras, of cylindric and polyadic algebras have all successively received attention; M. Stone, Tarski, and P. Halmos are closely associated with the central development here. The algebraic structures studied in this domain may be associated in a natural way with mathematical theories, and this association permits the use of very strong algebraic methods in the metamathematical analysis of these theories.

A fifth area of modern logical research concerns the so-called theory of models. Here effort is directed toward correlating mathematical properties possessed by a class of structures defined by means of given mathematical sentences with the structural properties of those sentences themselves.

A very early example is Garrett Birkhoff's result that, for a class of structures to be definable by means of a set of equational identities, it is necessary and sufficient that it be closed under formation of substructures, direct products, and homomorphic images. Characterizations of a similar nature were given for classes definable by universal elementary sentences (Tarski) and by any elementary sentences (J. Keisler).

A related type of result is R. Lyndon's theorem that any elementary sentence whose truth is preserved under passage from a model of the sentence to a homomorphic image of that model must be equivalent to a sentence which does not contain negation signs. In a different direction, E. Beth has shown that if a given set symbol or relation symbol is not definable in terms of the other symbols of an elementary axiom system, then there must exist two distinct models of these axioms which are alike in all respects except for the interpretation of the given symbol. (This proves the completeness of A. Padoa's method of demonstrating nondefinability.) A logical interpolation theorem of W. Craig's provides a close link for the results of Lyndon and Beth.

A sixth area which can be discerned in recent work on logic concerns the theory of proof. This is perhaps the oldest and most basic portion of logic, a search for systematic rules of proof, or deduction, by means of which the consequences of any propositions could be identified. In recent work, however, logicians have begun to depart in radical ways from the type of systems for which rules of proof were originally sought. For example, several attempts have been made to provide rules of proof for languages containing infinitely long formulas, such as sentences with infinitely many disjunctions, conjunctions, and quantified variables. Tarski, Scott, C. Karp, W. Hanf, and others have participated in such efforts. Curiously enough, while this direction of research seems at first very far removed from ordinary mathematics, one of the important results was used by Tarski to solve a problem, concerning the existence of measures on certain very large spaces, which had remained unsolved for many years.

The last area of logical research I should like to bring to your attention is a kind of converse study to what we have called algebraic logic. In the latter we are interested in applying methods of algebra to a system of logic. But there are also studies in which results and methods of logic are used to establish theorems of modern algebra. The first to have made such applications seems to have been the Russian mathematician A. Malcev, who in 1941 indicated how the completeness theorem for first-order logic could be used to obtain a result on groups. Subsequently the same technique was used by Tarski to construct various non-Archimedean ordered fields. Perhaps the best-known name in this area is that of Abraham Robinson, who formerly was associated with the University of Toronto in Canada. Among his contributions was the application of logical methods and results to improve a solution, given in 1926 by E. Artin, to Hilbert's 17th problem (17th of the famous list of problems presented in his address to the International Congress of Mathematicians in 1900). Robinson showed that when a real polynomial which takes only nonnegative values is represented as a sum of squares of rational functions, the number of terms needed for the representation depends only on the degree and number of variables of the given polynomial, and that it is independent of the particular coefficients.

Russell's Thesis in Perspective

I hope that this very brief sketch of some of the areas of contemporary logical research will give some idea of the ways in which logicians have reacted to the theorems of Gödel and Church which, in the period 1931 to 1936, dealt so harshly with earlier hopes. Speaking generally, one could describe this reaction as compounded of an acceptance of the impossibility of realizing the original hopes for mathematical logic, a relativization of the original program of seeking completeness and consistency proofs and decision methods, an incorporation of the new methods and constructs which appeared in the impossibility proofs, and the development of quite new interests suggested by generalization of early results.

Now with this background, let us return to Russell's thesis that all of mathematics can be reduced to logic. I would say that if logic is understood clearly to contain the theory of sets (and this seems to be a fair account of what Russell had in mind), then most mathematicians would accept without question the thesis that the basic concepts of all mathematics can be expressed in terms of logic. They would agree, too, that the theorems of all branches of mathematics can be derived from principles of set theory, although they would recognize that no fixed system of axioms for set theory is adequate to comprehend all of those principles which would be regarded as "mathematically correct."

But perhaps of greater significance is the consensus of mathematicians that there is much more to their field than is indicated by such a reduction of mathematics to logic and set theory. The fact that *certain* concepts are selected for investigation, from among all logically possible notions definable in set theory, is of the essence. A true understanding of mathematics must involve an explanation of which set-theory notions have "mathematical content," and this question is manifestly not reducible to a problem of logic, however broadly conceived.

Logic, rather than being all of mathematics, seems to be but one branch. But it is a vigorous and growing branch, and there is reason to hope that it may in time provide an element of unity to oppose the fragmentation which seems to beset contemporary mathematics—and indeed every branch of scholarship.

C. S. Peirce's Philosophy of Infinite Sets

Joseph W. Dauben

Joseph Warren Dauben was born in California in 1944 and received his Ph.D. in the history of science at Harvard in 1972. Since 1972 he has been associated with the City University of New York. He has been a fellow of the National Endowment for Humanities and a member of the Institute for Advanced Study at Princeton. He is the editor of *Historia Mathematica*.

This essay is much more than a guided tour through the catacombs of set theory. It is at once a brief but quite complete history of American mathematics up to the turn of the century, a succinct biography of one of the pioneers of that history, and an introduction to the philosophy of continuous processes. Rather a lot to attempt in a few pages, but Dauben manages it quite well.

Two aspects of the essay ought to be particularly noted: the description of set theory by Cantor and the idea of continuity. Cantor himself had, at least initially, some intuitive misgivings about his own creations. The reader should observe the methodology used to generate new sets from old ones. It is fair to ask if there is anything in the methodology of that generation that might put one on philosophically shaky grounds.

Another important topic is the idea of continuity. Peirce felt quite strongly that the set of real numbers had, in some philosophical way, not enough structure (substance may be better) to elicit even in aggregate the continuous line. Peirce's view of continuity springs from his Leibnizian notions of space and time. It is fascinating to observe that in the universe now created by quantum mechanics the line is too continuous. The quantum mechanistic universe is now discrete, an essentially finite assembly of indecomposable events that are only roughly approximated by the mathematics of the continuous, a hoary pre-Newtonian view of the world now essential to modern physics.

A final point: Peirce "filled in" his continuous line by creating a class of objects different from the usual real numbers. These new objects were much like the "infinitesimals" of the calculus of Newton and Leibniz. In Newton's day these strange quantities, greater than zero but less than any real number, were never rigorously defined and in time they became a decided embarrassment to the mathematical community. Nineteenth-century mathematicians devoted much effort to the liberation of the calculus from any notion of infinitesimals. By the end of that century infinitesimals were nowhere required in order to explain any mathematical idea. However, Peirce regretted their passing, felt that they were essential to the Leibnizian ideas of space and time, and tried to provide for them a rigorous mathematical definition. In this attempt Peirce was only partially successful. But the story does not end there. About 25 years ago A. Robinson, whose essay on the history of mathematics appears in Volume I, resurrected the idea of infinitesimals, gave them an indisputably rigorous mathematical definition, and used the resulting system to create the calculus which operated in precisely the way suggested by Newton and Leibniz some 300 years earlier.

Source: Joseph W. Dauben, "C. S. Peirce's Philosophy of Infinite Sets," *Mathematics Magazine* 50 (1977): 123–135. Reprinted by permission of the Mathematical Association of America.

I fear I might seem to talk gibberish to you, so different is your state of mental training and mine.[1]
CHARLES SANDERS PEIRCE

AMERICAN MATHEMATICS, LIKE American science generally in the nineteenth century, remained underdeveloped, depended heavily upon European models, and made few independent and recognized contributions of its own. Though presidents like Jefferson might take a pedagogical interest in mathematics and its teaching, and while Garfield, in fact, discovered an interesting variation on the many proofs of the Pythagorean theorem, American mathematics generally remained without support, either institutional or financial, until late in the century.[2]

Despite the lack of incentives to pursue a mathematical career in America, there were nevertheless some who made important contributions to mathematics in the United States. One of the most interesting of these, Charles Sanders Peirce, made fundamental discoveries, largely independent of his European counterparts, in set theory and mathematical logic. This paper explores the nature and significance of Peirce's contributions.

Though his study of continuity led him to produce results paralleling in some ways the contributions of Georg Cantor and Richard Dedekind in Germany, Peirce's work was dramatically different in its origins, inspiration, and ultimate mathematical character. In order to understand the fate of Peirce and his mathematical studies of continuity and infinity, it is necessary first to say something about the status of American science in general, and of American mathematics in particular, in the nineteenth century. Following a brief sketch of the major developments of set theory, largely in the hands of Cantor and Dedekind, we shall then turn to consider Peirce, his mathematics, and finally the reasons why his genius and multitudinous insights did not exert more influence upon his contemporaries than they did.

Mathematics in America in the Nineteenth Century

Alexis de Tocqueville, in assessing the status of science in America in the early nineteenth century, remarked that Americans found it easier to borrow their science from Europe than to pursue it earnestly themselves. "I am convinced," he wrote, "that if the Americans had been alone in the world . . . they would not have been slow to discover that progress cannot long be made in the application of the sciences without cultivating the theory of them."[3] Mathematics, as the handmaiden in particular to astronomy and physics, was as essential, but just as neglected, as the other basic sciences in America until well past mid-century. In large measure de Tocqueville found the unusual combination of democracy and economic opportunities responsible for America's indifference to basic science. By this he meant that the egalitarian ideal encouraged the idea that anyone, with hard work, could transform the nation's national resources into personal fortune. Thus if anything was sought in science, it was only the immediate means by which nature might be exploited. Europe had its monarchies and aristocracies to encourage pure science, but de Tocqueville was certain that it could flourish equally as well in the United States, if only constituted authorities here would give it encouragement and support.

Thus while utility was highly praised for reasons that were religious, political and entrepreneurial, little interest was paid to abstract study which seemed to offer no evidence of immediate usefulness.[4] Mathematics was no exception. In fact, most of America's mathematicians until the end of the century were individuals of means, and the case of Josiah Willard Gibbs is illustrative. Gibbs taught at Yale University for many years without pay. In a country where "success" was more often than not associated with financial prosperity, it is no wonder that scientists in America played virtually no role in government or public affairs, unlike their European counterparts. Even as late as 1902, the mathematician C. J. Keyser of Columbia University could write[5] that:

I know personally of six young men, five of whom have relinquished the pursuit of science and the (sixth) of whom told me only yesterday that he seriously contemplated doing so, all of them, for the reason that, as they allege, the university career furnishes either not at all, or too tardily a financial competence and consequent relief from practical condemnation to celibacy.

As for the American government, it consistently refused to support any national organization for science until after the Civil War, and it was only through the bequest of an Englishman that the Smithsonian Institution was finally established.[6] Often, in fact, Americans were better known abroad than at home. Nothing reflects so poorly upon the state of American science even towards the end of the century than a story J. J. Thomson[7] once told:

When a great university was founded in 1887, the newly elected President came over to Europe to find professors. He came to Cambridge and asked me if I could tell him of anyone who would make a good professor of molecular physics. I said, "You need not come to Europe for that; the best man you could get is an American, Willard Gibbs." "Oh," he said, "you mean Wolcott Gibbs," mentioning a prominent chemist. "No, I don't," I said, "I mean Willard Gibbs," and told him something of Gibbs' work. He sat thinking for a minute or two and then said, "I'd like you to give me another name. Willard Gibbs can't be a man of much personal magnetism or I should have heard of him."

Mathematicians in America could blame their lack of status on apathy and indifference. One mathematician assessing mathematical productivity in the United States echoed de Tocqueville's words when he noted that "educational and scientific activity shall come to be generally understood, and especially in proportion as we learn to value the things of mind, not merely for their utility, but for their spiritual worth."[8] The assessment was C. J. Keyser's, and in part he blamed the low level of productivity by American mathematicians before the turn of the century upon their isolation, saying that "in general there was no suspicion that, on the other side of the Atlantic, mathematics was a vast and growing science."[9]

Throughout the nineteenth century, mathematics, like the sciences generally, became more complex, more technical, more specialized. More formal training was required, more professionalization, and at first Americans clearly followed the pattern de Tocqueville had described in 1835. If Americans wanted to learn the newest techniques, to study the latest theories, they went to Europe, many to Germany, and to such centers for mathematics as Berlin and Göttingen. In rare instances, Europeans came to America. Perhaps no one was more influential for the future of American mathematics in this capacity than was J. J. Sylvester, whose arrival in America accompanied another significant development.[10] As a counterpart to the growing specialization of European science, advanced training at the graduate level was regarded increasingly as imperative. Consequently, following the examples of the great European schools like the *École Polytechnique* and the University of Berlin, America's first graduate school was founded in Baltimore.

In 1876 Johns Hopkins University opened, and one of its first great attractions was the English mathematician J. J. Sylvester. Both he and Johns Hopkins exerted a tremendous influence upon American mathematics, in part through the *American Journal of Mathematics*, edited by Sylvester and begun at Johns Hopkins in 1878. It was perhaps symptomatic that not only was the journal originally edited by an Englishman, but that to a great extent the journal's articles were written by foreigners. Since Johns Hopkins was primarily a graduate school, it served to encourage graduate studies at other U.S. universities. Two similar institutions were founded by the end of the century: Clark University in Worcester, Massachusetts, in 1889; and the University of Chicago in 1892, which was extremely influential in the Midwest.

But the single strongest factor in organizing and promoting mathematical research in America was the American Mathematical Society.[11] Its precursor, The New York Mathematical Club, had been founded in 1888, and at first was little more than a small group meeting at Columbia University. But soon the Mathematical Club became the New York Mathematical Society, publishing a monthly bulletin. In 1894 this organization was again transformed, becoming the American Mathematical Society with membership then at nearly four hundred. Bi-monthly meetings were held, summer meetings were scheduled around the country, and soon sections scattered from coast to coast were established. The first was the Chicago Section, chaired by E. H. Moore on April 24, 1897; five years later, in 1902, the San Francisco Section was chaired by Irving Stringham; and shortly thereafter, in 1906, the Southwestern Section was established in St. Louis by E. R. Hedrick. In terms of its societies, journals, and publishing mathematicians, mathematics in America had come a long way from its status early in the century, when arithmetic was still taught in the first year at Harvard College, and only became an entrance requirement in 1816. By the end of the nineteenth century, in many respects if not completely, the words of the French mathematician Laisant were in large measure true. As he surveyed the progress Americans had made in mathematics, he concluded[12] that:

Mathematics in all its forms and in all its parts is taught in numerous universities, treated in a multitude of publications, and cultivated by scholars who are in no respect inferior to their fellow mathematicians of Europe. It is no longer an object of import from the old world, but it has become an essential article of national production, and this production increases each day both in importance and in quantity.

Before turning to assess the character and significance of the contribution made by C. S. Peirce to American mathematics, in particular to various aspects of set theory, it is necessary to survey briefly the state of that art in Europe at the time. Above all, until about 1895 at least, the development of transfinite set theory was almost exclusively the work of the German mathematician Georg Cantor.

Georg Cantor (1845–1918)

Georg Cantor, creator of transfinite set theory, published a theorem in 1872 which brought him to the attention of the mathematical world, and which also marked the beginning of his work in

set theory. His theorem established the uniqueness of functional representations by trigonometric series over domains from which certain infinite sets of points could be excepted.[13] The only restriction limited the set of exceptional points to first species sets P, ones for which the nth derived set P_n was empty for some finite value of n. But in order to provide a satisfactory foundation for his proof, Cantor discovered that he was obliged to introduce a rigorous construction of the real numbers. He did so in terms of equivalence classes of infinite sequences of rational numbers subject to the Cauchy criterion for convergence, and was also led to formulate his Axiom of Continuity, which postulated the equivalence of the arithmetic and geometric continuums. In the same year, 1872, Richard Dedekind (1831–1916) published his construction of the real numbers in terms of his famous "cuts," and he did not fail to acknowledge the similar work Cantor had done in his paper on trigonometric series.[14] Cantor's unexpected results seem to have spurred his interest in the properties of continuous domains in general, and late in 1873 he discovered that the set of all real numbers was nondenumerable.[15] In 1879 he finally managed to publish a startling proof showing that any continuous space of n-dimensions could be mapped (though not continuously) in a one-to-one fashion onto the real line. Cantor was so unprepared for this discovery that it prompted one of his most oft-quoted remarks: "I see it, but I don't believe it."[16]

Cantor's first systematic presentation of his transfinite numbers was published in 1883. His *Grundlagen einer allgemeinen Mannichfaltigkeitslehre* was as much philosophy as it was mathematics,[17] a combination that was also to be characteristic of much of C. S. Peirce's research. In the *Grundlagen* Cantor introduced his transfinite ordinal numbers. He began by identifying two principles of generation. The first produced new ordinals by the successive addition of units, hence $1,2,3, \ldots, n, n + 1, \ldots$. The second principle was called upon to introduce a new number representing the totality of all ordinals generated by the first principle when such a sequence continued without coming to an end. For example, though it was not permissible to think of a last of all natural integers, one could posit a least number coming after *all* the natural numbers. This number Cantor defined as ω, and it represented the totality of all the positive integers in their natural order. It was then possible to apply the first principle of generation to produce higher transfinite ordinals: $\omega + 1$, $\omega + 2$, $\ldots$, $\omega + n$, $\ldots$. When this sequence continued without end, Cantor again called upon his second principle of generation to produce the least number following all those of the form $\omega + n$, namely the ordinal number 2ω, and so on. Later Cantor would define the second number class of such transfinite ordinals as the class $Z(\aleph_0)$, the totality of all order types α of well-ordered sets of cardinality $\aleph_0$. The power of this second number class $Z(\aleph_0)$ Cantor denoted by the second transfinite cardinal number $\aleph_1$.[18]

Cantor, of course, was not the only mathematician interested in the properties of infinite sets. In 1888, Richard Dedekind published a small pamphlet, *Was sind und was sollen die Zahlen*,[19] in which he introduced, among other things, the distinction between finite and infinite collections that has since become a classic:

A system S is said to be *infinite* when it is similar to a proper part of itself, in the contrary case S is said to be a *finite* system.

This definition is of particular interest for it seems that Peirce had been led to an equivalent distinction, even earlier, and for very different reasons.

In 1891 Cantor published his famous method of diagonalization, whereby it was possible to generate an unending sequence of sets of greater and greater cardinality.[20] In 1874 Cantor had shown only that the set of real numbers was nondenumerable. The result of 1891 was considerably more powerful, and impressively general, for he was able to show that for any exponent $\aleph$, the power $2^{\aleph} > \aleph$. If $\aleph_0$ be taken as the cardinality of the denumerable set of natural numbers, then $2^{\aleph_0}$ was a set of greater cardinality representing the set of all real numbers. Moreover, Cantor could show that there were sets of cardinality even greater than the real numbers, for example the set of all single-valued functions on the interval $(0, 1)$.

Between 1895 and 1897 Cantor's most ambitious and influential work appeared in the *Mathematische Annalen:* his "Beiträge zur Begrundung einer transfiniten Mengenlehre."[21] In Part I (1895) he presented his general theory of the order types of simply-ordered sets like the rationals taken in their natural order (type η), and the reals (type θ); in Part II (1897) he defined his transfinite cardinal numbers in terms of well-ordered sets, and explored in detail basic arithmetic properties of his transfinite numbers. He also took the opportunity to condemn the doctrine of infinitesimals in the recently published work of the Italian mathematician Giuseppe Veronese. Cantor had always been an ardent opponent of infinitesimals, and at one point called them the "infinitary cholera bacillus of mathematics."[22] Early in his career Cantor rejected the idea of infinitesimals, and when Mittag-Leffler asked if there might not be other kinds of numbers between the rational and real numbers, Cantor responded with an emphatic "no."[23] In 1887 Cantor published a proof of their logical impossibility, based not surprisingly upon the Archimedean character of what he called linear numbers, and some years later Peano published a similar proof against infinitesimals in his own journal, the *Rivista di matematica.*[24] To have admitted infinitesimals, it might be added, would have complicated greatly Cantor's continuum hypothesis, which asserted that the cardinality of the set of all real numbers, $2^{\aleph_0}$, was equal to that of his second number class, in other words, $2^{\aleph_0} = \aleph_1$. To allow infinitesimals in addition to the rationals and irrationals would have made this conjecture concerning the power of the continuum considerably more complicated.

By the end of the century, the status of Cantor's work was brought dramatically into question by discovery of the paradoxes of set theory. While Burali–Forti was the first to publish his paradox of the largest ordinal number, Cantor had discovered the paradoxes of both a largest ordinal and cardinal number even earlier, probably as early as 1895. Cantor sketched a proof for Dedekind in 1899, in which he concluded that it was a direct consequence of the paradoxical nature of the unending sequence of *all* cardinals that the continuum must be a set whose cardinality was one of Cantor's transfinite alephs.[25]

But in 1897 Burali–Forti drew a very different conclusion from his study of the collection of all ordinal numbers. Such a collection, he argued, must have an ordinal number δ greater than any ordinal in the collection. But if the set contained all ordinal numbers, then it must contain δ, and Burali–Forti was forced to the contradictory conclusion that $\delta > \delta$. From this he did not draw comfort, as did Cantor, in alleging that this was the key to solving much deeper problems of set theory. Instead, Burali-Forti concluded that mathematicians could only agree to abandon any hope of strict comparability between transfinite numbers.[26] In 1902 Bertrand Russell constructed a strictly logical paradox and shocked Frege by showing that there were certain antinomies inherently part of logic, and consequently of mathematics as a form of structured reason.[27]

In considering the paradoxes of set theory, in particular those of the greatest ordinal and cardinal numbers, Peirce agreed with Bertrand Russell that these were, properly speaking, questions of logic. The basic business of mathematics, for Peirce, was the formation of hypotheses.[28] In terms of set theory, this meant the determination of what grades of multitude between infinite collections were mathematically possible. And, as we shall see, Peirce drew from the paradox of the largest cardinal number a principle which he felt might help to resolve the question of the *true* nature of continuity.

Charles Sanders Peirce (1839–1914)

C. S. Peirce, the son of Benjamin Peirce, was born in Cambridge, Massachusetts, on September 10, 1839.[29] Benjamin Peirce, a professor of mathematics and natural philosophy at Harvard University, was careful to direct his son's schooling, and saw that young Charles had as rigorous a scientific education as he and the private schools of Boston could provide. When Peirce graduated from Harvard with an Sc. B. in chemistry, in 1863, he did so *summa cum laude*. But Peirce was not to go on immediately to devote himself to the study of pure science. His interests ran more to the study of method and logic, and in hopes of gaining more experience in the nature and

method of scientific investigation, he joined the U.S. Coast Survey. For more than thirty years Peirce remained with the Survey, and in addition to working on the nautical almanac, he conducted numerous pendulum experiments, was a special assistant in gravity research, and devoted a good deal of time to the observation of solar eclipses.

As for teaching, Johns Hopkins University made it possible for Peirce to lecture in logic from 1879 to 1884, and some of his earliest work of relevance to set theoretic problems dates from this period. In fact, in 1881, Peirce published a paper in the *American Journal of Mathematics*, "On the Logic of Number," in which (he was later always proud to emphasize) he had characterized the difference between finite and infinite sets well before Dedekind had done so in 1888.[30] Peirce asserted that Dedekind's *Was sind und was sollen die Zahlen* was doubtless influenced by his own paper, because Peirce had sent Dedekind a copy.[31] But the most interesting feature of Peirce's entire approach to mathematics was not the way in which it was like the research then being conducted in Europe, but in the ways it was unlike the approaches taken by Georg Cantor and Richard Dedekind to the problems of continuity and infinity.

Cantor, as we have seen, was motivated to study the continuum of real numbers as a result of his early study of the representation theorem for trigonometric series. Similarly, Dedekind's characterization of the continuum and his introduction of the now famous "Dedekind cut" to define the real numbers was also inspired by analysis. In trying to teach the basic elements of the differential calculus, particularly theorems involving limits, Dedekind realized that geometric intuition, though a guide, was not rigorously satisfactory. And so he turned to produce a purely arithmetic study of continuity and the irrational numbers.[32]

Peirce, on the contrary, took an entirely different approach. His inspiration was not analysis, and his interests were not in probing the foundations of mathematics in order to provide a certain, unshakable beginning from which function theory could proceed without difficulty. Instead, Peirce was led to study the mathematics of infinity, infinitesimals, and continuity as a result of his interests in logic and philosophy. In this difference lies the key to understanding why Peirce differed so markedly from Cantor and Dedekind in his approach to the problems of continuity and the infinite.

Peirce's first publication describing the difference between finite and infinite classes appeared in 1881, while he was lecturing in logic at Johns Hopkins. His paper[33] began with a definition (though insufficient) of continuity:

"A continuous system is one in which every quantity greater than another is also greater than some intermediate quantity greater than that other."

But since the rationals would be continuous under this definition, Peirce's description is inadequate, although it does represent a necessary feature of any continuum. Peirce, however, was only beginning his study of continuity at the time; the most interesting feature of his paper appeared towards the end, where he offered a distinction between finite and infinite collections. He announced that a set was finite if no one-to-one correspondence could be found between the set and any proper subset. Peirce's favorite example[34] was a syllogism which appeared in numerous equivalent forms throughout his mathematical and logical writings:

Every Hottentot kills a Hottentot,
No Hottentot is killed by more than one Hottentot,
Hence, every Hottentot is killed by a Hottentot.

The syllogism is true only if the set of Hottentots is finite. The form of the syllogism, Peirce noted, was due to De Morgan, who called it the *syllogism of transposed quantity*.[35] Thus Peirce's interest in the infinite was inspired by studies in logic and the consequences one might draw from the syllogism of transposed quantity.

In keeping with his interests, and in pushing his study of quantity, both finite and infinite, as far as he could, Peirce decided that a perfectly logical definition of continuity was needed, and in 1897, when he published "The Logic of Relatives" in *The Monist*, he wrote[36] that:

A perfectly satisfactory logical account of the conception of continuity is required. This in-

volves the definition of a certain kind of infinity, and in order to make that quite clear, it is requisite to begin by developing the logical doctrine of infinite multitude. This doctrine still remains, after the works of Cantor, Dedekind, and others, in an inchoate condition. For example, such a question remains unanswered as the following: is it, or is it not, logically possible for two collections to be so multitudinous that neither can be put into a one-to-one correspondence with a part or the whole of the other? To resolve this problem demands, not a mere application of logic, but a further development of the conception of logical possibility.

But what did Peirce mean by the need to define a certain kind of infinity before the concept of continuity could be accounted for logically? What was "inchoate" about the work of Cantor and Dedekind? Why was the comparability of cardinals, in Peirce's view, impossible to establish without developing further the concept of logical possibility? What, in fact, did Peirce mean by logical possibility? The answers to all these questions hinge on Peirce's view of the infinite, and upon a very important discovery, one he apparently made independently of Georg Cantor, and one for which Peirce was always, and justifiably so, very proud.

Peirce proved (though exactly when he did so for the first time is unclear) that the power of the set of all subsets of a given set is always greater than the power of the original set itself. In other words, for any exponent $\aleph$, $2^\aleph > \aleph$, a result, as Peirce put it, of "prime importance."[37] Beginning from the smallest infinite set, the set of all integers, he concluded that it was always possible to produce increasingly larger sets of greater and greater power. Peirce designated the collection of all integers "denumerable." The set of all real numbers comprised what he called the "first abnumeral" or the "primipostnumeral" multitude. The set of all subsets of the real numbers produced the "second abnumeral," or the "secundopostnumeral" multitude, and so on. Since one could always form from such sets the set of all subsets, Peirce noted that there could be no maximal multitude. But Peirce also commented that as for the second abnumeral, mathematics could offer no example of such a multitude, and added that in fact mathematics had no occasion to consider multitudes as great as this,[38] a comment that is somewhat puzzling, as we shall see, particularly in light of his construction of infinitesimals and his assertion that continua were greater in power than *any* postnumeral multitude.

In a letter to his friend E. H. Moore, Peirce commented[39] upon the significance of his discovery that there was no maximum multitude:

"Here we have a hint about continuity. . . . The continuum is a General. It is a General of relation. Every General is a continuum vaguely defined."

By a "General" Peirce seems to have meant that which was neither discrete nor definite, "General" as opposed to particular or to something completely specified. But what did Peirce see in all this to help solve the mystery of continuity?

Peirce argued that if a continuum did not contain all the points that it possibly could, then there would be gaps or discontinuities present.[40] Thus it was a problem of the utmost importance to determine what the maximum possible multitude *was* in order to determine the power of continua. But Peirce had already shown that there could be *no* such greatest possible multitude, that the process of forming power sets was unending, and that consequently it was a process that remained potential, indefinite. Similarly, if the continuum were to contain the maximum possible multitude of points, it had to be correspondingly potential, indefinite.

Since Peirce regarded the essence of multitudes to be their definiteness, thus making it possible to determine their powers or cardinalities, it was reasonable for him to assert that since the collection of all abnumerals was unending, potentially infinite, thus entirely indefinite, it could not properly be called a set. Or, in Peirce's terminology, it could not be called a multitude. Likewise, the elements constituting a continuum could not be regarded as comprising a set or multitude of objects. Thus the complete determination of continua was impossible, for Peirce regarded the concept as intrinsically potential, essentially general.[41]

Consequently, Peirce was led to reject Cantor's view that the geometric continuum was somehow made up of a multitude of points. Peirce realized that there were two features of such continua that had to be considered: one involved quantity, the other involved order. Cantor had published his analysis of what he called the simply-ordered type θ of the continuum of real numbers in 1895.[42] Peirce, however, disagreed on two counts. The collection of points comprising any continuum must be infinitely larger than any Cantor contemplated because, Peirce claimed, the real numbers R as defined by Cantor were grossly insufficient to account for the geometric continuum.[43] This was so, he argued, because of his discovery that the set of abnumerals was unending. Since the line must contain all points possible, and since the set R corresponded to the multitude represented by $2^{\aleph_0}$, it could not possibly, as a completed multitude, account for the nature of continuity. As for the question of the order of elements constituting a continuum, Peirce suggested that something like the proper idea was approximated if between every pair of rational numbers one inserted a sequence of irrational numbers. Between any two irrationals of this sequence one could pack yet another such sequence, and so on, without end. Thus Peirce thought it was possible that between any two points of the continuum, however close, one could always pack sets of points of higher and higher multitude. The continuum would eventually be "cemented together," and not by virtue of discrete points.[44]

Peirce illustrated his case by imagining a series of photographs.[45] No matter how close the intervals, no motion will appear in any of them. But our perception of motion in time shows that time must be more than a succession of instants. More than single, isolated point "instants" must be present to our consciousness. What is this something more? Peirce claimed that (1) in a sensible time there exists room for *any* multitude of distinct instants. (2) The instants are so close together they merge and cannot be distinct. And this view of time and its continuity greatly influenced Peirce's view of the continuum and the logical status of continuity. Just as parts of time merged to lose their identity, so too the points of a line. If continuity consisted of nothing but a special type of serial order, he argued that two continuous lines thought to intersect might actually "slip through" each other, this presumably being possible wherever spaces between one object and its "next" in the serial ordering on each line might occur.[46] This certainly suggests that Peirce had a very different way of thinking about continuity and serial order than did Cantor.

Peirce, as he put it himself, took the very word *continuity* to mean that the instants of time or the points of a line were everywhere "welded together."[47] As evidence of this, he seems to have been content to argue that its justification was nothing more than common sense. Peirce concluded that the instants of time did not constitute a multitude (or set, whose elements had to be distinct and definite). In fact, the collection of instants in any continuum of time had to be *more* than any multitude.

To illustrate his idea of continuity, Peirce outlined a procedure which he called interpolation on the unit interval, and which involved decimal representations given with only the digits 0 and 1. At step (I), there was only one interpolation, at step (II) there were 2, at step (III), there were four, at step (IV) there were 8, and at step (N) there would be 2^{N-1}. Schematically:

STEP (I)
0.000 . . .   .100 . . .   1.000 . . .
(II)   .010 . . .   .110 . . .
(III)   .001 . . .   .011 . . .   .101 . . .   .111 . . .

Here Peirce found, as he put it, a "premonition of continuity."[48] In carrying out this procedure, a nondenumerably infinite number of interpolations would be made. Somehow this process was to help Peirce explain how the continuum was able, in his words, to "stick together."[49] No finite collection could ever "stick together" in any order, nor could any denumerably infinite collection if considered in any well-ordered form. The difficulty in describing the continuity of the real line, Peirce believed, reduced to the fact that numbers *per se* could never account for continuity.[50] Numbers expressed nothing but the order, he believed, of discrete objects. Nothing discrete could possibly be multitudinous enough to account for the continuum.

For example, Peirce noted that in supposing the countable collection of the set of rational points to be completely present on the line, one was in effect supposing also the collection of irrational points in the sense that the irrationals could be considered as interpolated between the rationals.[51] Hence the denumerable set of rationals carried with it the existence of a nondenumerable collection of points, namely the first abnumeral multitude of irrational numbers. In exactly the same way, said Peirce, the system of irrational points on a line led to a secundo-postnumeral collection of points interpolated between the irrationals. This secundo-postnumeral collection for Peirce involved his infinitesimals, and it is possible to understand the role they played more clearly by returning for a moment to his diagram of decimal interpolations.

In a letter to M.F.C.S. Schiller of 1906, Peirce explained that by a Leibnizian infinitesimal of the first order he meant an assumed quantity smaller than any finite positive quantity.[52] It was the *first* quantity after the sequence .1, .01, .001, ... Peirce believed it was impossible to prove that there was *no* such quantity. In fact, he believed his infinitesimals were given an imprimatur of sorts by nature, since he took their existence to be necessary for physics.[53] To support this claim of the physical reality of infinitesimals, Peirce referred to the experience of memory. The perception of the flow of time must extend, he said, beyond a single instant. Yet Peirce could not see how such phenomena could be satisfactorily explained unless time were believed to be strictly infinitesimal. Moreover, there were reasons from physics which also established the necessary existence of infinitesimal magnitudes. In a letter written in 1908 to P. E. B. Jourdain,[54] Peirce struck up a theme which Cantor had sketched, but never developed, in a short article of 1885. Cantor had conjectured that in order to explain satisfactorily the phenomena of nature, one had to suppose two sorts of monads, material and aetherial. He conjectured that the power of the set of all material monads was denumerable, of cardinality $\aleph_0$, while the set of aetherial monads was equipotent with the second cardinal, $\aleph_1$. Peirce applied this idea in order to explain how matter could act on the brain to produce thought. Peirce posited two fluids, one vortex of matter-monads, and an infinitely subtler vortex of soul-monads, where the diameters of the soul-monads were to be taken as infinitesimals of infinite order, which Peirce felt was quite appropriate for the character of soul-monads. This theory was given the name of the "introvortical theory."[55] It all helped to convince Peirce that with physical counterparts for his logical infinitesimals, there was pragmatic justification for arguing their validity.

Peirce's most important reason for insisting that his infinitesimals were acceptable involved their self-consistency. Logically, being non-contradictory, there was no reason not to admit them into mathematics. Though Peirce did not undertake a careful arithmetic investigation of the properties of his infinitesimals, nor did he undertake any investigation of non-archimedean systems in general, he was a proto-proponent of nonstandard analysis in believing that there was perhaps more to understanding the nature of continuity than the rationals and irrationals together could manage to explain.

To make Peirce's point as clear as possible, it may be helpful, in closing, to sketch his reasons for arguing that the rationals and irrationals together were insufficient to account for the nature of continuity. While Cantor and Dedekind regarded the irrational numbers as completing the rationals, and thus conferring completeness on the real numbers, Peirce saw the relation between rationals and irrationals somewhat differently. He concluded that there was a kind of "nextness" in the reals which actually constituted a breach of continuity.[56] Suppose, he argued, that we do have a clear idea of a sequence of real numbers. If we have a clear idea of their order, it can be assumed that any set of objects sufficiently multitudinous can be similarly ordered. Assume each of these objects to be replaced with a sequence of points, similar in order to the real numbers on the open interval $(0, 1)$. But there is no reason to stop here, and Peirce went on to replace each point of such series by yet other series, and so on, without end. In his own words:[57]

The result is that we have altogether eliminated points. We have a series of series of series, *ad infinitum*. Every part, however closely designated, is still a series and divisible into further series. There are no points in such a line. There is no exact boundary between any parts.

It would be easier to interpret the significance Peirce attached to his infinitesimals for mathematics had he ever commented explicitly upon Cantor's and Dedekind's axioms of continuity, which hypothesized the equivalence of the standard Archimedean arithmetic continuum and the geometric continuum. But all we have is Peirce's allegation that the real numbers were insufficient to account for the continuity of space and time. As for analysis, however, it never had need to consider multitudes greater in magnitude than that of the first abnumeral, which meant that the set of real numbers was enough for the interests of analysis and presumably for all of mathematics.[58]

Peirce wanted to explore the logical boundaries of the possible in terms of the infinitely large and the infinitely small, and found no logical contradictions or constraints in either conception. Since his interests were primarily philosophical, it is perhaps easier to understand why he never submitted his ideas to a more searching mathematical analysis than he did.

Ultimately Peirce's infinitesimals remained vague rather than rigorously defined mathematical entities. He never suggested how they might be useful in analysis. But then Peirce's interests had never been inclined towards analysis. From the very beginning he had been inspired by the purely logical implications of the syllogism of transposed quantity, and the logic of relations. Thus, unlike Cantor, he was not concerned to develop the arithmetic properties of his ideas, since their existence as numbers was not for him of great consequence. He was interested in illuminating a deep philosophical problem of long standing, namely that of the continuum, and he felt that conceptually he had found an approach to the subject that was the most satisfying of all.

Finally, how can we now draw all of these ideas together in order to interpret Peirce's claim that "the continuum is a General," meaning that it could not be defined as a set in Cantor's sense of a collection of distinct elements, and Peirce's statement that "Infinity is nothing but a peculiar twist given to generality"?[59] Peirce took generality to involve the potential infinite, in that anything not general, anything specific, was completed in some sense or other. He also took infinity to be a potentiality, something never completed, and thus it too reposed upon generality. Reasoning about such matters, he noted with perhaps too little emphasis, was always exceedingly puzzling. Almost all metaphysicians, and even mathematicians, he added, had fallen into pitfalls concerning the infinite where the "ground was spongy."[60] Trouble inevitably stemmed from quantifiers like "all and every," but if one were always certain to determine *how* objects in question were to be selected, he believed that erroneous reasoning could easily be avoided. The trouble with the collection of all abnumerable multitudes was simply that it could never be considered as completed. It was self-generating, without end. Such collections were so great that they were no longer discrete, and not being complete, no definite determination of their magnitude could be given. They were potential and as such, general. In the same way the line was general, indeterminate, since between any of its points, Peirce imagined that more could be packed representing supermultitudinous collections. To quote Peirce directly:[61]

Such supermultitudinous collections stick together by logical necessity. Its constituent individuals are no longer distinct, or independent. They are not subjects but phases expressive of the properties of the continuum.

Peirce offered a graphic illustration. Suppose a collection of blades were to cut the line. So long as they did not comprise a supermultitudinous collection, the line would be cut up into bits, each of which was still a line. Peirce therefore urged mathematicians to discard all analytical theories about lines, and recommended that they begin from his view, a synthetic point of view.[62] By a simple mental experiment, he believed he had shown that the line refused to be cut up into points. But even if mathematicians refused to accept his arguments, Peirce insisted that only one thing mattered: his idea of continuity and of in-

finitesimals involved no contradiction. In closing, he warned:[63]

I am careful not to call supermultitudinous collections multitudes. Multitudes imply an independence of the individuals of one another which is not found in supermultitudinous sets. Here the elements are cemented together, they become indistinct.

Here Peirce had reached the potentiality, the generality that he had earlier said was essential if one were to understand properly the structure of continuity. For Peirce, the essence of continuity depended upon the supermultitudinousness of the elements of the line, and their "intrinsic arrangement which is inseparable from the particular grade of multitude in which those phenomena of cohesion are found."[64]

It is now possible to see what Peirce meant when he wrote to Paul Carus, editor of *The Monist*, to say that at last he had seen where Cantor had gone wrong.[65] Continuity could not come from any collection of points because points were discrete, determined, and if anything, points represented *discontinuities* when removed from the line. In summarizing his view for Judge Francis Russell in 1909, Peirce interpreted the essence of continuity in terms of the potential and completely general nature of the ideas involved. "As to a straight line not having any definition proper, it is demonstrable that it cannot be, properly speaking, defined."[66]

If we may take "properly speaking" to mean "mathematically speaking," then there was not much Peirce could hope to offer in such a view to his mathematical colleagues. But it is also true that he did not feel mathematics needed to go so far, apparently, in the analysis of the continuum as he had gone. Peirce was interested in pushing the logical consequences of his ideas to their ultimate conclusions for the sake of philosophy, but analysis, he seemed to say, could stop at something less.

For Peirce, such ideas justified themselves as a matter of instinct, of common sense.[67] He had always held that his intuitive understanding of the continuum, or the continuity of space and time, were the ultimate guides in his analysis of continuity. Nothing could have been further from the aims of Weierstrassian analysis, which sought to reject all such intuitions and aimed to base mathematics upon more certain foundations of arithmetic. Weierstrass had constructed examples of everywhere continuous, nowhere differentiable functions to show the inadequacy of intuition. But Peirce was not convinced, and once even commented that Weierstrassian mathematics, in showing a distrust of intuition, betrayed an ignorance of fundamental principles of logic.[68] Peirce followed his intuitions as far as they would carry him, and it may have been this feature of his thinking, as much as his interest in philosophical and metaphysical arguments, that prevented his being more readily accepted by those of his contemporaries even aware of his work.

ics of the nineteenth century, could have pursued the problem of continuity in the way he did. Out of touch with much of European mathematics, Peirce considered infinitesimals with an unprejudiced eye to affirm not only their existence, but to argue as well that the arithmetic continuum of real numbers was only a very incomplete picture of the actual richness of any continuum. Working in obscurity, penury, and isolation, he nevertheless saw, if only a glimmer, what later generations might be more willing to accept. In light of current research in non-standard analysis, it is now possible to consider, more rigorously than did Peirce, alternatives to the traditional nineteenth-century view of the standard Archimedean continuum.

Conclusion

Peirce once said that it was the business of science and mathematics to guess. For mathematics this reduced to the fabrication of hypotheses to be tested for logical self-consistency.[69] If no contradictions could be deduced, then the hypothesis, or the mathematical theory in question, stood as acceptable. This was the basis upon which Peirce argued most persuasively for the respectability of his ideas concerning infinitesimals and continuity. Kepler, to Peirce's mind, was the greatest guesser the history of science had ever seen. But in terms of American mathematics at the turn of the century, Peirce may easily have been an equally impressive guesser, producing the mathematical hypothesis of infinitesimals.

Kepler lacked sufficient mathematical techniques and a theory of gravitation to establish a convincing explanation of his laws, deficiencies Isaac Newton would later remedy. In much the same way, Peirce lacked sufficient techniques to produce a rigorous theory of non-Archimedean systems. But his hypotheses were eventually vindicated, in the twentieth century, by mathematicians like Schmieden, Laugwitz, Robinson, and Luxemburg.[70] Perhaps until the middle of this century, only a mathematician as interested in philosophy as was Peirce, and as isolated from the prevailing assumptions of established mathemat-

Notes

The single major reference cited below is C. Eisele, ed.: *The New Elements of Mathematics by Charles S. Peirce* (The Hague: Mouton, 1976); this reference is cited as Charles S. Peirce: *Mathematical Papers*.

1. Peirce: *Mathematical Papers,* volume 3, 109.
2. No recent study of mathematics in the United States has appeared. For two studies of an introductory sort, see G. A. Miller: *Historical Introduction to Mathematical Literature* (Macmillan, New York, 1921), and D. E. Smith and J. Ginsburg: *A History of Mathematics in America before 1900* (The Mathematical Association of America, New York, 1934).
3. Alexis de Tocqueville: *Democracy in America,* trans. H. Reeve (D. Appleton, New York, 1904), volume 2, 518.
4. R. H. Shryock: "American Indifference to Basic Science during the Nineteenth Century," *Archives internationales d'histoire des sciences,* 28 (1948–1949) 3–18.
5. C. J. Keyser: "Mathematical Productivity in the United States," *Educational Review,* 24 (November, 1902) 356.
6. For recent studies of Smithson and the history of the Smithsonian Institution, consult L. Carmichael: *James Smithson and the Smithsonian Story* (Putman, New York, 1965), and

W. Karp: *The Smithsonian Institution* (Smithsonian Institution, Washington, 1965). The significance of the Civil War for the fortunes of American Science has been studied by a number of historians, including I. B. Cohen: "Science and the Civil War," *Technology Review*, 48 (January, 1946), number 3; D. J. Struik: *Yankee Science in the Making* (Little, Brown, Boston, 1948), in particular Chapter XII in which Struik discusses the Civil War and the Morrill Act, pages 355–357; and A. H. Durpee: *Science in the Federal Government. A History of Policies and Activities to 1940* (Harvard University Press, Cambridge, 1957), especially Chapter IV, "The Fulfillment of Smithson's Will," and Chapter VII, "The Civil War."

7. J. J. Thomson: *Recollections and Reflections* (Macmillan, New York, 1937) 185–186.

8. Keyser (1902), 346. Miller also pointed directly to the major problem in America: "There is too much mathematical indifference," G. A. Miller: "American Mathematics," *Popular Science Monthly*, 79 (November, 1911), 461.

9. Keyser (1902), 347.

10. G. A. Miller (1911), 463, and Miller (1921), 30–32.

11. Keyser (1902), 350–352; Miller (1921), 33–35.

12. C. A. Laisant: *La mathématique, philosophie-enseignement* (G. Carré et C. Naud, Paris, 1898), translated by G. A. Miller (1911), 459.

13. G. Cantor: "Über die Ausdehnung eines Satzes aus der Theorie der trigonometrischen Reihen," *Math. Ann.*, 5 (1872) 123–132.

14. R. Dedekind: *Stetigkeit und irrationale Zahlen* (second edition, Vieweg, Braunschweig, 1892), translated by W. W. Beman: "Continuity and Irrational Numbers," *Essays on the Theory of Numbers*, (Dover, New York, 1963).

15. G. Cantor: "Über eine Eigenschaft des Inbegriffes aller reellen algebraischen Zahlen," *J. Reine Angew. Math.*, 77 (1874), 258–262. Consult as well the letters Cantor wrote to Dedekind in this period: E. Noether and J. Cavaillès, eds.: *Briefwechsel Cantor–Dedekind* (Hermann, Paris, 1937).

16. "Je le vois, mais je ne le crois pas," Cantor to Dedekind in a letter of June 29, 1877, *Briefwechsel Cantor–Dedekind*, 34.

17. G. Cantor: *Grundlagen einer allgemeinen Mannichfaltigkeitslehre. Ein mathematisch-philosophischer Versuch in der Lehre des Unendlichen* (B. G. Teubner, Leipzig, 1883).

18. G. Cantor: "Beiträge zur Begründung der transfiniten Mengenlehre," (Part I) *Math. Ann.*, 46 (1895) 481–512, translated by P. E. B. Jourdain: *Contributions to the Founding of the Theory of Transfinite Numbers* (Dover, New York, 1955), in particular section 6, 103–110; and (Part II) *Math. Ann.*, 49 (1897) 207–246, also translated by Jourdain. See in particular Cantor's discussion of the numbers of the second number class $Z(\aleph_0)$ in section 15 of Part II, in Jourdain's translation pages 160–169.

19. R. Dedekind: *Was sind und was sollen die Zahlen?*, translated by W. W. Beman: "The Nature and Meaning of Numbers," *Essays on the Theory of Numbers*, (Dover, New York, 1963), 31–115, in particular page 63.

20. G. Cantor: "Über eine elementare Frage der Mannigfaltigkeitslehre," *Jahresbericht der Deutschen Mathematiker-Vereinigung*, 1 (1891) 75–78.

21. Cantor (1895), in particular sections 9 and 11, and Cantor (1897).

22. Cantor in a letter to the Italian mathematician Vivanti, December 13, 1893, in H. Meschkowski: "Aus den Briefbüchern Georg Cantors," *Arch. History Exact Sci.*, 2 (1965) 505.

23. Mittag–Leffler raised the question in a letter to Cantor of February 7, 1883; consult H. Meschkowski: *Probleme des Unendlichen. Werk und Leben Georg Cantors*, (Vieweg, Braunschweig, 1967), 234. Cantor argued the inconsistency of infinitesimals in G. Cantor: "Mitteilungen zur Lehre vom Transfiniten," *Zeitschrift für Philosophie und philosophische Kritik*, 91 (1887) 81–125; 92 (1888), 240–265; in particular section VI.

24. G. Peano: "Dimostrazione dell'impossibilità di segmenti infinitesimi costanti," *Riv. Mat.*, 2 (1892) 58–62.

25. In 1899 Cantor corresponded with Dedekind on the subject of the paradoxes of set theory

and possible remedies. These were included in a poorly edited form in the edition of Cantor's collected works by E. Zermelo: *Georg Cantor. Gesammelte Abhandlungen mathematischen und philosophischen Inhalts* (J. Springer, Berlin, 1932), 443–450. See as well I. Grattan-Guinness: "The Rediscovery of the Cantor–Dedekind Correspondence," *Jahresbericht der Deutschen Mathematiker-Vereinigung*, 76 (1974) 104–139.

26. C. Burali–Forti: "Una questione sui numeri transfiniti," *Rend. Circ. Mat. Palermo*, 11 (1897), 154–164.

27. See Frege's discussion of the impact Russell's letter had upon his *Grundgesetze*, and Frege's attempt to repair the damage, in Appendix II to G. Frege: *Grundgesetze der Arithmetik, begriffsschriftlich abgeleitet*, II (Verlag Hermann Pohle, Jena, 1903), 127–143.

28. Peirce commented upon the relevance of hypotheses in mathematics in his correspondence, and in papers like "On Quantity," and "On Multitude," in *Mathematical Papers*, 3, pages 41 and 73, respectively. For letters in which Peirce discussed such matters, see those to Georg Cantor (December 21, 1900), to F. W. Frankland (May 8, 1906), to William James (December 28, 1909), and to E. H. Moore (November 21, 1904), all in *Mathematical Papers*, 3, pages 769, 785, 875, 916, respectively.

29. For studies of Peirce's life and work, consult C. Eisele: "Charles Sanders Peirce," *Dictionary of Scientific Biography*, ed. C. C. Gillispie (New York, 1974), X, 482–488; M. G. Murphey: *The Development of Peirce's Philosophy* (Cambridge, Mass., 1961); and P. P. Wiener and F. H. Young, eds.: *Studies in the Philosophy of Charles Sanders Peirce* (Cambridge, Mass., 1952).

30. C. S. Peirce: "On the Logic of Number," *Amer. J. Math.*, 4 (1881) 85–95, in *Collected Papers of Charles Sanders Peirce*, eds. C. Hartshorne and P. Weiss (Harvard University Press, Cambridge, Mass., 1960) volume III, 158–170. Hereafter, this edition of Peirce's papers will be cited as *Collected Works*, and the convention of citing *paragraphs* rather than pages will be followed. Thus the article "On the Logic of Number" would be cited as Peirce: *Collected Works*, 3.252–288.

31. Peirce in a letter to P. E. B. Jourdain, December 5, 1908, in *Mathematical Papers 3*, 883, and in the article "Multitude," in appendices to volume *3*, page 1117. Refer as well to a letter Peirce sent to the Editor of *Science* on March 16, 1900, "Infinitesimals," in *Collected Works*, 3.564.

32. Dedekind discusses his motives in the preface to his essay *Stetigkeit und irrationale Zahlen*, pages 1–3 in the translation cited in note 14.

33. C. S. Peirce: *Collected Works*, 3.256.

34. Peirce gave the Hottentot version of the syllogism in his letter to Georg Cantor of December 23, 1900: *Mathematical Papers*, 3, 772. In his paper of 1881, Peirce used Texans: *Collected Works*, 3.288.

35. A. De Morgan: "On the Syllogism and the Logic of Relatives," *Cambridge Philosophical Transactions*, 10 (1860).

36. C. S. Peirce: "The Logic of Relatives," *The Monist* 7 (1897) 161–217, in *Collected Works*, 3.526.

37. C. S. Peirce: *Mathematical Papers*, 3, 51. See as well Peirce's letters to Georg Cantor (December 23, 1900), and to F. W. Frankland (May 8, 1906), in *Mathematical Papers*, 3, 777 and 785, respectively. Peirce also discusses transfinite exponentiation and power sets in what appears to have been a draft for a lecture on "Multitude and Number," probably from 1897. Turn in particular to the section on "The Primipostnumeral," *Collected Works*, 4.200–212.

38. This suggests that Peirce was either unaware of, or did not fully appreciate, Cantor's paper of 1891, in which he showed that the set of all single-valued functions on the unit interval was greater in power than the set of all real numbers. G. Cantor (1891), cited above, note 20.

39. Peirce in a letter to E. H. Moore, March 20, 1902, in *Mathematical Papers*, 3, 925. For a discussion of "Generals," consult C. S. Peirce: "Notes on Symbolic Logic and Mathematics," in *Collected Works*, 3.642.

40. Refer to the note to pages 880, 881 of volume 3, *Mathematical Papers*.

41. *Mathematical Papers*, 3, 62, and Peirce in a letter to Francis Russell, April 15, 1909, *Mathematical Papers*, 3, 981.

42. Cantor (1895), cited in note 18 above.

43. C. S. Peirce, *Mathematical Papers*, 3, 122.

44. *Mathematical Papers*, 3, 98.

45. C. S. Peirce, "On Multitudes," *Mathematical Papers*, 3, 59.

46. *Mathematical Papers*, 3, 60–61.

47. *Mathematical Papers*, 3, 61–62.

48. *Mathematical Papers*, 3, 87–88.

49. *Mathematical Papers*, 3, 88.

50. C. S. Peirce, *Collected Works*, 3.568, and *Mathematical Papers*, 3, 93–94.

51. C. S. Peirce, "Multitude and Continuity," *Mathematical Papers*, 3, 94; and the draft of an addition Peirce meant for an article in the *Monist*, as given in the note to Peirce's letter to P. E. B. Jourdain, May 24, 1908, *Mathematical Papers*, 3, 880–881.

52. Peirce to F. C. S. Schiller, September 10, 1906, *Mathematical Papers*, 3, 989.

53. Peirce to C. J. Keyser, October 1–7, 1908, and to Josiah Royce, May 28, 1902, *Mathematical Papers*, 3, 898 and 957, respectively.

54. In addition to Peirce's letters to Keyser and Royce cited in note 53, turn to Peirce's "The Question of Infinitesimals," *Mathematical Papers*, 3, 123–124, and his article on "Infinitesimals," *Collected Works*, 3.570.

55. C. S. Peirce to C. J. Keyser, October 1–7, 1908, *Mathematical Papers*, 3, 896.

56. C. S. Peirce: "On Continuous Series and the Infinitesimal," and "The Question of Infini-tesimals," *Mathematical Papers*, 3, pages 125, 121–122 respectively.

57. C. S. Peirce, *Mathematical Papers*, 3, 126.

58. C. S. Peirce, *Mathematical Papers*, 3, 85.

59. C. S. Peirce to William James, June 8, 1903, in *Collected Works*, 8.268.

60. C. S. Peirce, *Mathematical Papers*, 3, 79.

61. C. S. Peirce, *Mathematical Papers*, 3, 95.

62. C. S. Peirce, *Mathematical Papers*, 3, 96.

63. C. S. Peirce, *Mathematical Papers*, 3, 87–89.

64. C. S. Peirce, *Mathematical Papers*, 3, 98–99.

65. C. S. Peirce to Paul Carus, August 17, 1899, *Mathematical Papers*, 3, 792.

66. C. S. Peirce to Francis Russell, April 15, 1909, *Mathematical Papers*, 3, 981.

67. C. S. Peirce, "On Quantity, with Special Reference to Collectional and Mathematical Infinity," *Mathematical Papers*, 3, section 20, page 56.

68. C. S. Peirce to Francis Russell, September 18, 1908, *Mathematical Papers*, 3, 968.

69. C. S. Peirce to C. J. Keyser, October 1–7, 1908, *Mathematical Papers*, 3, 893.

70. C. Schmieden and D. Laugwitz; "Eine Erweiterung der Infinitesimalrechnung," *Math. Z.*, 69 (1958) 1–39; W. A. J. Luxemburg: *Non-Standard Analysis* (Lecture Notes, California Institute of Technology, Pasadena, 1962; rev. ed. 1964); A. Robinson: *Non-Standard Analysis* (North-Holland, Amsterdam, 1966); W. A. J. Luxemburg and A. Robinson: *Contributions to Non-Standard Analysis* (North-Holland, Amsterdam, 1972).

Proof

Philip J. Davis and Reuben Hersh

Philip J. Davis and Reuben Hersh are introduced in Part Two of this volume.

Is mathematics synonymous with the notion of proof? If the two ideas are not identical it is difficult for most modern mathematicians to conceive of mathematics in the absence of proof. While a proof may not be a formal demonstration, the implication that mathematical fact A must follow from facts E, F, and G is essentially what mathematics is about. In Part One of Volume I the article by Richard J. Gillings indicated that even if the Egyptians did not write proofs as did the Greeks, they had a reasonable, well-defined format for suggesting why a mathematical procedure is valid. What the Egyptians had were proofs. It is important to mention the Egyptians in this regard since historians of mathematics have usually asserted that the ancient Egyptians had no notion of proof. The inference is that the Egyptians made some observations and then formulated general rules from these observations. Yet if we are to believe Gillings's examples, this inference seems to be false. Even the Egyptians wished to have some plausible demonstration for the validity of their mathematics.

Thus if the two notions of proof and mathematics are not the same, then they are virtually impossible to separate. To understand one requires some comprehension of the other, and it is the nature of proof that Davis and Hersh discuss in this essay. In developing an understanding of what constitutes a proof in mathematics the reader will have a better grasp of mathematics itself.

THE ASSERTION HAS been made that mathematics is uniquely characterized by something known as "proof." The first proof in the history of mathematics is said to have been given by Thales of Miletus (600 B.C.). He proved that the diameter divides a circle into two equal parts. Now this is a statement which is so simple that it appears self-evident. The genius of the act was to understand that a proof is possible and necessary. What makes mathematical proof more than mere pedantry is its application in situations where the statements made are far less transparent. In the opinion of some, the name of the mathematics game is proof; no proof, no mathematics. In the opinion of others, this is nonsense; there are many games in mathematics.

To discuss what proof is, how it operates, and what it is for, we need to have a concrete example of some complexity before us; and there is nothing better than to take a look at what undoubtedly is the most famous theorem in the history of mathematics as it appears in the most famous book in the history of mathematics. We allude to the Pythagorean Theorem, as it occurs in Proposition 47, Book I of Euclid's Elements (300 B.C.). We quote it in the English version given by Sir

Source: Philip J. Davis and Reuben Hersh, "Proof," in *The Mathematical Experience* (Boston: Birkhäuser, 1981), pp. 147–152. Reprinted by permission of Birkhäuser. (References omitted.)

Thomas Heath. The in-text numbers in brackets are references to previously established results or to "common notions."

Proposition 47.   In right-angled triangles the square on the side subtending the right angle is equal to the squares on the sides containing the right angle.

Let ABC be a right-angled triangle having the angle BAC right;

I say that the square on BC is equal to the squares on BA, AC.

For let there be described on BC the square BDEC, and on BA, AC the squares GB, HC; [1.46] through A let AL be drawn parallel to either BD or CE, and let AD, FC be joined.

Then, since each of the angles BAC, BAG is right, it follows that with a straight line BA, and at the point A on it, the two straight lines AC, AG not lying on the same side make the adjacent angles equal to two right angles; therefore CA is in a straight line with AG. [1.14]

For the same reason BA is also in a straight line with AH.

And, since the angle DBC is equal to the angle FBA; for each is right: let the angle ABC be added to each; therefore the whole angle DBA is equal to the whole angle FBC. [C.N. 2]

And, since DB is equal to BC, and FB to BA, the two sides AB, BD are equal to the two sides FB, BC respectively, and the angle ABD is equal to the angle FBC: therefore the base AD is equal to the base FC, and the triangle ABD is equal to the triangle FBC. [1.4]

Now the parallelogram BL is double of the triangle ABD, for they have the same base BD and are in the same parallels BD, AL. [1.41]

And the square GB is double of the triangle FBC, for they again have the same base FB and are in the same parallels FB, GC. [1.41]

[But the doubles of equals are equal to one another.]

Therefore the parallelogram BL is also equal to the square GB.

Similarly, if AE, BK be joined, the parallelogram CL can also be proved equal to the square HC; therefore the whole square BDEC is equal to the two squares GB, HC. [C.N. 2]

And the square BDEC is described on BC, and the squares GB, HC on BA, AC.

Therefore the square on the side BC is equal to the squares on the sides BA, AC.

Therefore etc. Q.E.D.

Now, assuming that we have read Euclid up to Proposition 47, and assuming we are able intellectually to get through this material, what are we to make of it all? Perhaps the most beautiful recorded reaction is that ascribed to Thomas Hobbes (1588–1679) by John Aubrey in his "Brief Lives":

He was 40 yeares old before he looked on Geometry; which happened accidentally. Being in a Gentleman's Library, Euclid's Elements lay open, and 'twas the 47 *El. libri* I. He read the Proposition. *By G—*, sayd he (he would now and then sweare an emphaticall Oath by way of emphasis) *this is impossible!* So he reads the Demonstration of it, which referred him back to such a Proposition; which proposition he read. That referred him back to another, which he also read. *Et sic deinceps* [and so on] that at last he was demonstratively convinced of that trueth. This made him in love with Geometry.

What appears initially as unintuitive, dubious, and somewhat mysterious ends up, after a certain kind of mental process, as gloriously true. Euclid, one likes to think, would have been proud of Hobbes and would use him as Exhibit A for the vindication of his long labors in compiling the Elements. Here is the proof process, discovered and promulgated by Greek mathematics, in the service of validation and certification. Now that the statement has been proved, we are to understand that the statement is true beyond the shadow of a doubt.

The backward referral to previous propositions, alluded to by Hobbes, is characteristic of the method of proof, and as we know, this can't go on forever. It stops with the so-called axioms and definitions. Whereas the latter are mere linguistic conventions, the former represent rock bottom self-evident facts upon which the whole structure is to rest, held together by the bolts of logic.

Also characteristic of the method is the considerable degree of abstraction that has occurred in the refinement of such concepts as triangle, right angle, square, etc. The figure itself appears here as a very necessary adjunct to the verbalization. In Euclid's presentation we cannot wholly follow the argumentation without the figure, and unless we are strong enough to imagine the figure in our mind's eye, we would be reduced to supplying our own figure if the author had not done it for us. Notice also that the language of the proof has a formal and severely restricted quality about it. This is not the language of history, nor of drama, nor of day to day life; this is language that has been sharpened and refined so as to serve the precise needs of a precise but limited intellectual goal.

One response to this material was recorded by the poet Edna Millay, in her line, "Euclid alone has looked on Beauty bare." A shudder might even run down our spines if we believe that with a few magic lines of proof we have compelled all the right triangles in the universe to behave in a regular Pythagorean fashion.

Abstraction, formalization, axiomatization, deduction—here are the ingredients of proof. And the proofs in modern mathematics, though they may deal with different raw material or lie at a deeper level, have essentially the same feel to the student or the researcher as the one just quoted.

Further reading of Euclid's masterpiece brings up additional issues. Notice that in the figure certain lines, e.g., BK, AL seem to be extraneous to a minimal figure drawn as an expression of the theorem itself. Such a figure is illustrated here: a right angled triangle with squares drawn upon each of its three sides. The extraneous lines, which in high school are often called "construction lines," complicate the figure, but form an essential part of the deductive process. They reorganize the figure into subfigures and the reasoning takes place precisely at this sublevel.

Now, how does one know where to draw these lines so as to reason with them? It would seem that these lines are accidental or fortuitous. In a sense this is true and constitutes the genius or the trick of the thing. Finding the lines is part of finding a proof, and this may be no easy matter. With experience come insight and skill at finding proper construction lines. One person may be more skillful at it than another. There is no guar-anteed way to arrive at a proof. This sad truth is equally rankling to schoolchildren and to skillful professionals. Mathematics as a whole may be regarded as a systematization of just those questions which have been pursued successfully.

Mathematics, then, is the subject in which there are proofs. Traditionally, proof was first met in Euclid; and millions of hours have been spent in class after class, in country after country, in generation after generation, proving and re-proving the theorems in Euclid. After the introduction of the "new math" in the mid-nineteen fifties, proof spread to other high school mathematics such as algebra, and subjects such as set theory were deliberately introduced so as to be a vehicle for the axiomatic method and proof. In college, a typical lecture in advanced mathematics, especially a lecture given by an instructor with "pure" interests, consists entirely of definition, theorem, proof, definition, theorem, proof, in solemn and unrelieved concatenation. Why is this? If, as claimed, proof is validation and certification, then one might think that once a proof has been accepted by a competent group of scholars, the rest of the scholarly world would be glad to take their word for it and to go on. Why do mathematicians and their students find it worthwhile to prove again and yet again the Pythagorean theorem or the theorems of Lebesgue or Wiener or Kolmogoroff?

Proof serves many purposes simultaneously. In being exposed to the scrutiny and judgment of a new audience, the proof is subject to a constant process of criticism and revalidation. Errors, ambiguities, and misunderstandings are cleared up by constant exposure. Proof is respectability. Proof is the seal of authority.

Proof, in its best instances, increases understanding by revealing the heart of the matter. Proof suggests new mathematics. The novice who studies proofs gets closer to the creation of new mathematics. Proof is mathematical power, the electric voltage of the subject which vitalizes the static assertions of the theorems.

Finally, proof is ritual, and a celebration of the power of pure reason. Such an exercise in reassurance may be very necessary in view of all the messes that clear thinking clearly gets us into.

Impossibility

Ian Richards

Ian Richards did his dissertation under Lars Ahlfors at Harvard in 1960 and then went to the Massachusetts Institute of Technology. He is currently at the University of Minnesota. Richards has held numerous NSF grants in analysis.

If there is one aspect of modern mathematics most difficult for nonmathematicians to grasp, it must be the notion of "impossibility" proofs. Some of the most important mathematical results of the past 200 years revolve around the rigorous demonstration that a particular mathematical process is impossible. The vital realization is that the process is proven impossible. Not that it has not yet been done, or that a certain attempt has failed, but that any attempt allowed by the rules of mathematics must fail. The next essay about Gödel's theorem is really an impossibility proof. Gödel proved that it is impossible to have a mathematical system that simultaneously contains the counting numbers 1, 2, 3, . . . and is also free of meaningful statements about those numbers whose truth cannot be determined. One can't have both counting numbers and no undecidable theorems—one or the other, but not both. Courant and Robbins's essay in Part Two of this volume mentioned the impossibility of trisecting any angle with compass and unmarked ruler; still others noted the impossibility of a general formula for solving polynomials of degree 5 or greater. These processes, and many others besides, are mathematically impossible.

In this essay Ian Richards presents some additional examples of the mathematically impossible and demonstrates why they are so. American business after World War II was guided by the slogan, "The difficult we do today, the impossible takes a little longer." This optimistic philosophy has disappeared in the 1980s as we have come to suspect as a nation that there are inherent limits to what can be accomplished. Realizing that there are important things that are in fact impossible and that can be known to be impossible could bring to a screeching halt much of the vacuous political and economic rhetoric spouted by various ideologies of left, center, and right.

While one man was proving it couldn't be done,
another man tried and he did it.

    (Children's verse)

HOW DOES ONE prove that something is impossible? Is anything impossible? Yes, of course, some things are. But let us momentarily play the devil's advocate. Conventional folk-wisdom teaches the opposite: that anything can be done if one is clever and tries hard enough. And common experience backs up that point of view. Things once believed to be impossible happen every day. There are two ways that this can come about, and the distinction is important to us here, since we are concerned with theory, not practice. Briefly:

  I. Sometimes the thing said to be impossible really isn't;

Source: Ian Richards, "Impossibility," *Mathematics Magazine* 48 (1975): 249–262. Reprinted by permission of the Mathematical Association of America.

II. And sometimes it is. However, even in this latter case it often happens that, *by bending the rules a little bit,* the situation can be altered, and the desired effect thereby achieved.

Type II represents what we call "mathematical impossibility"; type I is mere error. Consider some examples. When my father was a young biologist, working with a (then) new device called the electron microscope, several experts said that it was impossible to cut animal tissue into pieces thin enough for use with this instrument. The idea was that no knife edge, of any known material, was sharp enough to produce the necessary thin sections. My father succeeded in finding a suitable knife. He began by taking a raw carrot, quartered the carrot lengthwise, embedded the material to be cut into the edge of the carrot, and then gently drew a razor blade back and forth along this edge. (Today the same job is done with an instrument called a microtome, which incidentally costs several thousand dollars.)

My father's good fortune in doing what some people said couldn't be done, gives a typical example of type I; the "experts" were simply wrong. More important for our purposes is the type II situation, in which a problem really *is* unsolvable as stated, but a fortuitous change in the initial assumptions allows a "solution" to be found. Perhaps the most famous instance of this in all history is the story of Alexander the Great cutting the Gordian knot. Clearly he changed the rules! At a more mundane level, mathematicians have proved that one cannot trisect an arbitrary angle with ruler and compass; but of course that doesn't prevent engineers from trisecting angles when they need to. Another impossibility theorem (which we will discuss below) involves the "fifteen puzzle." A friend of mine showed this puzzle to his father, and explained that such and such a position could never be attained. His father reached the forbidden position by taking the toy down to his workshop, prying out one of the pieces, and putting it back in a different place—shades of Alexander!

However, some things really are impossible. In the Middle Ages, certain skeptics asked, "If God is omnipotent, can He make an object so heavy that He cannot move it?" The answer given by Thomas Aquinas and others was that "Even omnipotence cannot achieve contradiction."

Of course, this is how mathematicians prove that certain things are impossible. They show that the opposite assumption would lead to a contradiction. We should emphasize, however, that mathematics deals with precisely formulated problems. So, if something is proved impossible, it follows that there will never be a "type I" exception to the law—but, by bending the rules, the whole situation may be altered.

Thus it becomes clear that "impossibility theorems" have little or no practical significance. Nevertheless they are, in the author's opinion, among the most remarkable theorems in mathematics. For they have a certain mystifying quality. If trisecting a general angle *were* possible (as, e.g., bisecting one is), we could easily imagine what such a hypothetical solution would look like: presumably it would look rather like the construction for bisecting an angle, except that it would be more complicated. The reason why an impossibility proof seems mysterious (at least to me), is because of the following question: How do I know that there is not some intricate construction, involving perhaps thousands of steps, which my "proof" has overlooked? Clearly some general principle must be involved. In fact one is, and bringing out this underlying principle in several disparate situations is the main theme of this article.

[*Note.* The practical "uselessness" of impossibility proofs applies only if one takes a rather narrow viewpoint. For some of the *ideas* which have grown out of such investigations—e.g., group theory—have found practical application in other areas.]

A Summary of the Contents

In this paper we will consider seven problems in which "impossibility" plays a role. These are:

1. The rook's tour of a chessboard
2. The 15-puzzle
3. The knight's tour of a tic-tac-toe board
4. The magic five-pointed star
5. The trisection of an angle

6. The irrationality of all "nontrivial" linear combinations of nth roots (e.g., $\sqrt[3]{2} + \sqrt[4]{3} + \sqrt[5]{4}$)

7. The general quintic equation

The last three examples above involve Galois theory, and it would require too much space to include their proofs. We will content ourselves with some remarks about them. Also, in this connection, it seems impossible (no pun intended) to improve on the classic books of Artin [*Galois Theory*, Notre Dame Mathematical Lectures no. 2, 1942] and van der Waerden [*Algebra*, vol. 1, rev. ed., Ungar, New York, 1970]. (Each of these books treats Galois theory from a different viewpoint, and almost all later texts follow one or the other.)

The first four theorems concern elementary puzzles, and here I will give the proofs. However, in case the reader wants to work these problems out for himself, the proofs appear in a separate section, between Example 4 and Example 5. The point of the article is the common thread which runs through all seven examples, from the most elementary to the most advanced.

[*Note.* Although none of the results discussed here are new, one of the proofs is: for the magic star, number 4. In the discussion of this problem, reference is made to an earlier proof.]

Invariants

The common thread running through the seven problems mentioned above is the idea of an invariant. This idea, together with its cousin, the idea of a transformation, lies at the core of much modern mathematics. What is an invariant? To give a precise definition would be outside of the author's competence—the word belongs to logic and philosophy. However, the underlying idea is something like this:

An investigator is faced with a situation which is too complicated to analyze completely. So he finds a particular entity, the "invariant," which incorporates certain particular aspects of the situation. Hopefully the invariant will be easy to calculate. The investigator then shows that, under the sorts of transformations which are allowed in

the system, the invariant cannot vary. (This, of course, explains the name.) If "solving" a certain problem would require changing the invariant, then the solution is impossible.

Examples of invariants abound outside of mathematics. Energy, momentum, and angular momentum are standard physical invariants. Stretching a point, the human fingerprint could be called an anatomical invariant. In mathematics, some of the most common invariants are parity (odd versus even) and size (including number, length, area, etc.).

Here it might be worth pointing out that some of these mathematical invariants yield "impossibility theorems" which are so obvious as to escape notice. For example, it is impossible to break a square up into a finite number of triangular pieces, and then reassemble these pieces to form two squares, each having the same area as the original square. (To see the point, try proving this theorem using any idea *except* area.) In the examples which follow, the invariant is sometimes less obvious, but the basic principle is the same.

Examples of Impossibility Theorems

Example 1 (The Rook's Tour). Imagine a hypothetical piece which is allowed to make only those moves common to both the king and the rook in chess: that is, it can move *one square at a time horizontally or vertically* (but not diagonally, and never more than one square). This piece starts in the upper left-hand corner of a chessboard (see Figure 1) and is required to move over the whole board, occupying each square exactly once (and thus not re-entering the square from which it started). Furthermore, it must end its journey on the square marked "X" in the lower right-hand corner of the board. Prove that this is impossible.

[The solutions to the problems posed by Examples 1 to 4 are given after Example 4.]

Example 2 (The 15-Puzzle). A well-known toy involves 15 square pieces placed in a box

Start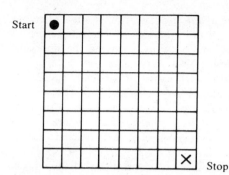

Stop

Figure 1   The rook's tour. The piece indicated by the black dot is restricted to move one square at a time, vertically or horizontally (and not diagonally). It must occupy each square exactly once.

which is 4 by 4 units on a side. Thus the box has 16 spaces, all but one of which are occupied by the pieces, and one space which is empty (see Figure 2). The pieces are numbered 1 through 15.

1	2	3	4
5	6	7	8
9	10	11	12
13	14	15	

empty

Figure 2a   The desired end position for the 15-puzzle.

1	2	3	4
5	6	7	8
9	10	11	12
13	15	14	

empty

Figure 2b   The "other" position. Here the pieces 14 and 15 have been reversed.

They may be moved by sliding an adjacent piece horizontally or vertically into the empty space. It is forbidden to take any of the pieces out of the box. Show that it is impossible to get from the position shown in Figure 2b to the one in Figure 2a, while staying within the rules of the game.

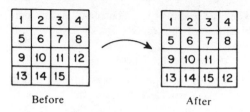

Before   After

Figure 2c   A typical move: the number 12 piece slides into the empty square.

Remark.   In the old 15-puzzle, popular in the nineteenth century, the pieces were wooden squares, which were loose and could be taken out of the box. These were shaken up and then placed in the box in a random order; the objective was to get the pieces into the "natural" order shown in Figure 2a. However, half of the time this was impossible—if the pieces were placed in the box so that Figure 2b could be reached, then Figure 2a could not. Furthermore (since this puzzle is fairly easy except when it is impossible), Figure 2b would usually be arrived at within a few minutes. Then the frustrated puzzle-solver might spend several fruitless hours trying to "make the last step," i.e., to interchange the 14-piece with the 15-piece. [In modern versions of the puzzle, the "impossible" case is avoided by having the pieces locked in the box with plastic flanges. Unfortunately, then there is a mechanical difficulty: the flanges rub against each other, and the pieces tend to twist and don't slide very well.]

Example 3 (Knight's Tour of a Tic-Tac-Toe Board).   Imagine four knights situated on the four corners of a 3 × 3 playing board. The knights in the lower left and lower right hand corners are colored white and black respectively, while the knights in the two upper corners are both red (see Figure 3). All four pieces move like a knight in chess, except that their moves are confined to the 3 × 3 board, and *they are not allowed to capture one another.* (Of course, two pieces cannot occupy the same square at the same time.) Prove that it is impossible to interchange the positions of the white and black knights, i.e., to have the white knight in the lower right corner

Red knights

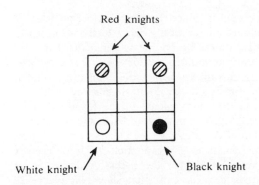

White knight   Black knight

Figure 3   The knight's tour.

and the black knight in the lower left at the same time. (It is NOT required that the red knights return to their original squares; interchanging the white and black knights is impossible no matter what positions the red knights occupy at the end of the game!)

Example 4 (The Magic Five-Pointed Star). Show that it is impossible to place the numbers 1 through 10 on the ten intersection points of a five-pointed star (see Figure 4a) in such a way that

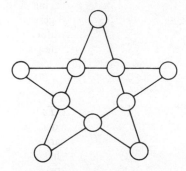

Figure 4a   A five-pointed star. In a magic star, each number from 1 to 10 would be used exactly once, and the sum of the four numbers on every line in the star would be the same.

each number is used exactly once, and the sum of the four numbers on any line in the star is the same.

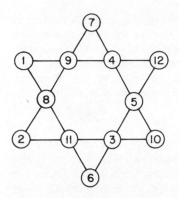

Figure 4b   A six-pointed magic star.

[A magic six-pointed star is shown in Figure 4b.]

Solutions to Examples 1, 2, 3, 4

Solution to Example 1 (The Rook's Tour of a Chessboard).   A hint is contained in the word "chessboard." You may have noticed that, in Figure 1 above, I didn't color the squares. If this were done (see Figure 5), then it would become

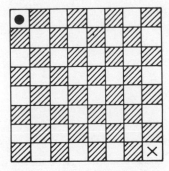

Figure 5   The chessboard of the rook's tour with its squares colored in.

clear that each move of our "rook-king" carries the piece from a white square to a black one or vice versa. Thus, to get from the starting point (a white square in Figure 5) to the finish (another white square), must involve an EVEN number of moves. However, the first square being occupied, there are 63 squares left to fill, an ODD number. Since the number of moves must, at the same time, be both odd and even, we have reached a contradiction, and the puzzle is impossible.

Solution to Example 2 (The 15-Puzzle). Here we use the same idea as in Example 1, plus one new idea. Firstly, each time a "move" is made in the 15-puzzle, *the empty square moves vertically or horizontally,* just like the "rook-king" in Example 1 (here see Figure 6). Thus, for the same reason as before, it must require an EVEN number of moves to bring the empty square back to its original position. However, it can be shown that interchanging the 14-piece with the 15-piece (if it could be done), would require an ODD number of moves. Thus we arrive at the same contradiction as in Example 1. The proof that the number of moves (if there were a solution) must be odd depends on some elementary facts about

permutations. Since the theory of permutations is included in practically every textbook on group theory, linear algebra, or determinants, I will not attempt to outline it in this space. For those who know this theory, here is the proof that the number of moves in the 15-puzzle must be odd:

Let the empty square in the 15-puzzle be labeled "square number 16." Then any possible position of the fifteen pieces plus the empty square corresponds to a permutation of the integers 1 through 16 (where the natural ordering is, of course, defined to be that shown in Figure 2a above). Thus the positions shown in Figures 2a and 2b correspond respectively to the permutations:

1, 2, 3, 4, 5, 6, 7, 8, 9, 10, 11, 12, 13, 14, 15, 16

and

1, 2, 3, 4, 5, 6, 7, 8, 9, 10, 11, 12, 13, 15, 14, 16

(note the inversion of 14 and 15 in the second case). The first permutation (the identity permutation) is even, and the second is odd. Now the theory of permutations tells us that to pass from

Before

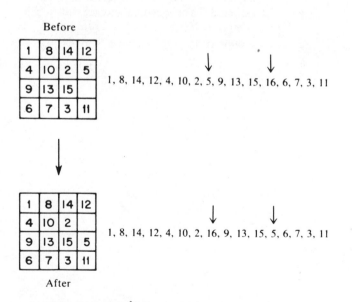

1, 8, 14, 12, 4, 10, 2, 5, 9, 13, 15, 16, 6, 7, 3, 11

1, 8, 14, 12, 4, 10, 2, 16, 9, 13, 15, 5, 6, 7, 3, 11

After

Figure 6   A typical move in the 15-puzzle: the number 5 piece changes places with the empty square (which we consider to be square number 16). The *permutations* of 1, · · · , 16 corresponding to these positions, are indicated to the right of the boxes.

an odd to an even permutation always requires an odd number of "MOVES" (where each "move" consists of exchanging two numbers, leaving the others fixed). In the 15-puzzle, each move amounts to an interchange of some piece with the empty square, number 16. This fits the situation required for the permutation-theorem just cited, and shows that the number of moves must be odd.

Solution to Example 3 (The Wandering Knights).   The square in the center of the 3 × 3 board is inaccessible to all of the knights. Number the remaining eight squares as shown in Figure 7a. Then the only possible moves for the

Figure 7a   The cycle 1, 2, 3, · · ·, 8, 1 and its inverse show the only possible moves for a knight on this 3 by 3 board.

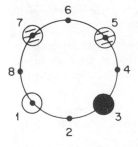

Figure 7b   The circular representation. Here each point on the circle corresponds to the point labeled with the *same number* on the square. (Thus the point 2, at the bottom of the circle, corresponds to a point at the top of the square.) In this representation, the allowable moves are simply to go one space sideways around the circle.

knights are from square 1 to 2 to 3 to 4 to 5 to 6 to 7 to 8 to 1, and backwards (the inverses of the preceding moves). Thus we may represent the playing board by eight points situated on a circle

(Figure 7b). In this *circular representation,* the allowable moves are simply to go one space clockwise or counterclockwise around the circle. In particular, since the pieces cannot occupy the same space and cannot capture, the pieces can never "jump" over one another. Now the invariant which solves the problem is seen to be topological: For, in order to interchange the positions of the black and white pieces, the two red pieces would have to be squeezed in between—i.e., the two red pieces would both end up occupying square number 2, which violates the rules.

[To make this argument precise, define the region "between" the black and white pieces to consist of all the positions on the circle traversed while moving in the *counterclockwise* direction *from* the black piece *to* the white one. Since the pieces can move only one space at a time (around the circle in Figure 7b), and cannot jump over one another, the two red pieces must remain "between" the black and the white one. Suppose, as required in the problem, the black piece moves to square number 1, and the white piece occupies square 3. Then the two red pieces must lie on squares "between" 1 and 3 (in the sense defined above); and the only such square is number 2.]

Solution to Example 4 (The Magic Star).   We give a proof based on the idea that the set of numbers 1, · · ·, 10 is too small to allow the two "extreme" numbers 1 and 10 to be balanced by the more "moderate" numbers in between. Thus here, size rather than parity plays the crucial role.

Step (i). If a solution were possible, the sum of the numbers in each line would be 22 (= 4 times the average 5.5 of the numbers 1 to 10). This is obvious.

Step (ii). If a solution existed, then the numbers 1 and 10 would have to lie on a single line.

Proof. Otherwise, take the six other numbers on the two lines passing through the point containing 1: These six numbers would have a sum $\leq 9 + 8 + 7 + 6 + 5 + 4 = 39$. But by step (i), their sum must be $21 + 21 = 42$.

Note. Figure 8 is drawn just to give some sort of picture. It will NOT matter in the proof exactly *where* the numbers 1 and 10 lie on the star.

The only fact that we need is that *any two lines in a five-pointed star intersect.*

Step (iii). Now assume that the numbers 1 and 10 are on a single line, which we call L_0 (see Figure 8). Call the two other lines through 1 and 10 respectively L_1 and L_{10}.

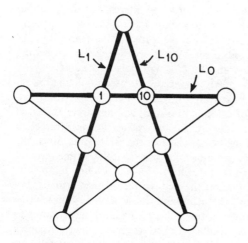

Figure 8   A five-pointed star, with the numbers 1 and 10 placed on particular points, and the three lines L_0, L_1, and L_{10} indicated. (Note: the proof which we give is independent of the actual location of the numbers 1 and 10; except that, after Step (ii), we know that 1 and 10 must lie on a single line.)

We must enumerate some possibilities; fortunately there are not very many. We list all of the possible combinations of numbers (1 and 10 are excluded) which could fill the *two empty spaces* on the line L_0 or the *three empty spaces* on the lines L_1 and L_{10}. (Recall that the sum of the four numbers along each line must be 22.) We go further: first we list all of the possibilities for L_0 (in the left hand column in Table 1); then *to the right of each L_0 entry, we list all of the L_1 and L_{10} combinations which are compatible with it.*

Thus, in the first case given in Table 1, the lines L_0, L_1, and L_{10} would contain the following sets of four numbers:

$$L_0 = \{1, 10, 9, 2\}, \quad L_1 = \{1, 8, 7, 6\},$$
$$L_{10} = \{10, 3, 4, 5\}.$$

Finally, we recall the fact that any two lines in a five-pointed star intersect. However, in each of

Table 1   Possible sets of numbers to fill the vacant spaces on L_0, L_1, and L_{10} in Figure 8. The sum of the four numbers along each line must be 22.

In L_0	In L_1	In L_{10}
(besides 1, 10)	(besides 1)	(besides 10)
9,2	8,7,6	3,4,5
8,3	9,7,5	2,4,6
7,4	none	none
6,5	9,8,4	2,3,7

the possibilities listed in Table 1, the lines L_1 and L_{10} have no common element. This contradiction proves the impossibility of constructing a five-pointed magic star.

Discussion

What invariants have been used so far? The idea of odd and even, obviously, in Examples 1 and 2; the topological notion of "betweenness" in Example 3, and the limitations forced by the sizes of the numbers in Example 4. There are also, in each problem, constructs (i.e., "tricks") designed to bring these invariants into play. Thus we have:

The operation of coloring the squares of the chessboard, in Example 1.

The idea of odd and even permutations, and the proposition that it requires an odd number of moves to turn one into the other, in Example 2.

The trick of turning the "knight's walk" around the tic-tac-toe board into a circular motion, in Example 3.

The method of looking at the two "extreme" numbers 1 and 10, in Example 4. There we also used the fact that any two lines in a five-pointed star intersect, which illustrates another kind of invariant.

In the problems which follow, based on Galois theory, the invariants are more complicated. As already stated, we cannot give the details here. We will attempt, in discussing these problems, to make comments which may be suggestive to a reader who does not know Galois theory, and (hopefully) clear to a reader who does.

Examples Depending on Galois Theory

Example 5 (Trisection of an Angle). The problem of deciding whether it is possible, using the "classical" instruments of Greek geometry, the straightedge and compass, to trisect an arbitrary angle, remained an open mathematical question for about two thousand years. It was finally settled around the year 1800, when it was proved that the construction is impossible. (Incidentally, this result seems to have the status of a "folk-theorem"—at least it is not generally attributed to any one man. It was certainly implicit in the work of Gauss, but may have been known earlier.)

Paul Erdös, in an offhand lecture given at the University of Minnesota, made some interesting comments on problems which remain untouched for hundreds of years. He remarked (the quote is a rough one, of course):

"Archimedes knew the impossibility of trisecting an angle. But he also knew that proving this proposition was not for his time, and so he concentrated his energies on problems that he could solve."

If so, Archimedes' judgment was sound, for at present, all known approaches to the trisection problem involve ideas from the so-called "modern algebra," a subject not highly developed until the eighteenth century. Indeed, it appears that the trisection problem really has very little to do with "geometry." In its solution, the geometric problem is immediately translated into a problem in algebra. We may outline the steps in the solution as follows:

[Here I will make free use of the language of contemporary algebra—hopefully this will convey something of the flavor of the argument, even to nonspecialists.]

1. The geometric problem is translated into a problem about numbers, using the sort of analytic geometry that is familiar to every calculus student today.
2. Each straightedge and compass construction generates certain points; these points have coordinates (via analytic geometry), and so they generate in turn a certain set of numbers.
3. These numbers (here is where the terminology gets thick) lie in what is called a "number field," which is an extension of the field of rational numbers. This number field is then viewed as a "vector space" over the subfield of rationals. *This allows us to speak of the DIMENSION of that vector space, which becomes an invariant arising out of the geometrical construction.*
4. It is shown that the "dimension" of these vector spaces over the rationals is always *a power of two.*

   [*Note.* The dimension need NOT be two; it can be 2, 4, 8, 16, $\cdots$. This corresponds to the fact that straightedge and compass constructions can be very complex. Such complexity would be reflected in the fact that the resulting number fields had very high dimension over the rationals. Here recall our earlier question: "How do we know that there is not some intricate construction, involving perhaps thousands of steps, which our proof has overlooked?"]
5. We have seen that straightedge and compass constructions give number fields whose dimension over the rationals must be a power of two. Now it turns out that, to trisect most angles, one requires number fields whose dimension is three, or a multiple of three. Since no power of two is ever, at the same time, a multiple of three, we have reached an impasse. Thus the assumption that it is possible, using the "classical instruments," to trisect an arbitrary angle, leads to a contradiction.

Remark. The reader might ask: Why use only the "classical instruments," the straightedge and compass? One answer is that it makes a good problem! Another answer is that those instruments are, after all, the simplest ones; both of them can be bought for under a dollar. (How much longer will this remain true?)

There are many other drawing instruments, of course. For a good discussion of these, I recommend the books of Felix Klein [*Famous Problems of Elementary Geometry*, repr. by Dover, New York, 1956] and Howard Eves [*A Survey of Geometry*, rev. ed. Allyn and Bacon, Boston, 1972]. Eves' book stresses the geometric aspects; Klein's book, the algebraic and analytic. Klein's book, incidentally, contains proofs of the impossibility of trisecting the angle, duplicating the cube, and squaring the circle.

Note. Like all "impossibility theorems," the one about trisecting angles is valid only if carefully formulated. Thus, the only instruments allowed are the straightedge (a ruler without markings) and the compass. Furthermore, an *exact* construction is required. (Approximate constructions abound.)

[Someone called the author once, and announced that he thought he had found a method for trisecting angles. However, he said, he had forgotten his high school trigonometry, and wondered whether I would be willing to do some calculations for him. When I informed him about the impossibility theorem, I expected some disagreement. Instead, the conversation ended on a rather surprising note. Evidently the fellow was much impressed by my abilities, for he asked me: "Say, this probably isn't your department, but do you know anything about mushrooms?" Unfortunately, I couldn't help him there.]

Example 6 (Linear Combinations of *n*th roots). The last two examples will be treated only very briefly. The reason for including them at all is that they follow, with increasing levels of sophistication, the pattern set by the trisection problem (Example 5).

[In technical language: the trisection problem involves only the idea of the *dimension* of a vector space. Example 6, when treated via Galois theory, requires somewhat more: the *noncommutativity* of a certain group. Finally, the classic problem of the quintic equation in Example 7, involves the full apparatus of Galois theory.]

Now to come to the question: Every student of mathematics learns the result that *n*th roots of integers, such as $\sqrt{2}$ or $\sqrt[3]{4}$, are irrational except in the trivial cases (like $\sqrt{4}$) when they reduce to whole numbers. A much more difficult problem is to treat *linear combinations* of *n*th roots, e.g.:

$$\sqrt[3]{3} + \sqrt[5]{4} + \sqrt[6]{72}. \qquad \text{(E)}$$

However, the result which one expects to be true does hold: Sums such as (E) are irrational whenever their terms do not "obviously" cancel out. It is not difficult to formulate this statement precisely; the technical version is as follows:

In the first place, by the "*n*th root" of a positive

integer, we mean here the real positive *n*th root. Now, for simplicity, we will state a special case of our theorem, involving 60th roots of integers whose only prime factors are 2 and 3. The reader who wishes to, will find no difficulty in devising a suitable generalization.

THEOREM. *Consider the set of positive real numbers:*

$$\sqrt[60]{2^a 3^b}, \qquad 0 \leq a < 60, \qquad 0 \leq b < 60.$$

These 3600 numbers are linearly independent over the rational field.

Remarks. The reader may be wondering what the above theorem has to do with "impossibility." To see the connection, let us take the four real numbers:

$$1, \sqrt[3]{3}, \sqrt[5]{4}, \sqrt[6]{72}.$$

These form a subset of the set of 3600 numbers mentioned in the theorem. To say that they are "linearly independent over the rationals" means that it is impossible to find rational numbers a, b, c, d, not all zero, such that

$$a + b\sqrt[3]{3} + c\sqrt[5]{4} + d\sqrt[6]{72} = 0.$$

(This, incidentally, shows that the number exhibited in (E) above is irrational.)

As I have said, the theorem is expected; much more surprising is the fact that it has, apparently, no elementary proof. (If one is content to consider only square-roots, and ignore cube-roots and higher radicals, then there are elementary solutions.) The theorem in its general form was first proved by Besicovitch. A treatment based on Galois theory has been given by the author. For extensions to number fields other than the rationals, see the paper of Siegel, and a paper by Schinzel to appear in Acta Arithmetica.

Example 7 (The Quintic Equation). As every student of high school algebra knows, there is a simple formula for solving the general quadratic equation:

if $ax^2 + bx + c = 0$, then
$$x = [-b \pm \sqrt{b^2 - 4ac}]/2a.$$

This formula involves, besides the rational operations (addition, subtraction, multiplication, and division), only the square-root. There are similar, but much more complicated, formulas for solving 3rd degree and 4th degree polynomial equations. Then, abruptly, the situation changes: there is no formula involving radicals (nth roots) for solving the general 5th degree equation.

Like many such results, this one was certainly suspected before it was proved. Important contributions were made by Lagrange, Gauss, Cauchy, Ruffini, Abel, and Galois. The approach used by Galois was the most far-reaching, and (having been, by now, greatly simplified) it is commonly taught in university courses in algebra today.

Unfortunately, such results are not accessible to anyone except a mathematical specialist. For teaching purposes, the puzzles given in Examples 1 to 4 above, may provide a reasonable introduction to this kind of mathematical thought. At least, the simple arguments which we gave there possess the essential ingredients of a mathematical proof—they are completely convincing!

To return to the children's platitude cited at the beginning of this article: "While one man was proving it couldn't be done, another man tried and he did it." If anyone does something which has *really* been proved to be impossible, then you may be sure that he cheated a little.

Added in Proof

William Pruitt has shown me a simplified proof for the magic five-pointed star (Example 4) which eliminates completely the "enumeration of cases" required in my solution. He follows my proof through Step (ii), in which it is shown that, if a magic five-pointed star did exist, then the numbers 1 and 10 would have to lie on the same line (again call it L_0). However, here he makes the following pretty observation: Step (iii*): *If a magic star did exist, then on no line in the star would there be two numbers whose sum is 11.* Clearly (iii*) contradicts (ii)!!!

Proof of (iii*).   Suppose such a line, call it L_0, did exist with four numbers u, $11 - u$, v, $11 - v$ on it. Let L_1, L_2, L_3, L_4 be the other four lines in the star, passing through the numbers u, $11 - u$, v, $11 - v$ respectively. (Here a glance at Figure 8 above may be helpful.) Consider the lines L_1 and L_2 as being "$+$" and the lines L_3 and L_4 as being "$-$." Then the algebraic sum of the numbers in these lines, counted according to multiplicity, and weighted with the "$+$" or "$-$" signs as indicated, would be $22 + 22 - 22 - 22 = 0$. Now let x be the number through which the pair of lines L_1 and L_2 intersect; similarly define y with reference to L_3 and L_4. We leave it to the reader to verify: The above "algebraic sum" $= 0 = u + (11 - u) - v - (11 - v) + 2x - 2y$ (all of the other numbers cancel out with one "$+$" sign and one "$-$" sign). Hence $2x - 2y = 0$, and $x = y$, a contradiction.

Analogies and Metaphors
to Explain Gödel's Theorem

Douglas R. Hofstadter

Douglas R. Hofstadter was born in New York City in 1945. He began his graduate studies at Berkeley but later turned to physics at the University of Oregon. He is currently associated with Indiana University and writes a monthly column for *Scientific American*. He was a Guggenheim Fellow to Stanford in 1980, the year that he won a Pulitzer prize for his book, *Gödel, Escher, and Bach: An Eternal Golden Braid*.

The historical and philosophical implications of Gödel's infamous theorem are hinted at throughout this volume. It would be inaccurate to liken the publication of this result to a bombshell; thermonuclear explosion comes closer to the truth, but even that rings a bit hollow. After all it is conceivable that some decades after the detonation of an atomic bomb life might almost be back to normal. In time essentially all traces of the explosion would be gone except for those deliberately preserved, as in Hiroshima. But mathematics will never be as it was before Gödel's theorem.

No matter how much the community of practicing mathematicians may ignore its presence, Gödel's theorem will not go away. Protestations to the contrary, Gödel's theorem influences the kinds of problems chosen to be treated and the approaches to such treatment. Problems not easily resolved are increasingly suspect of being formally undecidable or worse. The suggestion that an area may lead to undecidable questions is usually enough to send researchers at a trot to fields more readily harvested. Gödel's theorem has had a profound impact both in mathematics and in areas such as computer science where problems in artificial intelligence often must treat questions with the same self-referential character.

In this essay Douglas R. Hofstadter explains Gödel's theorem. His analogies and metaphors describe what the theorem asserts and how Gödel obtained a proof. It is a very effective exposition of a crucial part of modern mathematics. Indeed, without some insight into Gödel's theorem one cannot fully appreciate the philosophical problems of modern mathematics. Hofstadter is the author of Gödel, Escher, Bach: An Eternal Golden Braid, *a book for which he was awarded the Pulitzer Prize in general nonfiction in 1980. This essay is a condensation of material from that book.*

Source: Douglas R. Hofstadter, "Analogies and Metaphors to Explain Gödel's Theorem," *Two-Year College Mathematics Journal* 13 (March 1982):98–114. Reprinted by permission. This paper is a lightly edited transcript of the talk presented at the Fourth International Congress on Mathematical Education which was held in August of 1980 in Berkeley.

WHEN I WAS a graduate student at Berkeley in mathematics during 1966 and 1967, I found out, to my chagrin, that mathematics was too abstract for me. I had always thought that I was a pretty abstract thinker, but what I began to realize about that time in my life was that, in fact, all of my thoughts are very concrete. They all are based on images, analogies and metaphors. I really think only in concrete ideas, and I found that I couldn't attach any concrete ideas to some of the mathematics I was learning. I could learn the formal statements and theorems, I could prove theorems formally, but I really could not go beyond them. I was just not able to get the concepts without images, so I turned away from mathematics and went on to physics at the University of Oregon. Then my career went through variegated phases, and finally I wound up in computer science and artificial intelligence, which is not exactly an accident because my greatest interest in artificial intelligence nowadays is in understanding analogies. In a way I have come back to study, through computer science (and particularly through the branch of it called artificial intelligence), what these analogies are that I think with. So there is a little loop there that I have closed, and I feel very happy doing it.

My book illustrates particularly strongly my own predilection for thinking in metaphors, analogies, images, and so forth. Many of the images that I have produced in the book are connected with Gödel's theorem. Some of you may know and some of you may not know exactly what Gödel's theorem is. I will try to give you a flavor of what it is in this talk. It is not intended just for you to learn how to explain Gödel's theorem to other people, but possibly for you to learn some of the concepts directly right now from me. For those of you who already do know what the theorem is, I hope you will find some new variations of looking at it and how to think about it. Gödel's theorem depends on the idea of self-reference or level crossing, which you'll see in this paper. Its major impact upon mathematics is to show that formal systems have a certain kind of incompleteness. It really involves the concept of how self-reference, or mixing of different levels, can be brought into mathematics.

To begin with I will give you a little puzzle. It is a puzzle which delights me because it was something that happened to me as a real-life event. I was sitting at the edge of a swimming pool, and in the pool there were three balls, a small black one, a small white one, and a large white one. I was looking at them, and I thought,

Which Ball Is the Most Different?

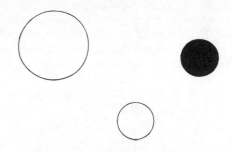

The obviously different one is the small white one. Two of them are the same color and two are the same size, and the only one that is in the intersection of those two sets is the small white one.

"How strange—the obviously different one is the small white one! Two of them are the same size and two are the same color, and the only one that is in the intersection of those two sets is the small white one. It is the most different because it is the most same!" Here we have a sort of mixing of levels. At some primitive level of observation, at the perceptual level, we have the categories of *size* and *color*, and there is no unique answer yielded at that level. But we have this more abstract view of the situation that says that size and color are two equally primitive things, so we can't choose between them. However, we do have an object that is different. We have one that differs in size, another that differs in color, and so there is one left over. So we are somehow changing in our level of description. We are moving to a more abstract level, and yet somehow we feel we really haven't cheated. I don't really know quite how to say this, but somehow there is a validity to this answer. Although it seems strange, there is some sense to this response and it is perfectly fair to move to this next abstract level and give this as our answer. This is the first example of how level mixing can appear in a simple context and can seem quite natural and amusing at the same time. Gödel's theorem deals primarily with this idea of self-reference, which is something that has fascinated people from all times and all places. Self-reference is something that occurs in many jokes: it is general and fascinates people.

Now I would like to give you some examples of self-reference outside Gödel's theorem. Some of them will be very simple, and some of them may be very familiar to you: they are intended to give you the flavor of it. My first example involves a question about a laser. What is the only place in a room that a laser cannot hit if you shine the beam? I have indicated it by the black dot in the figure. The only place that laser cannot hit is its own rear end. You can shine it to any other point in the room except that black dot. However, this matter is just a little bit trickier than that. You can actually get it to shine on that spot, depending on what you mean by "that spot." If I define it in coordinates *relative to the room*, then, of course, the laser can shine through it. If, though, I define it *in terms of self-reference*, in other words, with respect to the laser itself, then, of course, it can't ever shine on that particular point. This is reminiscent of an epigrammatic statement that was made about 200 years ago by the German man of letters Georg Lichtenberg. He said that the one place in a room that a fly can land with safety is on the handle of a flyswatter.

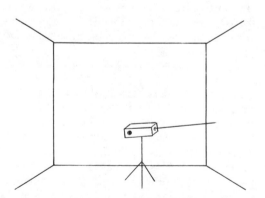
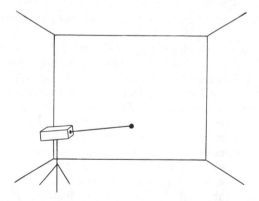

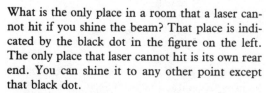

What is the only place in a room that a laser cannot hit if you shine the beam? That place is indicated by the black dot in the figure on the left. The only place that laser cannot hit is its own rear end. You can shine it to any other point except that black dot.

You can actually get it to shine on that spot, depending on what you mean by "that spot." If that spot is defined in coordinates *relative to the room*, then, of course, the laser can shine through it. If, though, it is defined *in terms of self-reference*, in other words, in terms of the laser itself, then, of course, it can't ever shine on that particular point.

Georg Lichtenberg's invulnerable fly. These days, perhaps the invulnerable fly sits on top of a malathion-spraying helicopter!

Here are three classic examples of self-reference that often appear in little signs that you can buy in stores.

THIMK	*I NEVER MAKE MISTEAKS*
1	2

PLAN Ahead

3

The first one is the most concise version of Gödel's theorem that I have ever seen. The second one does in fact contain a mistake, since "mistake" is misspelled. In the third one, it's implied that the signmaker did not plan ahead (but on second thought, of course, that's false). These are all variants of self-reference, but an interesting version of self-reference, in that the self-reference is *indirect*. In each case, it is left to the observer to perceive that what the sign is saying is related to the sign itself. It doesn't say anything such as "*This sign* contains a mistake." It doesn't refer to itself *directly*. Yet it does have an indirect self-reference.

Here are some *directly* self-referential statements:

Hofstadter's Law

It always takes longer than you expect, even when you take into account Hofstadter's Law.

The next one is very similar to Hofstadter's Law, and is, unfortunately, a sad fact:

One of the lessons of history is that no one ever learns the lessons of history.

Finally, we come to what is often regarded as the central self-referential statement, namely, the Epimenides Paradox:

Epimenides Paradox

This sentence is false.

Probably all of you have thought about the Epimenides Paradox, and realize that if it is true, then it is false. And if it is false, then it is true, and that gets you into a bind. Gödel's theorem is really based upon the Epimenides Paradox. I would now like to tell you what Gödel actually did, and then further illustrate Gödel's theorem.

In order to describe what Gödel did, I have to set the stage a bit and describe the state of the foundations of mathematics at the end of the last century. Mathematics was being axiomatized in an attempt to make very clear what *did*, and what *did not*, constitute a proof of a statement. Various axiomatic systems had been developed for Euclidean geometry, non-Euclidean geometry, projective geometry, etc. At that time, mathematicians such as Peano, Hilbert, and Frege were involved in axiomatizing mathematics. Perhaps the most ambitious attempts were made by Russell and Whitehead near the beginning of this century in their *Principia Mathematica*, in which they attempted to develop all of mathematics from the notions of logic and sets. The important thing about an axiomatization of any mathematical system is that it takes the set of concepts that one uses for thinking about these things and reduces them to a fixed and finite vocabulary, a finite set of symbols, and a finite set of axioms; or if you want, a finite set of axiom schemas (where schemas are like a mold for axioms) and a finite set of rules of inference. Thus, everything is collapsed down to a formal system, which involves expressing things in a fixed vocabulary according to a fixed grammar and then evolving theorems from axioms according to fixed rules. In other words, the result is a sort of typographical way of reasoning: reasoning is turned into a mechanical procedure—very similar to what computers do nowadays in manipulating symbols within themselves. This is what *Principia Mathematica* was all about: it tried to evolve all of mathematics in one system.

Then, Gödel, in 1930–31, twenty or so years after the publication of *Principia Mathematica* (1910–1913), realized that there was something going on here that could lead to some profound consequences. His idea was that the axiomatization of any branch of mathematics creates a very interesting formal object or formal structure, namely, the formal system itself. In other words, *Principia Mathematica* is not just a system in which mathematics is being done, but moreover it itself can become a mathematical object, in the sense that one can look upon its axioms, theorems, rules of inference and so forth as mathematical objects. The rules of inference are really things that are manipulating objects, the objects being strings of symbols. So this observation could have led Gödel to say, "Maybe I should invent a mathematics that applies to strings of symbols." He would have then been the inventor of something resembling a modern programming language, like Lisp, Snobol, and other languages that are called "string manipulation languages." But he didn't do that. He thought to himself, "There is no branch of mathematics that studies the properties of strings of symbols. However, there is a branch called number theory which studies the properties of integers. I can just replace all of these symbols by integers, and that way I can turn the study of *Principia Mathematica* as a mathematical object into a branch of number

theory. I can just replace all the strings in *Principia Mathematica* by numbers, and then I can describe what happens on each page as a sequence of transformations of numbers." So it becomes a little branch of number theory, which is an irony because *Principia Mathematica* was supposed to be a system in which all of mathematics was developed. But here Gödel is in a way turning around and saying, "But *Principia Mathematica* itself, its own structure, just forms part of number theory. If you think of the book and the system of theorems, the system in which the symbols are being manipulated, as a mathematical object, then it itself has been sort of "swallowed" by number theory, which is one of the subjects that it is supposed to be studying." That was the really tricky insight that Gödel had, the idea that one could turn a mathematical system on itself so that it could become its own object of study—slightly indirect because it involves replacing or coding symbols by numbers that stand for them. That's called *Gödel numbering*. That whole system had to be worked out in great detail to convince mathematicians that what he was doing was quite rigorous and not some made-up sleight-of-hand. Once you realize that *Principia Mathematica* (which includes number theory as one of its subjects) can talk about *Principia Mathematica* itself through this code called Gödel numbering, then you can get sentences that have *two levels of interpretation* rather than one. Earlier, a given sentence was only thought of as speaking about *numbers*. (It could say something like "641 is prime.") But now, there emerges a *second* level of interpretation, because *numbers represent statements*. Someone could say, "Really, this statement says something about strings in *Principia Mathematica*"!

The final trick is to find a specific string that can say something about *itself*. What Gödel found was that it was possible to find a sentence that said this: "This sentence is not provable." And this is where we come back to the Epimenides Paradox. The Epimenides Paradox states, "This sentence is false." In mathematics up until that time the idea of truth was exactly equated with provability. In particular, if one took the system of *Principia Mathematica* (which was supposed to be all-inclusive), the idea of *provability within Principia Mathematica* would have been synonymous with truth. So, to say "This sentence is not provable" would have been synonymous with saying "This sentence is not true," or, "This sentence is false." But if that were really what Gödel's sentence said, then *Principia Mathematica* would have a statement in it that was neither true nor false. This would be a statement about numbers, neither true nor false, and that seems impossible. It seems that if it's true, then it's false, and if it's false, then it's true. That just seems contradictory, and people had to think very hard to figure it out. (But Gödel perhaps didn't have to think too hard.)

Even after Gödel had made it very clear in his paper what the consequences of this were, a lot of people debated for many years about the differences between truth and provability. What Gödel showed was that there was actually a distinction between provability within any specific system and truth. Consider Gödel's sentence, for example:

Gödel's Sentence

"This sentence is not provable." (More precisely, "This sentence is not provable in formal system X.")

There are two possibilities. Either it is provable, or it is not provable. Those are the two possibilities. If it *is* provable, then it is true, so what it says has to be true, and it says it's *not* provable. That is really a contradiction, an absolute contradiction. If things were that way, then mathematics would be inconsistent, and that would be pretty much the end of mathematics. Thus that leaves us with only one alternative, namely, that the sentence is *not* provable (and that's what it says about itself). So it must be *true*. Now, here is the distinction—here is the trick. It could be true and yet not be provable, which would mean the system was not quite as strong as one had thought. That is, *Principia Mathematica* actually had a defect—it was not capable of proving all true statements. One really has to specify what one means by "provable." You can't just say

"provable" in some ethereal sense—you have to specify the system you mean.

In passing, I should also mention that Leon Henkin invented a different kind of sentence:

Henkin's Sentence

"This sentence is provable."

Henkin's sentence, by the way, is not the negation of Gödel's sentence. Do you see why?

I now want to give you an image to hold in your mind of a formal system in which one can express and prove mathematical statements. As in my book, I call the system Typographical Number Theory (TNT). That's appropriate because it sort of "blows up." I'm not going to present it by any means in full because it would take too much space, and I just want to give you the flavor of it. Here are five axioms of arithmetic written in its notation just so you have a sense of the way in which one can express statements in a formal system.

Typographical Number Theory (TNT):

A formal system in which one can express and prove mathematical statements

Five Axioms

1. $\forall a: \sim Sa = 0$
2. $\forall a: (a + 0) = a$
3. $\forall a: \forall a': (a + Sa') = S(a + a')$
4. $\forall a: (a \cdot 0) = 0$
5. $\forall a: \forall a': (a \cdot Sa') = ((a \cdot a') + a)$

and 18 rules of manipulation.

The upside-down A, "$\forall$" is a quantifier and means "for all," the colon is just a punctuation mark, and the little swirl, "$\sim$," called a tilde, means "not," and finally the capital "S" stands for the idea of "the successor of," or "one more than." So the first axiom says: "For all a, it is not the case that the successor of *a* equals 0," and in more understandable English, it says: "No number's successor is 0." Well, you could say "Minus one has a successor, and it is 0." But what this axiom is doing is telling you what the domain is, and it is saying, "Minus one is not in the domain. There is no number whose successor is 0." So it is basically saying "0 is the lowest number."

The second one is easier. It says: "For all *a*, *a* plus 0 equals *a*." The next one says something about the way addition works. It says: "If you have any two numbers *a* and *a'*, then *a* plus the successor of *a'* is equal to the successor of *a* plus *a'*." The next one says: "Multiplying by 0 gives you 0 always." Then the next one is a primitive form of the distributive law. It says: "If you multiply *a* with the successor of *a'*, then you get *a* times *a'* plus *a*." These axioms are to be considered as *strings*, as inviolate objects that are simply capable of being manipulated. You can start manipulating according to the 18 rules of manipulation (which I am not going to exhibit). They simply involve moving symbols to the right or to the left or taking symbols out and putting others in, and so forth. They are very formal, somewhat like a computer program acting on objects. Presumably those 18 rules of manipulation are well thought out, so that they never take you to a false statement if you started with true ones. That's the idea of Typographical Number Theory.

The idea that Gödel had was that because this is such a formal process, one can see this as a mathematical operation—the idea of manipulating symbols. Now he did not invent the idea of a string manipulation language. He simply said "Let's replace all these symbols by numbers, and then we'll have a *number* manipulation system." The way he chose to do it is not the way I am going to show you, but the way I am going to show you is just as good. It works just as well. One has to replace each symbol by some number. In the box, I show each symbol of TNT (and there are 20 of them) corresponding to a three-digit number so that one can "translate" a string of TNT symbols into a long numeral that consists of a sequence of three-digit numerals. (I'll soon show you how.) Once you grasp this idea of replacing symbols by numbers, long strings of symbols by bigger numbers and so forth, then you

The Gödel Isomorphism	
0	666
S	123
=	111
+	112
·	236
(	362
)	323
⟨	212
⟩	213
[	312
]	313
a	262
'	163
∧	161
∨	616
⊃	633
~	223
∃	333
∀	626
:	636

have the idea that the system can speak about itself in code. Once you understand that, you can go on to hypothesize that maybe some string could be invented that speaks about itself, and says about itself that it is not provable. I am going to come back to that question of how a statement can be constructed that speaks about itself at the end of the talk. Let's take that for granted for the moment. If you will assume that one can construct such a statement in the language of *Principia Mathematica* or in the language of TNT, or in any formal system of this sort, then you might ask this question, which is a very important question: Is Gödel's sentence really a statement about *numbers*, or a statement about *itself*? Remember it is a string in some formal system, and ostensibly that formal system contains statements about integers as did TNT.

For example, "*a* times 0 is 0 for every *a*." That's a statement about integers. Or you could say something like "17 is prime," in that language. Basically, that sounds like a statement about 17. So if you have a very long and complex statement that says something very complicated about *numbers,* how can it also say something about *itself?* Does it *really* say something about itself? It is a question of *level of description* and that's a very important idea.

Let me now take a minute to talk about computers. Everybody speaks of computers, at bottom, as manipulating "bits." "What you have in computers are 1's and 0's,"—that's what people say. "You move these 1's and 0's around in fancy ways, and that's really all a computer can do." That's sort of a strange way of speaking about it because we are also very happy to say that a computer manipulates *letters.* We talk about "text-handling programs" all the time. Is it wrong to say that computers manipulate texts? Do they *really* just manipulate 1's and 0's? Are they really just doing *binary arithmetic?* Of course, if you say they are just doing binary arithmetic, why should you stop there? You can say, "There are no 1's and 0's in a computer. All that's there is current going off and on. And so really all that a computer can do is manipulate *electrons.* It can't manipulate 1's and 0's. It can't do any arithmetic at all! It can just manipulate electrons!" There is a point at which you want to stop going down in the hierarchy of description. You might want to say that a computer can manipulate 1's and 0's. Or if it is convenient, you might want to stop *above* that level. You might want to say, "A computer can really manipulate *letters.*"

You might also want to stop for a minute and change gears to consider another image. You might ask: "What is a novel? Is a novel really a set of *letters?* Or is it a set of *words?* Or is it a set of *sentences?* Or is it a set of *ideas?* Or is it a set of *events?* What is a novel?" It would certainly be wrong to say a novel is a set of *letters* or *words,* because we say the novel could be translated into another language. Ultimately, when we remember a novel, we don't remember any of the letters, we don't remember any of the words (or only a few of them). We remember the *events.* But then—doesn't *style* count? It is very hard to determine the right answer to the question "What is a novel?" In some sense, all of the different answers are right. I am trying to make certain you understand my point of view. I'm not saying anything is wrong with saying Gödel's sentence is a statement about *numbers,* but by the same token one

shouldn't feel bad about saying it is a statement about *itself.* It's *both* of those things! It is both of these things simultaneously. Neither view of it is more right or more wrong than the other.

To give you a humorous version of Gödel's theorem, consider the "Wild Dance" version of Gödel's theorem. This is a real-life example which happened at a party. At the party, certain records could not be played. Actually, *most* of them couldn't be played, because people would dance to them. As soon as they danced, the floor would start to vibrate, the record player would shake, the needle would bounce all over the place, so it wouldn't be reproducing the music any more. It was a self-destroying dance! This gives us a question to ask. We have a set of "levels of translation" of the grooves. The question is: "Is the playing of a record *really:* a set of vibrations in a loudspeaker, or waves in the air, or shakings of the floor, or motions of people's feet, or quiverings of the table that the record player is on?" It's all of these things simultaneously. Whenever one of these things happens, the next one is set in motion. If you have dancers there, people will start dancing. When they start dancing, the floor vibrates. When the floor vibrates, the table vibrates. When the table vibrates, the phonograph will vibrate. When the phonograph vibrates, the record will vibrate. So the loop will close. All of these are valid descriptions of what a record, when played, is doing. This particular example of the record is a very interesting one because one can turn it into a kind of paraphrase of Gödel's theorem by saying: "For every record player, there are records that it can't play." One doesn't even require the dancers. After all, the sounds all by themselves will vibrate the record player itself. So one can say there is automatically some sort of self-destroying record. For every record player, there is a record that will make it vibrate and fall apart. After all, every record player has a special resonant frequency at which it will start vibrating more and more, and eventually it will break. You might say, "Oh, no, it doesn't. It might just be a very well made one." But certainly if you make a *loud enough* noise, *anything* will break. If you reproduce the sound of an atomic bomb in perfect fidelity, it will destroy the record player. Given any record player, there is some *bomb* that will

Gödel's Theorem (Wild Dance Version)
"This record cannot be played at this party"

↱ Grooves → Needle → Electricity → Loudspeaker → Air → Eardrums ↴
⌞ Phonograph ← Table ← Floor ← Muscles ← Nerves ← Brain ←⌟

Playing a record at a party can create a "strange loop"—a sort of generalized, level-crossing feedback—which unexpectedly prevents the record from being played. This is a real-life analogue to Gödel's construction of a self-referential (and self-undermining sentence) in a formal mathematical system. Both involve the fact that symbolic activity (musical vibrations or proving of theorems) has simultaneously several levels of interpretation, and these levels of interpretation, far from being just "different ways of looking at one thing," can actually interfere with each other and cause near-paradox (Gödel) or wreak havoc (at the party).

destroy it. You simply require that the record have the noise of that bomb in its grooves and then the record player will not be able to play that record in full fidelity. This is another image of how to think of Gödel's proof.

I have one more image of Gödel's proof that I would like to give you. The idea here involves likening symbol manipulation to the moving of railroad cars in a shunting yard [see figure *a*]. We have an engineer in a locomotive, and this engi-

(a) A train in a shunting yard. Or—is it a *long numeral* on a piece of paper? Or—is it the number of cigarettes smoked in all the galaxies in the universe since the Big Bang?

neer has been told to follow certain instructions in the shunting yard. He is blindly following these instructions. The instructions involve the numbers on the sides of the boxcars. He doesn't know what is inside the boxcars. All he knows is that he must follow certain rules, and he can move cars around in one way or another in the yard, and he tries to create certain trains according to the rules. For example, there is one rule that says you can detach any three cars that have the pattern, 626, ☐, 636, where the middle one can be anything (see figure b). That's one rule that he can obey. He can then detach them and they go away. He is left with the set of cars as shown in the figure.

Another rule that he can obey is this one: "Replace 262 by 666." Then he can replace that one as shown. The engineer is an intelligent guy, and as he is shunting these cars around, he realizes

that, in fact, he can think of just the numbers on the sides. He doesn't have to actually do the physical manipulation of the cars.

He can just think of these numbers on the side of the train and do it all in his head! Rather than talk about "assemblable trains" (because some trains are assemblable according to these rules, and others are not), he can just as well talk about "producible numbers." What I mean by a "producible number" is the long number that stands for any whole assemblable train. In this case (see figure c), the number would be 223,123,666,111,666. It would be a producible number because he started with the train in one position that *was* assemblable and did certain things according to the *rules*, and he came up with another train (i.e., number). Thus he could start thinking about the numbers that he was producing—these long, gigantic numbers—and ask if

(b) The engineer has a rule by which he can detach three cars whose sides exhibit the pattern 626, ☐, 636, so he does it, leaving a five-car train. This is describable either as a railroad shunting operation, or as the *typographical* manipulation of some numerals (strings of digits), or finally as the *calculation* of one number (magnitude) given another number, according to an *arithmetical* rule. The subtle difference between the last two is very significant.

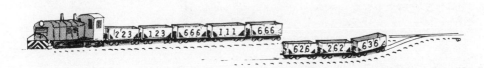

(c) Another rule says that a pattern such as 123 123 · · · 123 666 can be substituted for 262. So in the five-car train, the engineer performs the simplest of all such substitutions; namely, just 666 for 262. Thus we have mathematically converted one very large number, in two steps, into a somewhat smaller, but still huge, number. Or is it that we rearranged some *freight*, in a railroad shunting yard, into a different order? And what kind of freight might it be?

they had some number-theoretical property that distinguishes them from the *non-producible* numbers. Of course, the answer would have to be "yes," because if you think about it you will see all that he is doing are formal operations. But any formal operation on these numbers is really a *mathematical* operation. It is an operation that belongs within the discipline or the framework of number theory. It is a *number-theoretical* operation. The set of numbers attainable through these manipulations constitutes a set of numbers definable in number theory. Thus, he can become a number theorist instead of an engineer, and decide which trains are assemblable and which ones are not. This is something he finds quite fascinating. So he starts investigating the properties of these huge producible numbers, and, flipping the coin, of the non-producible numbers.

Quite coincidentally, he also happens to have studied TNT (Typographical Number Theory), and he is very interested in that, too, but that is just another idea to him. One day he happens to be taking a helicopter ride, and he gets a top view of what his trains look like. He gets to see what's inside the boxcars (see figure *d*). This one in particular has one of the five axioms of TNT in it: "For all *a*, it is not the case that the successor of *a* equals 0." Now remember that one of the things he was allowed to do was remove these three cars so that it left him with a shorter string, in which he then replaced the 262 by a 666. Well, the 666 cars all have 0's inside (see figure *e*). In

fact, the correspondence between a car's side number and the symbol it is carrying is exactly the one that I exhibited earlier—the one that had all the symbols of TNT with their three-digit codes, so that all the 666 cars carry 0's inside. So, in fact, what he had unknowingly started out with was an axiom-carrying train; and by manipulating a little bit, he came up with this new theorem-carrying train, which seen from above says, "It is not the case that 1 equals 0"—a true sentence that follows from the other one because the other one says: "No number's successor is 0." This one says: "It is not the case that the successor of 0 is 0," and I just call the successor of 0 "one." This new train says "It is not the case that 1 equals 0." This is a revelation because now he sees that although he had thought that all he was doing was constructing producible numbers, it turns out that from another (literally higher-level) viewpoint, he was actually *manipulating strings of TNT*. In fact, he was producing statements of number theory when seen from above! *From the side*, he was just producing numbers; but *from above* he was producing statements of number theory (and they were all true). Thus, he could conceive of the idea that some train, some very long train, might be talking about its *own* number, its own code number, and it might be saying something about the producibility of that number. Remember that producibility (like, say, primality) is a number-theoretical notion, and if our formal system is at all powerful, then it can cer-

(d) View from a helicopter of the train in (a). Here is our answer as to what kind of freight is involved. Each car is carrying a symbol of the formal system TNT! Shunting cars in the railroad yard is simultaneously an act of TNT symbol-manipulation (seen from above), and numerical computation (seen from the side). Theorem-proving in a formal system, as seen by Gödel (whose numbers adorn the sides of the cars), is equivalent to number-theoretical calculation according to certain computational rules.

(e) Helicopter view of the train in (c). This train expresses a theorem of TNT that is a direct consequence of the axiom seen in (d). The theorem says: "One is not zero." The engineer created this theorem *not* by thinking about how to deduce logical consequences of axioms, but by following rules governing numbers on the sides of the cars. Yet from an outsider's point of view, they are equivalent. No one could tell which way the engineer was thinking about his activity! This equivalence between doing reasoning *about* mathematics and doing mere calculation *within* mathematics yields a startling *level-crossing loop*, allowing a mathematical system to talk about itself. It's the gist of Gödel's insight that self-referential, paradoxical statements can be translated into formal mathematical systems, by means of *codes* where numbers stand for symbols.

tainly reason about this notion of producible numbers. Thus, some very long train might be talking about whether or not it itself is producible and might even say, "This train is not producible; this train is not assemblable." Now that is a very strange idea. I would like to suggest to you how that could happen.

This is very hard to figure out; it is the last trick that Gödel used. "How do you get a string of some formal system not just to speak about *other* strings in the formal system, but to speak exactly about *itself*? If you try naively to make something that speaks about itself, you might try to quote a sentence within itself. (I am speaking now of English.) If I try to make a sentence that talks about itself, there are two ways I might use. One is to say something like, "*This sentence* is false." Now how does that work? It is based on the convention that the phrase "this sentence" refers to the sentence it is contained in. Or I could say something like, "I am lying." That is using the convention that "I" stands for the speaker. We are using in a certain sense a sleight of hand. I don't know what you want to call it, but it is a kind of convention. There is another way of achieving self-reference, and that is more like the

one that said "THIMK," where the self-reference is more indirect, where the thing that is expressing something has the same *form* as the thing it is talking about.

If you want to have a sentence that talks about its own form without referring to itself directly, you have to have some sort of way of quoting it within itself, and you come to something like this example (see figure). We have here an attempt to create a sentence that speaks about itself, and it works. It talks about a quoted sentence which is infinitely long. So the sentence itself has to be infinitely long, and lo and behold! The quoted sentence is the sentence itself! It is a sequence of nested sentences, each of which is quoted within the outer one, and since it is an infinite structure we have the outermost one identical to the one that is one level in, and it's identical to the sentence one level further in, and so forth. But this is not going to satisfy us if we are trying to produce a *finite* sentence.

So how do you do it in a finite sentence? It might seem impossible. Gödel found a way to do it, and basically it involves the idea of *diagonalization* as in Cantor's argument that shows the real numbers are uncountable.

> The sentence
>   "The sentence
>   "The sentence
>   "The sentence
>   " • • • • • • • • • • • " is infinitely long."
>   is infinitely long."
>   is infinitely long."
>   is infinitely long.

I am going to show you a way of doing it in English. Instead of showing you via Cantor, the mathematician, I'll show you through Quine, the philosopher. Quine invented the following method. The idea is of *self-reference via form* not via convention such as "I" or "this sentence." "Quining" is what I called it in my book. (He certainly didn't call it that!) Quining is an operation that I define on any string of English. Take the string, put it in quotes, then take another copy and put it right after the quoted one.

So you have two copies of a string, and the first one is in quotes—that's all. Here is an example of a quined phrase:

> *"is a sentence with no subject"*
> *is a sentence with no subject.*

It is a perfectly true sentence. Neither half is a sentence, but the full thing is a sentence. (And it is a sentence *with* a subject, incidentally!) The next one, though, is a little trickier and is one where you get real self-reference.

> *"yields falsehood when preceded by its quotation"*
> *yields falsehood when preceded by its quotation.*

What is this really saying? The second part of the sentence is active: it's the thing that is speaking. It is referring to some phrase in quotes. What is it saying? It is saying that something, when you precede it by its quotation, yields a false statement. Well, what is that thing? That thing is the very thing that is speaking. And when you precede it by its quotation, you more or less "accidentally" have reconstructed the sentence itself. So, in fact, this sentence is talking about itself by means of form, not by convention.

Gödel figured out a way of doing that in mathematical systems. The way is very simple, because quoting something is very much like taking its Gödel number. Converting a string into a quoted string is very much like converting a string to its Gödel number. Gödel realized that one could parallel this construction precisely within a formal system and create self-reference this way. Actually, of course, it happened the other way around. Gödel didn't see this sentence by Quine. Quine invented it after Gödel's work. It was just meant to explicate what is going on in Gödel's proof.

My last picture shows a parallel phenomenon that happens inside life forms. The way self-reference happens in mathematics or formal mathematical systems is very similar to the way self-replication happens in living organisms. How does a fish reproduce itself along with its DNA inside? To give you a glimpse of what I am going to say, the fish is sort of like the unquoted string, and its DNA is like the quoted string. So first take the DNA out by itself (see figure). Now let the DNA develop according to certain *chemical processes*. (This is the analogue to the *typographical* process of quining.) The DNA develops, and we see it start to develop here, develop further, further, and you see what results? I will just say this is a sort of an answer to an age-old question. It is a very sexist question. It assumes that female ova play no role in reproduction of the species at all, that they are just there for food, and that really the sperms contain all the hereditary material. Just make this simplifying assumption: that a man contains sperms, and since his sperms are going to turn into people, they too must contain subsperms, and they must contain subsubsperms, etc., etc., ad infinitum. The medieval puzzler is: "Does a man contain all of his future progeny for all generations in some sort of infinite regress?" The answer is, no, not really, not even if reproduction went that way—no more than a fish's DNA is actually a fish.

DNA

DNA not only codes for the structure of the *fish*, but also programs its *own* replication. The method by which this is accomplished is analogous to the way in which self-reference can be achieved in a formal mathematical system.